AUSTRIA

BUSINESS AND INVESTMENT OPPORTUNITIES YEARBOOK

VOLUME 1

STRATEGIC, PRACTICAL INFORMATION AND OPPORTUNITIES

International Business Publications, USA
Washington DC, USA - Austria

AUSTRIA

BUSINESS AND INVESTMENT OPPORTUNITIES YEARBOOK

VOLUME 1 STRATEGIC, PRACTICAL INFORMATION AND OPPORTUNITIES

UPDATED ANNUALLY

We express our sincere appreciation to all government agencies and international organizations which provided information and other materials for this yearbook

Cover Design: **International Business Publications, USA**

2016 Edition Updated Reprint International Business Publications, USA
ISBN 1-4387-7618-7

For customer service and information, please contact:

in the USA: **International Business Publications, USA**
P.O.Box 15343, Washington, DC 20003
Phone: (202) 546-2103, Fax: (202) 546-3275.
E-mail: rusric@erols.com

Printed in the USA

AUSTRIA

BUSINESS AND INVESTMENT OPPORTUNITIES YEARBOOK

VOLUME 1

STRATEGIC, PRACTICAL INFORMATION AND OPPORTUNITIES

TABLE OF CONTENTS

STRATEGIC AND BUSINESS PROFILES

Capital and largest city	Vienna 48°12′N 16°21′E48.200°N 16.350°E
Official languages	German [a]
Ethnic groups (2012)	81.1% Austrians 2.7% Germans 2.2% Turks 8.9% other / unspecified
Demonym	Austrian
Government	Federal parliamentary republic
- President	Heinz Fischer
- Chancellor	Werner Faymann
- President of the National Council	Doris Bures
Legislature	Parliament
- Upper house	Federal Council
- Lower house	National Council
Independence	
- Margraviate of Austria	976
- Duchy of Austria	1156
- Archduchy of Austria	1453
- Austrian Empire	1804
- Austro-Hungarian Empire	1867
- First Republic	1918
- Federal State	1934
- Anschluss	1938
- Second Republic	since 1945
- State Treaty in effect	27 July 1955
Area	
- Total	83,879 km^2 (115th) 32,385.86 sq mi
- Water (%)	1.7
Population	
- 01.01.2015 estimate	8,579,747 (94th)
- Density	101.4/km^2 (106th) 262.6/sq mi
GDP (PPP)	2015 estimate
- Total	$402.420 billion
- Per capita	$47,031
GDP (nominal)	2015 estimate
- Total	$380.555 billion
- Per capita	$44,475
Gini (2011)	26.3 low
HDI (2013)	0.881 very high · 21st
Currency	Euro (€)[b] (EUR)

Time zone	CET (UTC+01)
- Summer (DST)	CEST (UTC+02)
Drives on the	right
Calling code	+43
ISO 3166 code	AT
Internet TLD	.at[c]

a. ^ Croatian, Czech, Hungarian, Romani, Slovak, and Slovene are officially recognised by the European Charter for Regional or Minority Languages (ECRML).

b. ^ Austrian schilling before 1999; Virtual Euro since 1 January 1999; Euro since 1 January 2002.

c. ^ The .eu domain is also used, as it is shared with other European Union member states.

Austria officially the **Republic of Austria** is a federal republic and a landlocked country of over 8.5 million people in Central Europe. It is bordered by the Czech Republic and Germany to the north, Hungary and Slovakia to the east, Slovenia and Italy to the south, and Switzerland and Liechtenstein to the west. The territory of Austria covers 83,879 square kilometres (32,386 sq mi) and has an alpine climate. Austria's terrain is highly mountainous, lying within the Alps; only 32% of the country is below 500 metres (1,640 ft), and its highest point is 3,798 metres (12,461 ft). The majority of the population speak local Bavarian dialects of German as their native language, and Austrian German in its standard form is the country's official language. Other local official languages are Hungarian, Burgenland Croatian, and Slovene.

The origins of modern-day Austria date back to the time of the Habsburg dynasty when the vast majority of the country was a part of the Holy Roman Empire. From the time of the Reformation, many Northern German princes, resenting the authority of the Emperor, used Protestantism as a flag of rebellion. The Thirty Years War, the influence of the Kingdom of Sweden and Kingdom of France, the rise of the Kingdom of Prussia, and the Napoleonic invasions all weakened the power of the Emperor in the North of Germany, but in the South, and in non-German areas of the Empire, the Emperor and Catholicism maintained control. During the 17th and 18th centuries, Austria was able to retain its position as one of the great powers of Europe and, in response to the coronation of Napoleon as the Emperor of the French, the Austrian Empire was officially proclaimed in 1804. Following Napoleon's defeat, Prussia emerged as Austria's chief competitor for rule of a larger Germany.

Austria's defeat by Prussia at the Battle of Königgrätz, during the Austro-Prussian War of 1866 cleared the way for Prussia to assert control over the rest of Germany. In 1867, the empire was reformed into Austria-Hungary. After the defeat of France in the 1870 Franco-Prussian War, Austria was left out of the formation of a new German Empire, although in the following decades its politics, and its foreign policy, increasingly converged with those of the Prussian-led Empire. During the 1914 July Crisis that followed the assassination of Archduke Franz Ferdinand of Austria, Germany guided Austria in issuing the ultimatum to Serbia that led to the declaration of World War I.

After the collapse of the Habsburg (Austro-Hungarian) Empire in 1918 at the end of World War I, Austria adopted and used the name the Republic of German-Austria (*Deutschösterreich*, later *Österreich*) in an attempt for union with Germany, but was forbidden due to the Treaty of Saint-Germain-en-Laye (1919). The First Austrian Republic was established in 1919. In the 1938 Anschluss, Austria was occupied and annexed by Nazi Germany. This lasted until the end of World War II in 1945, after which Germany was occupied by the Allies and Austria's former democratic constitution was restored. In 1955, the Austrian State Treaty re-established Austria as a sovereign state, ending the occupation. In the same year, the Austrian Parliament created the

Declaration of Neutrality which declared that the Second Austrian Republic would become permanently neutral.

Today, Austria is a parliamentary representative democracy comprising nine federal states. The capital and largest city, with a population exceeding 1.7 million, is Vienna. Austria is one of the richest countries in the world, with a nominal per capita GDP of $52,216 (2014 est.). The country has developed a high standard of living and in 2014 was ranked 21st in the world for its Human Development Index. Austria has been a member of the United Nations since 1955, joined the European Union in 1995, and is a founder of the OECD. Austria also signed the Schengen Agreement in 1995, and adopted the European currency, the Euro, in 1999

Austria - a small country with an area of 83.845 square kilometers (32.274 square miles) and 8 million inhabitants - is situated in the very heart of Europe. With no immediate access to the sea, Austria shares its borders with eight countries: Switzerland, Liechtenstein, Germany, the Czech Republic, the Slovak Republic, Hungary, Slovenia and Italy.

Due to this geographical position and out of a historical role as a link between the Orient and the Occident, Austria has successfully established its role as a stabilizing political factor in Central Europe and as a turn-table of East-West trade. Important international organizations, such as the International Atomic Energy Agency (IAEA), the United Nations Industrial Development Organization (UNIDO), and the Organization of Petroleum Exporting Countries (OPEC) have chosen Vienna, Austria's capital, as their headquarters.

As stated in its constitution, Austria is a democratic republic, composed of nine federal provinces. The legislative authority, on the federal level, lies in the hands of a two-chamber parliament: the first chamber, called *Nationalrat* (National Council), is elected at four year intervals, and at present consists of representatives from five political parties. The second chamber, the *Bundesrat*(Federal Council), represents the interests of the nine provinces. Laws passed by both chambers of the parliament must be signed by the Federal President, who is the head of state, elected in direct polls for a term of six years. The executive, on the federal level, is a government headed by the chancellor (*Bundeskanzler*). In each of the provinces there is a provincial legislative dealing with matters reserved to the provinces by the Federal Constitution, and a provincial government headed by a *Landeshauptmann*.

The capital, Vienna, is one of the nine provinces.

Austria's climate is moderate: the average temperatures during the summer (June to mid-September) are around 20° C/68° F, with occasional temperatures as high as 35° C/95° F; during winter (mid-November to February) it may get as cold as -15° C/4° F, but the average lies around -4° C/25° F. There may be heavy snowfall, in particular in the mountains (by the way, Austria's highest mountain is the *Großglockner* at 3.797 meters). Most of the rain is to be expected in May and June, but there is no distinct rainy season.

Approximately 19% of the total territory is arable land, 25% is grassland, 40% consists of forests, and the remaining 15% is mountain regions. Like in all Western industrialized countries, we also find in Austria the tendency towards concentration of population and settlements: 50% of the Austrian population live on 5% of the territory. The most important of these concentrations are the provincial capitals.

		Population	Province

Federal capital:	Vienna	1.609.000	Vienna
Provincial capitals:	Graz	240.000	Styria
	Linz	190.000	Upper Austria
	Salzburg	144.000	Salzburg
	Innsbruck	110.000	Tyrol
	Klagenfurt	90.000	Carinthia
	St. Pölten	49.000	Lower Austria
	Bregenz	26.000	Vorarlberg
	Eisenstadt	11.000	Burgenland

Once the center of power for the large Austro-Hungarian empire, Austria was reduced to a small republic after its defeat in World War I. After the annexation to Nazi Germany in 1938 and subsequent occupation by the victorious Allied powers, Austria's 1955 State Treaty declared the country "permanently neutral" as a condition of the Soviet military withdrawal. The Soviet collapse relieved the external pressure to remain unaligned, but neutrality had evolved into a part of Austrian cultural identity, which has led to an ongoing public debate over whether Vienna legitimately can remain outside of European security structures. A wealthy country, Austria joined the European Union in 1995 and, like many EU members, is adjusting to the new European currency and struggling with high unemployment.

GEOGRAPHY

Location: Central Europe, north of Italy and Slovenia
Geographic coordinates: 47 20 N, 13 20 E
Map references: Europe

Area:
total: 83,858 sq km land: 82,738 sq km water: 1,120 sq km

Area—comparative: slightly smaller than Maine

Land boundaries:
total: 2,562 km
border countries: Czech Republic 362 km, Germany 784 km, Hungary 366 km, Italy 430 km, Liechtenstein
35 km, Slovakia 91 km, Slovenia 330 km, Switzerland 164 km

Coastline: 0 km (landlocked)
Climate: temperate; continental, cloudy; cold winters with frequent rain in lowlands and snow in mountains; cool summers with occasional showers

Terrain: in the west and south mostly mountains (Alps); along the eastern and northern margins mostly flat or gently sloping

Elevation extremes:
lowest point: Neusiedler See 115 m
highest point: Grossglockner 3,797 m

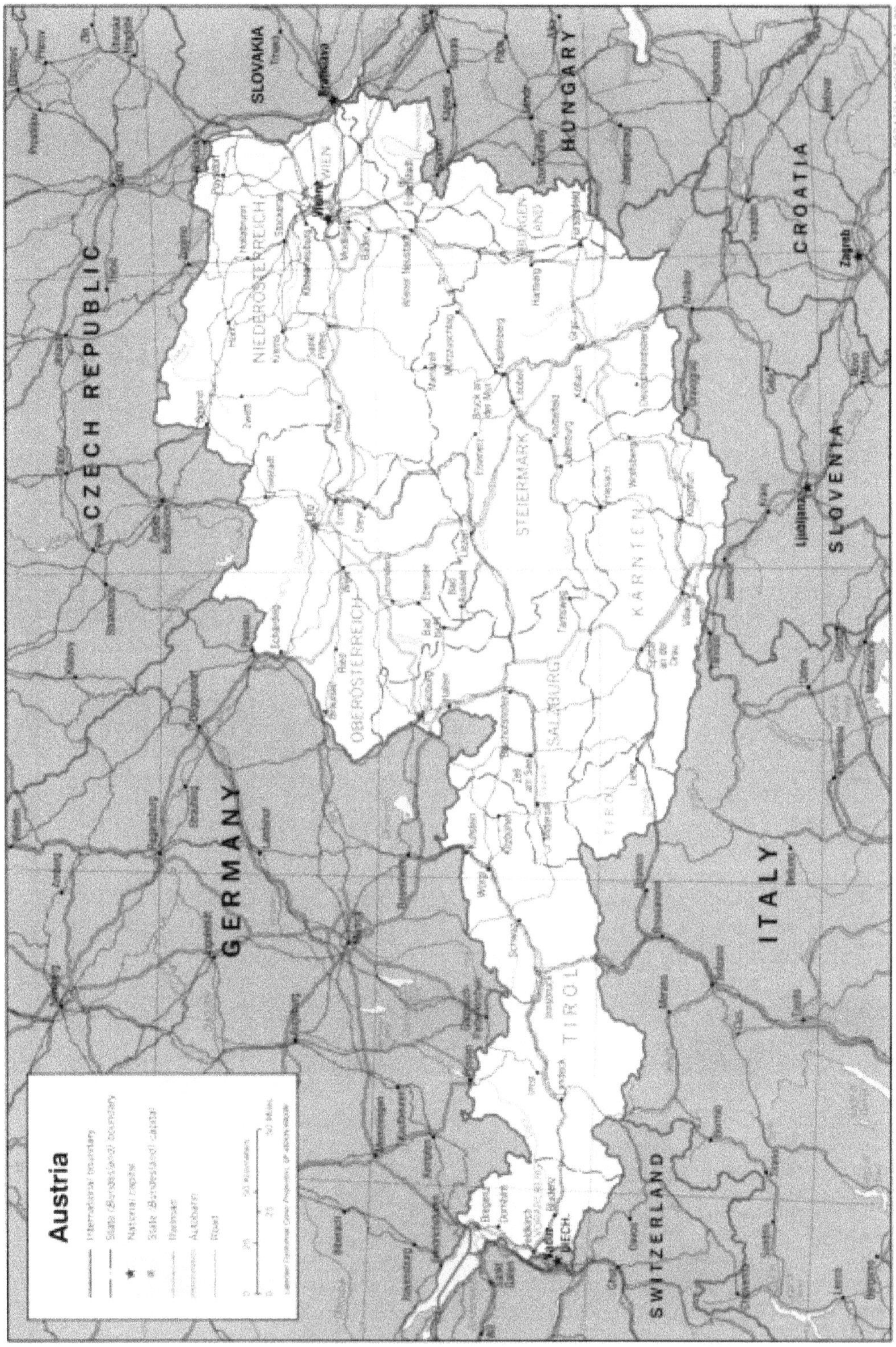

Natural resources: iron ore, oil, timber, magnesite, lead, coal, lignite, copper, hydropower

Land use:
arable land: 17% permanent crops: 1% permanent pastures: 23% forests and woodland: 39% other: 20%

Irrigated land: 40 sq km
Natural hazards: NA

Environment—current issues: some forest degradation caused by air and soil pollution; soil pollution results from the use of agricultural chemicals; air pollution results from emissions by coal- and oil-fired power stations and industrial plants and from trucks transiting Austria between northern and southern Europe

Environment—international agreements:
party to: Air Pollution, Air Pollution-Nitrogen Oxides, Air Pollution-Sulphur 85, Air Pollution-Sulphur 94, Air Pollution-Volatile Organic Compounds, Antarctic Treaty, Biodiversity, Climate Change, Desertification, Endangered Species, Environmental Modification, Hazardous Wastes, Law of the Sea, Nuclear Test Ban, Ozone Layer Protection, Ship Pollution, Tropical Timber 83, Tropical Timber 94, Wetlands, Whaling signed, but not ratified: Air Pollution-Persistent Organic Pollutants, Antarctic-Environmental Protocol, Climate Change-Kyoto Protocol

Geography—note: landlocked; strategic location at the crossroads of central Europe with many easily traversable Alpine passes and valleys; major river is the Danube; population is concentrated on eastern lowlands because of steep slopes, poor soils, and low temperatures elsewhere

PEOPLE

Population: 8,139,299

Age structure:
0-14 years: 17% (male 702,261; female 666,310)
15-64 years: 68% (male 2,792,484; female 2,713,397)

65 years and over: 15% (male 478,071; female 786,776)

Population growth rate: 0.09%
Birth rate: 9.62 births/1,000 population
Death rate: 10.04 deaths/1,000 population
Net migration rate: 1.32 migrant(s)/1,000 population

Sex ratio:
at birth: 1.05 male(s)/female
under 15 years: 1.05 male(s)/female
15-64 years: 1.03 male(s)/female
65 years and over: 0.61 male(s)/female
total population: 0.95 male(s)/female

Infant mortality rate: 5.1 deaths/1,000 live births

Life expectancy at birth:
total population: 77.48 years male: 74.31 years female: 80.82 years

Total fertility rate: 1.37 children born/woman

Nationality:
noun: Austrian(s)
adjective: Austrian

Ethnic groups: German 99.4%, Croatian 0.3%, Slovene 0.2%, other 0.1%
Religions: Roman Catholic 78%, Protestant 5%, other 17%
Languages: German

Literacy:
definition: age 15 and over can read and write
total population: 99%

GOVERNMENT

Country name:

conventional long form: Republic of Austria
conventional short form: Austria
local long form: Republik Oesterreich
local short form: Oesterreich
note: the name Oesterreich means "eastern realm" or "eastern march" and dates back to the 10th century; the designation refers to the fact that Austria was the easternmost extension of Bavaria, and in fact of all the Germans; the word Austria is a Latinization of the German name

Government type:

federal republic

Capital:

name: Vienna
geographic coordinates: 48 12 N, 16 22 E
time difference: UTC+1 (6 hours ahead of Washington, DC, during Standard Time)
daylight saving time: +1hr, begins last Sunday in March; ends last Sunday in October

Administrative divisions:

9 states (Bundeslaender, singular - Bundesland); Burgenland, Kaernten (Carinthia), Niederoesterreich (Lower Austria), Oberoesterreich (Upper Austria), Salzburg, Steiermark (Styria), Tirol (Tyrol), Vorarlberg, Wien (Vienna)

Independence:

12 November 1918 (republic proclaimed); notable earlier dates: 976 (Margravate of Austria established); 17 September 1156 (Duchy of Austria founded); 11 August 1804 (Austrian Empire proclaimed)

National holiday:

National Day, 26 October (1955); note - commemorates the passage of the law on permanent neutrality

Constitution:

several previous; latest adopted 1 October 1920, revised 1929, replaced May 1934 (authoritarian-corporate constitution), replaced by German Weimar constitution in 1938 following German annexation; latest reinstated 1 May 1945 (1920 constitution with 1929 revisions); amended many times, last in 2008 (2013)

Legal system:

civil law system; judicial review of legislative acts by the Constitutional Court

International law organization participation:

accepts compulsory ICJ jurisdiction; accepts ICCt jurisdiction

Suffrage:

16 years of age; universal

Executive branch:

chief of state: President Heinz FISCHER (SPOe) (since 8 July 2004)
head of government: Chancellor Werner FAYMANN (SPOe) (since 2 December 2008); Vice Chancellor Reinhold MITTERLEHNER (since 1 September 2014)
cabinet: Council of Ministers chosen by the president on the advice of the chancellor
elections: president elected for a six-year term (eligible for a second term) by direct popular vote and formally sworn into office before the Federal Assembly or Bundesversammlung; presidential election last held on 25 April 2013 (next to be held on 25 April 2016); chancellor formally chosen by the president but determined by the coalition parties forming a parliamentary majority; vice chancellor chosen by the president on the advice of the chancellor
election results: Heinz FISCHER reelected president; percent of vote - Heinz FISCHER 79.33%, Barbara ROSENKRANZ 15.24%, Rudolf GEHRING 5.43%
note: government coalition - SPOe and OeVP

Legislative branch:

description: bicameral Federal Assembly or Bundesversammlung consists of the Federal Council or Bundesrat (62 seats; members appointed by state parliaments with each state receiving 3 to 12 seats in proportion to its population; members serve 5- or 6-year terms) and the National Council or Nationalrat (183 seats; members directly elected in single-seat constituencies by proportional representation vote; members serve 5-year terms)
elections: National Council - last held on 29 September 2013 (next to be held by September 2018)
election results: National Council - percent of vote by party - SPOe 27.1%, OeVP 23.8%, FPOe 21.4%, Greens 11.5%, Team Stronach 5.8%, NEOS 4.8%, other 5.6%; seats by party - SPOe 53, OeVP 46, FPOe 42, Greens 22; Team Stronach 11, NEOS 9

Judicial branch:

highest court(s): Supreme Court of Justice or Oberster Gerichtshof (consists of 85 judges organized into 17 senates or panels of five judges each); Constitutional Court or Verfassungsgerichtshof (consists of 20 judges including 6 substitutes; Administrative Court or Verwaltungsgerichtshof - 2 judges plus other members depending on the importance of the case)
judge selection and term of office: Supreme Court judges nominated by executive branch departments and appointed by the president; judges serve for life; Constitutional Court judges nominated by several executive branch departments and approved by the president; judges serve for life; Administrative Court judges recommended by executive branch departments and appointed by the president; terms of judges and members determined by the president
subordinate courts: Courts of Appeal (4); Regional Courts (20); district courts (120); county courts

Political parties and leaders:

Alliance for the Future of Austria or BZOe [Josef BUCHER]
Austrian People's Party or OeVP [Reinhold MITTERLEHNER]
Communist Party of Austria or KPOe [Mirko MESSNER]
Freedom Party of Austria or FPOe [Heinz Christian STRACHE]
The Greens [Eva GLAWISCHNIG]
NEOS - The New Austria [Matthias STROLZ]
Social Democratic Party of Austria or SPOe [Werner FAYMANN]
"Team Stronach" [Frank STRONACH]

Political pressure groups and leaders:

Austrian Trade Union Federation or OeGB (nominally independent but primarily Social Democratic)
Federal Economic Chamber (OeVP-dominated)
Labor Chamber or AK (Social Democratic-leaning think tank)
OeVP-oriented Association of Austrian Industrialists or IV
Roman Catholic Church, including its chief lay organization, Catholic Action
other: three composite leagues of the Austrian People's Party or OeVP representing business, labor, farmers, and other nongovernment organizations in the areas of environment and human rights

International organization participation:

ADB (nonregional member), AfDB (nonregional member), Australia Group, BIS, BSEC (observer), CD, CE, CEI, CERN, EAPC, EBRD, ECB, EIB, EMU, ESA, EU, FAO, FATF, G-9, IADB, IAEA, IBRD, ICAO, ICC (national committees), ICCt, ICRM, IDA, IEA, IFAD, IFC, IFRCS, IGAD (partners), ILO, IMF, IMO, Interpol, IOC, IOM, IPU, ISO, ITSO, ITU, ITUC (NGOs), MIGA, MINURSO, NEA, NSG, OAS (observer), OECD, OIF (observer), OPCW, OSCE, Paris Club, PCA, PFP, Schengen Convention, SELEC (observer), UN, UNCTAD, UNESCO, UNFICYP, UNHCR, UNIDO, UNIFIL, UNTSO, UNWTO, UPU, WCO, WFTU (NGOs), WHO, WIPO, WMO, WTO, ZC

Diplomatic representation in the US:

chief of mission: Ambassador Hans Peter MANZ (since 2 December 2011)
chancery: 3524 International Court NW, Washington, DC 20008-3035
telephone: [1] (202) 895-6700
FAX: [1] (202) 895-6773
consulate(s) general: Chicago, Los Angeles, New York

Diplomatic representation from the US:

chief of mission: Ambassador Alexa Lange WESNER (since 22 October 2013)
embassy: Boltzmanngasse 16, A-1090, Vienna
mailing address: use embassy street address
telephone: [43] (1) 31339-0
FAX: [43] (1) 3100682

Flag description:

three equal horizontal bands of red (top), white, and red; the flag design is certainly one of the oldest - if not the oldest - national banners in the world; according to tradition, in 1191, following a fierce battle in the Third Crusade, Duke Leopold V of Austria's white tunic became completely blood-spattered; upon removal of his wide belt or sash, a white band was revealed; the red-white-red color combination was subsequently adopted as his banner

National symbol(s):

golden eagle, edelweiss, Alpine gentian; national colors: red, white

National anthem:

name: "Bundeshymne" (Federal Hymn)
lyrics/music: Paula von PRERADOVIC/Wolfgang Amadeus MOZART or Johann HOLZER (disputed)
note: adopted 1947; the anthem is also known as "Land der Berge, Land am Strome" (Land of the Mountains, Land on the River); Austria adopted a new national anthem after World War II to replace the former imperial anthem composed by Franz Josef HAYDN, which had been appropriated by Germany in 1922 and was thereafter associated with the Nazi regime; a gendered version of the lyrics was adopted by the Austrian Parliament in fall 2011 and became effective 1 January 2012

ECONOMY

Austria, with its well-developed market economy, skilled labor force, and high standard of living, is closely tied to other EU economies, especially Germany's. Its economy features a large service sector, a relatively sound industrial sector, and a small, but highly developed agricultural sector. Economic growth was anemic at less than 0.5% in 2013 and 2014, and; growth in 2015 is not expected to exceed 0.5%. Austria's 5.6% unemployment rate, while low by European standards, is at an historic high for Austria. Without extensive vocational training programs and generous early retirement, the unemployment rate would be even higher. Public finances have not stabilized even after a 2012 austerity package of expenditure cuts and new revenues. On the contrary, in 2014, the government created a "bad bank" for the troubled nationalized "Hypo Alpe Adria" bank, pushing the budget deficit up by 0.9% of GDP to 2.4% and public debt to 84.5% of the GDP. Although Austria's fiscal position compares favorably with other euro-zone countries, it faces several external risks, such as Austrian banks' continued exposure to Central and Eastern Europe, repercussions from the Hypo Alpe Adria bank collapse, political and economic uncertainties caused by the European sovereign debt crisis, the current crisis in Russia/Ukraine, the recent appreciation of the Swiss Franc, and political developments in Hungary.

GDP (purchasing power parity):

$386.9 billion (2014 est.)
$383 billion (2013 est.)
$382 billion (2012 est.)
note: data are in 2014 US dollars
country comparison to the world: 46

GDP (official exchange rate):

$436.1 billion (2014 est.)

GDP - real growth rate:

1% (2014 est.)
0.3% (2013 est.)
0.9% (2012 est.)
country comparison to the world: 189

GDP - per capita (PPP):

$45,400 (2014 est.)
$45,100 (2013 est.)

$45,100 (2012 est.)
note: data are in 2013 US dollars
country comparison to the world: 25

Gross national saving:

23.9% of GDP (2014 est.)
23.8% of GDP (2013 est.)
25.1% of GDP (2012 est.)
country comparison to the world: 49

GDP - composition, by end use:

household consumption: 55%
government consumption: 19.5%
investment in fixed capital: 21.1%
investment in inventories: 0.2%
exports of goods and services: 56.4%
imports of goods and services: -52.1%
(2014 est.)

GDP - composition, by sector of origin:

agriculture: 1.5%
industry: 28.6%
services: 69.8% (2014 est.)

Agriculture - products:

grains, potatoes, wine, fruit; dairy products, cattle, pigs, poultry; lumber

Industries:

construction, machinery, vehicles and parts, food, metals, chemicals, lumber and wood, paper and paperboard, communications equipment, tourism

Industrial production growth rate:

1.8% (2014 est.)
country comparison to the world: 137

Labor force:

3.778 million (2014 est.)
country comparison to the world: 96

Labor force - by occupation:

agriculture: 5.5%
industry: 26%
services: 68.5% (2012 est.)

Unemployment rate:

4.5% (2014 est.)
4.9% (2013 est.)
country comparison to the world: 42

Population below poverty line:

6.2% (2012)

Household income or consumption by percentage share:

lowest 10%: 4%
highest 10%: 22% (2011)

Distribution of family income - Gini index:

26.3 (2007)
31 (1995)
country comparison to the world: 131

Budget:

revenues: $212.3 billion
expenditures: $225.3 billion (2014 est.)

Taxes and other revenues:

48.7% of GDP (2014 est.)
country comparison to the world: 16

Budget surplus (+) or deficit (-):

-3% of GDP (2014 est.)
country comparison to the world: 116

Public debt:

80.2% of GDP (2014 est.)
74.5% of GDP (2013 est.)
note: this is general government gross debt, defined in the Maastricht Treaty as consolidated general government gross debt at nominal value, outstanding at the end of the year; it covers the following categories of government liabilities (as defined in ESA95): currency and deposits (AF.2), securities other than shares excluding financial derivatives (AF.3, excluding AF.34), and loans (AF.4); the general government sector comprises the sub-sectors of central government, state government, local government and social security funds; as a percentage of GDP, the GDP used as a denominator is the gross domestic product in current year prices
country comparison to the world: 27

Fiscal year:

calendar year

Inflation rate (consumer prices):

1.5% (2014 est.)
2.1% (2013 est.)

Commercial bank prime lending rate:

2.1% (31 December 2014 est.)
2.21% (31 December 2013 est.)
country comparison to the world: 181

Stock of narrow money:

$222.6 billion (31 December 2014 est.)
$225.8 billion (31 December 2013 est.)
note: see entry for the European Union for money supply for the entire euro area; the European Central Bank (ECB) controls monetary policy for the 18 members of the Economic and Monetary Union (EMU); individual members of the EMU do not control the quantity of money circulating within their own borders
country comparison to the world: 19

Stock of broad money:

$428.9 billion (31 December 2014 est.)
$439.3 billion (31 December 2013 est.)
country comparison to the world: 27

Stock of domestic credit:

$539.7 billion (31 December 2014 est.)
$559.3 billion (31 December 2013 est.)
country comparison to the world: 25

Market value of publicly traded shares:

$106 billion (31 December 2012 est.)
$82.37 billion (31 December 2011)
$67.68 billion (31 December 2013 est.)
country comparison to the world: 42

Current account balance:

$4.5 billion (2014 est.)
$11.25 billion (2013 est.)
country comparison to the world: 34

Exports:

$164.4 billion (2014 est.)
$165.1 billion (2013 est.)
country comparison to the world: 31

Exports - commodities:

machinery and equipment, motor vehicles and parts, paper and paperboard, metal goods, chemicals, iron and steel, textiles, foodstuffs

Exports - partners:

Germany 30.7%, Italy 6.6%, France 4.8%, US 4.4%, Switzerland 4.3%, Slovakia 4.2% (2013)

Imports:

$166.5 billion (2014 est.)
$165.2 billion (2013 est.)
country comparison to the world: 29

Imports - commodities:

machinery and equipment, motor vehicles, chemicals, metal goods, oil and oil products; foodstuffs

Imports - partners:

Germany 41.7%, Italy 6.4%, Switzerland 4.8%, Czech Republic 4.2% (2013)

Reserves of foreign exchange and gold:

$23.29 billion (31 December 2013 est.)
$23.29 billion (31 December 2013 est.)
country comparison to the world: 55

Debt - external:

$812 billion (31 December 2012 est.)
$786.1 billion (31 December 2011)
country comparison to the world: 18

Stock of direct foreign investment - at home:

$300.7 billion (31 December 2014 est.)
$286.3 billion (31 December 2013 est.)
country comparison to the world: 20

Stock of direct foreign investment - abroad:

$365.7 billion (31 December 2014 est.)
$346.5 billion (31 December 2013 est.)
country comparison to the world: 19

Exchange rates:

euros (EUR) per US dollar -
0.7489 (2014 est.)
0.7634 (2013 est.)
0.78 (2012 est.)
0.7185 (2011 est.)
0.755 (2013 est.)

ENERGY

Electricity - production:

69 billion kWh
country comparison to the world: 39

Electricity - consumption:

65.01 billion kWh
country comparison to the world: 40

Electricity - exports:

17.69 billion kWh
country comparison to the world: 10

Electricity - imports:

24.96 billion kWh
country comparison to the world: 8

Electricity - installed generating capacity:

22.36 million kW
country comparison to the world: 36

Electricity - from fossil fuels:

28.3% of total installed capacity
country comparison to the world: 184

Electricity - from nuclear fuels:

0% of total installed capacity
country comparison to the world: 43

Electricity - from hydroelectric plants:

51.8% of total installed capacity (2011 est.)
country comparison to the world: 45

Electricity - from other renewable sources:

19.9% of total installed capacity
country comparison to the world: 13

Crude oil - production:

20,240 bbl/day
country comparison to the world: 71

Crude oil - proved reserves:

48.5 million bbl (1 January 2014 est.)
country comparison to the world: 79

Refined petroleum products - production:

191,900 bbl/day
country comparison to the world: 57

Refined petroleum products - consumption:

263,300 bbl/day
country comparison to the world: 47

Refined petroleum products - exports:

43,010 bbl/day
country comparison to the world: 61

Refined petroleum products - imports:

123,900 bbl/day
country comparison to the world: 43

Natural gas - production:

1.369 billion cu m
country comparison to the world: 60

Natural gas - consumption:

8.528 billion cu m
country comparison to the world: 51

Natural gas - exports:

3.973 billion cu m
country comparison to the world: 33

Natural gas - imports:

10.41 billion cu m
country comparison to the world: 23

Natural gas - proved reserves:

9.656 billion cu m (1 January 2014 est.)
country comparison to the world: 80

Carbon dioxide emissions from consumption of energy:

66.68 million Mt

COMMUNICATIONS

Telephones - main lines in use:

3.342 million
country comparison to the world: 46

Telephones - mobile cellular:

13.59 million
country comparison to the world: 62

Telephone system:

general assessment: highly developed and efficient
domestic: fixed-line subscribership has been in decline since the mid-1990s with mobile-cellular subscribership eclipsing it by the late 1990s; the fiber-optic net is very extensive; all telephone applications and Internet services are available
international: country code - 43; satellite earth stations - 15; in addition, there are about 600 VSATs (very small aperture terminals) (2007)

Broadcast media:

Austria's public broadcaster, Osterreichischer Rundfunk (ORF), was the main broadcast source until commercial radio and TV service was introduced in the 1990s; cable and satellite TV are available, including German TV stations (2008)

Radio broadcast stations:

FM 65 (plus several hundred repeaters), shortwave 1 (2009)

Television broadcast stations:

9

Internet country code:

.at

Internet hosts:

3.512 million
country comparison to the world: 30

Internet users:

6.143 million
country comparison to the world: 42

TRANSPORTATION

Airports:

52
country comparison to the world: 90

Airports - with paved runways:

total: 24
over 3,047 m: 1
2,438 to 3,047 m: 5
1,524 to 2,437 m: 1
914 to 1,523 m: 4

under 914 m: 13

Airports - with unpaved runways:

total: 28
1,524 to 2,437 m: 1
914 to 1,523 m: 3
under 914 m:
24 (2013)

Heliports:

1

Pipelines:

gas 4,736 km; oil 663 km; refined products 157 km (2013)

Railways:

total: 6,399 km
standard gauge: 5,927 km 1.435-m gauge (3,853 km electrified)
narrow gauge: 384 km 1.000-m gauge (15 km electrified); 88 km 0.760-m gauge (10 km electrified)
country comparison to the world: 29

Roadways:

total: 124,508 km
paved: 124,508 km (includes 1,719 km of expressways) (2012)
country comparison to the world: 39

Waterways:

358 km
country comparison to the world: 89

Merchant marine:

registered in other countries: 3 (Cyprus 1, Kazakhstan 1, Saint Vincent and the Grenadines 1)
country comparison to the world: 134

Ports and terminals:

river port(s): Enns, Krems, Linz, Vienna (Danube)

MILITARY

Military branches:

Land Forces (KdoLdSK), Air Forces (KdoLuSK)

Military service age and obligation:

registration requirement at age 17, the legal minimum age for voluntary military service; 18 is the legal minimum age for compulsory military service (6 months), or optionally, alternative civil/community service (9-12 months); males 18 to 50 years old in the militia or inactive reserve are subject to compulsory service; in a January 2012 referendum, a majority of Austrians voted in favor of retaining the system of compulsory military service (with the option of alternative/non-military service) instead of switching to a professional army system (2015)

Manpower available for military service:

males age 16-49: 1,941,110
females age 16-49: 1,910,434 (2013 est.)

Manpower fit for military service:

males age 16-49: 1,579,862
females age 16-49: 1,554,130 (2013 est.)

Manpower reaching militarily significant age annually:

male: 48,108
female: 45,752

Military expenditures:

0.55% of GDP (2015 projected)
0.62% of GDP (2014)
0.63% of GDP (2013)
0.68% of GDP (2012)
0.7% of GDP (2011)
country comparison to the world: 115

TRANSNATIONAL ISSUES

Disputes - international:

none

Refugees and internally displaced persons:

refugees (country of origin): 11,906 (Afghanistan); 19,577 (Russia) (2014)
stateless persons: 604

Illicit drugs:

transshipment point for Southwest Asian heroin and South American cocaine destined for Western Europe; increasing consumption of European-produced synthetic drugs

IMPORTANT INFORMATION FOR UNDERSTANDING AUSTRIA

PROFILE

OFFICIAL NAME: Republic of Austria

Geography
Area: 83,857 sq. km. (32,377 sq. mi.); slightly smaller than Maine.
Cities: *Capital*--Vienna (1.6 million). *Other cities*--Graz, Linz, Salzburg, Innsbruck, Klagenfurt.
Terrain: Alpine (64%), northern highlands that form part of the Bohemian Massif (10%), lowlands to the east (26%).
Climate: Continental temperate.

People
Nationality: *Noun and adjective*--Austrian(s).
Population: 8,078,449.
Annual growth rate: 0.07%.
Ethnic groups: Germans 98%, Croats, Slovenes; other recognized minorities include Hungarians, Czechs, Slovaks, and Roma.
Religions: Roman Catholic 78%, Protestant 5%, Muslim and other 17%.
Language: German 92%.
Education: *Years compulsory*--9. *Attendance*--99%. *Literacy*--98%.
Health: *Infant mortality rate*--4.9 deaths/1,000. *Life expectancy*--men 74.7 years , women 80.9 years.
Work force (3.7 million): *Services*--67.2%; *agriculture and forestry*--0.8%.

Government
Type: Parliamentary democracy.
Constitution: 1920; revised 1929 (reinstated May 1, 1945).
Branches: *Executive*--federal president (chief of state), chancellor (head of government), cabinet. *Legislative*--bicameral Federal Assembly (Parliament). *Judicial*--Constitutional Court, Administrative Court, Supreme Court.
Political parties: Social Democratic Party, People's Party, Freedom Party, Greens, Liberal Forum.
Suffrage: Universal over 19.
Administrative subdivisions: Nine Laender (federal provinces).
Defense (2000): 0.8% of GDP.

PEOPLE

Austrians are a homogeneous people; 92% are native German speakers. Only two numerically significant minority groups exist--30,000 Slovenes in Carinthia (south central Austria) and about 60,000 Croats in Burgenland (on the Hungarian border). The Slovenes form a closely knit community. Their rights as well as those of the Croats are protected by law and generally respected in practice. The present boundaries of Austria, once the center of the Habsburg Empire that constituted the second-largest state in Europe, were established in accordance with the Treaty of St. Germain in 1919. Some Austrians, particularly near Vienna, still have relatives in the Czech Republic, Slovakia, and Hungary. About 78% of all Austrians are Roman Catholic. The church abstains from political activity; however, lay Catholic organizations are aligned with the conservative People's Party. The Social Democratic Party long ago shed its anticlerical stance. Small Lutheran minorities are located mainly in Vienna, Carinthia, and Burgenland.

The Austro-Hungarian Empire played a decisive role in central European history. It occupied strategic territory containing the southeastern routes to western Europe and the north-south routes between Germany and Italy. Although present-day Austria is only a tiny remnant of the old empire, it retains this unique position.

Soon after the Republic of Austria was created at the end of World War I, it faced the strains of catastrophic inflation and of redesigning a government meant to rule a great empire into one that would govern only 6 million citizens. In the early 1930s, worldwide depression and unemployment added to these strains and shattered traditional Austrian society. Resultant economic and political conditions led in 1933 to a dictatorship under Engelbert Dollfuss. In February 1934, civil war broke out, and the Socialist Party was outlawed. In July, a coup d'etat by the National Socialists failed, but Dollfuss was assassinated by Nazis. In March 1938, Austria was incorporated into the German Reich, a development commonly known as the "Anschluss" (annexation).

At the Moscow conference in 1943, the Allies declared their intention to liberate Austria and reconstitute it as a free and independent state. In April 1945, both Eastern- and Western-front Allied forces liberated the country. Subsequently, Austria was divided into zones of occupation similar to those in Germany. Under the 1945 Potsdam agreements, the Soviets took control of German assets in their zone of occupation. These included 7% of Austria's manufacturing plants, 95% of its oil resources, and about 80% of its refinery capacity. The properties were returned to Austria under the Austrian State Treaty. This treaty, signed in Vienna on May 15, 1955, came into effect on July 27, and, under its provisions, all occupation forces were withdrawn by October 25, 1955. Austria became free and independent for the first time since 1938.

GOVERNMENT

The Austrian president convenes and concludes parliamentary sessions and under certain conditions can dissolve Parliament. However, no Austrian president has dissolved Parliament in the Second Republic. The custom is for Parliament to call for new elections if needed. The president requests a party leader, usually the leader of the strongest party, to form a government. Upon the recommendation of the Federal Chancellor, the president also appoints cabinet ministers. No one can become a member of the government without the approval of the president.

The Federal Assembly (Parliament) is composed of two houses--the National Council (Nationalrat), or lower house, and the Federal Council (Bundesrat), or upper house. Legislative authority is concentrated in the National Council. Its 183 members are elected for a maximum 4-year term in a three-tiered system, based on proportional representation. The National Council may dissolve itself by a simple majority vote or it may be dissolved by the president on the recommendation of the Chancellor. The 64 members of the Federal Council are elected by the legislatures of the nine provinces for 4- to 6-year terms. The Federal Council only reviews legislation passed by the National Council and can delay but not veto its enactment.

The highest courts of Austria's independent judiciary are the Constitutional Court; the Administrative Court, which handles bureaucratic disputes; and the Supreme Court, for civil and criminal cases. Cases in the Administrative and Supreme Courts concerning constitutional issues can be appealed to the Constitutional Court. Justices of the three courts are appointed by the president for specific terms.

The governors of Austria's nine Laender (provinces) are elected by the provincial legislatures. Although most authority, including that of the police, rests with the federal government, the provinces have considerable responsibility for welfare matters and local administration. Strong provincial and local loyalties are based on tradition and history.

Principal Government Officials

Office	Holder	Party
Federal Chancellor Minister of the Chancellery for Arts, Culture, Media and Civil Servants	Werner Faymann Josef Ostermayer (de)	SPÖ
Federal Minister of Science, Research and Economy (de) Vice-Chancellor of Austria	Reinhold Mitterlehner	ÖVP
Federal Ministry for Europe, Integration and Foreign Affairs	Sebastian Kurz	ÖVP
Federal Minister of Family and Youth (de)	Sophie Karmasin (de)	Non-party
Federal Minister of Health (de)	Sabine Oberhauser (de)	SPÖ
Federal Minister of the Interior	Johanna Mikl-Leitner	ÖVP
Federal Minister of Justice	Wolfgang Brandstetter (de)	Non-party
Federal Minister of National Defence and Sport	Gerald Klug	SPÖ
Federal Minister of Agriculture, Forests, Environment and Water Management (de)	Andrä Rupprechter (de)	ÖVP
Federal Minister of Labour, Social Affairs and Consumer Protection (de)	Rudolf Hundstorfer (de)	SPÖ
Federal Minister for Education and Women	Gabriele Heinisch-Hosek	SPÖ
Federal Minister for Transport, Innovation and Technology	Alois Stöger	SPÖ
Federal Minister of Finance	Hans Jörg Schelling (de)	ÖVP

Austria maintains an embassy in the United States at 3524 International Court, NW, Washington, DC 20008 (te1. 202-895-6700). Consulates general are located in New York, Chicago, and Los Angeles, with honorary consulates in Atlanta, Boston, Buffalo, Cleveland, Denver, Honolulu, Houston, Miami, New Orleans, Newark, Philadelphia, St. Paul, San Francisco, San Juan, and Seattle.

POLITICAL CONDITIONS

Since World War II, Austria has enjoyed political stability. A Socialist elder statesman, Dr. Karl Renner, organized an Austrian administration in the aftermath of the war, and general elections were held in November 1945. In that election, the conservative People's Party (OVP) obtained 50% of the vote (85 seats) in the National Council (lower house of Parliament), the Socialists won 45% (76 seats), and the communists won 5% (4 seats). The ensuing three-party government ruled until 1947, when the communists left the government and the OVP led a governing coalition with the socialists (now called the Social Democratic Party or SPO) that governed until 1966. Between 1970 and 1999, the SPO has ruled the country either alone or in conjunction with the OVP, except from 1983-86, when it governed in coalition with the Freedom Party. In 1999, the OVP formed a coalition with the right wing-populist Freedom Party (FPO). The SPO, which was the strongest party in the 1999 elections, and the Greens now form the opposition. As a result of the inclusion of the FPO on the government, the EU imposed a series of sanctions on Austria. The U.S. and Israel, as well as various other countries, also reduced contacts with the Austrian Government.

The Social Democratic Party traditionally draws its constituency from blue- and white-collar workers. Accordingly, much of its strength lies in urban and industrialized areas. In the 1995 national elections, it garnered 38% of the vote. The SPO in the past advocated heavy state involvement in Austria's key industries, the extension of social security benefits, and a full-employment policy. Beginning in the mid-1980s, it shifted its focus to free market-oriented economic policies, balancing the federal budget, and European Union (EU) membership.

The People's Party advocates conservative financial policies and privatization of much of Austria's nationalized industry and finds support from farmers, large and small business owners, and lay Catholic groups, mostly in the rural regions of Austria. In 1995, it received 28% of the vote. The rightist Freedom Party attracts protest votes and those who desire no association with the other major parties. The party's mixture of populism and anti-establishment themes propagated by its aggressive leader Joerg Haider steadily gained support over the past years. It attracted about 27% of the vote in the 1999 elections. The Liberal Forum, founded on libertarian ideals, split from the Freedom Movement in February 1993. It received 5.5% of the vote in the 1999 election and, thus, failed to re-enter the national legislature. The Greens, a left-of-center party focusing on environmental issues, received 4.4% of the vote in 1999.

ECONOMY

Currency	Euro
Fiscal year	Calendar year
	Statistics
GDP	$385.5 billion (PPP)
GDP growth	0.6%
GDP per capita	€36,640 (
GDP by sector	agriculture: 1.7%; industry: 32.3%; services: 65.8%
Inflation (CPI)	2.6%
Population below poverty line	6.2%
Gini coefficient	26
Labour force	4.434 million
Labour force by occupation	agriculture: 5.5%; industry: 27.5%; services: 67%
Unemployment	4.4%
Average gross salary	€3,997/$5,395, monthly
Average net salary	€2,043/$2,758, monthly
Main industries	construction, machinery, vehicles and parts, food, metals, chemicals, lumber and wood processing, paper and paperboard, communications equipment, tourism
Ease-of-doing-business rank	29th
	External
Exports	$163.1 billion
Export goods	machinery and equipment, motor vehicles and parts, paper and paperboard, metal goods, chemicals, iron and steel, textiles, foodstuffs
Main export partners	Germany 31.4% Italy 7.0%

	France 4.7% Switzerland 4.5% United States 4.4%
Imports	$170.5 billion
Import goods	machinery and equipment, motor vehicles, chemicals, metal goods, oil and oil products; foodstuffs
Main import partners	Germany 42.1% Italy 6.6% Switzerland 5.1%
Gross external debt	$808.9 billion (30 September 2009)
Public finances	
Public debt	74.6% of GDP
Revenues	$191.7 billion
Expenses	$204.1 billion
Foreign reserves	$26.5 billion

Austria is one of the 11 richest countries in the world in terms of GDP (Gross domestic product) per capita, has a well-developed social market economy, and a high standard of living. Until the 1980s, many of Austria's largest industry firms were nationalised; in recent years, however, privatisation has reduced state holdings to a level comparable to other European economies. Labour movements are particularly strong in Austria and have large influence on labour politics. Next to a highly developed industry, international tourism is the most important part of the national economy.

Germany has historically been the main trading partner of Austria, making it vulnerable to rapid changes in the German economy. However, since Austria became a member state of the European Union it has gained closer ties to other European Union economies, reducing its economic dependence on Germany. In addition, membership in the EU has drawn an influx of foreign investors attracted by Austria's access to the single European market and proximity to the aspiring economies of the European Union. Growth in GDP accelerated in recent years and reached 3.3% in 2006.

In 2004 Austria was the fourth richest country within the European Union, having a GDP (PPP) per capita of approximately € 27,666, with Luxembourg, Ireland, and Netherlands leading the list.

Vienna was ranked the fifth richest NUTS-2 region within Europe (see Economy of Europe) with GDP reaching € 38,632 per capita, just behind Inner London, Luxembourg, Brussels-Capital Region and Hamburg.

Growth has been steady in recent years 2002–2006 varying between 1 and 3.3%

Austria has a well-developed social market economy with a high standard of living in which the government has played an important role. Many of the country's largest firms were nationalized in the early post-war period to protect them from Soviet takeover as war reparations. For many years, the government and its state-owned industries conglomerate played a very important role in the Austrian economy. However, starting in the early 1990s, the group was broken apart, state-owned firms started to operate largely as private businesses, and a great number of these firms were wholly or partially privatized. Although the government's privatization work in past years has been very successful, it still operates some firms, state monopolies, utilities, and services. The new government has presented an ambitious privatization program, which, if implemented, will considerably reduce government participation in the economy. Austria enjoys well-developed industry, banking, transportation, services, and commercial facilities.

Although some industries, such as several iron and steel works and chemical plants, are large industrial enterprises employing thousands of people, most industrial and commercial enterprises in Austria are relatively small on an international scale.

Austria has a strong labor movement. The Austrian Trade Union Federation (OGB) comprises constituent unions with a total membership of about 1.5 million--more than half the country's wage and salary earners. Since 1945, the OGB has pursued a moderate, consensus-oriented wage policy, cooperating with industry, agriculture, and the government on a broad range of social and economic issues in what is known as Austria's "social partnership." The OGB has announced tough opposition against the new government's program for budget consolidation, social reform, and improving the business climate, and indications are rising that Austria's peaceful social climate could become more confrontational.

Austrian farms, like those of other west European mountainous countries, are small and fragmented, and production is relatively expensive. Since Austria's becoming a member of the EU in 1995, the Austrian agricultural sector has been undergoing substantial reform under the EU's common agricultural policy (CAP). Although Austrian farmers provide about 80% of domestic food requirements, the agricultural contribution to gross domestic product (GDP) has declined since 1950 to less than 3%.

Austria has achieved sustained economic growth. During the 1950s, the average annual growth rate was more than 5% in real terms and averaged about 4.5% through most of the 1960s. Following moderate real GDP growth of 1.7%, 2.0% and 1.2%, respectively, in 1995, 1996, and 1997, the economy rebounded and with real GDP expansion of 2.9% in 1998 and 2.2% in 1999.

Austria became a member of the EU on January 1, 1995. Membership brought economic benefits and challenges and has drawn an influx of foreign investors attracted by Austria's access to the single European market. Austria also has made progress in generally increasing its international competitiveness. As a member of the Economic and Monetary Union (EMU), Austria's economy is closely integrated with other EU member countries, especially with Germany. On January 1, 1999, Austria introduced the new Euro currency for accounting purposes.

Starting January 2002, Euro notes and coins will be introduced and substitute for the Austrian schilling. Economists agree that the economic effects in Austria of using a common currency have been positive.

Trade with other EU countries accounts for almost 66% of Austrian imports and exports. Expanding trade and investment in the emerging markets of central and eastern Europe is a major element of Austrian economic activity. Trade with these countries accounts for almost 14% of Austrian imports and exports, and Austrian firms have sizable investments in and continue to move labor-intensive, low-tech production to these countries. Although the big investment boom has waned, Austria still has the potential to attract EU firms seeking convenient access to these developing markets.

Total trade with the United States in 1999 reached $6.6 billion. Imports from the United States amounted to $3.7 billion, constituting a U.S. market share in Austria of 5.4%. Austrian exports to the United States in 1999 were $2.9 billion or 4.6% of total Austrian exports.

FOREIGN RELATIONS

The 1955 Austrian State Treaty ended the four-power occupation and recognized Austria as an independent and sovereign state. In October 1955, the Federal Assembly passed a constitutional law in which "Austria declares of her own free will her perpetual neutrality." The second section of this law stated that "in all future times Austria will not join any military alliances and will not permit the establishment of any foreign military bases on her territory." Since then, Austria shaped its foreign policy on the basis of neutrality.

In recent years, however, Austria began to reassess its definition of neutrality, granting overflight rights for the UN-sanctioned action against Iraq in 1991, and, since 1995, contemplating participation in the EU's evolving security structure. Also in 1995, it joined the Partnership for Peace, and subsequently participated in peacekeeping missions in Bosnia. Discussion of possible Austrian NATO membership intensified during 1996. OVP and FPO aim at moving closer to NATO or a European defense arrangement. The SPO, in turn, believes continued neutrality is the cornerstone of Austria's foreign policy, and a majority of the population generally supports this stance.

Austrian leaders emphasize the unique role the country plays as East-West hub and as a moderator between industrialized and developing countries. Austria is active in the United Nations and experienced in UN peacekeeping efforts. It attaches great importance to participation in the Organization for Economic Cooperation and Development and other international economic organizations, and it has played an active role in the Organization for Security and Cooperation in Europe (OSCE).

Vienna hosts the Secretariat of the OSCE and the headquarters of the International Atomic Energy Agency, the UN Industrial Development Organization, and the UN Drug Control Program. Other international organizations based in Vienna include the Organization of Petroleum Exporting Countries and the International Institute for Applied Systems Analysis. Recently, Vienna added the Comprehensive Test Ban Treaty Organization and the Wassenaar Arrangement (a technology-transfer control agency) to the list of international organizations it hosts.

Austria traditionally has been active in "bridge-building to the east," increasing contacts at all levels with eastern Europe and the states of the former Soviet Union. Austrians maintain a constant exchange of business representatives, political leaders, students, cultural groups, and tourists with the countries of central and eastern Europe. Austrian companies are active in investing and trading with the countries of central and eastern Europe. In addition, the Austrian Government and various Austrian organizations provide assistance and training to support the changes underway in the region.

U.S.-AUSTRIAN RELATIONS

Austria's political leaders and people recognize and appreciate the essential role played by U.S. economic assistance through the Marshall Plan in the reconstruction of their country after World War II, and by the U.S. in promoting the conclusion of the Austrian State Treaty. It is in the interest of the U.S. that the present friendly relations be maintained and strengthened and that Austria's political and economic stability be maintained.

Principal U.S. Officials

Ambassador-- Alexa Wesner

Ambassador Alexa Wesner was born in Washington D.C. and grew up in Reston, Virginia. The daughter of immigrant parents, a German mother and Latvian father, she was the first in her family to attend a U.S. high school and university.

Deputy Chief of Mission--Christopher Hoh
Counselor for Economic and Political Affairs--Dean Yap
Counselor for Public Affairs, Acting--Robert Hugins
Counselor for Commercial Affairs--Christopher Quinlivan
Counselor for Management Affairs--Jeffry Olesen
Counselor for Agricultural Affairs--vacant
Consul General--Constance Anderson
Defense Attache--COL Ulises Soto
Office of Defense Cooperation--LTC Scott Dullea

The U.S. embassy in Austria is located at Boltzmanngasse 16, Vienna 1091, tel. (43) (1) 313-39 (After office hours: (43) (1) 319-5523). The U.S. Consular Agency in Salzburg is located at Alte Markt 1, 5020 Salzburg, tel. (43) (662) 848-776.

TRAVELING US STATE DEPARTMENT SUGGESTIONS

ENTRY REQUIREMENTS: A passport is required. A visa is not required for business or tourist stays up to three months. For further information concerning entry requirements for Austria, travelers should contact the Embassy of Austria at 3524 International Court, N.W.., Washington, D.C. 20008, tel. (202) 895-6767, or the nearest Austrian Consulate General in Chicago, Los Angeles, or New York. The Austrian Embassy to the United States maintains a web page in English that answers questions concerning the laws and regulations of Austria, including residency, driver's license requirements, and permission to work: http://www.austria.org/index.html.

In an effort to prevent international child abduction, many governments have initiated procedures at entry/exit points. These often include requiring documentary evidence of relationship and permission for the child's travel from the parent(s) or legal guardian not present. Having such documentation on hand, even if not required, may facilitate entry/departure.

CRIME: Austria has a low crime rate, and violent crime is rare. However, crimes involving theft of personal property have increased in recent years. Travelers can become targets of pickpockets and purse-snatchers who operate where tourists tend to gather; favorite spots include Vienna's two largest train stations and the pedestrian shopping area in the first district. The loss or theft of a U.S. passport overseas should be reported immediately to the local police and the nearest U.S. embassy or consulate. U.S. citizens can refer to the Department of State's pamphlet, *A Safe Trip Abroad*, for ways to promote a more trouble-free trip. The pamphlet is available from the Superintendent of Documents, U.S. Government Printing Office, Washington, D.C. 20402.

If you are the victim of a crime while overseas, in addition to reporting to local police, please contact the nearest U.S. embassy or consulate for assistance. The Embassy/Consulate staff can, for example, assist you to find appropriate medical care, to contact family members of friends, and explain how funds could be transferred. Although the investigation and prosecution for the crime is solely the responsibility of local authorities, consular officers can help you to understand the local criminal justice process and to find an attorney if needed.

MEDICAL FACILITIES AND INSURANCE: Good medical care is widely available. The Department of State strongly urges Americans to consult with their medical insurance company prior to traveling abroad to confirm whether their policy applies overseas and if it will cover emergency expenses such as a medical evacuation. U.S. medical insurance plans seldom cover health costs incurred outside the United States unless supplemental coverage is purchased. Further, U.S. Medicare and Medicaid programs do not provide payment for medical services outside the United States. However, many travel agents and private companies offer insurance plans that will cover health care expenses incurred overseas, including emergency services such as medical evacuations.

When making a decision regarding health insurance, Americans should consider that many foreign doctors and hospitals require payment in cash prior to providing medical service and that a medical evacuation to the United States may cost in excess of $50,000. Uninsured travelers who require medical care overseas often face extreme difficulties. When consulting with your insurer prior to your departure, please ascertain whether payment will be made to the overseas healthcare provider or if you will be reimbursed later for expenses that you incur. Some insurance policies also include coverage for psychiatric treatment and for the disposition of remains in the event of death.

Useful information on medical emergencies abroad, including overseas insurance programs, is provided in the Department of State's Bureau of Consular Affairs brochure, *Medical Information for Americans Traveling Abroad*, available via the Bureau of Consular Affairs home page or autofax: (202) 647-3000.

OTHER HEALTH INFORMATION: Information on vaccinations and other health precautions may be obtained from the Centers for Disease Control and Prevention's hotline for international travelers at 1-877-FYI-TRIP (1-877-394-8747); fax 1-888-CDC-FAXX (1-888-232-3299), or via their Internet site at http://www.cdc.gov.

TRAFFIC SAFETY AND ROAD CONDITONS: While in a foreign country, U.S. citizens may encounter road conditions that differ significantly from those in the United States. The information below concerning Austria is provided for general reference only, and it may not be totally accurate in a particular location or circumstance.

Safety of Public Transportation: Excellent
Urban Road Conditions/Maintenance: Excellent
Rural Road Conditions/Maintenance: Excellent
Availability of Roadside Assistance: Excellent

Road conditions in Austria are generally excellent. During the winter, however, roads in alpine areas may become dangerous due to snowfall, ice, or avalanches. Some mountain roads may be closed for extended periods, and tire chains are often required. Drivers should exercise caution during the heavily traveled vacation periods (December-February, Easter, and July-August). Extra caution is recommended when driving through autobahn construction zones, particularly on the A-1 East/West Autobahn. Reduced lanes and two-way traffic in these zones have resulted in several deadly accidents in recent years. Traffic information and road conditions are broadcast on the English language channel fm4, located between 91 and 105 FM depending on the locale.

A U.S. driver's license alone is not sufficient to drive in Austria. The U.S. driver's license must be accompanied by an international driver's permit (obtainable in the U.S. from American Automobile Association and the American Automobile Touring Alliance) or by an official translation of the U.S. driver's license, which can be obtained at one of the Austrian automobile clubs (OAMTC or ARBO). This arrangement is only acceptable for the first six months of driving in Austria, after which all drivers must obtain an Austrian license.

Austria requires all vehicles using the autobahn to display a highway tax sticker "Autobahn Vignette" on the inside windshield of the vehicle. The sticker may be purchased at border crossings, gas stations in Austria, as well as small "Tabak" shops located in Austrian towns. Fines for failing to display a valid autobahn vignette on the windshield of the car are usually around $120.00.

Austrian autobahns have a maximum speed limit of 130 km/hr, although drivers often drive much faster and pass aggressively. The use of hand-held cell phones while driving is prohibited. Turning right on red is also prohibited throughout Austria. The legal limit for blood alcohol content in Austria is .05 percent, and penalties for driving under the influence tend to be stricter than in many U.S. states.

Tourists driving rented vehicles should pay close attention to the provisions of their rental contract. Many contracts prohibit drivers from taking rented vehicles into eastern European countries. Drivers attempting to enter countries listed as "prohibited" on the car rental contract may be arrested, fined, and/or charged with attempted auto theft. The vehicle can be held by Austrian police for the car rental company.

Emergency roadside help and information may be reached by dialing 123 or 120 for vehicle assistance and towing services (Austrian Automobile Clubs), 122 for the fire department, 133 for police, and 144 for ambulance.

For additional general information about road safety, including links to foreign government sites, please see the Department of State, Bureau of Consular Affairs home page at http://travel.state.gov/road_safety.html. For specific information concerning Austrian driving permits, vehicle inspection, road tax and mandatory insurance, please contact the Austrian government website at http://www.austria.org/visa.html. Additional official tourist information can be obtained from the Austrian National Tourist Office in New York at tel. 212-944-6880 or in Los Angeles at tel. 818-999-4030.

AVIATION SAFETY OVERSIGHT: The U.S. Federal Aviation Administration (FAA) has assessed the Government of Austria's Civil Aviation Authority as Category 1 -- in compliance with international aviation safety standards for oversight of Austria's air carrier operations. For further information, travelers may contact the Department of Transportation within the United States at telepone 1-800-322-7873, or visit the FAA's Internet website at http://www.faa.gov/avr/iasa.htm. The U.S. Department of Defense (DOD) separately assesses some foreign air carriers for suitability as official providers of air services. For information regarding the DOD policy on specific carriers, travelers may contact the DOD at tel. (618) 256-4801.

CUSTOMS REGULATIONS: Austrian customs authorities encourage the use of an ATA (Admission Temporaire/Temporary Admission) Carnet for the temporary admission of professional equipment, commercial samples, and/or goods for exhibitions and fair purposes. ATA Carnet Headquarters, located at the U.S. Council for International Business, 1212 Avenue of the Americas, New York, NY 10036, issues and guarantees the ATA Carnet in the United States. For additional information, please call (212) 354-4480, or send an e-mail to atacarnet@uscib.org, or visit http://www.uscib.org for details.

DRUG PENALTIES: U.S. citizens are subject to the laws of the country in which they are traveling. Penalties for possession, use, or trafficking in illegal drugs in Austria are strict, and convicted offenders can expect jail sentences and fines.

CHILDREN'S ISSUES: For information on international adoption of children and international parental child abduction, please refer to our Internet site at http://travel.state.gov/children's_issues.html or telephone (202) 736-7000.

REGISTRATION AND EMBASSY/CONSULATE LOCATION: U.S. citizens are encouraged to register at the Consular Section of the U.S. Embassy in Vienna or at the Consular Agency in Salzburg and obtain updated information on travel and security within Austria. The U.S. Embassy in Vienna is located at Boltzmanngasse 16 in the Ninth District. The Consular Section of the U.S. Embassy is located in the Marriott Building, on the fourth floor of Gartenbaupromenade 2, in the First District. The telephone number for both the Embassy and the Consular Section is (43)(1) 31-339. There is also a Consular Agency in Salzburg at Alter Markt 1, tel. (43) (662) 84-87-76, open Monday, Wednesday, and Thursday from 9:00 a.m. to 12:00 noon. U.S. citizens in Salzburg who require assistance outside of these hours may contact the U.S. Embassy in Vienna. The Embassy also maintains a website, at http://www.usembassy-vienna.at with security updates and other information helpful to American citizens.

STRATEGIC AND PRACTICAL INFORMATION FOR CONDUSTRING BUSINESS IN AUSTRIA

INVESTMENT CLIMATE

A. HOST COUNTRY POLICIES AND PRACTICES

1. OPENNESS TO FOREIGN INVESTMENT

Government attitude toward foreign private investment:

The change in government in February 2000 breaking the 30-year political dominance of the Social Democratic Party (SPO) has, if anything, renewed Austrian openness to foreign investment. Both the right-of-center Peoples' Party (OVP) and the right-wing Freedom Party (FPO) are pro-business. The new coalition welcomes all foreign direct investment, particularly those investments that create new jobs in high technology, promote capital intensive industries, are linked with research activities, improve productivity, replace imports, increase exports, and do not have a negative impact on the environment. Plans include introducing additional tax incentives for industrial research and for international research organizations to locate in Austria. In some regions, Austria also offers special facilities and services ("cluster" packages) to foreign investors, for example, for manufacturers of chips, silicon and high-tech products or for automotive producers. Austria's basic policies toward foreign direct investment are not expected to change in coming years. A large number of foreign firms, including some 400 U.S. companies, have invested in Austria and most have expanded their original investment over time.

The new government is committed to economic and social reform and to improve the investment climate further. Economic goals included in the government program represent a very pro-business approach which some commentators have likened to the Reagan and Thatcher approaches. Priorities include reducing government expenditures and lowering the budget deficit; creating a more competitive business environment; increasing flexibility in labor and capital markets; lowering business costs; simplifying the Business Code; further streamlining permit procedures for new businesses; reducing regulatory red tape by centralizing permit approvals in one location; introducing more flexible work hours and shop opening hours; and fully liberalizing the electricity and gas sectors. The government is also in the process of implementing an ambitious privatization program; simplifying and streamlining the social welfare system; and reforming the pension system by lengthening the date for early retirement with parallel cuts in pension payments for early retirement.

Business costs in Austria continue to develop favorably. A 1999 KPMG study comparing business costs in Austria with the G-7 countries ranked Austria in the middle. Overall costs in Austria were similar to that of France and Italy, lower than in Germany and Japan, but higher than in the U.S., Canada and the U.K. The study designated Austria as the most attractive investment location in terms of low corporate tax rates. Since then, electricity and telecom costs have come down substantially in response to liberalization and competition. Large energy users are free to contract with foreign suppliers for their electricity needs. Firms have the option of selecting the most competitive from among a large number of private telecom suppliers. Strong productivity growth in combination with moderate wage increases have also resulted in lower costs for international investors.

There are no formal sectoral or geographic restrictions on foreign investment, although investment in sectors with excess capacity, such as steel, textiles, and paper, is not encouraged.

Financial and tax incentives within EU parameters are offered to firms undertaking projects in economically depressed areas and underdeveloped districts on Austria's eastern borders. Some of these geographic areas are also eligible for subsidies under EU programs. The only instances of local opposition to investment in the manufacturing sector have arisen out of environmental concerns. Potential U.S. investors need to factor into their decision-making process Austria's strict environmental laws. Austria's strong pro-environmental attitude is reflected in its tight restrictions on the introduction of biotechnology products, together with strict liability regulations for research, production, and distribution of genetically modified organisms (GMOs).

Acquisitions, mergers, takeovers, cartels:

International acquisitions and takeovers of domestic enterprises are permitted in Austria. As of January 1, 2000, investors confront stricter cartel regulations. International cartels are not prohibited, but are subject to oversight by the cartel court to prevent the abuse of market power. The consent of the cartel court must be obtained, requiring that the applicant refrain from market behavior that would limit or impede competition. Selling below the cost price is considered one possible abuse of a dominant market position. The cartel court must be notified of mergers and acquisitions if combined world-wide sales are in excess of Austrian schillings (AS) 4.2 billion (USD 325 million), if domestic sales exceed AS 210 million (USD 16.3 million), or if two of the firms involved each have world-wide sales exceeding AS 28 million (USD 2.2 million).

A new takeover law, in effect since January 1, 1999, provides investors better protection against insider trading. It applies to both friendly and unsolicited takeovers of corporations headquartered in Austria and listed on the Vienna Stock Exchange. Any shareholder obtaining a controlling stake in a corporation (thirty percent or more of all shares) is required to offer to buy out smaller shareholders at a defined "fair market" price. An independent takeover commission at the Vienna Stock Exchange oversees compliance.

Screening mechanisms:

Only those foreign investments with government financial assistance are subject to government overview. Screening is intended only to ensure compliance with EU regulations which limit such assistance to disadvantaged geographic areas.

Privatization:

In the ongoing privatization of public enterprises, foreign and domestic investors are, in principle, treated equally. The government has ambitious privatization plans and intends to sell 100 percent of the following companies: Austrian tobacco company, Dorotheum auction house and bank, federal printing company, Postal Savings Bank (PSK), Print Media company, Telekom Austria, and Vienna airport company. In a second phase the government will review full privatization of its shareholdings in the partly privatized companies Austrian Airlines, Boehler-Uddeholm, the postal service company, OMV petroleum company, Voest-Alpine steel, and Voest-Alpine technology. Despite the liberalization of electricity markets, the government is stuck with its 51 percent majority in the federal power company "Verbund" because selling these shares requires a two-thirds majority in Parliament and the Social Democratic Party refuses to approve such a move. A stated policy of "maintaining the Austrian interest" in banks and basic industries has so far not resulted in specific implementation of regulations. Thus, foreign investors have been successful in obtaining shares in important Austrian industry sectors, for example the telecom and energy sectors.

Treatment of foreign investors:

There is no discrimination against foreign investors. However, foreign investors are required to meet a number of regulations. Although participation by Austrian citizens in ownership or management is not required, at least one manager must meet residence and other legal qualifications. Non-residents must appoint a representative in Austria. Expatriates are allowed to deduct certain expenses (costs associated with moving, maintaining a double residence, education of children) from Austrian-earned income.

Investment incentives:

Forty-one percent of Austria's land area is eligible for support under various EU structural fund programs. The Austrian federal, provincial, and local governments also provide financial incentives within EU parameters to promote investments in Austria. Incentives under these programs are equally available to domestic and foreign investors and range from tax incentives to preferential loans, guarantees and grants. Most of these incentives are available only if the planned investment meets specified criteria (e.g., implementation of new technology, reducing unemployment, etc.).

2. Conversion and Transfer Policies

There are no restrictions on converting or transferring funds associated with foreign investment. The Austrian National Bank (ANB) has fully liberalized all cross-border capital transactions for non-residents and residents, including the acquisition of Austrian securities, debt service, and the repatriation of profits, interest payments, dividends, and proceeds from the sale of an investment.

The Austrian schilling is a freely convertible currency. On January 1, 1999, Austria became one of the eleven founding members of the Economic and Monetary Union (EMU) and has adopted the common Euro currency, which will fully replace the Schilling for all transactions at the beginning of 2002. Effective March 1, 2002, the Austrian Schilling will no longer be an official payment instrument. On December 31, 1998, the exchange rate for Euro 1.00 was irrevocably fixed at Austrian Schillings 13.7603. Investors will therefore be shielded from any exchange rate risk of the Schilling against the ten other participating currencies during the transition to the Euro in 2002.

Since the start of the EMU on January 1, 1999, the European Central Bank (ECB) has been responsible for setting monetary policy in the EMU area. The ECB's primary goal in defining monetary policy is to maintain price stability. The Austrian National Bank has one seat and one vote on the ECB's Governing Council.

3. Expropriation and Compensation

Expropriation of private property in Austria is rare and may proceed only on the basis of special legal authorization. It can be instigated only when no other alternative for satisfying the public interest exists; when the action is exclusively in the public interest; and when the owner receives just compensation. The expropriation process is fully transparent and non-discriminatory towards foreign firms.

4. Dispute Settlement

The Austrian legal system provides an effective means for protecting property and contractual rights of nationals and foreigners. Additionally, Austria is a member of the International Center for the Settlement of Investment Disputes. Enforcement of foreign arbitration awards in Austria is also granted by the New York Convention of 1958. There have been no recent reports of bilateral investment disputes.

5. Performance Requirements/Incentives

Austria is in compliance with World Trade Organization Trade Related Investment Measures (TRIMS) agreement notification. There are virtually no restrictions on foreign investment in Austria and there is no discrimination against foreign investors, however, some requirements exist. For example, at least one manager must meet residency and other legal qualifications. Non-residents must appoint a representative in Austria.

Although not required in order to gain access to tax incentives, performance requirements may be imposed when foreign investors seek financial or other assistance from the Austrian government. There is no requirement, however, that nationals hold shares in foreign investments, that the share of foreign equity be reduced over time, or that technology be transferred.

The U.S. and Austria are signatories to a 1931 Treaty of Friendship, Commerce, and Consular Rights. A new immigration law went into effect in Austria in 1998 which brought relief on burdensome visa requirements to the American business community in Austria. While the new law cut down on the overall number of immigration slots, other categories, such as key managers, intra-company transferees and management trainers – and their families – have benefited from a newly created category of temporary visas with no numerical limitations. Recruitment of long-term overseas specialists or those with managerial duties is under quota-controls. As a result of this reform, an American Chamber of Commerce's 1998 survey showed that investors were generally satisfied in getting key non-Austrian staff into the country. Companies still express some concern about availability of visas for non-managerial staff, especially for long-term trainee positions for third-country nationals.

6. Right to Private Ownership and Establishment

Foreign and domestic private enterprises are free to establish, acquire, and dispose of interests in business enterprises, with the exception of television, railroads, some utilities, and state monopolies. As the government continues to pursue privatization, some of these industries are gradually being opened up to private investment as well. For example, legal changes were implemented in 1997 to allow private radio on a limited number of licenses. The postal monopoly for wire-transmitted voice telephony and infrastructure was dismantled in 1998 and the Austrian electricity market was liberalized in February 1999. The ambitious privatization program of Austria's new government, approved by Parliament in May 2000, foresees full or partial privatization of many important Austrian companies.

In most business activities, 100 percent foreign ownership is permitted. Foreign direct investment is restricted only when competing with state-owned companies, monopolies, and utilities. License requirements, such as in the banking and insurance sectors, apply equally to domestic and foreign investors. The latter, however, is dependent on reciprocity. Specific regulations on requirements for joint ventures do not exist.

7. Protection of Property Rights

The Austrian legal system protects secured interests in property, both movable and real. Mortgages are recognized, if they are registered in the land register and the underlying contracts are valid. The land register provides a reliable system for recording interests in property. For any real estate agreement to be effective, the agreement must be entered with the land register. This requires approval of the land transfer commission or the office of the provincial governor. Any interested party has access to the land register.

Austria has laws to protect intellectual property rights, including patent and trademark laws, a law protecting industrial designs and models, and a copyright law, all of which offer the holder protection. Legislation also protects three-dimensional semiconductor chip layout design.

Austria is a party to the World Intellectual Property Organization (WIPO) and several international property conventions, including the European Patent Convention, the Patent Cooperation Treaty, the Madrid Trademark Agreement, the Budapest Treaty on the International Recognition of the Deposit of Microorganisms for the Purpose of Patent Procedure, the Universal Copyright Convention, the Brussels Convention Relating to the Distribution of Program-Carrying Signals Transmitted by Satellite, and the Geneva Treaty on the International Registration of Audiovisual Works. In compliance with the World Trade Organization Treaty on Intellectual Property (TRIPS), Austria extended patent terms so that patents on inventions are valid up to 20 years after application. Since both the United States and Austria are members of the "Paris Union" International Convention for the Protection of Industrial Property, American investors are entitled to the same kind of protection under Austrian patent legislation as are Austrian nationals. In accordance with the Madrid Agreement, Austria's protection period for trademarks is ten years, with the option to extend for another ten years, if registration is renewed before expiration.

Trade secrets are protected by various regulations. For example the right to privacy, data protection regulations, and the federal statistics law prevent publication of production data, provided there are four producers or less.

Austrian copyright law grants the author the exclusive right to publish, distribute, copy, adapt, translate, and broadcast his work. Infringement proceedings, however, can be time consuming and complicated. Austria's copyright law is in conformity with the EU directives on intellectual property rights.

8. Transparency of the Regulatory System

The Austrian government has long recognized the need to streamline its complex and time consuming regulatory environment. Its cumbersome permit and paperwork requirements have served as disincentives to foreign investment. Some of the attempts to streamline the regulatory process are reflected in the Business Code of 1997, which provides for simplified and faster administrative procedures to obtain business permits and reduces considerably the number of business categories. However, plans to implement a "one-stop shop" for business permits failed. The new government plans to finally introduce the one-stop-shopping principle for all business permits, even by way of electronic means. Plans also include further reform of the Business Code with the goal of speeding up establishment of new businesses, facilitating access by reducing the number of trades to two categories (free trades and trades requiring official approval), and simplifying qualification requirements.

Despite bureaucratic problems, both tax and labor laws, as well as health and safety standards, are applied uniformly and do not influence the sectoral allocation of investments. The Austrian investment climate has become more conducive for business since Austria became a member of the EU. The adoption of regulations to foster competition, including more liberal shopping hours and flexible worktime have provided benefits for employers, employees and consumers alike. The new government plans to implement even more flexible worktime regulations by introducing flex-time and gender-neutral regulations for night work by 2001 in compliance with the EU agreement.

Plans are also for more liberal regulations for shop opening hours, but shops will remain closed on Sundays.

9. Efficient Capital Markets and Portfolio Investment

A broad variety of credit and portfolio investment instruments are traded in an open capital market. Foreign firms have access to this local market without restrictions and are free to use foreign credit markets as well. The Vienna Stock Exchange, established as a private corporation in 1997, undertook major reforms in 1998 to facilitate investment. In November 1999, the Vienna Exchange expanded trading hours and initiated cooperation with the Frankfurt Stock Exchange by connecting its cash market to Xetra, Frankfurt's electronic trading system. Traders world-wide now have on-screen information and direct access to all stocks listed in Vienna. Quotations on the Vienna Stock Exchange are in the Euro currency and the fee system is transparent. All listed companies are required to publish quarterly reports. Criminal penalties for insider trading are in place. The "Austrian Securities Authority" (an Austrian version of the U.S. Securities and Exchange Commission), established in 1998, is working hard to police irregularities on the stock exchange, but suffers from limited staff and budget.

New buy-back regulations, in place since 1999, have considerably expanded the previously very limited possibilities for issuers to acquire their own shares. Austria's regulations comply with international standards permitting buy-backs as an instrument to influence a company's capital structure, to reduce excess liquidity, or to prepare for listings on exchanges abroad.

The legal, regulatory, and accounting systems are transparent and consistent with international norms. Austrian regulations governing accounting standards will provide U.S. investors with improved and internationally standardized financial information. Austrian-based companies, including subsidiaries of U.S. parent companies, are required to present their consolidated financial statements in accordance with International Accounting Standards (IAS) or Generally Accepted Accounting Principles (US-GAAP).

Austria has a highly developed and sound banking system with worldwide correspondent relationships, as well as representative offices and branches in the United States and other major financial centers. Total assets of Austria's five largest banks amounted to AS 2,450 billion (USD 190 billion) in 1999.

10. Political violence

There have been no incidents of politically motivated damage to foreign businesses. Civil disturbances are extremely rare.

11. Corruption

The Austrian penal code contains penalties for bribery, which include a fine of up to USD 350 per day for up to 360 days or up to two years imprisonment for the briber and up to five years imprisonment for the bribee. Under the penal code, any person who bribes a civil servant, a foreign official or a manager of an Austrian public enterprise is subject to criminal penalties. Austria completed ratification of the OECD Anti-Bribery Convention May 20, 1999, when the Austrian government deposited the ratification instrument with the OECD in Paris. The Convention entered into force July 19, 1999. Corresponding penal code legislation has been in place since summer 1998.

Prior to the implementation of the OECD Convention, the tax deductibility of bribes and any gray market payments (regardless of their title as operating, income-related or other expenses) was abolished. The non-deductibility covers all payments and other material grants, the granting or accepting of which is subject to legal penalties.

The Federal Ministry of Justice has the primary responsibility for prosecuting acts of corruption, but in the case of public tenders, the Federal Chancellery may also become involved. No records exist yet to assess the degree of enforcement. The U.S. Embassy in Vienna has never received any reports from U.S. firms about corruption as an obstacle to either doing business or investing in Austria.

B. BILATERAL INVESTMENT AGREEMENTS

Austria has bilateral investment agreements in force with Albania, Argentina, Bulgaria, Cape Verde, China, Croatia, Czech Republic, Estonia, Hong Kong, Hungary, Kuwait, Latvia, Lithuania, Malaysia, Morocco, Paraguay, Poland, Romania, South Africa, South Korea, former Soviet Union, Tunisia, Turkey, Ukraine, Vietnam, and former Socialist Federal Republic of Yugoslavia (SFRY). The agreement with former Czechoslovakia currently still applies to Slovakia and the agreement with the former SFRY applies to Slovenia. Agreements with Bolivia, Chile, Croatia, and Mexico have been signed, but are not yet in effect. Additional agreements with Algeria, Armenia, Belarus, Cuba, Georgia, Kyrgyzstan, Mongolia, Philippines, Uzbekistan and the Federal Republic of Yugoslavia (FRY) have been initialed. Negotiations with the Russia for a new agreement have been initiated, the old agreement with the former Soviet Union continues to apply. Under these agreements, investment disputes that cannot be settled amicably may be submitted to the International Center for Settlement of Investment Disputes or an arbitration court according to the UNCITRAL arbitration regulations.

The U.S. and Austria are parties to a new bilateral double taxation treaty covering income and corporate taxes, which went into effect on February 1, 1998. Another bilateral double taxation treaty covering estates, inheritances, gifts and generation-skipping transfers has been in effect since 1982.

C. OPIC AND OTHER INVESTMENT INSURANCE PROGRAMS

OPIC programs are not available for Austria. OPIC has a cooperation agreement with Austria's Finance Guarantee Company, enabling U.S. firms to secure joint-venture investments with Austrian partners in Central and Eastern Europe. Since May 1997 Austria has been a member of the Multilateral Investment Guarantee Agency (MIGA).

D. LABOR

Austria has a highly educated labor force of 3.7 million people. Depending on labor demand, government policies limit the number of foreign workers to between 8 and 10 percent of the salaried workforce. In 1999, the number of "guest workers" averaged 305,800. While demographic trends indicate little growth in the labor force over the next few years, other factors, such as productivity gains, industrial restructuring, federal employment incentives for women, and measures to raise the retirement age serve to offset the demographics. However, shortages of highly specialized laborers are likely to occur in specific sectors such as telecom, new media, data processing and software. A recent study by the American Chamber of Commerce in Austria found that American firms have no problems in finding the required staff in the Austrian labor market, with the exception of two fields, tourism and information technology. While there is wide disagreement on the total shortage of personnel, there is unanimous agreement that the deficit in the information technology area is very high. According to the study, U.S. firms in Austria find that Austrian employees meet their workplace requirements very well (30 percent) or well (38 percent). The study also showed that U.S. firms generally rated the Austrian educational system highly.

Compared to other EU countries, Austria had a relatively low unemployment rate of 3.7 percent in 1999, according to EU calculations. Predictions for 2000 call for a further decline to 3.5 percent. Legislation enacted in early 1996 and again in 1999 is designed to counteract the rising unemployment among older workers. It provides financial bonuses for companies hiring workers age 50 and above, and envisions penalties for businesses laying off workers within this age group.

Like other EU members, Austria submitted a national employment plan to the EU in April 1998. Its stated aim is to create 100,000 new jobs over a 5-year period, and to reduce unemployment from 4.5 to 3.4 percent. The plan does not focus on any single employment strategy, but contains a policy mix of federal employment programs and work incentives, particularly for young workers and women. Current strong economic growth is expected to help the government achieve the target unemployment rate of 3.4 percent by 2001.

Terms of employment are closely regulated by law in Austria. Working hours, minimum vacation time, holidays, maternity leave, juvenile work allowances, statutory separation notice, protection against dismissal, and the right to severance pay are all secured by law. However, the requirements of EU membership has promoted an increase in work flexibility. For example, the night shift ban for women will be completely phased out by 2001 in line with pertinent EU regulations.

Austrian social insurance is compulsory and comprises health insurance, old-age pension insurance, unemployment insurance, and accident insurance. Social insurance contributions are a percentage of total monthly earnings and are shared by employers and employees.

High non-wage payroll costs (70 percent of direct wage costs) are frequently cited as a reason for Austria's relatively high labor costs and were highlighted by the results of the 1997 U.S. Investor Confidence Survey. The new government is committed to cut these costs, despite challenges from organized labor. Planned measures to reduce employer costs include tightening leave policies and reducing employer social welfare contributions.

About 50 percent of the work force is unionized. Shop stewards must be consulted on various issues. Co-determination rights of employees are regulated by law. At least one-third of the members of a corporation's board of directors must come from the firm's staff. Labor-management relations are generally harmonious and strikes are rare. However, the new government's program of economic reform and privatization is expected to meet strong resistance from the labor chamber and the trade unions, which have threatened with strikes and work slow-downs.

In June 2000 the railway workers held a "warning" strike that lasted one hour to demonstrate their concerns over pension reforms. Despite these threats, the government obtained parliamentary approval for its reform program, in effect by-passing social partnership institutions that have traditionally relied on consensual decision-making. While initial strike threats seemed more saber rattling than substantive, the chances for strike actions in the near future, in particular in sensitive areas such as the federal railroads or the postal service, have clearly increased. Thus, Austria's so far peaceful social climate could become more confrontational in the future.

Collective bargaining revolves mainly around wage adjustments, fringe benefits, and reduction of the work week. While the law still provides for a maximum of 40 hours per week, collective bargaining agreements provide for a work week of 38 or 38.5 hours per week for more than half of all employees. A legal framework for flexible working hours was introduced several years ago, and in those sectors where it has been implemented, it has proven very popular. Legislation for more flexible work hours has been in place since 1997. The new government plans to authorize introducing of flex-time by individual or company agreements. Gender-neutral regulations for night work will be introduced by 2001 in compliance with EU requirements. Plans also include more liberal shop opening hours, but with shops remaining closed on Sundays.

List of Major Foreign Investors

More than 340 U.S. firms hold investments in Austria, which range from simple sales offices to major production facilities.

The following is a short list of U.S. firms holding major investments in Austria:

The following is a brief list of firms, headquartered in countries other than the U.S., holding major investments in Austria:

Web Resources

http://www.awsg.at/portal/ Austria Wirtschaftsservice - the government's "one-stop shop" institution providing financial incentives.

Labor continues to push for a minimum wage of AS 168,000 (USD 13,000) per year (including Christmas and vacation bonuses), but growing competition among job seekers is expected to exert downward pressure on most wages. Austrian labor is skeptical about adopting the "Dutch model" which relies on a high proportion of part-time workers.

E. FOREIGN-TRADE ZONES/FREE PORTS

Austria has four foreign trade zones. In Vienna-Freudenau, Linz, Graz, and Bad Hall near Innsbruck there are zones where products of foreign origin may be stored, displayed, sampled, mixed, sorted, repacked or re-exported without the obligation to pay duty. Their impact has been limited, and foreign investors have shown little interest.

F. FOREIGN DIRECT INVESTMENT STATISTICS

In 1999, the inflow of new foreign direct investment reached AS 38 billion (USD 2.9 billion), equal to 1.4 percent of GDP, and pushed the value of the foreign direct investment stock in Austria to AS 298 billion (USD 24.1 billion), equal to 11.4 percent of GDP.

Note: The 1999 annual average exchange rate for USD 1.00 was Austrian Schillings (AS) 12.91.

Source: Austrian National Bank statistics on Austrian outward and inward direct investment at the end of 1997, published in August 1999. Available 1998 and 1999 data are from the Austrian National Bank's current account statistics.

Table 1:

LIST OF MAJOR FOREIGN INVESTORS:

Some 400 U.S. firms hold investments in Austria, which range from simple sales offices to major production facilities. The following is a short list of U.S. firms holding major investments in Austria.

American Express Bank Ltd.
Baxter International Inc.
Chrysler International Corp.
Citibank Overseas Investment Corp.
The Coca-Cola Company
Eastman Kodak Company
Exxon Corporation
General Electric Capital Corporation
General Motors Corp.
Harman International Industries Inc.
Hercules Inc.
Honeywell Inc.
IBM World Trade Corp.
Johnson and Johnson Int.
McDonald's Corporation
Mars Inc.
Merrill Lynch and Co., Inc.
Mobil Oil Corporation
Nalco Chemical Company
Otis Elevator Co.
Philip Morris Companies Inc.
Pioneer Overseas Corp.
PQ International Inc.
Schlumberger Ltd.
Starwood Hotels and Resorts Worldwide, Inc. (Sheraton Hotels)
WEA International Inc.

Following is a brief list of firms headquartered in other countries than the U.S. holding major investments in Austria.

AEG AG, Germany
Alcatel, France
Allianz AG, Germany
Amer, Finland
Asea Brown Boveri, Switzerland and Sweden
Assicurazioni Generali, Italy
Axel Springer Verlag, Germany
BASF, Germany
Bayer AG, Germany
Bayerische Landesbank, Germany
Bayerische Motorenwerke (BMW), Germany
Bayerische Vereinsbank AG, Germany
Bombardier, Canada
Robert Bosch AG, Germany
Continental Gummiwerke AG, Germany
Deutsche Bank, Germany
Deutsche Telekom, Germany
Electricite de France, France

Electrolux, Sweden
Ericsson, Sweden
Hafslund Nycomed, Norway
Henkel, Germany
Hipp, Germany
Hoechst AG, Germany
Interhoerbiger, Switzerland
Kone Oy, Finland
Koramic, Belgium
Liebherr, Germany
Magna, Canada
MAN, Germany
Mannesmann AG, Germany
Mazda Corp., Japan
Nestle S.A., Switzerland
Novartis, Switzerland
NV Koninklijke KNP Paper Company, Netherlands
Papierwerke Waldhof Aschaffenburg, Germany
Philips Gloeilampenfabrieken, Netherlands
Renault, France
Rewe, Germany
Rhone-Poulenc, France
Riunione Adriatica Di Sicurta (RAS), Italy
Rothenberger, Germany
Russian Central Bank, CIS
Shell Petroleum N.V., Netherlands
Siemens, Germany
Smurfit Group, Ireland
Solvay Et Cie, Belgium
Sony, Japan
Sueddeutscher Verlag, Germany
Svenska Cellulosa Ab, Sweden
Telecom Italia, Italy
Unilever N.V., Netherlands
Voith, Germany
Westdeutsche Allgemeine Zeitung (WAZ), Germany
Westdeutsche Landesbank, Germany

AUSTRIA AND THE EUROPEAN UNION

Austria is a member of the EU since 1995. As a consequence Austria adopted the common external tariff .

The average import duty applied by the European Union amounts to only 5.4%; in addition roughly 60% of the merchandise from outside the EU is imported duty free into the European Union.

PRINCIPLES OF AUSTRIAN IMPORT REGULATIONS

The common customs regulations apply in each EU-member state and have priority over national law.

The Austrian customs tariff is based on the "TARIC" (Integrated Tariff of the EU). The customs duties have to be paid at customs clearance. However, tariffs for certain commodities and products may be suspended by the EU if there is no production of these goods within the EU. Tariff quotas, in turn, are granted in the case that the supply within the EU falls short of demand.

In addition, the Generalized System of Preferences (GSP) lays out the rules for the utilization of preferential duties granted for imports from developing countries. Furthermore, the EU has entered a number of agreements with European and overseas countries which provide for preferential customs treatment of certain products of those countries. In order to be able to benefit from these lower tariff rates the goods have to be accompanied by certificates of origin as set forth in the agreements.

FOREIGN TRADE POLICY

The foreign trade of the EU can be considered as principally liberalised. There are, however, exceptions and restrictions in the form of import-quotas, surveillance measures as well as safeguard measures against dumping and illegal subsidies. In addition, trade embargos decided by the UN and the EU are respected.

Imports of textile and apparel products from a number of countries are subject to restrictions and monitoring, based on bilateral agreements between the EU and supplier-countries. For the whole textile sector cerificates of origin are necessary.

The EU has reached agreements on quotas for some textile and apparel products with some countries - mainly from Asia -, which are controlled by the authorities of the respective export country and the EU.

With other countries surveillance measures for the export of textiles and apparel products without quotas have been agreed upon.

All these restrictions are based on a double control system: The national authorities in the EU member states issue the import license upon presentation of the export license of the respective exporting country.

Certain iron and steel products originating from outside the EU, Norway, Iceland and Switzerland require an import document or license, which is issued in Austria by the Ministry of Economic Affairs.

Once issued this document is valid throughout the EU.

A "double-licensing system" is in force for iron and steel products from certain countries. The importer in the EU needs an export license issued by the authorized institution from these countries in order to obtain the EU import license.

Further information on import quotas and licenses may be obtained from:

Bundesministerium für wirtschaftliche Angelegenheiten
Sekt. II/A/2
A-1030 Vienna, Landstrasser Hauptstrasse 55-57
Tel.: +43/1/711 02-354 Fax: +43/1/715 83 47

Some agricultural products such as wine, milk, wheat, meat, rice and products thereof require import licenses issued by:

Agrarmarkt Austria - AMA
A-1200 Vienna, Dresdner Strasse 70
Tel.: +43/1/331 51-0 Fax: +43/1/331 51-199

In addition to possible import quotas for agricultural products, regulations concerning labeling and packaging of food and beverages under the Austrian food legislation have to be observed.

IMPORT DOCUMENTATION

In order to bring goods from outside the EU into Austria and thus into the EU market, a customs declaration must be made by a resident of the EU. A written declaration is not necessary for shipments valued at less than ATS 11.500,-.

A full description of the imported goods including weight, dimensions and quantity, country of origin, shipper, consignee and exporting country must be included in the commercial invoice. Two copies of the commercial invoice have to be forwarded together with the airway bill or bill of lading to the customs authorities.

Additional information is needed for textiles according to the specific import regulations: type of textile fabric (fibre content); width of the material and weight per square meter.

In order to be able to benefit from preferential customs treatment certificates of origin have to be submitted.

Phytosanitary certificates have to be presented upon bringing certain plants into the EU.

According to the International Convention for the Protection of Endangered Species certain animals are prohibited from importation.

The transport of live animals is subject to a special regulation with mandatory rests for the animals.

MARKING AND LABELING

Certain products imported into Austria are subject to special regulations regarding the manner in which they must be marked or labeled at the time of sale to indicate composition, content or country. Mainly wine, textiles, apparel (washing instructions), detergents and other household chemicals have to comply with labeling and marking legislation.

The certification of safety ("CE" mark) applies to machines, construction material, telecommunication devices, medical and sports equipment, explosives, and toys. The CE label certifies only the compliance with the respective EU regulations. It is therefore not a quality or a standardisation label. The CE label is obtained by the producer or his authorized agent or importer in the EU.

MOST IMPORTANT TRADE FAIRS AND EXHIBITIONS

Information on important trade fairs and exhibitions is supplied by the

Wirtschaftsförderungsinstitut
Wiedner Hauptstrasse 63
A-1045 Vienna,
Telephone: +43/1/501 05-3656
Fax: +43/1/501 05-254.

The most important fair venues are Vienna and Salzburg.

COMMERCIAL BANKS

Bank Austria AG
Vordere Zollamtsstrasse 13
A-1030 Vienna
Tel.: +43/1/711 91
Fax: +43/1/711 91-6155

BAWAG
Seitzergasse 2-4
A-1010 Vienna
Tel.: +43/1/534 53-0
Fax: +43/1/534 53-2840

Raiffeisen Zentralbank Österreich AG
Am Stadtpark 9
A-1030 Vienna
Tel.: +43/1/717 07
Fax: +43/1/717 07-1715

Creditanstalt-Bankverein AG
Schottengasse 6-8
A-1010 Vienna
Tel.: +43/1/531 31-0
Fax: +43/1/531 31-44699

Die Erste österreichische Spar-Casse AG
Graben 21
A-1010 Vienna
Tel.: +43/1/531 00-0
Fax: +43/1/531 00-2272

Österreichische Postsparkasse>
Georg-Coch-Platz 2
A-1018 Vienna
Tel.: +43/1/514 00-0
Fax: +43/1/514 00-1700

EXPORT-IMPORT REGULATIONS

Austria is heavily dependent on its export activities. Important areas of exports are the steel and engineering industries, agricultural products, chemical products and machinery. As described in further detail below, there exists a general policy of promoting export.

A. General

Austria has an export promotion scheme which consists of two parts, i.e., export guarantees and export financing. This export promotion is available to any enterprise or corporation registered or incorporated in Austria, irrespective of any foreign (even wholly-owned) participation.

Although the EC Treaty rules on state aid generally prohibit any aid granted by a member state which distorts or threatens to distort competition and affects trade between member states (which may well be the case when aid is granted for exports to third countries), the Commission has authorized soft aid to small and medium enterprises related to the development of export markets. With regard to export credit insurance, the EC Commission has not yet applied the state aid rules since most member states operate such a system. Austria has notified the EC Commission of its export promotion regime and has not received any objections.

The administration of the Austrian export promotion scheme lies with the Österreichische Kontrollbank Aktiengesellschaft ("ÖKB"), acting as trustee and agent for the Republic of Austria.

B. Export Guarantees

The various export guarantees available from the ÖKB under the Austrian export promotion scheme cover political and commercial risks for export of Austrian goods and services and for their financing. Since 1995, Austria has defined goods as being Austrian when such goods or services qualify for an Austrian certificate of origin in conformity with the EC rules of origin. ÖKB export guarantees also cover political risks of investments in foreign countries by Austrian enterprises. Despite its name, the legal nature of an export guarantee is that of an insurance rather than that of an irrevocable and unconditional bank guarantee or stand-by letter of credit.

Export guarantees are issued on the basis of the General Business Conditions of the ÖKB. Rarely do any individual guarantees deviate from these conditions.

A guarantee fee is payable quarterly. The application fee is paid only once. Guarantees do not usually provide for participation by the beneficiary in a loss due to a "political risk event." The beneficiary's participation in losses due to "economic risk events" usually amounts to 10-30 %.

C. Export Financing

The ÖKB manages the financing of exports of Austrian goods and provides services on a medium to long-term basis. The facilities are granted in order to finance the manufacturing of Austrian goods and/or the payment terms extended to foreign buyers.

The ÖKB operates basically as a refinancing institution: there is usually no direct relationship between the exporter and ÖKB. The exporter is extended a credit by its banking connection, which in turn is granted refinancing by ÖKB. The financing scheme also covers credit lines extended by Austrian banks to foreign buyers and/or foreign banks to finance the purchase of Austrian goods and services. In certain instances, the ÖKB will even grant direct buyer credits to assist Austrian exports.

Export financing is granted only if the basic transaction is covered by an export guarantee. Such financing is limited to the amount of the guarantee.

Export financing is made available at fixed (preferable for long-term loans) and at variable (preferable for short-terms loans) interest rates. However, beginning in 1995, the ÖKB stopped granting export financing for short-term marketable risks.

The actual amount of the loan, i.e., the percentage of the underlying transaction that is financed and the interest rate charged, depends on various factors, including the proposed term of the financing. The interest rate is often split for a so-called "base financing" at a fixed interest rate and a remaining portion at a variable interest rate.

A special committee, The Export Financing Committee, established within the ÖKB is competent to decide on applications under the export financing scheme.

EXCHANGE CONTROLS

Under the Foreign Exchange Act ("Devisengesetz"), the Austrian National Bank - otherwise acting as the Austrian central bank - is responsible for administering the exchange control system. As a general rule, the Austrian National Bank is empowered to regulate all foreign exchange transactions. In theory, Austria has imposed a very strict foreign exchange control. In practice, however, the burden upon the business community has been significantly eased. The Austrian National Bank has been granted the power by the legislature to issue general regulations, whereby it generally grants its approval to specific kinds of transactions ("general approval"). The advantage of this system is that it allows swift adjustment to the applicable legal framework when necessitated by changes in the international or national financial environment. In 1991, the Austrian National Bank made use of this power when it liberalized foreign exchange transactions in accordance with EC directive 88/361. As a result, it is now fair to say that in normal cross-border transactions, the average business person is hardly aware that Austria has an exchange control system at all.

If the Austrian National Bank grants a general approval, no further approval must be solicited for a particular transaction.

Regulations of the National Bank are frequently altered and/or amended so that every description of the foreign exchange regulations is obsolete after a short period of time. For financial transactions, it is thus recommendable to turn to Austrian credit institutions or to a local counsel which will procure all such approvals as may be required under foreign exchange regulations. Since the Foreign Exchange Act entails very grave sanctions for violations, it is advisable under all circumstances to secure the assistance of a legal counsel in the case of complex transactions. The Austrian National Bank has granted a general approval for all business transactions which were originally subject to the regulations of foreign exchange laws. There are a few exceptions to this general rule, particularly concerning banking transactions and accounts of Austrians abroad. Certain regulations concern credit and loan transactions. Various notification requirements are to be obeyed in financial transport or transactions.

Austria has no restrictions on the convertibility of the Austrian currency. Foreign exchange may be freely purchased. No particular capitalization is required before a dividend can be paid. There are no special taxes on dividends to foreign shareholders except those under the Austrian general Income Tax Act. Income repatriation does not trigger any exchange control related taxes, fees or duties of any kind. No limitations whatsoever exist on capital remittances when operations are decreased or dissolved. Also, no exchange regulations require payment of employees, suppliers, etc. in local currency. However, payments by an Austrian company, whether it is a subsidiary or branch of a foreign entity, to its employees might be required in local currency under labor law rules.

XIV. TAX

A. Categorization of Taxes

The most important taxes for businessmen and business entities are:
- corporate income tax for legal entities (Körperschaftssteuer);
- municipality tax on payroll (Kommunalsteuer)
- value-added tax (Mehrwertsteuer); and
- personal income tax (Einkommensteuer).

1. Corporate Income Tax

Companies and other legal entities in Austria are subject to corporate tax. Unlimited tax liability exists in Austria for corporate entities whose seat or management is located in Austria. Such resident corporations are subject to tax on their worldwide income. Limited tax liability only exists in the case of

a) corporations which have neither their place of management nor principle office nor branch in Austria, in which case such

corporations are taxed only on income derived from certain Austrian sources;
b) foreign corporations with a branch in Austria, not including those mentioned in a), are taxed only on income generated by the branch office; or
c) tax-exempt corporations with domestic income on which withholding tax is levied.

The total taxable income of a resident corporation is taxed at a uniform rate of 34 %. The portion of the income of a non-resident corporation subject to Austrian corporation tax is determined either by way of annual assessment or by way of deduction at the source (in the event the non-resident corporation derives its income from commercial or technical consultation carried out in Austria, dividends from an Austrian corporation, or royalties for patents, licenses, know-how, or copyright utilized in Austria). Under Austrian tax law, all income received by a company is classified as business income. No special rates apply to capital gains or losses. If a corporation operates in more than one state, double taxation agreements usually stipulate that the place of effective management gives rise to unlimited tax liability (OECD-model).

2. Municipality Tax on Payroll
The municipality tax on the company payroll applies to any business enterprise which is conducted in order to generate income. The tax amounts to 3 % of the payroll. Wages and salaries paid to employees in an independent profession are also subject to this tax.

3. Value-Added Tax (VAT)
VAT liability is imposed on so-called "entrepreneurs" for their taxable transactions and on imports from countries other than EU Member States. "Entrepreneur" for VAT purposes is any individual or corporation, irrespective of its legal form, that carries on a business or professional activity producing income, even if this is done without a profit motive.

The main taxable events are the delivery (sale) of goods and the performance of services for consideration by a commercial enterprise within Austria as well as the importation of goods by an Austrian entrepreneur from an entrepreneur not located in an EU Member State; the withdrawal of goods and services as well as the withdrawal of an entire business or part thereof by a businessman for purposes unconnected with the conduct of his business ("Eigenverbrauch"). Consolidated corporations ("Organgesellschaften") are recognized for VAT purposes so that related companies (including foreign subsidiaries or parent companies) are treated as one taxpayer.

Presently, the normal VAT rate is 20 %, with a reduced rate of 10% for certain transactions. A tax rate of 12% applies to wine and some motor vehicles.

4. Personal Income Tax
Only natural persons ("natürliche Personen") are subject to income tax. Generally, individuals residing in Austria are subject to unlimited tax liabilities; non-residents are subject to limited tax liability (i.e., only on certain categories of income from Austrian sources). An individual is usually deemed a resident if his stay in Austria exceeds six months or if he maintains a house or apartment in Austria.

There are seven categories of income in Austria:
Income from agricultural and forestry activities;
Income from professional or self-employed activities;
Income from conducting a business;
Income from dependent employment;
Income from capital investments;

Income from rentals and leasing; and
Other income as specified in the Income Tax Act (including certain recurring income; gains on so-called speculative transactions, gains on sale of holdings of more than 10 % in stock corporations and limited liability companies).

Income not falling under one of these specific categories is not taxable. For example, capital gains (with certain exceptions), private lottery winnings, receipts from gifts and donations and private insurance payments (if not made in the form of recurring payments) are not taxable income in Austria.

Taxable income of resident taxpayers is taxed at graduated marginal rates ranging from 10 % to 50 %. Income tax on wages and salaries of non-resident individuals is taxed at the standard Austrian rates. An exception exists for artists, sportsmen, writers or those in similar professions, whose income is subject to a 20 % withholding tax.
Unless otherwise stipulated in the relevant tax treaty, foreign withholding tax on passive income from other countries is usually credited against the Austrian income tax.
5. Other Taxes
Real Property Tax: Real property is subject to tax based on the assessed unit tax value which, in general, is substantially lower than the market value of the real property. The rates vary among the municipalities because they each have the authority to tax.

Capital Transfer Tax: A capital transfer tax of 1 % is levied on the issue of stock or on any increase of capital stock or other capital holding of a corporation.

Stock Exchange Turnover Tax: The transfer of securities within Austria is subject to a stock exchange turnover tax. Shares in a limited liability company are taxed at 2.5 %; shares in a stock corporation at 0.15 %. The tax can be reduced by 50 % if the transfer is executed abroad and only one party to the transaction is an Austrian resident.

B. Tax Treaties
Austria has concluded numerous double taxation conventions, which normally closely follow the OECD Model Convention. Either the exemption or the tax credit, or some mixed method, are applied for avoiding double taxation.
Austria has concluded tax treaties with the following countries:
Argentina, Australia, Belgium, Brazil, Bulgaria, Canada, China, Cyprus, Czech Republic, Denmark, Finland, France, Germany, Greece, Hungary, India, Indonesia, Ireland, Israel, Italy, Japan, Korea, Liechtenstein, Luxembourg, Malaysia, Malta, Netherlands, Norway, Pakistan, Philippines, Poland, Portugal, Romania, Slovenia, South Africa, Spain, Sweden, Switzerland, Thailand, Tunisia, Turkey, United Arab Republic, United Kingdom, USA, Successor States of the former USSR.

C. Intercompany Transactions
Intercompany transactions must be conducted at arms-length. Any amounts paid in excess of standard market rates are deemed a hidden distribution of profit and disallowed as a deduction in determining taxable income.
Under the international affiliation privilege ("Schachtelprivileg"), dividends paid by a foreign subsidiary to a resident parent company are not taxable if the following conditions are met:
the Austrian resident corporate entity must have unlimited tax liability in Austria and must have owned directly and continuously at least 25 % of the share capital of the foreign distributing stock corporation for at least a period of 12 months prior to the end of its accounting period; and
the foreign company must have a legal form comparable to an Austrian corporation.

In contrast to the affiliation privilege, another means of mitigating the tax burden is through consolidated enterprises ("Organgesellschaften"). In the case of a consolidation, a subsidiary, although a separate legal entity according to corporate law, is treated as a branch of the parent for tax purposes. This allows the losses of one company to be offset against profits of another.

Pre-conditions to establish consolidated corporations are:

the parent (controlling) company must be a corporate entity with unlimited tax liability;

the subsidiary (dominated) company must also be a corporate entity with unlimited tax liability;

the dominated company must be financially, organizationally and economically integrated into the parent company; and

an agreement between the parent and the subsidiary regarding the pooling of these subsidiaries' profits and losses (Ergebnisabführungsvertrag) must exist.

D. Private Foundations

Enacted on 1 September 1993 in order to avoid further transfer of private assets abroad, the Austrian Private Foundations Act offers a similar legal concept to that of private foundations in other jurisdictions, such as Liechtenstein. Private foundations under the Austrian Private Foundations Act may directly or indirectly serve any legal purpose. However, a private foundation may not run a business itself but is limited to deriving its income from participations. The minimum property to be conveyed to the private foundation is ATS 1 million.
Beneficiaries must either be specifically nominated, defined in a general way or if not named, a mechanism for selection must be chosen.

Private foundations are subject to the tax regime of the Austrian Corporate Income Tax Act (their worldwide income is taxed at a regular flat corporate income tax rate of 34 %). Certain income is tax exampt at the level of the foundation and is taxed at the level of the beneficiaries only. Thus, considerable tax advantages can be achieved from deferred payment of taxes if income is retained with the foundation for a certain period of time.

The following income from capital investments and from participations is tax exempt:

income from bonds and convertible bonds offered to the public if the institution processing payment is located in Austria,

income from cash deposits and other receivables to Austrian banks,

income from investments in domestic and foreign investment funds according to the Investment Fund Act if generated from investments as listed above,

income from distributions of participations in domestic (Austrian) corporations,

alienation of participations in Austrian corporations if held for at least one year,

income from comparable foreign capital investments and participations unless the tax payable is reduced by a double tax treaty.

XV. LABOR AND EMPLOYMENT

A. General

Industrial relations in Austria are characterized by a high degree of centralization and a strong tendency towards compromise. The Austrian Federation of Trade Unions, which represents roughly 60 % of all Austrian employees, is probably the most influential and powerful voluntary association in Austria and is regarded as one of the most highly centralized trade unions in the western world. The heads of employer and employee organizations have a close working relationship and there are, as a result, almost no strikes or lockouts in Austria. The "Social Partnership" ("Sozialpartnerschaft"), which is the informal label for this working relationship, has become known in the world as an effective means of successful cooperation between employers and employees.

B. Sources of Law
Austrian labor law stems from a wide variety of sources on different levels. A great number of federal statutes regulate Austrian labor relations and the individual rights and duties of employer and employee. Collective bargaining agreements may further regulate terms and conditions of employment. They are binding on the individual employer and employee even though they are concluded between employers and employees organizations. Additionally, a plant agreement, which is a written contract concluded between an individual employer and the works council, deals with matters reserved to such agreements by statutory law or by a collective agreement. Within such limits a plant agreement has the legal force of a statute, granting individual rights to employees.

Since these sources of law provide for rather detailed rights and duties of the employer and the employee, few employees have concluded employment contracts in writing and these are seldom more than several pages in length.

C. Social and Unemployment Insurance
All employees working in Austria are automatically insured under the social insurance system, which covers health, occupational and pension insurance. In addition, an employee will also be insured under the unemployment insurance system. It is the employer's duty to file registration with the social insurance carrier once an employee has started work. Moreover, the employer has to pay a part of the social insurance contributions and channel both the employer's and employee's contribution directly to the social insurance carrier.

D. Foreign Employees
Foreign employees may only be employed in Austria if the employer has either obtained a work permit or the employee is in possession of a work authorization ("Arbeitserlaubnis") or a "certificate of dispensation ("Befreiungsschein"). If these policies are violated, the local employment office may levy fines against the employer (in the amount of ATS 5,000 to ATS 120,000 per employee; in case of repeated violation the latter amount may be doubled).
A work permit will be issued if the current state and development of the labor market permits employment of foreigners and if there are no other important public or economic reasons to preclude such employment. Generally, several criteria have to be met before a work permit will be issued, such as the foreign employee may not be hired out to another employer, the work council has to be informed, housing of usual standards must be available.

Work permits are issued for a particular position and are valid for up to one year.
A foreign employee may not be treated disparately as to his terms of employment. However, if the work force in the plant has to be reduced, the foreign employee has to be terminated first. For several branches and regions, the Federal Minister of Labor and Social Affairs may issue quotas for foreign labor; the quota disposes of the need to check on the general requirements for a work permit in an individual case.

E. General Conditions of Employment
1. Hours
Working hours in Austria are regulated by the Act on Working Hours ("Arbeitszeitgesetz"). In addition, collective bargaining agreements frequently limit working hours and/or increase compensation for certain periods of working time (in particular for overtime). A standard work week is 40 hours, although certain industries have introduced the 38.5 hour work week. Flexible working hours, where allocation of working time is partly left to the employee ("Gleitzeit"), may be established by plant agreement or, in the absence of a works council, by written agreement with the employer. The statutory provisions in working hours do not apply to managerial employees with decisive management functions.

2. Wages
Statutory labor law provides almost no regulation regarding how wages are determined. The subject of wages is mainly left to collective bargaining agreements and, above that, to individual agreement. As a general rule, therefore, employers are rather unrestricted in how compensation is calculated as long as it is in compliance with the minimum wages set out in the collective bargaining agreements. The great majority of Austrian employees are paid on the basis of hours on the job, which is usually paid out in a monthly salary. Compensation levels in Austria vary greatly, even as outlined in collective agreements. Minimum wages for white collar workers depend on the type of work performed and to a large extent on seniority. Very roughly, minimum wages for white collar employees range from about ATS 8,000 per month for junior and low qualified employees up to ATS 30,000 per month for senior and higher qualified employees. Almost all employees in Austria receive their monthly salary 14 times a year, the 13th and 14th distribution is based on the historical practice of granting additional salaries for summer vacation time and Christmas. Minimum wage for blue collar workers generally does not depend on seniority but only on the type of work performed. Very roughly, the minimum wage ranges from ATS 50 to ATS 100 per hour with considerable differences among the branches of business.

3. Equal Treatment

Austrian labor law contains two sets of rules that provide some general protection against discrimination by an employer: As a matter of statutory law, the Austrian Equal Treatment Act ("Gleichbehandlungsgesetz) has been largely brought into line with the relevant EC directives. The Act now prohibits any gender discrimination by the employer with regard to hiring, working conditions, compensation, fringe benefits, promotion, schooling and training, and termination. As a matter of case law, over the years Austrian courts have established the legal principle that an employer may not treat a single employee (or a small group of employees) worse than other employees with regard to working conditions without good cause. The rule mainly applies to compensation and fringe benefits.

4. Termination
Termination of employment contracts is highly regulated. At any time, the parties are free to terminate the employment by mutual consent. Contracts for a definite period will end when the contract period has elapsed. Employment contracts for an indefinite period can be terminated by ordinary termination, which usually does not require any cause and is subject to notice periods that depend on the length of employment and on the kind of work performed (white collar work or blue collar work) and in part on the individual agreement. The notice period for the termination of white collar employees varies from six weeks to five months. For blue collar employees the applicable notice periods are laid down in the collective agreements and are usually not less than two weeks. In all plants which regularly employ at least five employees, all employees are entitled to some protection against ordinary termination, including the right to appeal the termination. Every employment relationship can be terminated by either side if continuation of employment becomes unreasonable for one party. In such a case, immediate termination takes place without undue delay. If employment has lasted for three or more years, the employee is entitled to receive severance payment in case of termination. The amount depends upon the time of service spent with the employer and ranges from two months' to one year's salary.

5. Paid Holidays and Vacations

All employees in Austria are legally entitled to 13 statutory paid holidays and an annual paid vacation of 25 working days increasing to 30 working days after 25 years of service.

XVI. INSOLVENCY

The Austrian insolvency law, which entered into force January 1, 1983 and was subsequently amended, embraces the three features of business reorganization, bankruptcy and debt recomposition.

A. Business Reorganization
The business reorganization ("Unternehmensreorganisation") is a proceeding to enable businesses in temporary financial difficulties but basically healthy and fit to stay in business, to continue to carry out their activities after having undergone a restructuring procedure based on sound business principles.

Only the debtor itself can apply for the opening of these proceedings and only if it is still solvent. If the directors or certain representative officers, who run a business and face bankruptcy or debt recomposition proceedings, fail to timely file an application for the opening of a business reorganization proceeding, they may be held liable for the company debts under stringent and complicated regulations. Upon application to the insolvency court, the debtor must submit sufficient proof as to the need for reorganization and a reorganization plan. The court then appoints a temporary reorganization auditor who initiates the business reorganization proceedings. The court then issues a resolution which will not be publicly announced. The temporary reorganization auditor examines the reorganization plan and inquires as to whether the debtor is still solvent. If the debtor is still solvent, the auditor files an expert opinion within 30 days upon receipt of the reorganization plan regarding the ability of the plan to remedy the temporary incapacity of the debtor to meet his financial obligations. If the temporary reorganization auditor approves the plan, the court will suspend the business reorganization proceeding.

While the reorganization plan is in force, the business owner must report the status of its business and the measures and steps taken under the reorganization plan to those parties involved in the plan. This report is due every 6 months and immediately after circumstances pertinent to the implementation of the plan have changed. If the temporary reorganization auditor has been appointed to supervise the implementation of the reorganization plan, he must report to the court.

The court will terminate the business reorganization proceedings if

- the debtor becomes insolvent;
- the debtor is late in submitting the reorganization plan;
- the debtor fails to deposit the advance of the temporary reorganization auditor's fees;
- the debtor violates its duty to cooperate under the plan; or
- if the temporary reorganization auditor reaches the opinion that the suggested reorganization plan fails to serve its purpose and lacks any chance of success.

Prior to a resolution to cease the business reorganization proceeding, the court must instruct the business owner as to its duty to file an application for the opening of bankruptcy proceedings, provided the material requirements are met.

B. Bankruptcy
Bankruptcy ("Konkurs") proceedings must be raised against debtors that are incapable of meeting their financial obligations, i.e., that outstanding receivables cannot be settled within due time or in the event of "overindebtedness", i.e., whenever the liabilities exceed the assets.
Another requirement for opening bankruptcy proceedings is the existence of sufficient assets to cover the anticipated costs caused by the bankruptcy proceeding; in the lack thereof, an advance on costs may be deposited with the court. If the debtor is a legal entity, the individuals with statutory representation power are personally liable for the deposit of the advance.

An application for initiation of the bankruptcy proceedings must be filed either by the debtor itself or by a creditor. If the debtor is a legal entity and incapable of meeting its financial obligations or is overindebted, it is the obligation of each individual with statutory representation power, e.g., managing directors or the members of the board of management, to file an application without delay. In other cases the duty to file for bankruptcy rests with the sole proprietor of the business

or with the partners of a partnership. Failure to meet this obligation exposes these parties to criminal prosecution and personal liability towards the creditors under civil law.
Upon initiation of bankruptcy proceedings, the debtor is deprived of all rights to make any dispositions with respect to its property. Pending litigation and any steps for the enforcement of claims against the debtor are temporarily suspended.

Along with its decision to open bankruptcy proceedings, the court appoints a receiver ("Masseverwalter"). Under the supervision of the court and, in some cases, a creditors' committee, the receiver is fully in charge of the bankruptcy estate. The first task is usually to determine the true economic situation of the debtor's business and whether there are any possibilities to carry on the business. If there are no prospects for doing so, the receiver is obligated to sell all assets and distribute them to the creditors. It should be pointed out that under Austrian law a distribution of the debtor's assets does not discharge the debtor definitively of its debts towards the creditors; the debtor remains liable for all unsettled debts for a thirty-year period.

All claims filed with the court are, with some exceptions, treated equally and settled proportionally to the entire body of claims filed and acknowledged in the course of the bankruptcy proceeding. Any third parties' property in the debtor's possession at the time of initiation of the bankruptcy proceedings, however, is subject to segregation from the bankrupt estate.

C. Debt Recomposition
Whereas bankruptcy proceedings ultimately lead to the distribution of the debtor's assets, with the debtor remaining liable for its debts, debt recomposition proceedings ("Ausgleich") are aimed at enabling the debtor to continue its activities and to be discharged from a part of its debts.
An application for the opening of debt recomposition proceedings can only be filed by the debtor. The substantive requirements for the opening of bankruptcy proceedings apply mutatis mutandis to the initiation of debt recomposition proceedings. If bankruptcy proceedings have already been initiated, the application for debt recomposition proceedings must be dismissed. The application must contain an accurate and complete report of the debtor's current financial status and suggestions as to the percentage of the debts the debtor is willing to settle, the time frame within which it intends to accomplish this goal, and the ways and modes of raising the necessary funds. The minimum statutory limit of debts to be settled is 40 % of the creditors' claims within two years.
Unlike bankruptcy proceedings, the debt recomposition proceedings do not deprive the debtor of its ability to carry on transactions with respect to its assets, although the court appointed receiver ("Ausgleichsverwalter") has a right to veto any ordinary transaction of the debtor and must expressly agree to any transaction of the debtor beyond the ordinary course of business. The debtor will be discharged of a part of its debts if this proposal is approved by both the creditors and the court and is fulfilled by the debtor.

D. Private Bankruptcy
A change in Austrian insolvency law introduced bankruptcy proceedings for individuals, irrespective of whether the individuals are engaged in a trade or business or not. The general provisions of the Bankruptcy Code also apply to personal bankruptcy proceedings unless specified otherwise. The basic aim of personal insolvency proceedings is to oblige the insolvent individual to make a reasonable contribution from future earnings towards his creditors.

E. Aspects Applicable to Foreigners
Proceedings are equally applicable to foreign- and domestic-owned companies. Foreign creditors in insolvency proceedings must appoint an Austrian-based agent for the service of process. Foreign companies must also conform in the original registration or later on to certain requirements regarding the guarantee of debts.

XVII. INTERNATIONAL RELATIONSHIPS

Austria was a founding member of the OEEC and later joined its successor, the Organization for Economic Cooperation and Development (OECD). Austria has also been a member of the General Agreement on Tariffs and Trade (GATT) since 1951, and joined its successor, the World Trade Organization (WTO) when it was established in 1995.

Since 1973, Austria has been associated with the European Community through a free trade agreement. Together with other member states of the European Free Trade Association (EFTA), Austria joined the European Economic Area (EEA) when it was set up in 1994, thereby participating in the EC Single Market. Austria applied for EC membership in 1989 and, following a very short period of negotiations in 1993/94 and a successful referendum (66 % pro), joined the European Union on January 1, 1995 (together with Finland and Sweden).

With the opening of the Eastern European economies in the late 1980s and Austria's excellent commercial and personal relations to trade and industry in these countries, new chances for the Austrian economy with respect to foreign enterprises doing business in Eastern Europe and to Austrian subsidiaries were created. These long lasting connections - frequently based on historical family ties - provide the Austrian business community with a valuable entrance to the ideas and customs of the business community in Eastern Europe. This is reflected by important investments of the Austrian industry in Eastern Europe, in particular in its neighboring states Czech Republic, Slovakia and Hungary. In reviewing the raw figures, such as the number of joint ventures of foreign companies in Eastern European countries, it is evident that Austria is among the leading foreign investors, with a participation which is by far disproportional to the size of its population and industry. There is no doubt that Austria is willing to provide large financial, technical and marketing expertise and support to Eastern Europe.
Austria maintains trade commissions in all industrial countries and in most developing nations which provide a network to the foreign investor seeking advice on any questions concerning the Austrian business community. Being part of the Austrian Federal Chamber of Commerce system, the Austrian trade commissions usually have the most extensive information available and are also able to provide third country information and connections through an efficient network.

KEY GOVERNMENT AGENCIES AND EMBASSIES:

BUNDESKANZLERAMT
Office of the Federal Chancellor
Ballhausplatz 2, 1010 Vienna
Telephone: 531 15, Telefax: 535 03 38

BUNDESMINISTERIUM FÜR AUSWÄRTIGE ANGELEGENHEITEN
Ministry of Foreign Affairs
Ballhausplatz 2, 1010 Vienna
Telephone: 531 15, Telefax: 535 45 30

BUNDESMINISTERIUM FÜR FINANZEN
Ministry of Finance
Himmelpfortgasse 4-8, 1010 Vienna
Telephone: 514 33, Telefax: 512 512 78 69

BUNDESMINISTERIUM FÜR WIRTSCHAFTLICHE ANGELEGENHEITEN
Ministry of Economic Affairs
Stubenring 1, 1010 Vienna
Telephone: 711 00, Telefax: 713 93 11

BUNDESMINISTERIUM FÜR INNERES
Ministry of the Interior
Herrengasse 7, 1010 Vienna
Telephone: 531 26 31, Telefax: 531 26-39 10
BUNDESMINININISTERIUM FÜR JUSTIZ
Ministry of Justice
Museumstraße 7, 1070 Vienna
Telephone: 521 52, Telefax: 521 52-727

BUNDESMINISTERIUM FÜR ARBEIT UND SOZIALES
Ministry of Labor and Social Services
Stubenring 1, 1010 Vienna
Telephone: 711 00 Telefax: 713 79 95

BUNDESMINISTERIUM FÜR ÖFFENTLICHE WIRTSCHAFT UND VERKEHR
Ministry of Public Economy and Transport
Radetzkystraße 2, 1030 Vienna
Telephone: 711 62 Telefax: 713 78 76

BUNDESKAMMER FÜR GEWERBLICHE WIRTSCHAFT
Federal Chamber for Industry and Trade
Haus der Wirtschaft, Wiedner Hauptstraße 63, 1040 Vienna
Telephone: 501 05, Telefax: 502 06-250

AMERIKANISCHE BOTSCHAFT
American Embassy
Boltzmanngasse 16, 1090 Vienna
Telephone: 31 55 11, Telefax: 31 00 486

AMERIKANISCHES KONSULAT
American Consulate
Gartenbaupromenade 2, 1010 Vienna
Telephone: 514 51, Telefax: 51 34 351

BRITISCHE BOTSCHAFT
British Embassy
Jauresgasse 12, 1030 Vienna
Telephone: 713 15 75, Telefax: 75 78 24

FINANCIAL INSTITUTIONS:

WIENER BÖRSE/WIENER BÖRSEKAMMER
Vienna Stock Exchange
Wipplingerstraße 34, 1010 Vienna
Telephone: 534 99
ÖSTERREICHISCHE NATIONALBANK
National Bank, Foreign Exchange Control Authority
Otto Wagner-Platz 3, 1090 Vienna
Telephone: 43 60

LARGE AUSTRIAN BANKS AND SUBSIDIARIES OF FOREIGN BANKS:

Creditanstalt Bankverein AG

Österreichische Länderbank AG
Bank der Österreichischen Postsparkasse Aktiengesellschaft - P.S.K.
Bank Bank für Arbeit und Wirtschaft AG
Bank Winter & Co. AG
Raiffeisen Zentralbank Österreich AG
Internationale Bank für Außenhandel AG
Österreichische Volksbanken-AG
Österreichisches Credit-Institut, AG
Schoeller & Co. Bankaktiengesellschaft
Bank für Oberösterreich und Salzburg
Bankhaus Krentschker & Co. AG
Hauptverband der Österreichischen Sparkassen Girozentrale und Bank der Österreichischen Sparkassen, Aktiengesellschaft
DIE ERSTE Österreichische Spar-Casse Bank Zentralsparkasse u Kommerzialbank Wien
Österreichische Volksbanken Aktiengesellschaft
American Express Bank Ltd
Algemene Bank Nederland (Österreich) AG
Westdeutsche Landesbank (Austria) AG
Sanpaolo Bank (Austria) AG
Royal Trust Bank (Austria)
Chase Manhattan Bank (Austria) AG
Citibank (Austria) AG
Deutsche Bank (Austria) AG
Adria Bank AG
Banco do Brasil AG
Central Wechsel- und Creditbank AG
Centro Internationale Handelsbank Aktiengesellschaft
Donau-Bank AG Elsässische Bank AG

COMMERCIAL INSTITUTIONS AND OTHER ORGANIZATIONS:

AMERIKANISCHE HANDELSKAMMER IN ÖSTERREICH
American Chamber of Commerce in Austria
Türkenstraße 9, 1090 Vienna
Telephone: 31 57 51, Telefax: 310 16 32

AMERIKANISCHES KULTURINSTITUT
Austrian-American Cultural Institute
Schmidgasse 14, 1080 Vienna
Telephone: 31 55 11
BRITISCHE HANDELSKAMMER
British Trade Council in Austria
Müllwaldplatz 1/12, 1040 Vienna
Telephone: 505 43 03, Telefax: 75 78 24

BRITISCHES KULTURINSTITUT
British Cultural Insitute
Schenkenstraße 4, 1010 Vienna
Telephone: 533 26 16

VEREINIGUNG ÖSTERREICHISCHER INDUSTRIELLER
Association of Austrian Industrialists
Schwarzenbergplatz 4, 1030 Vienna
Telephone: 711 35-0

ICD GESELLSCHAFT FÜR INDUSTRIEANSIEDLUNG UND INDUSTRIELLE KOOPERATION GESELLSCHAFT MBH ICD
Corporation for Industrial Location Policy and Industrial Cooperation
Opernring 3 - 5, 1010 Vienna
Telephone: 588 58-0, Telefax: 56 86 59

SALZBURGER BETRIEBSANSIEDELUNGSGESELLSCHAFT
Association for Plant Location Policy in Salzburg
Jakob Haringer Straße 1, 5020 Salzburg
Telephone: 0662/54 88883, Telefax: 0662/54 889

ÖSTERREICHISCHER RECHTSANWALTSKAMMERTAG
Austrian Bar Association
Rotenturmstraße 13, 1010 Vienna
Telephone: 535 12 75

ÖSTERREICHISCHE NOTARIATSKAMMER
Chamber of Notaries Public
Landesgerichtsstraße 20, 1010 Vienna
Telephone: 42 45 09

KAMMER DER WIRTSCHAFTSTREUHÄNDER
Chamber of Independent Accountants
Bennoplatz 4, 1080 Vienna
Telephone: 42 16 72-0

INGENIEURKAMMER FÜR WIEN, NIEDERÖSTERREICH UND BURGENLAND
Chamber of Engineers for Vienna, Lower Austria and Burgenland
Karlsgasse 9, 1040 Vienna
Telephone: 505 17 81

FREMDENVERKEHRSVERBAND FÜR WIEN
Tourist Board for Vienna
Kinderspitalgasse 5, 1090 Vienna

Telephone: 43 16 08

INVESTING IN AUSTRIA

The investment climate in Austria is favorable to starting up and expanding business relations. The main advantages are: full access to the European Union market, well-established business ties to Central and Eastern Europe, an excellent socio-political climate, a highly skilled workforce, and a high standard of living.

INITIAL STEPS FOR STARTING A BUSINESS

Non-Austrian nationals intending to reside in Austria for longer than 3 months must hold a residence visa ("Aufenthaltsgenehmigung"). Application for residence must be made at an Austrian Embassy or Consulate outside of Austria. Detailed information about the necessary documentation for this visa can be obtained from any Austrian Embassy or Consulate.

All residents of Austria, including foreign nationals, must be registered with the police. This is done at the police station in the district of residence. Proof of registration (*Meldezettel*) is a basic form of identification required for most official transactions.

The legal existence of a corporation, partnership and sole proprietorship begins with its registration in the commercial register (*Firmenbuch*), which is open to the public. This is normally done with the assistance of an Austrian lawyer or notary public.

Costs associated with the registration of a company include a corporate tax, court costs, fees for incorporation, an announcement in the semi-official Austrian newspaper *Die Wiener Zeitung*, and the fees of an attorney or notary public.

A number of business activities in Austria are regulated and require that an application be made for a business license (*Gewerbeschein*). Evidence of proficiency is required for most businesses; usually a passing score on an examination or evidence of prior experience in the field is sufficient. In the case of a corporation it is necessary to name a person who meets the proficiency requirements for the type of business to be carried out. This person must either be a person authorized to represent the corporation or an employee working at least halftime for the corporation (*gewerberechtlicher Geschäftsführer*).

For business activities which do not require proof of proficiency, the business licence is granted automatically upon registration of the business. Information about businesses which require proof of proficiency is available from the Economic Chamber of the province where the business will be located.

TYPES OF COMPANIES

There are several options available as to how a company can be organised; the most common are the following:

A Limited Liability Company (*GmbH*) has to be formed by at least two shareholders. No requirements for shareholders regarding citizenship or residence apply. The Articles of Association have to be notified at an Austrian notary public and must include: name, seat, share capital and initial contribution by each shareholder. The minimum share capital is ATS 500.000,- (approx. US$ 47.000,-). 50% of the share capital must be paid in cash. Under certain conditions, the capital may be paid solely in non-money assets. Shares in a *GmbH* can be transferred only by means of a notarial deed . Such a transfer is also subject to a 2.5 percent tax.

The requirements of a Stock Corporation (*Aktiengesellschaft*), a legal entity, are laid down in the Austrian Stock Corporation Act (*Aktiengesetz*). The minimum stock capital is ATS 1 million (approx. US$ 94.000,-). As opposed to a Limited Liability Company, the shares of a Stock Corporation may be transferred without a notarial deed. A transfer tax , albight somewhat lower, applies also in this case.

The major differences between a Limited Liability Company and a Stock Corporation are the following:

- an *AG* must always have a supervisory board and an auditor
- the managers of a *GmbH* may be appointed or recalled at any time
- the shareholders may give binding directives in all management issues to the managing directors of a *GmbH*
- every general meeting of an *AG* must be recorded by a notary public

A General Partnership (*OHG*) consists of two or more individuals or corporations both with full liability. The *OHG* is presented by its partners and may acquire rights, real estate, incur liabilities and be party in a lawsuit.

Limited Partnerships (*KG*) are formed by at least one general partner (*Komplementär*) with unlimited liability and at least one limited partner (Kommanditist) whose liabilty is limited by his invested share. The general partner conducts the business.

TAXATION

Companies

The formation of a partnership or corporation is subject to a fee/tax of 1% of the capital. Real estate transactions including transfer of real estate upon formation of a company are subject to a 3.5% tax. The registration fee in the land register is 1%.

Corporate profits are subject to a corporation tax (*Körperschaftssteuer*) at a rate of 34%.

The income tax rate on dividends paid by corporations to their individual shareholders is 25% without any further income tax being levied.

Austria has signed double taxation treaties with many countries following the OECD Model Convention.

Municipal tax is levied on all entrepreneurs who have employees, the rate is 3% of the payroll.

Similar to the municipal tax, there is an obligatory contribution to the child allowance fund in the amount of 4.5% of the payroll.

Value Added Tax (VAT)

The Austrian sales tax is a value added tax (VAT), which means that it relates only to the additional value created within the enterprise for a certain product. The method is the following: sales tax is assessed on the full sales price and therefore paid by the buyer and collected by the seller. The seller may, however, deduct the VAT (input tax) which he has paid at the time of the acquisition. Consequently, he remits to the fiscal authorities only the difference. Therefore, the Austrian VAT normally does not constitute an expense item for the company owner. The actual tax burden is borne by buyers not eligible for a refund of the VAT.

The standard rate on goods and services is 20 percent. A reduced rate of 10 percent applies, inter alia, to foodstuffs, agricultural products and residential property rentals. Luxury goods such as perfumes,furs,jewelry and stereo equipments carry a VAT rate of 32 percent.

Exports to non-EU-countries are completely exempt from VAT. Imports effected by an Austrian company from third countries are subject to import tax. However, the VAT paid by the importer may be recovered as import input tax.

It is important to note that all export sales (including sales whose place of delivery and settlement is outside Austria) are completely exempt from VAT in Austria. Imports effected by the Austrian subsidiary from, say, the foreign parent company are effectively not subject to VAT either.

Although the VAT is paid by the Austrian importer, it will be recovered by the Austrian subsidiary, since VAT payable upon importation of the goods may be recovered as import input tax.

LEGAL INFORMATION

Austria's laws are embedded in a hierarchical system, in which each category of law with regard to validity is based on, and limited by, the superior category. The Austrian Federal Constitution stands at the top of this system. Subordinated to the constitution are ordinary laws with an extent of jurisdiction on a federal or limited to a provincial level. Ordinances based and limited on the respective law can be issued by state authorities. Decisions by administrative authorities addressed to an individual are called orders. Judgements by Austrian Courts do not have, as opposed to the British or American legal system, any normative power beyond the parties of the disputes. Judgements are, however, commonly used in legal arguments.

Austria's accession to the European Union had far-reaching consequences for its legal system. In order to safeguard homogenous economic development within the European Union, a common adaptation of the various legal systems is indispensable. Trade, agricultural and anti-trust policy falls almost entirely in the sole competence of the European Commission. Mutual competence on a national and EU level is applicable in health, consumer and environmental protection, trans-european networks, research and development, the cohesion fund and social policy matters. The European Union is allowed to act only when the envisaged targets cannot be achieved on a national level (principle of subsidarity).

PATENT RIGHTS, TRADEMARK LAW

Patent rights are applicable on recent technical inventions which are based on inventive research and are intended for commercial use. A patent registration can be filed at the:

Patentamt
Kohlmarkt 8-10
A-1010 Vienna/AUSTRIA
Tel.: +43/1/534 24-0
Fax: +43/1/533 85 97

Registration for persons without permanent residence in Austria is possible only through an Austrian lawyer. In accordance with the Paris Agreement on the Protection of Commercial Properties any invention which has already been registered in a signatory state of the Paris Agreement will be treated as if the registration has been filed at the same time as in the respective signatory state, provided the later application is made within 12 months after the first application. The patent right has a validity of 20 years from the day of registration.

In accordance with the European Patent Convention patent rights can be obtained in all signatory states (Belgium, France, the Netherlands, Germany, Great Britain, Italy, Switzerland, Denmark, Ireland, Monaco, Portugal, Luxembourg, Austria, Sweden, Liechtenstein, Spain, Greece) by a single application. A European patent grants the bearer the same rights as each single national patent of a signatory state. Applications in Austria can be filed at the above mentioned address.

Utility Models (Gebrauchsmuster) are considered useful for the protection of smaller technical inventions. They grant less protection than a patent but are easier to obtain and less costly. Utility

Models grant an exclusive usage right for three years. An extension of up to eight years is possible. The registration must be filed at the Patentamt.

Trademarks have a validity of ten years. Extensions of up to 20 years are possible. A third person can apply for the annulment of a trademark if it has been registered and not been in use for five years.

PROPRIETARY RIGHTS

Retention of title ("Eigentumsvorbehalt") is broadly regarded as the most popular security in Austria. It does not require disclosure. The seller maintains ownership until the purchase price has been fully paid. An agreement of retention of title has to be concluded between buyer and seller before the merchandise is dispatched.

Bails, letters of responsibility, bank guarantees, transfer of titles and mortgages are other commonly used legal forms for securing the proprietor's rights. Their application depends on the type and character of the respective business transaction.

INSOLVENCY LAW

Insolvency proceedings in Austria are initiated either by the involved company itself or a creditor. The management of a company has to file for insolvency proceedings without any delay if the company is insolvent or its liabilities exceed its assets. Within a period of sixty days the management can then try to negotiate a solution with the creditors. An administrator is appointed at the same time by the Court who assumes control over the company. All creditors have to file their claims at court to obtain a pro rata payment.

Insolvency proceedings can take one of two forms:

A composition settlement (Ausgleichsverfahren) is possible if at least 40% of the creditors' claims can be satisfied and the creditors agree. Upon acceptance and fulfilment of the composition proceeding the company will be discharged from all liabilities.

If not even 40% of the creditors' claims can be satisfied or the creditors do not agree, the management of the company has to file for bankruptcy proceedings (Konkursverfahren).

PROCEDURAL LAW

A litigation case has to be presented in Austria in writing and in addition orally to the court. In case of a litigation amount exceeding ATS 52.000,- (about US$ 4.500) the parties have to be represented by lawyers.

In countries with whom Austria has signed treaties on the enforcement of foreign judgment, Austrian court decisions are enforceable and vice versa.

ARBITRATION

Austria signed the agreement on the acknowledgement and enforcement of foreign arbitration decisions (New York Agreement). Austrian arbitration decisions are therefore valid in any signatory state of the New York Agreement. The appointment of the competence of national (e.g. Austrian Federal Economic Chamber) or international arbitration courts (e.g. of the ICC, Paris,

France) is acceptable. The same applies for ad-hoc arbitration courts according to the ECE or UNCITRAL arbitration rules.

EXCHANGE CONTROL

The Austrian National Bank (ANB) is in charge of foreign exchange control which is considered as rather liberal. Usually general permits are issued by the ANB. Notifications are still necessary in various cases merely for statistical purposes. Within the European Union free circulation of capital is in force and no restrictions are applied there.

TRADE LAWS AND REGULATIONS

Most business activities in Austria require a trade license *(Gewerbeberechtigung)* under the Trade Act *(Gewerbeordnung)*. The requirements for obtaining a trade license depend on the type of business. A **certificate of proficiency** *(Befähigungsnachweis)* is usually required to prove that the person planning to engage in a trade fulfills certain educational criteria and has gained previous practical experience. An exemption from the certificate of proficiency *(Nachsicht vom Befähigungsnachweis)* by the Trade Authority is possible. Other activities *(freie Gewerbe)* do not require such certificate of proficiency.

Provided that the above-mentioned requirements are met, the **filing of a notification** is sufficient to start a business. However, a limited number of professions require an authorization *(Bewilligung)*.

If the trade is conducted by a **corporation**, it is further necessary to name an **individual** who meets the proficiency requirements for the type of business to be carried out. This person must either be a person authorized to represent the corporation (managing director of a *GmbH* or member of the board of directors of an *AG*) or an employee working at least half-time for the corporation. This person is responsible for the correct conduct of the business and is commonly referred to as the ***"gewerberechtlicher Geschäftsführer"***.

An **industrial license** *(Betriebsanlagenbewilligung)* has to be obtained if the business operates a plant or factory. The Trade Authority issuing the industrial license usually imposes a number of conditions which the owner of the plant or factory must fulfill during operation. Even after an industrial license has been issued, the authorities may impose additional conditions if new safety or environmental considerations arise. Usually strict limits on permissible noise, dust, smoke and other forms of pollution as well as on interference in connection with neighbors are prescribed and regulations for the protection of employees are imposed.

Breaches of trade law may constitute an offence punishable by the administrative authorities. Furthermore, competitors may sue for cease and desist of the non-observance of trade law under the Unfair Competition Act.

PRIVATIZATION

ÖIAG *(Österreichische Industrieverwaltungs Aktien-gesellschaft)* is a 100 % state-owned company, which holds shares in a number of important Austrian industrial enterprises and is responsible for the privatization of state assets.

In 1992, the state-run railways (ÖBB) were transformed into a company with legal personality *(Bundesbahngesetz 1992)*, but the government still holds 100 % of its shares. In May 1994, the Gulf emirate of Abu Dhabi was found as a partner for *OMV*, the, at the time, partially privatized

(28 %) integrated oil and chemicals group. *ÖIAG* sold 20 % of its stock for about ATS 5 billion to Abu Dhabi's International Petroleum Investment Company (IPIC). In May 1996, another 14.9 % of OMV stock was sold so that *ÖIAG* now holds 35 %. *ÖIAG* achieved record profits of ATS 6.33 billion in 1997 by the sale of salt mines and the partial flotation of *Austria Tabak*, although 1998 was by no means as successful. The company, however, did advise on the sale of *Dachstein Fremdenverkehrs AG* to a consortium. The government share in **Bank Austria** was disposed of in February 1998. Dresdner Bank paid ATS 7.8 billion, and their investment banking branch, Dresdner Kleinwort Benson, placed the international tranche of 4.5 million shares with domestic and foreign institutional investors. The remaining two million shares were publicly offered in Austria and spread among many small investors. In 1999 *Austrian Airlines' capital* was increased to ATS 3.4 billion and a second tranche of 9.4 % of *Austria Tabak* shares was sold on the stock market. By Summer 2001 a further tranche of 41.1 % shares of Austria Tabak should be sold to a strategic investor. 100 % of the shares of ***Postsparkasse*** (postal savings bank) were sold by the state-owned postal holding company PTBG to BAWAG (approximately 75 %) and KSP Unternehmensbeteiligungsgesellschaft m.b.H. (approximately 25 %). The privatization of *Vienna International Airport* and the government printing office *(Österreichische Staatsdruckerei)* have been completed at the beginning of 2001. Another scheduled privatization project for 2001 includes *Dorotheum* auction house.

The biggest privatization in Austrian history occurred in the **telecommunications sector**. A close-run contest between Telecom Italia and Ameritech for the strategic partnership with *Telekom Austria* was decided in Italia's favor when it acquired a blocking minority holding of 25 % plus one share for the record price of ATS 27.226 billion. An advantage was the already existing share held by STET (a subsidiary of Telecom Italia) in *Mobilkom*, a subsidiary of *Telekom Austria*, thus keeping Austria's mobile and terrestrial phone networks under one roof and facilitating integration of the two. The high sales price was justified according to telecommunications experts: liberalization of markets is expected to result in two-digit growth rates and prices lowered through competition will see a great rise in demand for telecommunications services.

In November 2000 another tranche of 28 % of *Telekom Austria* shares were publicly sold at the Vienna and New York stock exchange (NYSE) making *Telekom Austria* the first Austrian company to list its shares on the NYSE. The participation of private investors constituted a further record with approximately 91,000 shareholders. This exceeded the previous most successful participation, that of *Austria Tabak* with 62.000 shareholders, by 47 %. The ÖIAG now holds 44.4 % of *Telekom Austria* shares, Telecom Italia holds 29.8 % due to an agreement to the ÖIAG and 25.8 % is publicly held. With approximately 91,000 shareholders, *Telekom Austria* is the largest publicly held company in Austria. The ÖIAG derived approximately ATS 16 billion out of this transaction.

All in all, Austria has made substantial progress towards full liberalization of its markets over the past years.

NEW TECHNOLOGIES

Austria has implemented the EC Directive concerning **Electronic Signatures** intended to remove one of the main remaining obstacles to cross-border electronic commerce by adopting the Electronic Signature Act *(Signaturgesetz)*, which entered into force on January 1, 2000. Electronic signatures can be used in the public sector within national and Community administrations and in communications between such administrations and citizens and economic operators, for example in matters relating to public procurement, taxation, social security, or the health and justice systems. Any electronic signature may be legally valid and effective. Specially certified signatures will fulfill the writing requirement and the requirement of personal signature which is prescribed by law for certain legal acts.

Before January 17th, 2002 Austria will have to enact national legislation to comply with EC Directive 2000/13/EC on certain Legal Aspects of Information Society Services in particular **Electronic Commerce**. A bill on e-commerce is currently drafted by the Ministry of Justice.

For information on EC Directives on Distance Contracts and on financial services see 17.

In 1999 a **fourth mobile phone license** (in addition to *Telekom Austria*, *max-mobil* and *one*) has been granted. The tender of this mobile phone licence was finished in May 1999. The Telecommunications Control Commission has assigned 2x14.8 MHz from the frequency band DCS 1800 to *tele.ring Telekom Service GmbH & Co KG*. The price of this fourth mobile licence was ATS 1.35 billion.

In November 2000 six **UMTS mobile phone licenses** were publicly auctioned. The auction ended after two days with a total bid of ATS 11.443 billion (EUR 832 million). Each of the six bidders - *Telekom Austria, max-mobil, Connect Austria/One, tele.ring, Telefonica,* and *Hutchison Whampoa* - acquired 2 x 10 MHz in the paired spectrum. Of the five unpaired frequency packages, *max-mobil* and *Telekom Austria* each acquired one, the other three were allotted to *max-mobil, Telekom Austria* , and *Hutchison* by the drawing of lots.

As per 1st April 2001 the Act on the Austrian Communications Authority (*KommAustria-Gesetz*) established a new regulatory authority for the control and regulation of the broadcasting and telecommunications sector, the **Austrian Communications Authority** (*Kommunikationsbehörde Austria - KommAustria*), whose operating arm and agent is the **Telecommunications and Broadcasting Regulation GmbH** (*Rundfunk und Telekom Regulierungs-GmbH*). The **Telecommunications and Broadcasting Regulation GmbH** assumes also the responsibilities of the former **Telekom Control GmbH**, including the administrative support of the **Telecommunications Control Commission** (*Telekom-Kontroll-Kommission*

EXPORT AND IMPORT CONTROL

Since Austria's accession to the European Union (EU), the EU's foreign trade regime has been applicable to Austria. However, under the **Foreign Trade Act** *(Außenhandelsgesetz 1995)* imports and exports, excepting those of EU member states, can be restricted. The Minister of Economic Affairs may issue regulations stipulating that imports or exports of certain goods require a licence. Such restrictions may be imposed for legal or economic reasons. A breach of such a regulation may result in prosecution. The transfer of modern technologies is regulated both by the Austrian Foreign Trade Act and the Dual-Use Regulation of the EU, the latter having replaced the COCOM List in 1995.

UNCITRAL SALES LAW

The **United Nations Convention on Contracts for the International Sale of Goods** (**UNCITRAL Sales Law** - *UN-Kaufrecht*) is usually applicable to sales agreements concluded between Austrians and foreigners and prevails over Austrian civil law. However, the applicability can be excluded by agreement. UNCITRAL Sales Law does not differentiate between impossibility, warranty, default etc: if a party fails to perform its contractual obligations, this constitutes a breach of contract. The buyer has to give notice within a reasonable time after having discovered the lack of conformity or after he ought to have discovered it, in any case within a period of two years from the time the goods were actually handed over to him. The buyer may then require performance. He may also require the seller to repair the goods. He may only insist on the delivery of substitute goods if the lack of conformity constitutes a fundamental breach of contract. Furthermore, the law provides for a reduction in the price in case the goods do not conform with the contract. The seller may require the buyer to pay the price and to take delivery. Damages for breach of contract include the loss of profit; liability is not based on fault.

VALUE ADDED TAX (VAT)

Since 1973 Austria's **VAT** *(Umsatzsteuer, Mehrwertsteuer = USt, MWSt)* system has been similar to that of the EU. A new VAT Act 1994 *(Umsatzsteuergesetz 1994)* came into force on January 1, 1995, when Austria joined the EU. It brought the Austrian VAT regime in line with EU directives.

The **standard rate** on goods and services is 20 %. A reduced rate of 10 % is valid for food, agricultural products, rental of residential property and the transportation of passengers. Exports, airlines and certain services related to exports and imports are zero-rated, whereas the banking and insurance industries are exempt from VAT, as is the rental of immovable property besides residential property, though the lessor may elect otherwise (see 12.4). Hospitals, doctors and dentists are exempt from VAT.

Entrepreneurs not exempt from VAT can **recover VAT** paid provided they have invoices which meet certain formal requirements. Non-resident entrepreneurs may opt out of VAT, thus being relieved of filing requirements, while at the same time losing the right to recover input VAT.

Entrepreneurs have to make **monthly VAT payments** which are due on the fifteenth of the second month following the month the goods or services were supplied. An additional prepayment is due on December 15. A tax return must be filed annually. The tax is assessed by the tax authorities *(Finanzamt)* and prepayments are credited against the annual VAT liability.

Specific rules apply to the **intra-EU supplying of goods and rendering of services** (see 22.2). Particularly, for most purchases by private individuals the country-of-destination principle has been replaced by the country-of-origin principle, i.e., VAT accrues in the country in which the goods are bought and not in the country to which the goods are taken. Mail orders in excess of certain thresholds and motor vehicle sales remain subject to the country-of-destination principle. Information on intra-EU supplies must be provided regularly to the Austrian tax authorities.

STAMP DUTIES

Stamp duties *(Gebühren)* are levied on numerous legal acts if they are manifested by a written document. Stamp duties are either payable in stamps (e.g. on bills of exchange, power of attorney) or payable in cash after an assessment is made by the tax authorities, in certain cases after a self-assessment. The following written agreements - *inter alia* - attract stamp duty:

- lease and rental agreements (1 %)
- loans, overdraft facilities (0.8 % or 1.5 %)
- assignments of rights, e.g. receivables (0.8 %)
- suretyships (1 %)

The Stamp Duty Act contains a number of **anti-avoidance rules**, the most stringent ones on loans and overdraft facilities. However, it is still possible to avoid stamp duties in some cases.

INHERITANCE AND GIFT TAX

Austrian **inheritance tax** *(Erbschaftssteuer)* is attracted where either the deceased or the heir was resident in Austria at the time of the deceased's death. Austria has concluded tax treaties with some countries to avoid double taxation on estates (see Annex 1).

Gifts are subject to **gift tax** *(Schenkungssteuer)* at the same rates as inheritances. In most cases, gifts do not fall under the scope of the above-mentioned tax treaties.

The **tax rate** ranges from 2 % to 60 %, depending both on the relationship between transferor and transferee and the value of the estate or gift. A surcharge of 2 % to 3.5 % is levied on the transfer of real estate. If cash, bonds or shareholdings of less than 1 % in domestic or foreign companies that are deposited or custodied with an Austrian bank are among the assets of an estate, they are exempt from inheritance tax. It should be noted that this exemption does not apply to gifts. Gifts of cash deposited with an Austrian bank are exempt from tax if the gift is made before July 1st, 2002.

The transfer of assets to an Austrian **foundation** attracts inheritance tax at a flat rate of 5 % (if real estate is transferred plus a 3.5 % surcharge, both based on 300 % of the property's assessed value).

It should be noted that inheritance and gift taxes were generally based on the assets' value determined under specific rules. In particular, the **assessed value** *(Einheitswert)* of real estate located in Austria is below market value (see 12.4). Since 2001 the basis of the inheritance and gift taxes is the **threesome assessed value**, unless it exceeds the fair market value.

▲

OTHER TAXES

The first registration of a **car** in Austria attracts a duty (Normverbrauchsabgabe) based on the purchase price. The rate depends on the standard fuel consumption of the car and can reach up to 16 %.

Insurance premiums are subject to **insurance tax** *(Versicherungssteuer)* at rates ranging between 1 % and 11 %. The fivefold rate (maximum 50 %) applies when the premium is paid to an insurance company resident outside of the EU or the EEA.

The 10 % tax on the sale of **beverages and ice cream** to consumers *(Getränkesteuer)* was abolished following a decision of the European Court of Justice.

With effect from June 2000 a new federal 5 % **advertising tax** *(Werbeabgabe)* replaced the old system of taxation which was governed by provincial law. Some municipalities collect **parking fees** and **tourism contributions**.

Please note that Austria has such a wide range of taxes that it is impossible to enumerate them in this brochure, instead the main taxes of interest to the foreign investor are emphasized here.

CONTRIBUTIONS TO THE AUSTRIAN FEDERAL ECONOMIC CHAMBER

Every partnership and company that has a business licence is required to pay mandatory contributions *(Kammerumlagen)* to the Austrian Economic Chamber (Wirtschaftskammer Österreich), which are collected by the federal tax authorities. The contributions are levied in two ways:

- 0.44 % to 0.52 % contribution based on gross wages and salaries *(Zuschlag zum Dienstgeberbeitrag [DB])*
- a contribution of 0.39 % based on total input VAT from both purchases and imports

TAX TREATIES

Austria has concluded tax treaties with the following countries:

Argentina
Australia
Belgium
Brazil
Bulgaria
Canada
China
Cyprus
Czechoslovakia
The tax treaty with Czechoslovakia is now being applied to both the Czech Republic and to Slovakia.
Denmark
Egypt
Finland
France
Germany
Greece
Hungary
India
Indonesia
Republic of Ireland
Israel
Italy
Japan
Republic of Korea
Liechtenstein
Luxembourg
Malaysia
Malta
The Netherlands
Norway
Pakistan
The Philippines
Poland
Portugal
Romania
Slovenia
South Africa
Spain
Sweden
Switzerland
Thailand
Tunisia
Turkey
UK
Ukraine
USA
USSR
The tax treaty with the USSR is now being applied to all states that formerly belonged to the Soviet Union, except the Baltic States.

The purpose of the above treaties is to avoid double taxation. For royalties, interest and dividends the credit method, in which the country of residence grants a tax credit for tax paid at source is generally used. With regard to other income, under some treaties the exemption method is used, in which the country of residence exempts other income from taxation. In a few cases the credit method applies to all types of income. Tax treaties regularly reduce the rate of withholding taxes on royalties, interest and dividends.

Austria has entered into tax treaties with regard to **inheritance tax** with

France
Germany
Hungary
Liechtenstein
Sweden
Switzerland
USA

If no treaty exists, the Ministry of Finance may grant unilateral relief from double taxation.

AUSTRIA CUSTOMS SYSTEM: IMPORTANT INFORMATION AND REGULATIONS

AUSTRIA CUSTOMS BASICS

IMPORT REGULATIONS BY AUSTRIA CUSTOMS

Import:

Tobacco products
200 cigarettes or
100 cigarillos or
50 cigars or
250 grams of tobacco

Alcohol:
1 liter of spirits over 22 % vol. or
2 liters of fortified wine or sparkling wine
2 liters of still wine

Perfume:
50 Grams

Eau de toilette:
250 ml

Other goods: Up to a value of 175 Euro

Restricted Imports:

Products of animal origin:
Apart from some exceptions the Community rules do not allow the importation of meat, meat products, milk and milk products by travellers.

Animal or plants:
Travellers must be aware that certain wildlife animals or plants and parts thereof are protected by the Convention of Washington (CITES). The importation of these specimens is strongly restricted following the Community rules implementing the CITES-Convention.

Pets:
Pet owners have to respect the Community rules on movements of pet animals.

Prohibitions and restrictions in the following areas are covered by national legislation
-Drugs
-Medicines
-Weapons
-Explosive Material
-Pornographic Materials
If you need more information, please contact the competent authorities of your country of destination.

Currency Controls In/Out:
Travellers entering or leaving the Community and carrying any sum equal to or exceeding *

10,000 (or its equivalent in other currencies or easily convertible assets such as cheques drawn on a third party) to make a declaration to the customs authorities.

CUSTOM DUTIES

EU customs law has been in force since Austria's accession to the European Union on January 1, 1995. At the same time, save a few transitional provisions, the most important parts of the Austrian customs law, e.g. the Austrian Customs Act (Zollgesetz), ceased to be applicable. The Foreign Trade Promotion Fee *(Außenhandelsförderungsbeitrag)* - prior to Austria's accession to the EU levied at a rate of 0.3 % of the value of exported or imported goods - ceased being collected. The Free Trade Agreement between Austria and the EEC of 1972 and Austrian membership in EFTA were terminated. Generally, the advantages of the EU Common Market cannot be cumulated with those under, e.g., bilateral free trade agreements between Austria and third parties. Consequently, Austria's bilateral customs agreements, aside from those on mutual administrative assistance in customs matters (e.g. with Hungary), were terminated. On the other hand, as a member of the EU Austria has to implement the bilateral and multilateral agreements (e.g. free trade agreements) concluded by the EU with third countries. The EEA Agreement remains applicable to non-EU parties (e.g. Norway) to this agreement.

According to the principle of the **free movement of goods** no customs duties are levied on trade of goods - both industrial and agricultural - between member states. For statistical purposes, however, trade movements are registered (INTRASTAT).

In general, goods entering the EU are subject to European customs duties as stipulated in the Common Customs Tariff, which is patterned after the **Harmonized Tariff System**. European customs law also provides for customs exemptions and preferences in various forms and for different purposes (e.g. aid to developing countries). With regard to export of goods, *inter alia*, export licences and subsidies on exports of certain agricultural products are stipulated. The large number of international agreements concluded by the EU makes it impossible to provide even a concise outline of all provisions.

The EU as well as the member states are members of the **World Trade Organization (WTO)**, which was established on January 1st, 1995, after completion of the Uruguay Round of negotiations which lasted from 1986 until 1994. The WTO is the decision-making body and administrative institution based on the GATT 1994. The European Customs Tariff and the Harmonized Tariff System have recently been adapted to the requirements of GATT provisions.

IMPORT VALUE-ADDED TAX

Import value-added tax *(Einfuhrumsatzsteuer)* is collected by the customs authorities. It is levied on imported goods, at the normal VAT rate (currently 10 or 20 %,

Austria has already adopted legislation implementing EU directives on VAT in the common market in the **VAT Act** *(Umsatzsteuergesetz)*. According to EU law on VAT, Austrian entrepreneurs can supply goods and services to undertakings in other EU member states free of Austrian VAT, provided the recipient of the goods or services has a **VAT identification number *(UID)***. Similarly, entrepreneurs from other member states can supply goods and services to Austrian entrepreneurs free of VAT, again provided the Austrian entrepreneur has a VAT identification number. In this case, the Austrian entrepreneur has to pay the applicable amount of VAT to the Austrian tax authorities. In both cases, as a general rule the business which has paid local VAT can claim this amount as a credit against its VAT liability. Different VAT rules apply in the Common Market for goods and services supplied to non-entrepreneurs, i.e. consumers.

When entering Austria from EU Member States, the previously accustomed permanent customs checks are over. It is only occasionally that you have to expect these checks at the border or when traveling through Austria.

A new feature is that you may import your purchases, made in the enlarged EU, without having to pay any charges or customs duties. As has been the case so far with imports from Germany or Italy, you are able – as of that date - to bring any of your personal belongings or articles of use to Austria, without having to pay customs duties or other charges in Austria.

Please mind the following regulations when importing tobacco products from neighboring countries: When coming to Austria by car or ship, the ceiling of 25 cigarettes continues to apply. Limited quantities also apply when importing tobacco products from Estonia and Lithuania, or when you arrive by plane from one of the adjoining new states. Please pay special attention to these regulations, so that you will be able to enter Austria without any problems. Please be aware that you will continue to need a passport when traveling to EU Member States.

his information is intended to assist you in determining whether you may bring the goods that you carry with you to Austria duty-free, and whether and/or which formalities have to be observed on entering Austria.

In addition, the most important bans and restrictions on imports are listed so that you can be informed in advance about possible barriers and/or requirements in connection with the import of goods.

DEFINITIONS

When you enter Austria, the statutory regulations and formalities basically differentiate between persons coming from an EU country or a non-EU country. Depending on whether you have an EU domicile or a non-EU domicile, different provisions need to be observed. Whether you enter Austria for private or business purposes, however, does not matter.

HOW DO YOU DEFINE "DOMICILE"?

The main point in connection with having an EU domicile or a non-EU domicile is the permanent center of your interests. This center is the result of looking at your personal and occupational circumstances, with your personal bonds binding of decisive significance. In most cases, the permanent center of your interests is the place where also you family is domiciled. This also applies to cases in which persons, for occupational reasons, must alternately stay in different places inside or outside the EU. However, unless you regularly return to your family's domicile (e.g. less than once every month), your regular domicile is where you work. Whenever you stay in a place for occupational reasons in order to carry out a task of a definite duration or to attend school or university, your regular domicile will always be the family's domicile.

WHAT ARE BANS AND RESTRICTIONS ON IMPORTS?

Certain goods must not be imported at all into Austria or the EU. Other goods may be imported but require specific import documents, such as certificates, confirmations or permits, which you must obtain either at your holiday destination prior to your entry into Austria, or from the competent authorities in Austria. The bans and restrictions on imports are primarily intended to prevent any risk to the health of persons, animals or plants, caused by the goods brought to Austria. However, they also serve, for example, to maintain public order, safety and security or to protect the environment. Bans and restrictions on imports may also be applied when entering Austria from EU countries. Moreover, similar regulations generally also apply to the entry into the country of your holiday destination.

TRADE REGULATIONS, CUSTOMS AND STANDARDS

IMPORT TARIFFS

EU import tariffs vary depending on the product, however for most U.S. exports the tariffs are relatively low. In fact, over half of all products from non-EU countries enter without any tariff. The average EU tariff level for manufactured goods is relatively low at 3.5 percent, but some goods are taxed at a higher rate. For example, passenger cars and office machines have duties of about 10 percent. For certain kinds of shoes and special motor vehicles, the rate may be up to 18 percent. U.S. exporters can obtain EU import tariff rates at the following websites: http://europa.eu.int/comm/taxation_customs/databases/database.htm or http://ec.europa.eu/comm/taxation_customs/common/databases/taric/index_en.htm.

TRADE BARRIERS

In general, officially there are no non-tariff barriers for U.S. companies entering the Austrian market. However, certain practices in certain sectors should be a concern to certain U.S. industries. For an exhaustive analysis of non-tariff barriers (especially in the pharmaceutical, telecom, biotechnology, refrigerant, and legal and accounting services sectors) in Austria and throughout the European Union, please refer to the National Trade Estimate Report on Foreign Trade Barriers, published by USTR and available through the following website: http://www.ustr.gov/ or http://useu.usmission.gov. Information on agricultural trade barriers can be found at the following website: http://www.useu.be/agri/usda.html. To report existing or new trade barriers and get assistance in removing them, contact either the Trade Compliance Center at http://www.trade.gov/tcc or the U.S. Mission to the European Union athttp://www.buyusa.gov/europeanunion.

Some goods are subject to tariff-rate quotas, whereby after a certain quantity of the product has entered the EU at a low or zero duty rate, the rate is increased. These are primarily goods determined to be useful to the European economy only in certain quantities, generally raw materials or parts. The most important tariff quotas for manufactured goods are on chemicals and electronics. Both are administered on a first-come, first-served licensing basis. The Austrian importer can get information about the extent to which the quota has been filled through the Customs Office Suben, which has an on-line connection to Brussels, as well as through the Main Customs Offices (Hauptzollaemter) or via the internet at www.europa.eu.int/comm/taxation_customs/databases/database.htm.

IMPORT REQUIREMENTS AND DOCUMENTATION

When a delivery is made to Austria, the products become subject to the import value-added tax (Einfuhrumsatzsteuer) upon entry into the Austrian customs area. The import value-added tax is assessed according to the customs value of imported goods. The importer is entitled to claim a refund of the import value-added tax from the tax office once the product is sold again in the distribution chain.

Finally, the end-user is subject to the Value Added Tax (VAT), which generally amounts to 20 percent in Austria. For food products the VAT is 10 percent only. Alcoholic beverages fall into the 20 percent VAT category.

The rates for the import value-added tax and the VAT are identical. The VAT is a pure tax on transactions that is ultimately absorbed by the end-user or consumer.

The European Union, and therefore Austria, requires import licenses for a number of products, first and foremost for agricultural produce and products. This holds for all originating countries, including the United States. Special rules apply for imports of particular products and countries, such as shoes from China. European Union import quotas are managed through the granting of import licenses to qualified firms. In general, an Austrian importer must possess an export license from the supplier country, and then obtain permission to import from the Austrian authorities (Einfuhrbewilligung). For imports of agricultural products, importers should contact Agrar Markt Austria (AMA), Dresdner Strasse 70, A-1201 Vienna, tel: +43 1 331 51-0. (www.ama.at). The licensing authority for most other goods is the Austrian Ministry of Economics and Labor.

The import of war materiel requires a license and individual approval of each shipment. The licensing authority responsible for these products is the Austrian Ministry of the Interior (www.bmi.gv.at).

IMPORT LICENSES

The Integrated Tariff of the Community, referred to as TARIC (acronym for "Tarif Intégré de la Communauté"), is designed to show various rules applying to specific products being imported into the customs territory of the EU or, in some cases, when exported from it. To determine if a license is required for a particular product, check the TARIC.

The TARIC can be searched by country of origin, Harmonized System (HS) Code, and product description on the interactive website of the Directorate-General for Taxation and the Customs Union. The TARIC is updated annually.

It is important to note that the World Customs Organization has released the third update in more than 20 years to the HS Code. There are major production classification revisions to chapters 84 and 85. This affects not just the EU, but all 121 contracting parties to the HS starting January 2007.

In addition, many EU Member States maintain their own list of goods subject to import licensing. For example, Austria's "Import List" (Einfuhrliste) includes goods for which licenses are required, their code numbers, any applicable restrictions, and the agency that will issue the relevant license. The Import List also indicates whether the license is required under Austrian or EU law.

Key Link: http://ec.europa.eu/taxation_customs/common/databases/taric/index_en.htm

IMPORT DOCUMENTATION

Non-agricultural Documentation

The official model for written declarations to customs under "Normal Procedure" is the Single Administrative Document (SAD). European Free Trade Association (EFTA) countries including Norway, Iceland, Switzerland, and Liechtenstein also use the SAD. However, other forms may be used for this purpose. Information on import/export forms is contained in Title VII, of Council Regulation (EEC) No. 2454/93, which lays down provisions for the implementation of Council Regulation (EEC) No. 2913/92 establishing the Community Customs Code (Articles 205 through 221). Articles 222 through 224 provide for computerized customs declarations and Articles 225 through 229 provide for oral declarations.

Additional information on import/export documentation can be found in Title III, of Council Regulation (EEC) No. 2913/92 of October 12, 1992, establishing the Community Customs Code (Articles 37 through 57).

Goods brought into the customs territory of the Community are, from the time of their entry, subject to customs supervision until customs formalities are completed.

Goods presented to customs are covered by a summary declaration, which is lodged once the goods have been presented to customs. The customs authorities may, however, allow a period for lodging the declaration, which cannot be extended beyond the first working day following the day on which the goods are presented to customs. The summary declaration can be made on a form corresponding to the model prescribed by the customs authorities. However, the customs authorities may permit the use, as a summary declaration, of any commercial or official document that contains the particulars necessary for identification of the goods. Shippers are encouraged to make the summary declaration in computerized form.

The summary declaration is to be lodged by:

- the person who brought the goods into the customs territory of the Community or by any person who assumes responsibility for carriage of the goods following such entry; or
- the person in whose name the person referred to above acted.

Non-EU goods presented to customs must be assigned a customs-approved treatment or use authorized for such non-Community goods. Where goods are covered by a summary declaration, the formalities for them to be assigned a customs-approved treatment or use must be carried out:

- 45 days from the date on which the summary declaration is lodged in the case of goods carried by sea;
- 20 days from the date on which the summary declaration is lodged in the case of goods carried other than by sea.

Where circumstances so warrant, the customs authorities may set a shorter period or authorize an extension of the period.

Batteries

New EU battery rules came into force on September 26, 2006 following the publication of the Directive on batteries and accumulators and waste batteries and accumulators (Directive 2006/66) in the EU's Official Journal. This new Directive replaces the original Battery Directive of 1991 (Directive 91/157). The new Directive applies to all batteries and accumulators put on the EU market including automotive, industrial and portable batteries. It aims to protect the environment by restricting the sale of batteries and accumulators that contain mercury or cadmium (with an exemption for emergency and alarm systems, medical equipment and cordless power tools) and by promoting a high level of collection and recycling. It places the responsibility on producers to finance the costs associated with the collection, treatment, and recycling of used batteries and accumulators. The Directive also includes provisions on the labeling of batteries and their removability from equipment. EU Member States must implement the EU Directive into their national law by September 26, 2008. For more information, see our market research report: http://www.buyusainfo.net/docs/x_8086174.pdf

The law itself (in German) Batterienverordnung.

WEEE & RoHS

EU rules on waste electrical and electronic equipment (WEEE), while not requiring specific customs or import paperwork, may require U.S. exporters to register the products with a national WEEE authority, or arrange for this to be done by a local partner. Similarly, related rules for EEE restricting the use of the hazardous substances (RoHS) lead, cadmium, mercury, hexavalent chromium, PBBs, and PBDEs, do not entail customs or importation paperwork. However, U.S. exporters may be asked by a European RoHS enforcement authority or by a customer to provide evidence of due diligence in compliance with the substance bans on a case-by-case basis. U.S. exporters seeking more information on WEEE and RoHS Regulations should visit:http://www.buyusa.gov/europeanunion/weee.html

Agricultural Documentation

Phytosanitary Certificates: Phytosanitary certificates are required for most fresh fruits, vegetables, and other plant materials.

Sanitary Certificates: For commodities composed of animal products or animal by-products, EU countries require that shipments be accompanied by a certificate issued by the competent authority of the exporting country. This applies regardless of whether the product is for human consumption, for pharmaceutical use, or strictly for non-human use (e.g., veterinary biologicals, animal feeds, fertilizers, research). Many of these certificates are uniform throughout the EU, but the harmonization process has not been finalized yet. During this transition period, certain Member State import requirements continue to apply. Up-to-date information on harmonized import requirements can be found on the following website: http://www.useu.be/agri/certification.html.

Sanitary Certificates (Fisheries): Since April 2006, the EU has accepted the U.S. seafood inspection system as equivalent to the European one. Consequently, a specific public health certificate must accompany U.S. seafood shipments. EU Decision 2006/199/EC places specific conditions on imports of fishery products from the U.S. Sanitary certificates for shellfish are covered by Commission Decision 1996/333/EC and must be used for gastropods, bivalve mollusks, tunicates, and echinoderms. The two competent Authorities for issuing sanitary certificates are the FDA and the U.S. Department of Commerce, National Marine Fisheries Service (NMFS/USDC).

Since May 1, 2004, aquaculture products coming from the United States are subject to specific animal health legislation, i.e. Regulations 2003/804/EC and 2003/858/EC. An animal health certificate, in addition to a public health certificate, must accompany shipments of aquaculture live bivalve mollusks and finfish. This animal health certificate is not required in the case of live bivalve mollusks intended for immediate human consumption. For further information, please contact the NOAA Fisheries office at the U.S. Mission to the EU.

On November 20, 2006, the Commission published an amendment to Regulations 2003/804/EC and 2003/858/EC. Decision 2006/767/EC, in force as of November 27, 2006, modifies the conditions of imports of aquaculture live bivalve mollusks as well as fishery products for human consumption.

A new EU Hygiene law has been in force since January 1, 2006. This new set of Regulations aims at simplifying existing rules and at guaranteeing safer food. To facilitate the implementation of the revised rules, the Commission recently published implementing measures and transitional arrangements that are also effective as of January 1, 2006. These guidelines can be found below:

- Commission Regulation 2073/2005
- Commission Regulation 2074/2005
- Commission Regulation 2076/2005

From May 1, 2007, a second set of new hygiene laws will be in place. They will greatly modify import requirements for animal and animal products.

For detailed information on import documentation for seafood, please see the following web site: http://www.nmfs.noaa.gov or http://www.cfsan.fda.gov/.

U.S. EXPORT CONTROLS

Austria is a member of the Australia Group, the Missile Technology Control Regime, the Nuclear Supplier Group and the Wassenaar Arrangement. Exporting to Austria is not subject to any special licensing requirements. For more information about export licensing, please visit the Bureau of Industrial Security

TEMPORARY ENTRY

There are no tariffs imposed on goods that enter Austria on a temporary basis for a particular purpose, such as transit goods or goods intended for demonstration or exhibition at trade fairs. A refundable security deposit is required equal to applicable import duties.

In the case of a commodity that is imported on a temporary basis to be used and returned (such as machinery), a compensatory levy of 3 percent per month applies if the commodity would be dutiable if imported permanently into Austria. If replacement parts for warranty or non-warranty repairs of a product are brought into Austria on a temporary basis and the products are re-exported after repair, no duties and taxes will be charged for this transaction. This would be handled by a carnet in the so-called excise bond procedure.

LABELING AND MARKING REQUIREMENTS

This chapter provides some general information about labeling. Important note: labeling is always linked to the product itself! Labels appear in the form of text or numerical statements that may be required but are not necessarily recognized on a universal basis. Labels typically indicate more specific information about a product, such as measurements, or an indication of materials. There are mandatory and voluntary labels for the Austrian market.

The use of language on labels has been the subject of a Commission Communication, which encourages multilingual information, while preserving the freedom of Member States to require the language of the country of consumption. In Austria, language requirements for labeling and marking of products depend on the type of product and the intended use. For some product categories, especially those with a health or environmental impact, it is mandatory to label products in German. Although not required for all products sold in Austria, for marketing purposes it is advisable to include German on all labels.

Products that require labels but are not adequately labeled (Kennzeichnungspflicht) are stopped at the border and must be labeled correctly within three weeks. The company importing the product bears the responsibility to ensure that products are certified and properly marked before they are offered for sale.

For detailed information about the labeling of your products, please contact the U.S. Commercial Service in Austria at:

Email: Vienna.Office.Box@mail.doc.gov

More detailed information about labeling can be found at:
http://www.buyusainfo.net/docs/x_4171929.pdf

An overview of EU mandatory and voluntary labeling and marking requirements has been compiled in a market research report that is available on

http://www.export.gov/mrktresearch/index.asp

The subject is also covered in the section on standards in this chapter (see below).

PROHIBITED AND RESTRICTED IMPORTS

The import of certain commodities into Austria is prohibited, usually the result of international sanctions and the like. A variety of goods and commodities are subject to import (and export) restrictions to protect the safety and lives of humans, animals and plants, safeguard national security, or to protect artistic, cultural or intellectual property. Examples would be restrictions and controls on the import of certain foodstuffs, wines, drugs, pharmaceuticals, seeds, war materiel, and antiques.

The Integrated Tariff of the European Communities, referred to as the TARIC, is designed to show various rules applying to specific products being imported into the customs territory of the EU or, in some cases, being exported from it, with their codes and customs duty rates. To determine if a product is prohibited or subject to restriction, refer to column five of the TARIC register for the specific product and look for the following codes:

CITES - Convention on International Trade of Endangered Species
PROHI - Import Suspension
RSTR - Import Restriction

For information on how to access the TARIC, see the Import Requirements and Documentation Section above.

Key Link: http://ec.europa.eu/taxation_customs/common/databases/taric/index_en.htm

CUSTOMS REGULATIONS AND CONTACT INFORMATION

Austria is a member of the European Union (EU), and therefore the Austrian Customs regime is based on the EU's TARIC system, which is determined in Brussels. The TARIC register can be searched by country of origin, Harmonized System Code, and product description on the interactive website of the EU Directorate-General for Taxation and the EU Customs Union. The TARIC is updated annually in April.

For further information please contact:

Hauptzollamt Wien (Central Customs Office-Vienna)
Schnirchgasse 9
A-1030 Vienna, Austria
Tel.: (0043 1) 795 90 3200
Fax: (0043 1) 795 90 2399
Website: http://www.bmf.gv.at

Tariff information via phone (Monday–Friday from 6:00 am to 10:00 pm):
Zolldokumentationsstelle Villach
Tel.: (0043 4242) 33 233 420 or 421 or 422
E-mail: post.425-ztv.zaktn@bmf.gv.at

Regulation 648/2005 is the "Security Amendment" to the Customs Code (Regulation 2913/92) and outlines the implementing provisions for Authorized Economic Operators, risk management procedures, pre-departure declarations, and improved export controls.

Tariffs and Import Taxes: Information on customs valuation is contained in Title II, Chapter Three, of Council Regulation (EEC) 2913/92, establishing the Community Customs Code, titled, "Value of Goods for Customs Purposes" (Articles 28 through 36). The primary basis for determining customs value set out in Articles 29 is:

"... the transaction value, that is, the price actually paid or payable for the goods when sold for export to the customs territory of the Community..."

Article 29 lists the following conditions which must be met in determining customs value:

- There are no restrictions as to the disposal or use of the goods by the buyer, other than restrictions which are imposed or required by a law or by the public authorities in the community, which limit the geographical area in which the goods may be resold, or which do not substantially affect the value of the goods;
- The sale or price is not subject to some conditional consideration for which a value cannot be determined with respect to the goods being valued;
- No part of the proceeds of any subsequent resale disposal or use of the goods by the buyer will accrue directly or indirectly to the seller, unless an appropriate adjustment can be made in accordance with Article 32; and
- The buyer and seller are not related, or, where the buyer and seller are related, that the transaction value is acceptable for customs purposes.

The "price actually paid or payable" in Article 29 refers to the price for the imported goods. Thus the flow of dividends or other payments from the buyer to the seller that do not relate to the imported goods is not part of the customs value.

Articles 32 and 33 provide for adjustments to the value for customs purposes. Article 32 lists charges that are added to the customs value, such as, commissions and brokerage, costs of containers, packing, royalties and license fees, and the value of goods and services supplied directly or indirectly by the buyer in connection with the production and sale for export of the imported goods. Article 33 lists charges that are not included in the customs value, such as charges for transport, charges incurred after importation, charges for interest under a financing arrangement for the purchase of the goods, charges for the right to reproduce imported goods in the Community, and buying commissions.

Effective July 1, 1995, the Commission amended Article 147(1) of Regulation 2454/93 of the Customs Code which affects valuation in the case of successive sales. This amendment "defaults" valuation to the last sale, but allows the value of an earlier sale if it can be demonstrated that such a sale took place for export to the EU. The evidentiary requirements to support the authenticity of any earlier sales will be based upon commercial documents such as purchase orders, sales contracts, commercial invoices, and shipping documents.

Key Link: http://ec.europa.eu/taxation_customs/customs/index_en.htm

For contact information at national customs authorities, please visit:

http://ec.europa.eu/taxation_customs/common/links/customs/index_en.htm

STANDARDS

Overview

Austria is a signatory to the WTO (GATT) Agreement on Product Standards. As a member of the European Union, Austria is obligated to adopt European standards. While some European standards are already legally binding, others may still be in a transition phase, and still others may be awaiting national implementation. In the absence of a European standard, the national standard will apply.

National Standards: Austrian national standards are prepared and administered by the Austrian Bureau of Standards (Oesterreichisches Normungsinstitut - ON), a private non-profit organization incorporated by the Austrian Parliament in the Standards Act of 1971 as the only Austrian body to issue and endorse Austrian standards. The ON can also provide information on nongovernmental standards.

Products tested and certified in the U.S. to American standards are likely to have to be retested and re-certified to European Union (EU) requirements because of the EU's different approach to the protection of the health and safety of consumers and the environment. Where products are not regulated by specific EU technical legislation, they are always subject to the EU's General Product Safety Directive as well as to possible additional national requirements.

European Union standards created in recent years under the New Approach are harmonized across the 27 EU member states and European Economic Area countries in order to allow for the free flow of goods. A feature of the New Approach is CE marking. While harmonization of EU legislation can facilitate access to the EU Single Market, manufacturers should be aware that regulations and technical standards might also become barriers to trade if U.S. standards are different from those of the European Union.

EU standard-setting is a process based on consensus initiated by industry or mandated by the European Commission and carried out by independent standards bodies, acting at the national, European or international level. There is strong encouragement for non-governmental organizations, such as environmental and consumer groups, to actively participate in European standardization.

Many standards in the EU are adopted from international standards bodies such as the International Standards Organization (ISO). The drafting of specific EU standards is handled by three European standards organizations:

CENELEC, European Committee for Electrotechnical Standardization

ETSI, European Telecommunications Standards Institute

CEN, European Committee for Standardization handling all other standards

Standards are created or modified by experts in Technical Committees or Working Groups. The members of CEN and CENELEC are the national standards bodies of the member states, which have "mirror committees" which monitor and participate in ongoing European standardization. CEN and CENELEC standards are sold by the individual member states standards bodies as well as through the American National Standards Institute (ANSI). ETSI is different in that it allows direct participation in its technical committees from non-EU companies that have interests in Europe and gives away its individual standards at no charge on its website. In addition to the three standards developing organizations, the Commission of the European Union plays an important role in standardization through its funding of the participation in the standardization process of small and medium-sized companies and non-governmental organizations, such as environmental and consumer groups. It also provides money to the standards bodies when it mandates standards development to the European Standards Organization for harmonized standards that will be linked to EU technical regulations. All EU harmonized standards, which provide the basis for CE marking, can be found on http://www.newapproach.org/.

Due to the EU's vigorous promotion of its regulatory and standards system as well as its generous funding for its business development, the EU's standards regime is wide and deep -- extending well beyond the EU's political borders to include affiliate members (countries which anticipate becoming full members in the future) such as Albania, Bulgaria, Croatia, Romania, FYR of Macedonia, and Turkey. Another category, called "partner standardization bodies," includes the standards organizations of Russia, Bosnia-Herzegovina, Tunisia, Egypt, Serbia/Montenegro and Ukraine, which are not likely to join the EU or CEN any time soon, but which have an interest in participating in specific CEN technical committees. They agree to pay a fee for full participation in certain technical committees and agree to implement the committee's adopted standards as national standards. Many other countries are targets of the EU's technical assistance program, which is aimed at exporting EU standards and technical regulations to developing countries such as the Mediterranean and Balkan countries, some Latin American countries, China, and Russia.

To know what CEN and CENELEC have in the pipeline for future standardization, it is best to visit their websites. CEN's "business domain" page provides an overview by sector and/or technical committee, whereas CENELEC offers the possibility of searching its database. ETSI's portal leads to ongoing activities.

With the need to adapt more quickly to market needs, European standards organizations have been looking for "new deliverables" which are standards-like products delivered in a shorter timeframe. While few of these "new deliverables" have been linked to EU regulation, expectations are that they will eventually serve as the basis for an EU-wide standard. For further information, refer to: http://www.cenorm.be/cenorm/workarea/sectorfora/isss(ict)/index.asp.

STANDARD ORGANIZATIONS

Following is the Austrian Organization that develops standards:

Oesterreichisches Normungsinstitut (ON)
(Austrian Bureau of Standards)

Heinestrasse 38, Postfach 130
A-1021 Vienna, Austria
Tel: (43 1) 213 00-613
Fax: (43 1) 213 00-650
Web: http://www.on-norm.at/

The ON prepares standards in a variety of fields: ores and metals, mechanical engineering, building and construction, health and medical equipment, non-metallic materials, chemical and allied industries, special technologies, personal safety, food, environment, and waste management.

About 90 percent of the standards ON prepares are voluntary. The ISO 9000 series of quality management standards is one of the most important voluntary standards in Austria, and has become almost a requirement in many industries.

NIST Notify U.S. Service

Member countries of the World Trade Organization (WTO) are required under the Agreement on Technical Barriers to Trade (TBT Agreement) to report to the WTO all proposed technical regulations that could affect trade with other Member countries. Notify U.S. is a free, web-based e-mail subscription service that offers an opportunity to review and comment on proposed foreign technical regulations that can affect your access to international markets. Register online at Internet URL: http://www.nist.gov/notifyus/.

Testing

The most important testing organization in Austria is TueV Oesterreich, Krugerstrasse 15, A-1015 Vienna, Austria. Phone: +43 1 514 07-0; Fax: +43 1 514 07-6005.

CONFORMITY ASSESSMENT

Conformity Assessment is a mandatory step for the manufacturer in the process of complying with specific EU legislation. The purpose of conformity assessment is to ensure consistency of compliance during all stages of the production process to facilitate acceptance of the final product. EU product legislation gives manufacturers some choice with regard to conformity assessment, depending on the level of risk involved in the use of their product. These range from self-certification, type examination and production quality control system, to full quality assurance system. You can find conformity assessment bodies in individual Member state countries in this list by the European Commission http://europa.eu.int/comm/enterprise/nando-is/home/index.cfm. To promote market acceptance of the final product, there are a number of voluntary conformity assessment programs. CEN's certification systems are the Keymark, the CENCER mark, and the European Standard Agreement Group. CENELEC has its own initiative. ETSI does not offer conformity assessment services.

PRODUCT CERTIFICATION

To sell their product on the EU market of 27 member states as well as Norway, Liechtenstein and Iceland, U.S. exporters are required to apply CE marking whenever their product is covered by specific product legislation. CE marking product legislation offers manufacturers a number of choices and requires decisions to determine which safety/health concerns need to be addressed, which conformity assessment module is best suited to the manufacturing process, and whether or not to use EU-wide harmonized standards. There is no easy way for U.S. exporters to understand

and go through the process of CE marking, but hopefully this chapter provides some background and clarification.

In the eighties, the New Approach was launched to overcome the lengthy adoption process of "old approach" type legislation. The goal of the European Union's harmonization program under the New Approach is to streamline technical harmonization and the development of standards for certain product groups, including, among others, machinery, toys, construction products, electromagnetic compatibility, personal protective equipment, non-automatic weighing instruments, medical devices, gas appliances, hot water boilers, and radio and telecommunications terminal equipment (RTTE). Under the New Approach, Directives cover essential safety, health and environmental requirements. The three regional European standards organizations, CEN, CENELEC and ETSI, are mandated by the Commission to develop technical standards that are consistent with the essential requirements of EU Directives.

Products manufactured to standards adopted by CEN, CENELEC and ETSI, and published in the Official Journal as harmonized standards, are presumed to conform to the requirements of EU Directives. The manufacturer then applies the CE Marking and issues a declaration of conformity. With these, the product will be allowed to circulate freely within the European Union. A manufacturer can choose not to use the harmonized EU standards, but must then demonstrate that the product meets the essential safety and performance requirements. Trade barriers occur when design, rather than performance, standards are developed by the relevant European standardization organization, and when U.S. companies do not have access to the standardization process through a European presence.

The CE marking addresses itself primarily to the national control authorities of the Member States, and its use simplifies the task of essential market surveillance of regulated products. Although CE marking is intended primarily for inspection purposes by EU Member State inspectors, the consumer may well perceive it as a quality mark.

The CE mark is not intended to include detailed technical information on the product, but there must be enough information to enable the inspector to trace the product back to the manufacturer or the authorized representative established in the EU. This detailed information should not appear next to the CE marking, but rather on the declaration of conformity, the certificate of conformity (which the manufacturer or authorized agent must be able to provide at any time, together with the product's technical file), or the documents accompanying the product.

ACCREDITATION

Independent certification bodies, known as notified bodies, have been officially accredited by competent authorities to test and certify to EU requirements. Under the U.S./EU Mutual Recognition Agreements (MRAs), however, notified bodies based in the United States and referred to as conformity assessment bodies will be allowed to test in the United States to EU specifications, and vice versa. The costs will be significantly lower and U.S. products will, as a result, become more competitive. At this time, the U.S./EU MRAs cover the following sectors: EMC (in force), RTTE (in force), medical devices (in transition), pharmaceutical (in transition), and recreational craft (in force). The U.S. Department of Commerce, National Institute of Standards and Technology (NIST), has a link on its website to American and European Conformity Assessment bodies operating under a mutual recognition agreement.

Accreditation is handled at Member state level. European Accreditation is an organization representing nationally recognized accreditation bodies. Membership is open to nationally recognized accreditation bodies in countries in the European geographical area that can demonstrate that they operate an accreditation system compatible with EN45003 or ISO/IEC Guide 58.

The Austrian Accreditation Body:

Bundesministerium fuer Wirtschaft und Arbeit
(Austrian Federal Ministry for Economy and Labor)
Abteilung I/12
Dampfschiffstrasse 4
A-1030 Vienna, Austria
Contact: Dipl-Ing. Guener P. Friers
Tel.: (0043 1) 711 00-82 48
Fax: (0043 1) 714 35 82
E-mail: guenter.friers@bmwa.gv.at
E-mail: akkreditierung@bmwa.gv.at

The accreditation of laboratories is required for any sector in Austria.

Technical Regulations

The Official Journal is the official gazette of the European Union. It is published daily and consists of two series covering draft and adopted legislation as well as case law, questions from the European Parliament, studies by committees, and more (http://europa.eu.int/eur-lex/lex/JOIndex.do?ihmlang=en). It lists the standards reference numbers linked to legislation (http://www.newapproach.org/Directives/DirectiveList.asp). National technical Regulations are published on the Commission's website http://ec.europa.eu/comm/enterprise/tris/ to allow other countries and interested parties to comment.

Member countries of the World Trade Organization (WTO) are required under the Agreement on Technical Barriers to Trade (TBT Agreement) to report to the WTO all proposed technical regulations that could affect trade with other member countries. Notify US is a free, web-based e-mail subscription service that offers U.S. companies an opportunity to review and comment on proposed foreign technical regulations that can affect their access to international markets. Companies may register on-line at: http://tsapps.nist.gov/notifyus/data/index/index.cfm

LABELING AND MARKING

Manufacturers should be mindful that, in addition to the EU's mandatory and voluntary schemes, national voluntary labeling schemes might still apply. These schemes may be preferred by consumers, and thus be essential for marketing purposes.

Manufacturers are advised to take note that all labels require metric units, although dual labeling is also acceptable until the end of December 2009. The use of language on labels has been the subject of a Commission Communication that encourages multilingual information, while preserving the freedom of Member States to require the use of the language of the country of consumption.

The EU has mandated that certain products be sold in standardized quantities. Council Directive 80/232/EC provides permissible ranges of nominal quantities, container capacities, and volumes for a variety of products. Please note that this legislation is currently being reviewed in an effort to simplify it.

Key Link:

http://eur-lex.europa.eu/LexUriServ/LexUriServ.do?uri=CELEX:31980L0232:EN:HTML

THE ECO-LABEL

EU legislation of 1992, revised in 2000, distinguishes environmentally friendly products and services through a voluntary labeling scheme called the Eco-label. Currently, the scheme applies to seven product groups: cleaning products, appliances, paper products, clothing, lubricants, home and garden products and tourism services. The symbol, a green flower, is a voluntary mark. The Eco-label is awarded to producers who can show that their product is less harmful to the environment than similar products. This "green label" also aims to encourage consumers to buy green products. However, the scheme does not establish ecological standards that all manufacturers are required to meet in order to place a product on the market. Products without the EU Eco-label can still enter the EU as long as they meet existing health, safety, and environmental standards and regulations.

The EU Eco-label is an expensive scheme (costing up to EUR 1,300 for registration and up to EUR 25,000 per year for the use of the label, with a reduction of 25 percent for SMEs) and has therefore not been widely used so far. However, the Eco-label can be a good marketing tool and, given the growing demand for green products in Europe, it is likely that the Eco-label will more and more become a reference for green consumers.

Key Links: http://buyusainfo.net/docs/x_4284752.pdf
http://ec.europa.eu/comm/environment/ecolabel/index_en.htm
http://www.eco-label.com/.

In June 2005, the European Commission tabled a Communication designed to launch a debate on the best way ahead regarding the eco-labeling of fishery products. This initiative follows a growing interest by non-governmental environmental organizations and increased interest by the public in food products associated with environmental sustainability. A number of eco-labeling schemes have already been established with regard to fishery products, and other initiatives are being developed. It is not always easy to determine the reliability of eco-labeling claims. International guidelines on eco-labeling have recently been adopted by the Food and Agriculture Organization (FAO) (www.fao.org), and discussions f these issues and their potential effect on free trade are taking place in other international fora such as the World Trade Organization (WTO) (www.wto.org).

Companies selling a broad range of electrical goods in Europe are required to comply with the Waste Electrical and Electronic Equipment Directive (WEEE), and since July 2006 they need to conform to the Restriction on Use of certain Hazardous Substances Directive (RoHS). One of the requirements is that electrical goods be marked so that consumers do not throw them away with municipal waste. For details on WEEE and RoHS requirements and implementation, please see the following website:http://www.buyusa.gov/europeanunion/weee.html.

Manufacturers and distributors should be aware of specific requirements regarding the labeling and traceability of foodstuffs, including seafood, which are covered by several EU Regulations:

- Regulation 178/2002/EC
- Directive 2000/13/EC, last amended by Directive 2003/89/EC as regards indication of the ingredients present in foodstuffs.
- Commission Directive 2005/26/EC.

- Council Regulation 104/2000/EC (seafood)
- Commission Regulation 2065/2001/EC (seafood, only for retail channels)

CONTACT INFORMATION

U.S. Mission to the E.U.
Foreign Commercial Service
Rue Zinner 13
B - 1000 Brussels, Belgium
Fax: 32 2 513 1228

Gwen B. Lyle – Standards Attaché
Tel: 32 2 508 2674
gwen.lyle@mail.doc.gov

Sylvia Mohr – Standards Specialist
sylvia.mohr@mail.doc.gov
Tel: 32 2 508 2675
Fax: 32 2 513 1228

CEN – European Committee for Standardization
Rue de Stassart 36
B – 1050 Brussels, Belgium
Fax: 32 2 550 08 19
Tel: 32 2 550 08 25 / 550 08 11
http://www.cen.eu/cenorm/index.htm

CENELEC – European Committee for Electrotechnical Standardization
Rue de Stassart 35
B – 1050 Brussels, Belgium
Tel: 32 2 519 68 71
Fax: 32 2 519 69 19
http://www.cenelec.org

ETSI - European Telecommunications Standards Institute
Route des Lucioles 650
F – 06921 Sophia Antipolis Cedex, France
Tel: 33 4 92 94 42 12
Fax: 33 4 93 65 22 99
http://www.etsi.org

European Commission
Enterprise Directorate - General
Rue de la Science 15
B – 1040 Brussels, Belgium
Mail: Office: SC15 02/09 B – 1049 Brussels
Tel: 32 2 299 56 72
Fax: 32 2 299 16 75
http://europa.eu.int/comm/enterprise/standards_policy/

EFTA – European Free Trade Association
Rue de Trèves 74

B – 1040 Brussels
Tel: 32 2 286 17 41
Fax: 32 2 286 17 42
http://www.efta.int/

NORMAPME – European Office of Crafts Trades and Small and Medium-Sized Enterprises for Standardization
Rue Jacques de Lalaing 4
B – 1040 Brussels, Belgium
Tel: 32 2 282 05 31
Fax: 32 2 282 05 35
http://www.normapme.com

ANEC - European Association for the Co-ordination of Consumer Representation in Standardization
Avenue de Tervueren 36, Box 4
B – 1040 Brussels, Belgium
Tel: 32 2 743 24 70
Fax: 32 2 706 54 30
http://www.anec.org

ECOS – European Environmental Citizens Organization for Standardization
Boulevard de Waterloo 34
B – 1000 Brussels, Belgium
Tel: 32 2 289 10 93
Fax: 32 2 289 10 99

EOTA – European Organization for Technical Approvals
(for construction products)
Avenue des Arts 40
B – 1040 Brussels, Belgium
Tel: 32 2 502 69 00
Fax: 32 2 502 38 14
info@eota.be ww
w.eota.be

REACH is a new EU regulatory framework for the Registration, Evaluation and Authorization of Chemicals (REACH), which will enter into force in Austria on June 1, 2007. The aim is to improve protection of health and the environment through better and earlier identification of the properties of chemical substances. The REACH Regulation also gives industry greater responsibility to manage the risks from chemicals and to provide safety information on substances. Manufacturers and importers will be required to gather information on the properties of their substances, which will help them manage them safely, and must register the information in a central database. A chemicals agency in Helsinki will act as the central point in the REACH system: it will manage the databases necessary to operate the system, co-ordinate the in-depth evaluation of suspicious chemicals, and be responsible for a public database in which consumers and professionals can find information on hazards.

For more information about REACH, please look at: http://www.buyusa.gov/austria/en

TRADE AGREEMENTS

As an EU member, Austria participates in the European Economic Area (EEA). Austria is also a member of the World Trade Organization (WTO). Although Austria has no bilateral free trade agreements, as an EU member it participates in all EU trade agreements, including:

- Association agreements involving political and economic elements in addition to tariff reductions with Bulgaria, Switzerland, Czech Republic, Hungary, Iceland, Liechtenstein, Norway, Poland, Romania, Slovak Republic, South Africa.
- Free trade agreements primarily involving reductions in tariffs. Agreements are in place with Estonia, Latvia, Lithuania, and Mexico.
- Cooperation agreements concentrating on increasing trade and cooperation, in place with Belarus, Kazakhstan, Kyrgystan, Moldova, Russia, and Ukraine.

In addition, there are trade agreements in place with Cyprus, Malta, Morocco, Tunisia, Egypt, Syria and Israel. There are Customs Union agreements with Turkey, San Marino and Andorra. The EU extends Customs preferences to many African and Caribbean states.

EXPORT PROMOTION

Exporting goods and services is of vital significance for each economy in an increasingly inter-linked and globalised world. In Austria, the total of exported goods during 2003 amounted to approx. € 78.8 billion. Currently, approx. 7% of all Austrian exports are covered within the scope of the Austrian export promotion system.

However, "export promotion" should not be understood as the granting of subsidies, financial aid or direct payments to exporters. Instead, this system consists of state-supported export guarantees. They insure against certain risks arising when dealing with international contract partners as far as such risks cannot be covered appropriately by private export credit insurers. This type of hedging in the form of guarantees by the Federal Minister of Finance enables exporters the access to favourable financing conditions for their export businesses .

In today's international competitive environment exporting companies intending to succeed have to offer - in addition to their goods and services - adequate risk coverage and financing options. Projects might be large, situated in riskier countries outside the OECD and require multisourcing. Private export credit insurance and financing instruments do not offer sufficient facilities. This is the main reason why states with exporting companies run state-supported export credit systems (EU and OECD countries, also emerging markets such as India, Brazil, South Africa, etc.). The Austrian export promotion system enables Austrian exporters to participate under fair competitive conditions in international markets .

The Oesterreichische Kontrollbank AG ("OeKB") has been authorised by the Republic of Austria to act as its handling agent for the Austrian export guarantee system.

To facilitate financing exports covered by guarantees, the Federal Minister of Finance is also authorised to assume liabilities for capital taken up by the authorised OeKB on national and international finance markets. These funds are then made available to exporting companies by OeKB's export financing scheme .

The Austrian export promotion system is in accordance with relevant international rules (OECD–, WTO- and EU- rules and regulations). It is designed to be self-supporting due to its fee structure. Exporters have to pay risk adequate guarantee fees.

The so called "Paris Club" (multilateral forum of creditor states) deals with payment difficulties in the field of state-guaranteed export credits and development aid credits. Based on a Paris Club agreement, solutions are implemented bilaterally.

EXPORT REGULATIONS BY AUSTRIA CUSTOMS

Currency Controls In/Out:
Travellers entering or leaving the Community and carrying any sum equal to or exceeding ?10,000 (or its equivalent in other currencies or easily convertible assets such as cheques drawn on a third party) to make a declaration to the customs authorities.

Exports:
Travellers holding a valid ticket for a destination outside the EU (and certain areas within the EU, such as the Canary Islands) can buy goods free of duty and tax in so-called "tax-free shops" in airports and ports. There are no limits as to the quantity or value of the goods that can be purchased duty and tax free. Travellers should however bear in mind that the importation of these goods in the country of destination will be subject to duty and tax allowances, similar to those applying to travellers that enter the EU from a non Member State.

Abolition of duty free goods within the EU
On 30 June 1999, the sale of duty-free alcohol and tobacco at airports and at sea was abolished in all of the original 15 EU member states. Of the 10 new member states that joined the EU on May 1st 2004, these rules already apply to Cyprus and Malta. There are transitional rules in place for visitors returning to one of the original 15 EU countries from one of the other new EU countries. But for the original 15, plus Cyprus and Malta, there are now no limits imposed on importing tobacco and alcohol products from one EU country to another (with the exceptions of Denmark, Finland and Sweden, where limits are imposed). Travellers should note that they may be required to prove at customs that the goods purchased are for personal use only.

AUTHORIZED ECONOMIC OPERATORS (AEO)

In April 2005, the European Parliament and the Council of the European Union passed an amendment to the Customs Code (Regulation (EC) No 648/2005) with the objective of increasing security when importing and exporting goods into and out of the European Community while also simplifying customs clearance for ‘authorised economic operators’ (AEOs). The details of this security amendment were regulated in the amendment to the Customs Code Implementing Regulation (Regulation (EC) No 1875/2006).

Measures should now be gradually implemented by the end of 2013 to harmonise customs controls and improve the protection of the EU’s external borders. The concept of the ‘secure supply chain’ will increasingly affect customs administrations and operators involved in customs activities.

The concept of the authorised economic operator (AEO) should simplify customs clearance for economic operators while also making it possible to implement customs controls more efficiently and in a more targeted manner and to tighten authorisation procedures for customs simplifications.

AEO CERTIFICATES SINCE 1 JANUARY 2008

Since 1 January 2008, economic operators based in the EU and certain third country operators have been able to apply for AEO status. AEO status is awarded by the customs authorities in the form of certificates and has the advantages of facilitation with regard to customs regulations and/or simplifications with regard to security-related customs controls. Before certifying a company with AEO status, the customs authorities must review whether the economic operator has previously properly observed customs regulations, has a satisfactory accounting system, is demonstrably solvent and has suitable security standards.

In addition to the binding legal regulations, the Commission has also published guidelines to ensure the harmonised assessment and evaluation of AEO criteria by customs authorities throughout the EU.

THE FOLLOWING AEO CERTIFICATES CAN BE AWARDED:

- 'AEOC' – for customs simplifications
- 'AEOS' – for facilitation with regard to security-related customs controls
- 'AEOF' – for a combination of customs simplifications and facilitation with regard to security-related customs control

INFORMATION ON THE AEO APPLICATION PROCEDURE

Since 1 January 2008, it has been possible to apply to customs offices for AEO certificates. The sections below provide you with key information and tips on the AEO application procedure.

RESPONSIBILITY

Economic operators based **in** Austria and subject to the jurisdiction of the Austrian customs administrations must submit their application to the customs office responsible for the area in which the applicant's residence or registered office is based. Economic operators based **outside** Austria and subject to the jurisdiction of the Austrian customs administrations must submit their application to the Innsbruck customs office. The scope of jurisdiction of the Austrian customs administration is regulated in the Customs Code Implementing Regulation.

WHAT DOES SELF-ASSESSMENT MEAN?

In addition to general requirements, authorised economic operators must also fulfil specific criteria (AEO criteria). Depending on the specific type of certificate being applied for, these are:

- previous adherence to customs regulations;
- a satisfactory accounting system;
- demonstrable financial solvency;
- where applicable, appropriate security and safety standards.

Before issuing the AEO certificate, the customs authorities must check whether all the prerequisites have been fulfilled. Economic operators who have decided to apply for AEO status are advised to conduct a self-assessment **before** submitting the formal application in order to internally determine whether the criteria have been met and all the necessary information is available. The self-assessment enables the economic operator and the customs authorities to conduct an upfront risk assessment and minimises the scope of the pre-audit at the company to check for potential risks.

In the interests of an efficient risk analysis process, a risk-oriented self-assessment questionnaire has been developed, which can be completed electronically on the BMF website. You are advised to only send your application and the result of this self-assessment to the customs office once you have fully completed the self-assessment. Without the self-assessment, the customs authorities are unable to maintain an effective, efficient certification procedure.

ELECTRONIC PROCESSING OF APPLICATIONS AND SELF-ASSESSMENTS

The Austrian customs administration endeavours to process all applications as quickly and efficiently as possible. To reduce costs and administration, applications and self-assessments can be electronically completed on the BMF website. At the moment, the IT-supported application must still be printed out, signed and submitted to the responsible customs office for legal reasons; however, the application details are also sent to the responsible customs office electronically. The self-assessment, which does not form part of the application, can be conducted as a completely paperless process and all the electronic files can be sent to the responsible customs office.

The Austrian customs administration requests that you only complete a paper-based application and self-assessment in well-justified exceptional cases. In such cases, the necessary forms can be requested from the *Zoll- und Verbrauchsteuerverfahren* [customs and excise] competence centre via e-mail (AEO-Austria@bmf.gv.at). The sample application and self-assessment forms provided in PDF-format below are for further information only.

APPLICATION AND SELF-ASSESSMENT TIPS

- The AEO concept is not only a customs matter. Agree on the decision to become an AEO within your company or group before applying.
- Familiarise yourself with both the legal regulations on the AEO concept and the AEO Guidelines.
- Collate all the documents and information required for the application and self-assessment in your company in good time.
- Give yourself plenty of time for the self-assessment and conduct it carefully.
- Only submit your application once all the data is available and you have prepared all the information for the self-assessment.
- Incomplete or superficially complete applications and self-assessments waste time and can substantially delay the application procedure and the pre-audits.
- The numbers in the self-assessment questionnaire correspond to the questionnaire in the AEO Guidelines. Each question is based on a potential risk, which is described under the same number in the AEO Guidelines. The AEO Guidelines also specify particular focus areas and provide examples of measures that can be taken to minimise potential risks.
- The self-assessment questionnaire has been designed for all supply chain participants and companies of all sizes. However, this means that some questions will not be applicable to all economic operators. In such cases, it is not necessary to answer these questions. To make the risk analysis easier for the customs authorities, you should, however, provide a brief explanation as to why the question is not applicable, unless this is already obvious.
- If you have any technical questions about the electronic process, please contact the *Zoll und Verbrauchsteuerverfahren* competence centre.

- Work together with the customs office to organise the temporal schedule of the pre-audit and ensure that the important contact persons are available for information at the necessary time. This can substantially ease the temporal requirements of the audit.

SECURITY DECLARATIONS

If an application is made for an 'AEOS' or an 'AEOF certificate', when concluding new contractual relationships with a business partner, the authorised economic operator should urge the business partner to evaluate and improve the supply chain security and – providing this is compatible with the company model – expressly indicate this in the contractual agreements. **One** way of implementing this requirement is by using security declarations. Further information on security declarations can be found in the AEO Guidelines and in the document 'Frequently Asked Questions on the AEO concept (FAQs)'. The European Commission has recommended the use of the template-based security declarations throughout the EU. PDF versions that can be saved will be available under the Customs Forms section in the next few days.

ECONOMIC OPERATORS REGISTRATION AND IDENTIFICATION (EORI): GENERAL INFORMATION ON THE EORI APPLICATION PROCEDURE

WHAT IS THE PURPOSE OF AN EORI NUMBER?

The EORI number:

- uniquely identifies economic operators and other persons in their dealings with the customs authorities;
- must be quoted in all communications (applications during the customs procedure, customs declarations, appeals etc.) between the economic operator or other persons and the customs authorities (including in other member states);
- is also used when exchanging information with other customs authorities and other authorities.

WHO HAS TO REGISTER?

All economic operators who conduct activities (including passively) within the scope of their business activities that are subject to customs law (e.g. as an importer, exporter, declarant, authorisation holder during customs procedures or similar) and that have their registered office or residence in the customs territory of the Community (specifically, in Austria) must register with the Austrian customs administration to be allocated an EORI number.

Non-economic operators (e.g. private individuals) can also register.

Each economic operator is allocated a single EORI number, which must then be used by the economic operator and, where applicable, by branches of the economic operator throughout the European Union.

REGISTRATION APPLICATION

To register for an EORI number, an application must be submitted.

Each economic operator must complete its own registration application; hauliers cannot submit applications for each of their customers.

The registration application must be completed online.

The economic operator will then receive an e-mail with the application information in the form of an EORI application, which must be printed out, signed and returned by post or fax to the customs office responsible for the economic operator's registered office.

IMPORTANT!

If the hard copy of the EORI application is not signed and forwarded to the responsible customs office, the electronically recorded data is not processed and no registration will take place.

REGISTRATION PROCESS

The customer service team in the customs office responsible for your company reviews the accuracy of the information in your application. Once the accuracy has been confirmed, an EORI number will be issued by the customer administration competence centre.

You will then be sent the registration decision on the allocation of an EORI number.

SUBMIT YOUR REGISTRATION IN PLENTY OF TIME!

Registration applications take at least 10 working days to process. At the start of the registration phase in particular, the customs offices may receive a higher workload, which will result in the registration procedure taking longer.

To ensure that the economic operator is registered on time and issued the EORI number, we ask that you commence the registration procedure as soon as possible.

This will save you subsequent hassle and prevent customs clearance delays.

EXCISE MOVEMENT & CONTROL SYSTEM (EMCS)

The EMCS (Excise Movement and Control System) is an EU project with the objective of replacing the paper-based documents currently required for intra-Community movements of excise goods (alcohol, tobacco products and energy products) under an excise duty suspension arrangement by electronic messages. The computerised system introduced in accordance with the decision of the European Parliament and the Council (Decision No 1152/2003/EC) will modernise and accelerate the procedure. It will also provide the Member States with real-time information on consignments moving under suspension of excise duties , enabling them to plan any necessary checks and inspections in advance.

The computerised system should also be used for the electronic exchange of information envisaged within the scope of the improved mutual assistance arrangements.

The EMCS has to be introduced in '1+3' phases (phase 0 and phases 1, 2 and 3) by 2013. Phase 0 encompasses the support and maintenance of the existing systems used in the excise field (SEED, MVS and EWSE) pending the introduction of the EMCS. Phase 1 is the preparation phase. The main activity during this phase is the creation of the system specifications. The development and implementation of the system are set to take place in phases 2 and 3. By 1 April 2013 EMCS will become operational at Community level.

At Community level, the European Commission (DG TAXUD, Directorate D) is responsible for the project.

The European Trade Federations have been involved with the development of the EMCS. To keep them informed about the project's progress, joint meetings are organized and their comments are considered in so far as possible during further developments.

LEGAL INFORMATION

The following legal bases and documents are important with regard to the development of the EMCS:

EU LEVEL

- Decision No 1152/2003/EC of the European Parliament and the Council of 16 June 2003 on computerising the movement and surveillance of excisable products, OJ L 162/5 of 1 July 2003.
- Council Directive 2008/118/EC of 16 December 2008 concerning the general arrangements for excise duty and repealing Directive 92/12/EEC, OJ L 9 of 14 January 2009 in the current version (applicable from 1 April 2013)
- Council Directive 92/12/EEC of 25 February 1992 on the general arrangements for products subject to excise duty and on the holding, movement and monitoring of such products (system directive), OJ L 76/1 of 23 March 1992 in the current version
- Commission Regulation (EC) No 684/2009 of 24 July 2009 implementing Council Directive 2008/118/EC as regards the computerised procedures for the movement of excise goods under suspension of excise duty, OJ L 197 of 29 July 2009 in the current version (applicable from 1 April 2013)
- Commission Regulation (EEC) No 2719/92 of 11 September 1992 on the accompanying administrative document for the movement under duty-suspension arrangements of products subject to excise duty, OJ L 276/1 of 19 September 1992 in the current version
- Council Regulation (EC) No 2073/2004 of 16 November 2004 on administrative cooperation in the field of excise duties, OJ L 359/1 of 4 December 2004

- Decision No 1152/2003/EC
- Council Directive 2008/118/EC
- Council Directive 92/12/EEC
- Commission Regulation (EC) No 684/2009
- Commission Regulation (EEC) No 2719/92
- Council Regulation (EC) No 2073/2004

NATIONAL LEVEL

To comply with the provisions of Community legislation, the Austrian Excise Duty Acts (Mineral Oils Tax Act; Alcohol Tax Act; Beer Tax Act; Sparkling Wine Tax Act; Tobacco Tax Act) have been amended by the **Abgabenänderungsgesetz 2009**, published in the Federal Gazette I Nr. 151/2009. Further details and procedural rules for movements of excise goods under a duty suspension arrangement, in particular concerning the submission of the electronic administrative document and the rules and procedures relating to the necessary exchange of data, will be laid down in an Implementing Regulation to the said Excise Duty Acts.

The Austrian Act on mutual administrative assistance has no longer been applicable to excise duties since the entry into force of the Council Regulation (EC) Nr. 2073/2004 on administrative cooperation in the field of excise duties on 1 July 2005. The EU Regulation is directly applicable in all Member States.

PRACTICAL INFORMATION FOR BUSIENSS AND INVESTMENT

DOING BUSINESS IN AUSTRIA

MARKET OVERVIEW

This Country Commercial Guide (CCG) presents a comprehensive look at Austria's commercial environment, including economic, political and market analysis. It is provided as a tool for U.S. companies intending to do business in Austria. The CCG is prepared annually at the U.S. Embassy in Vienna through the combined efforts of several United States Government agencies and includes substantial input from the U.S. Mission to the European Union. It is a living document and its contents are updated during the year, as necessary and appropriate.

Austria, with a population of 8.4 million, is a dynamic European Union member country offering export opportunities for U.S. companies of all sizes. For U.S. firms looking to expand in Southeast Europe, Austria offers attractive features as regional headquarters location, and recent Austrian governments have sought to increase encourage this through economic reforms and by highlighting Austria's historical and economic ties to the surrounding region. At present, approximately 350 U.S. firms have subsidiaries, affiliates, franchisees, and licensees in Austria. About 150 of these companies have regional responsibilities for Central European, Eastern European, or Balkan countries.

According to Statistik Austria, overall imports to Austria grew by 4.7% in 2008. U.S. exports to Austria amounted to $5.0 billion, representing a 9.0% decrease from 2007. By comparison, U.S. imports from Austria in 2008 were reported to be $7.6 billion, down 9.9% from 2007. U.S. exports to Austria comprised 2.9% of the total amount of imports to Austria in 2008.

Principal U.S. exports to Austria are motor vehicle parts and accessories, aircraft, machinery, medical devices, pharmaceuticals, and computer equipment and parts. Principal Austrian exports to the U.S. include specialized industrial machinery, automobiles, pharmaceuticals, glassware, electric power machinery and some food products.

After the deepest recession in more than 50 years, Austria's economy has started to recover, but the upward trajectory will be slow, with setbacks to be likely. GDP will grow only around 1.5% in 2013 and 2011–insufficient to prevent unemployment from rising to a projected 5.2-5.7%. Economists say that growth of 2% or more is not on the horizon, meaning that there will be little or no improvement in Austria's labor market. Despite its growth trajectory, albeit slow, the Austrian government will have to turn its attention to scaling back large deficits and burgeoning public debt.

Since mid 2008, some 56,000 jobs have disappeared in Austria despite a bank rescue package, stimulus measures and labor market programs. With slow economic growth and even with the return to full time work of some 100,000 workers currently on reduced working hours (or in training , which is not included in current unemployment statistics), the number of unemployed is projected to rise from an annual average of about 260,000 to about 300,000 in 2011. Unemployment rates (Eurostat methodology) are projected to rise to 4.7-5.0% in 2009, to 5.2-5.4% in 2013 and 5.2-5.7% in 2011.

Despite lingering downside factors, the overall economy appears to be rebuilding strength. U.S. exporters will find opportunities to gain market position within a great majority of Austrian industry sectors.

MARKET CHALLENGES

Austria is a good export market for U.S. technology and services, and presents no significant trade barriers. Qualified Austrian agents and distributors can be found for nearly every kind of product. Given the size of the country, Austria represents a desirable, affluent pilot market for U.S.-made products and services. Because of Austria's geographic location and history, many Austrian agents and distributors sell regionally–covering several markets in Southeast Europe, in addition to Austria.

When establishing a business in Austria, U.S. companies may still encounter troublesome bureaucratic barriers. Some Austrian provinces have established one-stop-shops for investors, and they are competing with each other in an effort to eliminate red tape.

Most business activities in Austria are regulated and require that a separate application be made for a business license and registration in the commercial register. Evidence of proficiency in running a business is required for most businesses. Usually a passing score on an examination or evidence of prior experience in the field is sufficient. For those business activities that do not require proof of proficiency, the business license is granted automatically upon registration of the business.

Austria welcomes foreign direct investment that does not have a negative impact on the environment. The Government particularly welcomes those investments that create new jobs in high technology fields, promote capital-intensive industries, and have links to R&D activities, for which special tax incentives are available.

MARKET OPPORTUNITIES

To overlook Austria would be to overlook one of the world's most prosperous nations (on a per capita basis). Doing business in and from Austria presents certain advantages. The introduction below summarizes four advantages that will be particularly relevant in the future.

First, Austria is at an international crossroad, bordering on eight European countries: Germany, Italy, Switzerland, Slovenia, Hungary, Slovakia, Czech Republic, and Liechtenstein. This gives it a logistical advantage over the other countries in the region. Four of Austria's neighbors joined the EU in May 2004 (Czech Republic, Slovakia, Slovenia, and Hungary), transforming Austria geographically from a country on the eastern frontier of the EU to one occupying a more central position within the enlarged EU. The addition of two other Eastern European countries to the EU at the beginning of 2007, Romania and Bulgaria, strengthened Austria's central position.

Austria is a member of the Schengen agreement and offers U.S. companies access to growing markets in Eastern and Southeastern Europe. Some question whether Austria will continue to play a role as a gateway to the East in attracting U.S. exports and investment, or whether U.S. firms will bypass Austria and go directly to the more growth-oriented and often more pro-business new EU members. The answer depends on many factors, and American firms are wise to assess all aspects and options. Many U.S. businesses continue to view Austria as a prime location and distribution hub. The country has financial and transportation links to the Eastern European and Balkan region, and its banks and service providers understand regional business practices. Partnerships with Austrian firms who have a presence in regional markets may be an attractive option for some U.S. companies.

A second advantage for Austria is its well-diversified and relatively resilient economy. The Austrian government has sought to remain competitive by pursuing investment in high-potential industries such as telecommunications, non-agricultural biotechnology, medical and pharmaceutical research, and electronics. For U.S. companies in these industry sectors, Austria represents a good opportunity for export, joint ventures, and investment. Under pressure from the newest EU members, who offer lower corporate tax rates, Austria lowered its corporate tax rate in 2005 from 34% to 25%. This step reflected a commitment by the government to compete with its new EU neighbors. Furthermore, numerous 'soft facts' such as excellent school systems and a very high standard of living, make Austria even more attractive to expatriate business managers.

A third plus for Austria is its membership in the EU and the Euro currency zone. The Euro has been the common currency for Austria since 2002. It has already facilitated trade and promoted economic stability for U.S. companies, helping them to manage pricing, balance accounts, and move products within Austria and throughout EU member countries. It should be noted that some U.S. firms have found Austria's implementation of EU rules unnecessarily burdensome, bureaucratic and non-transparent, and have threatened to cut back on their investment in Austria as a result. Nevertheless, for U.S. exporters, the unified EU market and the still favorable exchange rate between the Euro and the dollar mean that U.S. goods should be able to compete on advantageous terms in the coming year.

A fourth advantage Austria offers is that the United States is its fifth largest trading partner and its largest trading partner outside of Europe. U.S. companies entering the market for the first time will benefit from the strong trading relationship already established between the two countries. Austria is a very attractive market demanding high product quality, excellent after sales service, and competitive prices. Although Austrian buyers may give preference to the supplier who is closest geographically and speaks German, many U.S. products and services can compete well with those from Germany and other EU member countries.

MARKET ENTRY STRATEGY

The best strategy for an American exporter to Austria is usually to select one distributor or agent for the entire Austrian market. Some companies appoint distributors in Germany who cover all of German-speaking Europe, including Germany, Austria, and most of Switzerland. But this works best for U.S. exporters with a limited number of customers and end-users in Austria. In such cases, a distributor might be located in Munich instead of Vienna. Austrian buyers are sensitive to agents or distributors based elsewhere and may give priority to competitors with a more dedicated Austrian presence.

SELLING U.S. PRODUCTS AND SERVICES

USING AN AGENT OR DISTRIBUTOR

Qualified Austrian agents and distributors can be found for nearly every kind of product. Because of Austria's geographic location and history, many Austrian agents and distributors sell regionally, covering several markets in Central and Eastern Europe, in addition to Austria.

Companies wishing to use distribution, franchising and agency arrangements need to ensure that the agreements they put into place are in accordance with both European Union (EU) and Austrian law. Council Directive 86/653/EEC establishes certain minimum standards of protection for self-employed commercial agents who sell or purchase goods on behalf of their principals. In essence, the Directive establishes the rights and obligations of the principal and its agents; the agent's remuneration; and the conclusion and termination of an agency contract, including the notice to be given and indemnity or compensation to be paid to the agent. U.S. companies should be particularly aware that the Directive states that parties may not derogate certain requirements. Accordingly, the inclusion of a clause specifying an alternate body of law to be applied in the event of a dispute will likely be ruled invalid by European courts.

The European Commission's Directorate General for Competition enforces legislation concerned with the effects on competition in the internal market of "vertical agreements." Most U.S. exporters are small- and medium-sized companies (SMEs) and are therefore exempt from the Regulations because their agreements likely would qualify as "agreements of minor importance," meaning they are considered incapable of effecting competition at the EU level but useful for cooperation between SMEs. Generally speaking, companies with fewer than 250 employees and an annual turnover of less than EUR 50 million are considered small- and medium-sized undertakings. The EU has additionally indicated that agreements that affect less than 10% of a particular market are generally exempted as well (Commission Notice 2001/C 368/07).

The EU also looks to combat payment delays with Directive 2000/35/EC. This covers all commercial transactions within the EU, whether in the public or private sector, primarily dealing with the consequences of late payment. Transactions with consumers, however, do not fall within the scope of this Directive. In sum, the Directive entitles a seller who does not receive payment for goods/services within 30-60 days of the payment deadline to collect interest (at a rate of 7% above the European Central Bank rate) as compensation. The seller may also retain the title to goods until payment is completed and may claim full compensation for all recovery costs. The current legislation is undergoing review.

Companies' agents and distributors can take advantage of the European Ombudsman when victim of inefficient management by an EU institution or body. Complaints can be made to the European Ombudsman only by businesses and other bodies with registered offices in the EU. The Ombudsman can act upon these complaints by investigating cases in which EU institutions fail to act in accordance with the law, fail to respect the principles of good administration, or violate fundamental rights.

ESTABLISHING AN OFFICE

Establishing a business in Austria may lead to some bureaucratic challenges, however, great progress has been made on behalf of the Austrian government to reduce the paperwork involved and the effort has continued to accelerate. Some regions have moved to set up one-stop shops for entrepreneurs, but it is unclear how much of the red tape these offices can really eliminate.

Most business activities in Austria are regulated and require that separate applications be made for a business license (Gewerbeschein) and for registration in the commercial register (Firmenbuch). Evidence of proficiency is required to operate most businesses. sufficient. For business activities that do not require proof of proficiency, the business license is granted automatically upon registration of the business.

Austrian office. These include public corporations, limited liability companies, limited or unlimited commercial partnerships, silent partnerships, branches of foreign enterprises, cooperative societies, and sole proprietorships. Most foreign-owned businesses choose to operate as a limited liability private company (Gesellschaft mit beschraenkter Haftung or Ges.m.b.H.). online at www.aba.gv.at/ . It is an excellent source of information on all subjects related to opening an office or a production facility in Austria. In addition, all nine Austrian provinces maintain official investment offices. To get into contact with these institutions, please consult the U.S. Commercial Service Vienna at the following E-Mail address: vienna.office.box@mail.doc.gov the processing of personal data. Austrians are well aware of this legislation and are highly sensitive to violations of their privacy.

This opt-out should be available at the time of collection and at any point thereafter. This general legislation is supplemented by specific rules set out in the "Directive on the processing of personal data and the protection of privacy in the electronic communications sector" (2002/58/EC). This requires companies to secure the prior consent of consumers before sending them marketing emails. The only exception to this opt-in provision is if the marketer has already obtained the intended recipient's contact details in the context of a previous sale and wishes to send them information on similar products and services.

Personal data can only be transferred outside the EU if adequate protection is provided for it or if the **unambiguous consent** of the data subject is secured. The European Commission has decided that a handful of countries have regulatory frameworks in place that guarantee the adequate protection of data transferred to them–the United States is NOT one of these.

The Department of Commerce and the European Commission negotiated the Safe Harbor agreement to provide U.S. companies with a simple, streamlined means of complying with the adequacy requirement. It allows those U.S. companies that commit to a series of data protection principles (based on the Directive), and who publicly state that commitment by "self-certifying" on a dedicated website, to continue to receive personal data from the EU. Signing up is voluntary but the rules are binding on those who do. The ultimate means of enforcing Safe Harbor is that failure to fulfill the commitments will be actionable as an unfair and deceptive practice under Section 5 of the FTC Act or under a concurrent Department of Transportation statute for air carriers and ticket agents. While the United States as a whole does not enjoy an adequacy finding, companies that join up to the Safe Harbor scheme will. Companies whose activities are not regulated by the FTC or DoT (e.g. banks, credit unions, savings and loan institutions, securities dealers, insurance companies, not-for-profit organizations, meat packing facilities, or telecommunications carriers) are not eligible to sign up to the Safe Harbor.

EU based exporters or U.S. based importers of personal data can also satisfy the adequacy requirement by including data privacy clauses in the contracts they sign with each other. The Data Protection Authority in the EU country from where the data is being exported must approve these contracts. To fast track this procedure the European Commission has approved sets of model clauses for personal data transfers that can be inserted into contracts between data importers and exporters. The most recent were published at the beginning of 2005; work to update these and develop new ones is ongoing. Most transfers using contracts based on these model clauses do not require prior approval. Companies must bear in mind that the transfer of personal data to third countries is a processing operation that is subject to the general data protection Directive regardless of any Safe Harbor, contractual or consent arrangements.

EU countries' Data Protection Authorities (DPAs) and large multinational companies are also developing a third major approach to compliance with EU rules on transfers of personal data to countries outside the EU. This is based on country-by-country approval of "binding corporate rules" (BCRs). Companies that set up BCRs that satisfy European DPAs will be able to use the presumption of conformity that these approvals provide to transfer personal data from the EU to any location in the world – not just the United States. BCRs can be a tool for compliance with privacy rules on a global scale. The process of negotiation and approval of the BCRs is currently lengthy and complex, and has not been attempted by small or medium-sized companies.

FRANCHISING

Compared to the dominance of franchising in the United States, franchising as a business model is a relatively small factor in the Austrian economy, accounting for an estimated 5% of retail sales. After a period of stagnation in the late 1990's, Austria's franchising sector is again experiencing respectable growth: the franchise association estimates a yearly growth in the number of franchise systems at around 10%, and the number of new franchise unit owners to be growing at 16%.

Around half of the franchise businesses operating in this country are of local origin. The top foreign participant in the Austrian franchising economy is Germany, with around 25% of franchises, followed by the United States, with about 10% of all franchises operating in Austria. Most German franchisers either set up a headquarters in Austria or franchise directly over the border, whereas most American franchisers choose to expand their operations in Austria through a master franchise partner, a solution that has had mixed results.

Some of the best prospects for franchising include business and personal services, schooling and training, and specialty retailing.

The Austrian Franchise Association collects data, maintains an informative web site, and co-organizes seminars as well as a yearly trade show together with various local partners such as 'Gewinn' magazine.

Oesterreichischer Franchise-Verband
Contact: Ms. Silvia Perl
Am Heumarkt 10, A - 1030 Vienna, Austria
Tel.: 0664/2407878, Fax: 0664/741136127
Web: **http://www.franchise.at/html_seiten/franchising.htm**
e-Mail: **oefv@franchise.at**

DIRECT MARKETING

Within limits set by Austrian law, telephone and direct mail solicitation are very much in evidence in Austria. Telecommunications regulations forbid most forms of e-mail direct marketing. Some U.S. companies have established themselves in the Austrian market with multi-level marketing systems.

There is a wide range of EU legislation that impacts the direct marketing sector. Compliance requirements are stiffest for marketing and sales to private consumers. Companies need to focus, in particular, on the clarity and completeness of the information they provide to consumers prior to purchase and on their approaches to collecting and using customer data. The following gives a brief overview of the most important provisions flowing from EU-wide rules on distance selling and on-line commerce. Companies are advised to consult the information available via the hyper-links, to check the relevant sections of national Country Commercial Guides, and to contact the Commercial Service at the U.S. Mission to the European Union for more specific guidance.

Processing Customer Data

The EU has strict laws governing the protection of personal data, including the use of such data in the context of direct marketing activities. For more information on these rules, please see the privacy section above.

Distance Selling Rules

The EU's Directive on distance selling to consumers (97/7/EC) sets out a number of obligations for companies doing business at a distance with consumers. It can read like a set of onerous "do's" and "don'ts," but in many ways it represents nothing more than a customer relations good practice guide with legal effect. Direct marketers must provide clear information on the identity of themselves as well as their supplier, full details on prices including delivery costs, and the period for which an offer remains valid – all of this, of course, before a contract is concluded. Customers generally have the right to return goods without any required explanation within seven days, and retain the right to compensation for faulty goods thereafter. Similar in nature is the Doorstep Directive (85/577/EEC) which is designed to protect consumers from sales occurring outside of a normal business premises (e.g., door-to-door sales) and essentially assure the fairness of resulting contracts.

Financial services are the subject of a separate Directive that came into force in June 2002 (2002/65/EC). This piece of legislation amends three prior existing Directives and is designed to ensure that consumers are appropriately protected in respect to financial transactions taking place where the consumer and the provider are not face-to-face. In addition to prohibiting certain abusive marketing practices, the Directive establishes criteria for the presentation of contract information. Given the special nature of financial markets, specifics are also laid out for contractual withdrawal.

Direct Marketing over the Internet

The e-commerce Directive (2000/31/EC) imposes certain specific requirements connected to the direct marketing business. Promotional offers must not mislead customers and the terms that must be met to qualify for them have to be easily accessible and clear. The Directive stipulates that marketing e-mails must be identified as such to the recipient and requires that companies targeting customers on-line must regularly consult national opt-out registers where they exist. When an order is placed, the service provider must acknowledge receipt quickly and by electronic means, although the Directive does not attribute any legal effect to the placing of an order or its acknowledgment. This is a matter for national law. Vendors of electronically supplied services (such as software, which the EU considers a service and not a good) must also collect value added tax (see Electronic Commerce section below).

JOINT VENTURES/LICENSING

Joint ventures and licensed production arrangements in Austria offer U.S. firms several advantages, including access to the E.U. market, improved access to Central and Eastern European markets, reduction of transportation costs to European destinations, and high quality production. Joint ventures may be formed as companies, partnerships, or other legal entities.

Austrian companies are receptive to licensing arrangements, especially as a source of technology. Royalty and license fee payments may be freely transferred out of Austria.

In addition to the assistance offered by the U.S. Commercial Service Vienna, U.S. firms seeking joint venture or license partners in Austria will receive valuable information from the Austrian Government's investment organization:

ABA – Invest in Austria

Contact: Mr. Hans Nagl
Opernring 3, A-1010 Vienna, Austria
Tel.: ++43 1 588 58 12, Fax: ++43 1 586 86 59
Web: **http://www.aba.gv.at**
e-Mail: **h.nagl@aba.gv.at**

SELLING TO THE GOVERNMENT

The Bundesbeschaffung GmbH (BBG) was created in June, 2001 and acts as a central procurement agency for the federal government of Austria in compliance with EU legislation. The agency is run as a limited liability company (thus is outside the federal budget), but is owned by the Austrian Ministry of Finance. More information is available online (in German) at: https://bbg.portal.at/Internet/Startseite/_start.htm

The Austrian Government adheres to the WTO (GATT) Agreement on Government Procurement. Austria's Federal Procurement Law complies with EU guidelines. Austria does not have Buy National laws, but as with any political decision, the economic impact of any new contract is taken into consideration. In addition, some major contracts are negotiated by invitation, and limited tenders and offset requirements are common in defense contracts. For assistance with specific tenders, please contact this office (The U.S. Commercial Service Vienna) or our CS EU office in Brussels.

The EU public procurement market, including EU institutions and Member States, totals around EUR 1,600 billion. This market is regulated by three Directives:

Directives on remedies cover legal means for companies who face discriminatory public procurement practices. These directives are implemented in the national procurement legislation of the 27 EU Member States.

The US and the EU are signatories of the World Trade Organization's (WTO) Government Procurement Agreement (GPA), which grants access to most public supplies and some services and works contracts published by national procuring authorities of the countries that are parties to the Agreement. In practice, this means that U.S.-based companies are eligible to bid on supplies contracts from European public contracting authorities above the agreed thresholds.

However, there are restrictions for U.S. suppliers in the EU utilities sector both in the EU Utilities Directive and in the EU coverage of the Government Procurement Agreement (GPA). The Utilities Directive allows EU contracting authorities in these sectors to either reject non-EU bids where the proportion of goods originating in non-EU countries exceeds 50% of the total value of the goods constituting the tender, or that they are entitled to apply a 3% price difference to non-EU bids in order to give preference to the EU bid. These restrictions are applied when no reciprocal access for EU companies in the U.S. market is offered. Those restrictions however were waived for the electricity sector.

For more information, please visit the U.S. Commercial Service at the U.S. Mission to the European Union website dedicated to EU public procurement. This site also has a database of all European public procurement tenders that are open to U.S.-based firms by virtue of the Government Procurement Agreement. Access is free of charge.

DISTRIBUTION AND SALES CHANNELS

Picture1.jpg

Austria enjoys a multitude of distribution and sales channels, including traditional agents, wholesalers and retailers, catalog and e-commerce channels, direct marketing, franchising, joint ventures, and other licensing agreements. Manufacturer's representative agreements as we know them in the United States, however, are uncommon.

It may be useful to think of Austria in terms of the following five marketing or distribution areas:

The business and government center as well as the most populous region.

These are Styria, Lower Austria, and Upper Austria, where most industrial and agricultural production takes place.

These are Carinthia, Tyrol, and Salzburg, which rely heavily on tourism.

This province in the far western Alps on the Swiss border has a small but wealthy population.

This province in the eastern flatlands of Austria is the least developed part of the country.

Many Austrian firms distribute to the neighboring markets of Central and Eastern Europe at the wholesale level, and some Austrian retail chains are beginning to build networks in those countries as well. In the same way, German and international retail giants have been building a presence in Austria over the past several years.

Selling Factors/Techniques

Possibly because of the many years of shortage during World War II and the post-war period, and certainly due to Austria's monarchical authoritarian history, the traditional buyer-seller relationship in Austria may seem strange to the American. The logic in the Austrian relationship holds that the customer wants or needs something and is on unequal footing with the seller, who, holding the item that the customer wants, is in a position of power. Though it is true that this traditional interpersonal part of the commercial relationship is losing its hold here as the older generations move into retirement and more sophisticated communications and competition take hold, the sense that the customer is asking a favor of the seller still persists throughout the Austrian market to some degree.

Why is this information important? Because it will help U.S. firms avoid making simple mistakes when communicating with potential partners and customers. Two rules of thumb are worth remembering: First, U.S. companies should refrain from hard sell practices, which could backfire if the Austrian customer feels that the products are less desirable because of a strong sales approach. And second, companies should stick to simple American friendliness and transparency, which usually make a good impression.

Another interesting difference in the way Austrians make purchasing decisions is the relative importance of preciseness. While Americans like a product to be tough and easy to use, Austrians want a product to be perfectly engineered and very precise.

In addition to cultural considerations, price has become a key factor in purchasing. More and more sectors are now price-driven, a development that has accelerated with the globalization of the local economy. Where product quality and personal relationships once played a dominant role in purchasing decisions, the focus has shifted increasingly to pricing and the bottom line. However, emphasis on quality and personal relationships still play a comparatively stronger role in purchasing decisions in Austria compared to the U.S.

ELECTRONIC COMMERCE

In 2009, 98% of Austrian businesses with more than 10 employees used the internet, and 80% maintained a website. Around 75% of firms with more than 10 employees have a broadband connection, and 38% access the internet using a mobile connection (cell phone/netbook). Almost 40% of Austrian businesses report purchasing goods or services online, reporting a total of $67.6 billion in online sales.

In 2009, 70% of all Austrian households had internet access, 58% via broadband. Of all Austrians aged 16-74, 72% reported using the internet regularly and 41% reported having purchased something online in the past 12 months, up from 37% in 2007.

In July 2003, the EU started applying Value Added Tax (VAT) to sales by non-EU based companies of Electronically Supplied Services (ESS) to EU based non-business customers. U.S. companies that are covered by the rule must collect and submit VAT to EU tax authorities. European Council Directive 2002/38/EC further developed the EU rules for charging VAT. These rules were indefinitely extended following adoption of directive 2008/8/EC

U.S. businesses mainly affected by the 2003 rule change are those that are U.S. based and selling ESS to EU based, non-business customers or those businesses that are EU based and selling ESS to customers outside the EU who no longer need to charge VAT on such transactions. There are a number of compliance options for businesses. The Directive created a special scheme that simplifies registering with each Member State. The Directive allows companies to register with a single VAT authority of their choice. Companies have to charge different rates of VAT according to where their customers are based but VAT reports and returns are submitted to just one authority. The VAT authority responsible for providing the single point of registration service is then responsible for reallocating the collected revenue among the other EU VAT authorities.

TRADE PROMOTION AND ADVERTISING

After growing a respectable 6.4% in 2007, the advertising industry in Austria was able to book another excellent year in 2008, recording growth of 5.4% and a $4.7 billion result for the year. The relative distribution of advertising in Euros among the various media and marketing channels has been changing slowly over the past several years.

Spending Breakdown

Daily papers, regional publications, magazines, industry publications, and other print media continue to account for the lion's share of advertising spending, capturing 45.7% in 2008. Direct mail and flyers together account for 19% of the advertising pie, slightly down from 20% in 2007. Television remained steady at just below 19% of the total. Billboard advertising remains a constant feature of Austrian marketing, with around 6% of the total, the same market share as radio advertising. The fastest growing venue for advertising is online advertising, which grew by 34% between 2007 and 2008 but still accounts for only 3% of total spending on advertising.

Truth in Advertising

A Consumer Forum was established by the Austrian Economics Ministry to ensure truth in advertising. The Forum is made up of representatives of political parties, business organizations, labor unions, and business associations. A subcommittee for commercial advertising examines posters and TV, radio and newspaper ads, as well as entire sales campaigns, for their truthfulness, information value, and ethnic sensitivity. The Forum can initiate proceedings against advertisers who make false claims. Anyone transgressing established commercial usage laws may be sued. The government recently lifted the regulation that prohibited comparative advertising, thus enabling advertisers to make direct comparisons between their products and services and those of their competitors.

Trade Promotion

Annually, between 100 and 150 national and international trade fairs representing many industry sectors are organized in Austria. Most of the Austrian fairs are open to the general public and thus fulfill an advertising function. However, most of these fairs are not the best choice for business to business marketing. Austrian business entities generally attend the major European trade fairs, especially those in Germany. Austria hosts many industry-specific congresses with a global or regional focus. Many of these offer opportunities for small scale promotion.

General EU Legislation

Laws against misleading advertisements differ widely from Member State to Member State within the EU. To respond to this imperfection in the Internal Market, the Commission adopted a Directive, in force since October 1986, to establish minimum and objective criteria regarding truth in advertising. The Directive was amended in October 1997 to include comparative advertising. Under the Directive, misleading advertising is defined as any "advertising which in any way, including its presentation, deceives or is likely to deceive the persons to whom it is addressed or whom it reaches and which, by reason of its deceptive nature, is likely to affect their economic behavior or which for those reasons, injures or is likely to injure a competitor." Member States can authorize even more extensive protection under their national laws.

Comparative advertising, subject to certain conditions, is defined as "advertising which explicitly or by implication identifies a competitor or goods or services by a competitor." Member States can, and in some cases have, restricted misleading or comparative advertising.

The EU's Audiovisual Media Services Directive lays down legislation on broadcasting activities allowed within the EU. From 2009 the rules allow for US-style product placement on television and the three-hour/day maximum of advertising will be lifted. However, a 12-minute/hour maximum will remain. Child programming will be subject to a code of conduct that will include a limit of junk food advertising to children.

Following the adoption of the 1999 Council Directive on the Sale of Consumer Goods and Associated Guarantees, product specifications, as laid down in advertising, are now considered as legally binding on the seller. (For additional information on Council Directive 1999/44/EC on the Sale of Consumer Goods and Associated Guarantees, see the legal warranties and after-sales service section below.)

The EU adopted Directive 2005/29/EC concerning fair business practices in a further attempt to tighten up consumer protection rules. These rules outlaw several aggressive or deceptive marketing practices such as pyramid schemes, "liquidation sales" when a shop is not closing down, and artificially high prices as the basis for discounts in addition to other potentially misleading advertising practices. Certain rules on advertising to children are also set out.

Medicine

The advertising of medicinal products for human use is regulated by Council Directive 2001/83/EC. Generally speaking, the advertising of medicinal products is forbidden if market authorization has not yet been granted or if the product in question is a prescription drug. Mentioning therapeutic indications where self-medication is not suitable is not permitted, nor is the distribution of free samples to the general public. The text of the advertisement should be compatible with the characteristics listed on the product label, and should encourage rational use of the product. The advertising of medicinal products destined for professionals should contain essential characteristics of the product as well as its classification. Inducements to prescribe or supply a particular medicinal product are prohibited and the supply of free samples is restricted.

Nutrition and Health Claims

On July 1, 2007, a new regulation on nutrition and health claims entered into force. Regulation 1924/2006 sets EU-wide conditions for the use of nutrition claims such as "low fat" or "high in vitamin C" and health claims such as "helps lower cholesterol". The regulation applies to any food or drink product produced for human consumption that is marketed on the EU market. Only foods that fit a certain nutrient profile (below certain salt, sugar and/or fat levels) will be allowed to carry claims. Nutrition and health claims will only be allowed on food labels if they are included in one of the EU positive lists. Food products carrying claims must comply with the provisions of nutritional labeling directive 90/496/EC . From 2013, only nutrition clams in the Annex will be allowed.

The development of nutrient profiles, originally scheduled for January 2009, is being delayed due to the 2009 Parliamentary elections and the appointment of a new Commission. Once they have been set, there will be another two-year period before the nutrient profiles begin to apply to allow food operators time to comply with the new rules. Nutrition claims can fail one criterion, i.e. if only one nutrient (salt, sugar or fat) exceeds the limit of the profile, a claim can still be made provided the high level of that particular nutrient is clearly marked on the label. For example, a yogurt can make a low-fat claim even if it has high sugar content but only if the label clearly states "high sugar content". Health claims cannot fail any criteria.

The deadline of January 31, 2013, for compiling a list of well-established health function claims such as 'calcium is good for your bones' will not be met due to the vast amount of applications that have to be screened by EFSA. Disease risk reduction claims and claims referring to the health and development of children will require an authorization on a case-by-case basis, following the submission of a scientific dossier to EFSA. A simplified authorization procedure has been established for health claims based on new scientific data. GAIN Report E48055 describes how application dossiers for authorization of health claims should be prepared and presented. A guidance document on how companies can apply for health claim authorizations can be downloaded from EFSA's website at:
http://www.efsa.europa.eu/EFSA/ScientificPanels/NDA/efsa_locale-1178620753812_1178684448831.htm

Food Supplements

Regulation 1925/2006, applicable as of July 1, 2007, harmonizes rules on the addition of vitamins and minerals to foods. The regulation lists the vitamins and minerals that may be added to foods. This list was most recently revised in November 2009. A positive list of substances other than vitamins and minerals has not been established yet, although it is being developed. Until then, Member State laws will govern the use these substances.

Tobacco

The EU Tobacco Advertising Directive bans tobacco advertising in printed media, radio, and internet as well as the sponsorship of cross-border events or activities. Advertising in cinemas and on billboards or merchandising is allowed though these are banned in many Member States. Tobacco advertising on television has been banned in the EU since the early 1990s and is governed by the TV without Frontiers Directive.

PRICING

Austrian prices are among the highest in the European Union, reflecting the high cost of labor, extensive agricultural subsidies, the small size of the market, and high taxes. High labor costs include the cost of social benefits such as mandatory health insurance and pension fund contributions for employees. The value-added tax (VAT) on most products and services is 20% and is charged at point of sale. Special taxes are levied on luxury goods, fuel, drinks, tobacco, and other items. These costs and taxes should be taken into account when pricing products for sale in Austria.

SALES SERVICE/CUSTOMER SUPPORT

Customer service and support in Austria gained attention with EU integration. Starting on January 1, 2002, the basic warranty for consumer purchases was increased from six months to two years, and the burden of proof was reversed. The customer is no longer required to prove that he did not break the item; rather, the store must show that he did. Despite this change in the warranty rules, a customer who purchases a defective product cannot in most cases bring it back to the store for replacement, but instead must wait while the product is shipped for repair. Stores often impose more restrictive exchange policies for articles purchased on sale or with a credit card. American-style guarantees and customer service are gradually becoming more common and publicizing them is a popular marketing tool.

Business customers demand a high level of support and most wholesalers or distributors offer excellent support. If a part on a machine breaks, the customer will demand that it be replaced or repaired within 24 hours, which may present logistical problems for smaller U.S. suppliers who cannot warehouse replacement parts in Europe.

Conscious of the discrepancies among Member States in product labeling, language use, legal guarantee, and liability, the redress of which inevitably frustrates consumers in cross-border shopping, the EU institutions have launched a number of initiatives aimed at harmonizing national legislation. Suppliers within and outside the EU should be aware of existing and upcoming legislation affecting sales, service, and customer support.

EU Regulation

Conscious of the discrepancies among Member States in product labeling, language use, legal guarantee, and liability, the redress of which inevitably frustrates consumers in cross-border shopping, the EU institutions have launched a number of initiatives aimed at harmonizing national legislation. Suppliers within and outside the EU should be aware of existing and upcoming legislation affecting sales, service, and customer support.

Product Liability

Under the 1985 Directive on liability of defective products, amended in 1999, the producer is liable for damage caused by a defect in his product. The victim must prove the existence of the defect and a causal link between defect and injury (bodily as well as material). A reduction of liability of the manufacturer is granted in cases of negligence on the part of the victim.

Product Safety

The 1992 General Product Safety Directive introduces a general safety requirement at the EU level to ensure that manufacturers only place safe products on the market. It was revised in 2001 to include an obligation on the producer and distributor to notify the Commission in case of a problem with a given product, provisions for its recall, the creation of a European Product Safety Network, and a ban on exports of products to third countries that are not deemed safe in the EU.

Legal Warranties and After-Sales Service

Under the 1999 Directive on the Sale of Consumer Goods and Associated Guarantees, professional sellers are required to provide a minimum two-year warranty on all consumer goods sold to consumers (natural persons acting for purposes outside their trade, businesses or professions), as defined by the Directive. The remedies available to consumers in case of non-compliance are:

http://ec.europa.eu/comm/consumers/cons_int/safe_shop/guarantees/index_en.htm

Other issues pertaining to consumers' rights and protection, such as the New Approach Directives, CE marking, quality control and data protection are dealt with in Chapter 5 of this report.

PROTECTING YOUR INTELLECTUAL PROPERTY

IPR Climate in Austria

Austria is a member of all international intellectual property rights (IPR) agreements, and IPR is well respected. To begin the process of registering a patent in Austria or in the EU, contact the U.S. Commercial Service in Vienna (tel. +43 1 313 39 2243) or the Austrian Patent Office:

Dresdner Straße 87, 1200 Vienna, Austria
Tel.: ++43 1 534-24-0, Fax: ++43 1 534-24-53
Web: **http://www.patentamt.at/Home/index.htm**
e-Mail: **info@patentamt.at**

Linke Wienzeile 4/1/9, A-1060 Vienna, Austr
Tel.: ++43 1 523 4382, Fax: ++43 1 523 4382 1
Web: **http://www.patentanwalt.at**
e-Mail: **info@oepak.at**

First, it is important to have an overall strategy to protect IPR. Second, IPR is protected differently in Austria than in the U.S. Third, under local laws, rights must be registered and enforced in Austria. Companies may wish to seek advice from local attorneys or IP consultants. The U.S. Commercial Service can provide a list of local lawyers upon request.

U.S Government generally cannot enforce rights for private individuals in Austria. It is the responsibility of the rights' holders to register, protect, and enforce their rights where relevant, retaining their own counsel and advisors. While the U.S. Government is willing to assist, there is little it can do if the rights holders have not taken these fundamental steps necessary to securing and enforcing their IPR in a timely fashion. Moreover, in many countries, rights holders who delay enforcing their rights on a mistaken belief that the U.S. Government can provide a political resolution to a legal problem may find that their rights have been eroded or abrogated due to doctrines such as statutes of limitations, laches, estoppels, or unreasonable delay in prosecuting a law suit. In no instance should U.S. Government advice be seen as a substitute for the obligation of a rights holder to promptly pursue its case.

A good partner is an important ally in protecting IPR. Keep an eye on your cost structure and reduce the margins (and the incentive) of would-be bad actors. Projects and sales in Austria require constant attention. Work with legal counsel familiar with Austrian laws to create a solid contract that includes non-compete clauses, and confidentiality/non-disclosure provisions.

For information about patent, trademark, or copyright issues -- including enforcement issues in the US and other countries -- call the STOP! Hotline: 1-866-999-HALT

Austria is a member of all international IPR agreements, and IPR is well respected. To begin the process of registering a patent in Austria or in the EU, contact the U.S. Commercial Service Vienna (Tel.: ++43 1 313 39-2205) or the Austrian Patent Office:

Oesterreichisches Patentamt (Austrian Patent Office)
Dresdner Straße 87, 1200 Vienna, Austria
Tel.: ++43 1 534-24-0, Fax: ++43 1 534-24-535
Web: **http://www.patentamt.at/Home/index.html**
e-Mail: **info@patentamt.at**

Copyright

The EU's legislative framework for copyright protection consists of a series of Directives covering areas such as the legal protection of computer programs, the duration of protection of authors' rights and neighboring rights, and the legal protection of databases. Almost all Member States have fully implemented the rules into national law; and the Commission is now focusing on ensuring that the framework is enforced accurately and consistently across the EU.

The on-line copyright Directive (2001/29/EC) addresses the problem of protecting rights holders in the online environment while protecting the interests of users, ISPs and hardware manufacturers. It guarantees authors' exclusive reproduction rights with a single mandatory exception for technical copies (to allow caching), and an exhaustive list of other exceptions that individual Member States can select and include in national legislation. This list is meant to reflect different cultural and legal traditions, and includes private copying "on the condition right holders receive fair compensation."

Patents

EU countries have a "first to file" approach to patent applications, as compared to the "first to invent" system currently followed in the United States. This makes early filing a top priority for innovative companies. Unfortunately, it is not yet possible to file for a single EU-wide patent that would be administered and enforced like the Community Trademark (see below). For the moment, the most effective way for a company to secure a patent across a range of EU national markets is to use the services of the European Patent Office (EPO) in Munich. It offers a one-stop-shop that enables rights holders to get a bundle of national patents using a single application. However, these national patents have to be validated, maintained and litigated separately in each Member State.

Trademarks

The EU-wide Community Trademark (CTM) can be obtained via a single language application to the Office of Harmonization in the Internal Market (OHIM) in Alicante, Spain. It lasts ten years and is renewable indefinitely. For companies looking to protect trademarks in three or more EU countries the CTM is a more cost effective option than registering separate national trademarks.

On October 1, 2004, the European Commission (EC) acceded to the World Intellectual Property Organization (WIPO) Madrid Protocol. The accession of the EC to the Madrid Protocol establishes a link between the Madrid Protocol system, administered by WIPO, and the

Community Trademark system, administered by OHIM. As of October 1, 2004, Community Trademark applicants and holders are allowed to apply for international protection of their trademarks through the filing of an international application under the Madrid Protocol. Conversely, holders of international registrations under the Madrid Protocol will be entitled to apply for protection of their trademarks under the Community Trademark system.

Designs

The EU adopted a Regulation introducing a single Community system for the protection of designs in December 2001. The Regulation provides for two types of design protection, directly applicable in each EU Member State: the registered Community design and the unregistered Community design. Under the registered Community design system, holders of eligible designs can use an inexpensive procedure to register them with the EU's Office for Harmonization in the Internal Market (OHIM), based in Alicante, Spain. They will then be granted exclusive rights to use the designs anywhere in the EU for up to twenty-five years. Unregistered Community designs that meet the Regulation's requirements are automatically protected for three years from the date of disclosure of the design to the public.

Trademark Exhaustion

Within the EU, the rights conferred on trademark holders are subject to the principle of "exhaustion." Exhaustion means that once trademark holders have placed their product on the market in one Member State, they lose the right to prevent the resale of that product in another EU country. This has led to an increase in the practice of so called "parallel importing" whereby goods bought in one Member State are sold in another by third parties unaffiliated to the manufacturer. Parallel trade is particularly problematic for the research-based pharmaceutical industry where drug prices vary from country to country due to national price regulations. Community wide exhaustion is spelled out in the Directive on harmonizing trademark laws. In a paper published in 2003, the Commission indicated that it had no plans to propose changes to existing legal provisions.

Due Diligence

The Austrian economy is highly regulated, which means that there are checks and controls against fraud, however they do not stop all fraudulent activity. Due diligence is important in Austria, as it is anywhere. Basic information on a company, such as confirmation of registration and confirmation that no bankruptcy proceedings are in process, is readily available from official and semi-official sources. Excellent commercial background checks on a company can be obtained through the U.S. Commercial Service Vienna, as well as though private sector resources.

LOCAL PROFESSIONAL SERVICES

The same professional services that are available in other highly developed market economies are readily available locally in Austria. Business service providers known to this office (the U.S. Commercial Service Vienna) are offered through an on-line listing on the U.S. Commercial Service website. The website is a good source for such service providers.

Local service providers focusing on EU law, consulting, and business development can be viewed on the website maintained by the Commercial Service at the U.S. Mission to the European Union at: http://www.buyusa.gov/europeanunion/services.html

For information on professional services located within each of the EU member states, please see EU Member State Country Commercial Guides which can be found at the following website: http://www.export.gov/mrktresearch/index.asp under the Market Research Library.

Resources

Web Resources

There are innumerable web resources available in Austria and the EU, some of which have some English content. Following are the most important sites:

http://www.buyusa.gov/austria/en

The website of the U.S. Commercial Service in Vienna, containing market research on Austria in English, as well as contact points, a list of business service providers, upcoming events, and information on CS services.

http://www.amcham.or.at/ American Chamber of Commerce in Austria is a good source of information on U.S. companies operating in Austria. The AmCham also lists information about upcoming events.

http://portal.wko.at/

The website of the Austrian Federal Economic Chamber, containing information on the Chamber and contact points in German, and basic information in English

http://www.virtualvienna.net/

A website in English designed for expatriates living in Austria and for prospective transferees to Austria, introducing the reader to life in Austria. http://www.austria.org/

The official Austrian government source of information on Austria for readers in the United States.

Regulation on late payment http://www.ombudsman.europa.eu/home/en/default.htm

European Ombudsman http://ec.europa.eu/justice_home/fsj/privacy/index_en.htm

Contact

U.S. Commercial Service Vienna, Austria
Marta Haustein, Commercial Specialist
e-Mail: marta.haustein@mail.doc.gov

LEADING SECTORS FOR U.S. EXPORT AND INVESTMENT

ADVERTISING SERVICES (ADV)

The Austrian advertising industry consists of:

The advertising and PR service provider market is dominated by a few large Austrian-based firms, several international and multinational advertising agencies with Western European mother companies, and American agencies. The majority of the advertising agencies are also active in the PR business, in addition to the several PR firms operating in Austria. Some advertising agencies penetrate the Austrian market from abroad, especially from Germany and Switzerland. A variety of Austria-based agencies do business in the neighboring countries of Central/Eastern Europe, especially in cooperation with local joint-venture partners.

In 2008, $4.7 billion was spent on advertising in Austria, an increase of 5.4% from 2007. The 2008 classic advertising market was dominated by print and TV media. Austrian advertising expenditures were shared among the following:

In 2008, online media showed an especially high rate of growth, with advertising revenues increasing by 33.8%. Fourteen marketing organizations and advertising platforms (according to their own estimate) cover 75% of the market in question, and reported $128.2 million in gross revenues. However, it is also necessary to note that this figure does not include search engine marketing, and that no reliable indicators of the difference between reported and net revenues are available. In any case, it can be observed that practically all of Austria's major media companies are beginning to promote online presentations more heavily, often under the same brand name, and are stepping up cross-media marketing with combinations of print and online advertising or television and online advertising.

For the year 2008, the media analysis firm "FOCUS Media Research" reported growth in gross advertising revenues for the sixth consecutive year, with an increase of 5.1% for the overall market and 6.7% for conventional advertising media. There is no doubt that advertising was heavily influenced by three key events in 2008, each of which had very different effects: First, in June 2008, the Euro 2008 football (soccer) championship was held in Vienna, Salzburg, Klagenfurt and Innsbruck as well as a number of cities in Switzerland. This event met expectations in tourism, but the resulting advertising stimulus was rather limited due to the conditions imposed by the organizers (FIFA) and international sponsors. Also, at the end of September, early elections to the National Council (one of the chambers of the Austrian parliament) took place, which generated additional business for the outdoor advertising segment and this time for private broadcasters as well. As a result, the second-highest growth rate of the year was recorded in September (+8.0%), while April showed the highest rate (+13.6% in nominal terms).

However, late September also saw the spectacular failure of the U.S. investment bank Lehman Brothers, and since that time the worldwide financial markets have been in a state of crisis. From December 2008 to February 2009, "FOCUS Media Research's" advertising monitoring data clearly shows that advertising spending dropped in three consecutive months, each time more drastically.

Best Products and Services

American advertising agencies hold an excellent position in this market. We estimate that about 30% of Austria's total advertising revenues are generated by 13 U.S. agencies. The most successful and largest subsidiaries of U.S. agencies in Austria are:

Opportunities

Looking to the future, additional market opportunities in the Austrian market can be found for innovative American advertising agencies. A great share of the 350 Austrian subsidiaries of U.S. companies is already clients of U.S. owned advertising agencies.

The online advertising market certainly offers future best prospects in Austria and the majority of the large U.S. owned online advertising firms such as Google, Yahoo!, Facebook, MySpace, YouTube, etc. are already well established on the Austrian market.

Resources

Web Resources

http://www.fachverbandwerbung.at/	Fachverband Werbung und Marktkommunikation
	Wirtschaftskammer Oesterreich (Austrian Federal Economic Chamber)
http://www.publicrelations.at/	Public Relations Verband Austria (PRVA)
http://www.amma.at/	Austrian Multimedia Association (AMMA)
http://www.dmvoe.at/	Dialog Marketing Verband Oesterreich (Association for Dialogues in Austrian Marketing)
http://www.creativclub.at/	Creativ Club Austria
http://www.werberat.at/	Oesterreicher Werberat (Austrian Council for Advertising)
http://www.marketingclub.at/	Marketing Club Austria
http://www.wgonline.at/	Oesterreichische Werbewissenschaftliche Gesellschaft (Austrian Society for the Study of Marketing and Advertising)
http://www.vmoe.at/	Verband der Marktforscher Oesterreichs (Association of Market Researchers in Austria)
http://www.vmd.at/	Vereinigung Oesterreichischer Dekorature (Austrian Coalition for Visual Marketing)
http://www.emba.co.at/	Event Marketing Board Austria
http://www.vrm.at/	Verband der Regionalmedian Oesterreichs (Assocation of Regional Media in Austria)
http://www.iab-austria.at/	IAB (Internet Advertising Bureau Austria)

Contact
U.S. Commercial Service Vienna, Austria
Manfred Weinschenk, Commercial Specialist
e-Mail: **manfred.weinschenk@mail.doc.gov**

AIRCRAFT AND PARTS (AIR)

	Aircraft and Parts Data Table (in $ million)		
	2008	2009 (estimated)	2013 (estimated)
Total Market Size	1479.1	1553.0	1630.6
Total Local Production	145.6	152.9	160.5
Total Exports	721.2	757.3	795.2
Total Imports	2,054.7	2,157.4	2,265.3
Imports from the U.S.	701.5	736.5	773.4

Civil Sector

The Austrian market for civil aviation aircraft amounted to $1,479.1 million in 2008 and is expected to grow by 5% in 2009, while Austrian aircraft and parts imports in 2008 amounted to $ 2.05 billion. With domestic-based manufacturing limited to one company, Diamond Aircraft Industries, the vast majority of the market is served by imports.

The major aircraft industry suppliers to Austria in 2008 were Germany with 50.2%, the United States with 34.1%, Canada with 6.0% and France with 1.4%.

The Austrian general aviation market is characterized by imports. Diamond Aircraft Industries is the sole Austrian manufacturer, and it produces only motor gliders. The Federal Statistical Office gives only import/export figures for civil aircraft and related parts and equipment. No official civil aircraft production figures are available. Production figures and market demand estimates are based on sales figures obtained from the Civil Aviation Office and Diamond Aircraft Industries.

Diamond Aircraft Industries, in Wiener Neustadt, rolled out 243 single-engine two-seater and four-seater propeller-driven avgas aircraft in 2008. 95% of Diamond's production is exported. In 2008, Diamond rolled out 3% more aircraft than in 2007. Diamond uses diesel engines from the Austrian firms Austro Engines and Rotax. Suppliers for avionics are the U.S. companies King and Garmin.

We project an average annual growth rate of 5% for the Austrian aircraft market. Growth rates are problematic because of the critical importance of government and military contracts and the incidence of large, one-time orders that greatly skew the statistics.

Aircraft leasing companies have become major factors in the industry as aircraft development and production costs escalate. For the airlines, leased aircraft offer the advantages of low capital investment and greater flexibility in adjusting to changing market conditions.

In line with the dimensioning of the fleet, the Austrian Airlines Group (AAG) sold all of its A340-300 in 2008. Moreover, the AAG is going to add two Fokker 100 planes to its operation and will drop four Airbus A330-200 models from service.

Austria imported 47 twin-engine aircraft over 5.7 tons in 2008, which was an increase of 18% compared to 2007.

The principal end-users of civil aviation aircraft, parts and equipment are in the Austrian Airlines Group, which includes Austrian Airlines, Lauda Air, Austrian Arrows and Rheintalflug, as well as other charter airlines. Emergency medical services and the police use civilian helicopters. The market for corporate fleets and business charter operators appears saturated because of the low prices for flights available commercially. However, industry experts forecast a growth for this sector in 2013.

In the very important category of single aircraft up to 2 tons, U.S. aircraft are dominant. A total of 671 units were registered in 2008. The largest share of this market is held by Piper, Cessna and Beech Aircraft. A strong competitor is Diamond. In 2008, 104 light aircraft (2 to 5.7 tons) were registered in Austria. A total of 14 twin-engine aircraft (up to 5.7 tons) were imported in 2008. This segment had the highest import increase. Private Austrian pilots register their aircraft for business use in order to gain tax advantages. Other end-users are air taxi and charter services.

The outlook in 2009 for new light aircraft in the category up to 2 tons is rather dim due to a glut of used aircraft on the market. However, demand for new aircraft in the category up to 5.7 tons is expected to rise again in 2013 as older equipment is replaced. The only reason for postponing the replacement of the older equipment could be the economic downturn, which may delay it for some time.

Hope for future expansion of the civil helicopter market is not optimistic, due to the small size of the Austrian market. Most new purchases simply will replace old equipment. The industry's efforts now focus on emergency medical services, police and military. The market leader is EUROCOPTER, followed by AGUSTA Bell, Hughes, Robinson and Aerospatiale.

Market Access

Austrians are generally well disposed toward Americans. Following a few general rules of Austrian etiquette will help maintain this positive feeling. Appointments should be made either by telephone or in writing well in advance, and prospective buyers or distributors should be given the option of determining the date and place of the meeting. Prompt response to letters and faxes is very important. Some local firms have reported negative experiences in trying to contact U.S. firms, having to go through too many organizational layers and sometimes never getting a response at all. The exporter who can communicate in German will be much rewarded, even though most Austrians speak English.

Austrians tend to place more emphasis on quality than price, especially for larger purchases. The quality of a product should therefore be its main selling point. Austrians are generally looking for long-term business relationships rather than immediate sales and profit. Hard selling is generally counterproductive.

Best Products and Services

The best sales potential during the period 2013-2011 for U.S. aircraft and equipment is expected to be for satellite navigation systems and GPS, aircraft 5.7 – 14 tons and aircraft engines.

Opportunities
MOD's 18 SAAB105 replacement program.
No special other projects or specific opportunities are available at the present time.

Resources

Web Resources

http://www.austrocontrol.at	Austro Control (Air Traffic Control Authority)
http://www.luftfahrt.or.at	Federal Economic Chamber – Aviation Department
http://www.viennaairport.com	Vienna International Airport
http://www.aci-europe.org	Airport Council International
http://www.bmvit.gv.at	Civil Aviation Airport Authority, Federal Ministry of Transportation, Innovation and Technology
http://www.aua.com	Austrian Airlines Group
http://www.diamond-aircraft.at/	Diamond Aircraft Industries

Contact

U.S. Commercial Service Vienna, Austria
Ingeborg Doblinger, Commercial Specialist
e-Mail: **ingeborg.doblinger@mail.doc.gov**

AUDIO VISUAL EQUIPMENT (AUV)

	Audio Visual Equipment Data (AV) Data Table (in $ million)		
	2008	2009 (estimated)	2013 (estimated)
Total Market Size	1,821.6	1,904.0	1,961.1
Total Local Production	423.3	436.0	449.1
Total Exports	1,052.5	1,056.3	1,088.0
Total Imports	2,450.8	2,524.3	2,600.0
Imports from the U.S.	192.0	197.8	203.7

Austria's media population is 8.4 million with 3.5 million households. In 2008 there were a total of 3.4 million TV households and 2.7 million DVD households registered. Free-to Air TV is very popular: a very large number of German language channels are available for free on digital and analogue satellite and cable. At the end of 2008, a total of 86% of TV households received TV by satellite (43%) or cable (39%). Terrestrial TV offers six Austrian channels that are broadcasted nationwide or nearly nationwide.

Austrian broadcasters must prove themselves in a highly competitive market, where German channels are available to cable- or satellite households. The public service broadcaster ORF (Austrian Broadcasting Corporation) is dominant in the TV market. The two channels ORF 1 and ORF 2 had an average market share of combined 72.3% in 2008, by far leading the ranking list. The German channel SAT.1 followed in 2008 with a market share of 13.4%, Puls 4 with a market share of 5.0% and gotv with a market share of 0.9%.

There are four Austrian-originated commercial TV broadcasters: ATV, Puls 4, Austria 9 and gotv. As all of them are quite new in the market, their market shares are still marginal. ATV started in 2003 as Austria's first commercial broadcaster and is the most successful within this group with an average market share of only 3.0% in 2008.

ATV and Puls 4 can be received nationwide via satellite, cable or antenna. Austria 9 and the special interest channel gotv (music) can be received by either digital satellite or via cable. Another special channel named ORF sportplus is an additional offer from ORF and dedicated to sports and travel programs. It is broadcasted for satellite, cable- and antenna reception.

Several regional TV broadcasters produce one or two hour programs, which are updated daily or weekly and are constantly repeated.

Premiere Austria is the only pay TV operator and is a local version of Premiere Germany. It had approximately 2.4 million subscribers in Germany and Austria by the end of 2008. The number of Austrian subscribers is not available. The operator has key movie Pay TV rights and also offers the Austrian Soccer League.

Mobile

In June 2008 mobile TV was launched on the basis of the digital broadcast-standard DVB-H for handheld devices. Over 50% of the Austrian population has access to this technology with 15 Austrian and German channels offered, of which four are especially designed for mobile. In addition, four radio programs are also transmitted.

Equipment

The total import of audio and infrastructure equipment in 2008 amounted to $2.45 billion, an increase of 14.2% vis-à-vis 2007, while the total import of conferencing and home cinema equipment including TV sets valued $1,123.0 million in 2008–an increase of 12.8% from 2007. The total import of security systems in 2008 amounted to $252.0 million.

Demand for audio and infrastructure equipment will be increasing in 2009/2013 according to industry experts, while demand for conferencing and home cinema equipment including LCD or Plasma TV sets will continue to increase at a double digit rate. There will also be significant growth for security equipment, since emphasis has been placed in Austria on homeland security and the protection of critical infrastructure. The greatest potential is to be realized in the retail and public sectors. Additional growth possibilities exist for residential alarms and video cameras, ICT security (firewall, anti-virus, spam filters) and protection systems.

Best Products and Services

Media

Titles that benefited from strong marketing support and promotions during the previous release windows continue to be top titles in VOD, which remains a hit driven market.

Free content helps to grow numbers of orders, but on demand usage is increasing on a transactional basis as well.

Equipment

Households are prepared to pay more for quality equipment. The consumer electronics entertainment segment of the AV market including HIFI stereo equipment and TV sets (digital-ready and HDTV compatible sets) is the fastest growing segment. Products of high demand include home entertainment systems, LCD and Plasma TVs, DVD players/recorders, Digital Portable Audio Players (mp3). The demand for LCD projectors for home cinema is also increasing. Industry experts also forecast a growth for smart security systems.

Businesses are looking increasingly at DLP technology and for large displays. LCD rather than plasma is in demand. In addition, they are looking for integration services such as image projection and manipulation related software and audio integration solutions. Popular AV products in the conference room and public stations (e.g. subway stations), include electronic display systems, control systems and beamers. Demand for wireless, portable products is growing.

The industry forum of FEEI (Association of the Electric and Electronic Industries) dealt with a wide range of key issues over the past year. The FEEI cooperated closely with the media regulator RTR and the Austrian Broadcasting Corporation (ORF) for the launch of HDTV, including the publication of an HDTV brochure together with ORF containing all relevant information on the new technology. FEEI also prepared a statement for the consumer protection association "Verein für Konsumenteninformation" about a test report on flat-screen TVs.

Opportunities

Opportunities for audio visual equipment exist at public facilities, for instance train stations, hospitals, medical offices, day spas and clinics. Opportunities exist for media and equipment, but will face stiff competition. While German-made media content is very popular, primarily due to the German language, U.S. produced content is also very popular. U.S. produced media content will find a good market in Austria. Likewise, U.S. equipment will find a good market.

Resources

Web Resources

http://www.feei.at/ Fachverband der Elektro und Elektronikindustrie (Association of the Electrical and Electronics Industries)

http://www.rtr.at/ RTR – Rundfunk und Telekom Regulierungs GmbH (Regulator)

http://www.upc.at UPC Telekabel

Contact
U.S. Commercial Service Vienna, Austria
Ingeborg Doblinger, Commercial Specialist
e-Mail: **ingeborg.doblinger@mail.doc.gov**

COMPUTER AND PERIPHERALS (CPT)

	Computer and Peripherals Data Table (in $ million)		
	2008	2009 (estimated)	2013 (estimated)
Total Market Size	2,975.7	2,560.9	2645.4
Total Local Production	63.1	57.8	59.7
Total Exports	698.6	693.0	715.9
Total Imports	3,431.2	3,196.1	3,301.6
Imports from the U.S.	248.7	246.0	254.1

The Austrian computer hardware market in 2008 totaled EUR 2.0 billion (USD 2.8 billion), a decline of 7.5% vis-a-vis 2007. Hardware accounted for 29.5% of total IT spending in 2008.

While statistics are not yet available, industry experts project that the IT market declined 0.2% to reach $9.5 billion in 2009. Over the five-year forecast period, the Austrian IT market should expand at a compound annual growth rate (CAGR) of 3.3% with the strongest growth to be seen in the IT services segment.

Sales for the entire computer hardware sector are expected to show an 8.4% decrease in 2009; however for 2013 industry experts have already forecasted an increase of 3.3%.

Server sales reached $280.8 million in 2008, PC desktops sales reached $1.1million, and PC notebooks sales amounted to $278.8 million and storage system sales were $180.3 million. Peripheral sales totaled $399.8 million and networking equipment sales reached $610.1 million. Hardware accounted for 29.5% of the total IT market in 2008. For 2009, we believe statistics will show a decline for all hardware segments. Peripheral sales will also decline in 2009.

The current credit crunch is having an impact on Austria's IT market starting with a drop in hardware sales and leading to a related negative trend to almost all areas, including services.

Austria's economy contracted through most of 2009, although forecasts are more optimistic for 2013. The more severe cuts in IT budgets will be aimed at hardware or software projects, but many companies will also look for ways to reduce spending on IT services.

On the consumer side, the focus clearly shifted to notebooks, as lower prices continue to attract more and more individual users. Consumer notebook sales in 2008 recorded a growth of 11.6%.

The Austrian disk systems market is highly competitive with a relatively low volume of annual array sales. The $171.5 million in disk systems revenue represented 8.9% decline over the previous year.

New shipments of disk storage systems declined 8.7% in 2008. Storage spending was also driven by projects intended to increase data resiliency and to reduce data recovery and restore times. Such trends would certainly support the shift towards networked storage, which when appropriately designed and implemented, provides end-users with a much more resilient and efficient storage ecosystem.

A large portion of recent storage spending was in the financial services, telecom services, government, and healthcare industries.

A weakened economy will delay some IT projects and other investments. While companies realize the need to support their ongoing IT operations, additional technology investments will be postponed at least until there is better understanding of magnitude and possible duration of the current economic crisis. Investment delays are predicted to especially impact the IT implementation of IT projects.

Blades will remain the engine of growth for x86 servers, primarily for the datacenters. Cloud computing will become an important IT technique to reduce capex while containing opex associated with IT staff costs. Datacenters where hosting is occurring will gain much of the new-generation infrastructure. Other challenges will be around power cooling, which will be a top priority for many customers in 2013. Virtualization and multicore technologies will increasingly be combined as x86 server platforms take on increasingly heavy enterprise workloads.

The level of participants involved in IT decisions in Austrian companies has increased as a result of the alignment of IT with business. Corporate management teams have growing influence in the final IT investment decision, and the decision-making process is becoming slower and more complex. In general, enterprises have more of this inter-relation and need more time to make their choices.

The good news for this industry is that nearly 40% of Austrian end users are absolutely positive that IT can help them to deal with the effects of the financial crisis. An additional 32% believe IT can help them weather the financial crisis.

The United States is the main source of imports, followed by Germany. Overall, sales for the entire computer hardware sector are expected to increase by 3.3% in 2013.

Best Products and Services

The best opportunities of sales for U.S. manufactured IT hardware products are disk storage systems, servers (x86), peripherals, networking equipment, smart handheld devices and notebooks with special features.

Web Resources

http://www.adv.at	ADV – EDP Association
http://www.ocg.at	Austrian Computer Society
http://www.computer-buerosysteme.at	Vienna Chamber of Commerce – Dept. ICT
http://www.statistik.at	Statistik Austria

Contact
U.S. Commercial Service Vienna, Austria
Ingeborg Doblinger, Commercial Specialist
e-Mail: **ingeborg.doblinger@mail.doc.gov**

COMPUTER SOFTWARE AND SERVICES (CSF/CSV)

Overview

	2008	2009 (estimated)	2013 (estimated)
Total Market Size	5,899.7	5,954.9	6,113.8
Total Local Production	N/A	N/A	N/A
Total Exports	N/A	N/A	N/A
Total Imports	N/A	N/A	N/A
Imports from the U.S.	2,802.4	3,963.0	4,076.2

In 2008, total packaged software sales reached approximately $ 1,974.9 million (EUR 1,420.8 million) of which application software represented $ 938.9 million (EUR 675.5 million) and systems infrastructure software represented $ 525.1 million (EUR 377.8 million).

The value of IT services totaled $ 3.9 billion (EUR 2.8 billion) in 2008. Of this total operations management accounted for $ 871.9 million (EUR 627.3 million; system implementation accounted for $ 1.5 billion (EUR 1.1 billion); support services $ 975.6 million (EUR 701.9 million); planning $ 415.1 (EUR 298.6 million); and IT training and education $ 137.6 million (EUR 99.0 million).

The expected annual growth rate for 2009 for software was 2% and 2.2% for services. In 2013, the annual growth rate is estimated at 2.9% for software and 3.4% for services.

Software as a service (SaaS) is becoming a formidable offering now, particularly in the CRM, collaboration, and security segments as the cost structure makes it attractive for customers trying to reduce spending. As a result, SaaS will gain momentum on the Austrian IT market and will require services related to integration with other applications.

Virtualization is still driving the services transition in datacenters, especially around storage and servers, and will emerge as a viable solution for clients (desktop). As Austrian companies of all kinds seek to cut costs and maintain service levels, they will turn to virtualization, which will enable them to reduce new hardware spending and increase flexibility via a smaller datacenter farm (storage and servers). In the desktop space, virtualization will not be adopted as quickly, but the security aspect and centralized control over the desktop makes virtualization attractive nonetheless.

Regulatory demands and uncertain economic conditions are forcing companies to invest in business continuity solutions and to put policies and systems in place to manage risk. Due to the financial turmoil, industry experts expect to see new regulations on financial markets in 2009 and

2013. Therefore, experts consider compliance to be one of the few recession-resilient segments; services around governance, risk and compliance will continue to increase and provide opportunities. On the infrastructure side, risk assessments, network investments and back-up and disaster recovery solutions will benefit.

The outsourcing market seems to be the winner of the economic crisis, or is at least doing better than the other market segments. The outsourcing market typically expands with economic challenges, and cost cutting becomes the main motivation behind procurement of outsourcing services. The current economic downturn will therefore bring greater opportunities for outsourcing, as well as new customers.

The outlook for the IT services market in Austria for 2009 was conservative, with growth rates expected to be minimal, coupled with a reduction in billing rates. Industry experts had expected many project delays, as well as reductions in project scopes. Despite delays, IT spending-related decisions, projects aimed at increasing cost efficiencies were seen as more likely to be approved. Although pricing pressures will also impact an outsourcing market, this market will show healthy growth due to the preference for the effectiveness of operational management.

Industry experts forecast that most IT deploy and support services spending will be trimmed to the absolute minimum, resulting in a massive drop in this segment. In addition, hardware shipments and software license rates are expected to decline sharply.

IT services accounted for 47.9% and software for 22.4% of IT spending in Austria in 2008.

IBM is the largest IT vendor in Austria. However, there are approximately 50 additional U.S. IT firms selling their products and services in Austria. In addition, there is strong competition from European and Asian suppliers in this market.

Enterprise security remains a fundamental aspect of a company's IT infrastructure, and is reflected in spending on IT services around security. Nevertheless, it is difficult to determine exact security budgets, as expenditure is spread across many departments within a company. Themes such as physical security, information and transaction security and business continuity are being taken seriously, which creates a market for contingency planning, needs assessment, risk assessment, and management services. The market for security software totaled $ 169.6 million in 2008 an increase of 24.5% vis-à-vis 2007.The estimated growth rate for 2009 is 8.2%.

Best Products and Services

Accelerated adoption of virtualization will create opportunities for vendors of infrastructure software that deliver products that manage this increasingly virtualized IT environment, particularly around performance monitoring, provisioning, compliance reporting, cluster visibility, and change and configuration management.

Demand for multifunctional security solutions and security software is rising significantly. Security technology is an important foundational element for many of the leading growth drivers in the IT market today, including Web services and digital identity services.

Opportunities

The best opportunities for sales of U.S. software in Austria appear to be in the Internet systems engineering and applications consultancy, data bank and communications software/office automation, security, education, CASE, CIM and quality control. The primary end-users are industry, financial services, public administration, trade, health, energy, production, distribution and electronic banking.

Web Resources

http://www.adv.at	ADV – EDP Association
http://www.ocg.at	Austrian Computer Society
http://www.idc-austria.at	IDC Austria

U.S. Commercial Service Vienna, Austria
Ingeborg Doblinger, Commercial Specialist
e-Mail: **ingeborg.doblinger@mail.doc.gov**

DRUGS AND PHARMACEUTICALS (DRG)

	2008	2009 (estimated)	2013 (estimated)
Total Market Size	2,198.1	2,209.1	2,284.8
Total Local Production	2,430.3	2,442.5	2,526.2
Total Exports	4,376.6	4,398.5	4,549.3
Total Imports	4,144.4	4,165.1	4,307.9
Imports from the U.S.	464.8	471.8	492.8

Given the present economic crisis, 2009 Austrian production of pharmaceuticals is expected to stay the same as the previous year and a slight increase is projected for 2013. An estimated annual real growth rate of 2% of total market size over the next 3 years seems realistic. More than half of all pharmaceuticals approved for sale in Austria are imported. The Austrian health-care system directly employs approximately 170,000 people. Another 180,000 are indirectly engaged in the industry.

Pharmaceutical expenditures in Austria account for about 13% of total health care spending. Around 70% of health-care spending is publicly financed. International comparison shows that drug consumption in Austria is significantly below the European average with regard both to expenditures in Euros and to the number of packages sold. Annual per capita consumption amounts to 22 packages valued at approximately $250. Self-medication accounts for about 10% of the market, placing Austria in the lower third among other European countries. Increased life expectancy and the growth in private health care insurance are expected to have a positive impact on the market.

European drug prices are 25% to 35% lower than U.S. prices. Europe spends 60% less per capita on pharmaceuticals than does the United States – a gap that has roughly doubled since 1992, when European governments spent about 30% less per capita than the United States.

Austrian pharmacy sales prices for pharmaceuticals are about the European average, whereas factory prices are below the European average. As of January 1, 2009, the Government of Austria reduced the Value Added Tax (VAT) on drugs and pharmaceuticals from 20% to 10% which has been a long-term claim by the U.S. Commercial Service Vienna, and the Association of Research-Based Pharmaceutical Companies (FOPI).

Suppliers of drugs to the Austrian population include 1,234 public pharmacies, 46 hospital pharmacies, and 962 self-dispensing doctors who receive their pharmaceutical products from public pharmacies and dispense medicine directly to patients.

The Austrian pharmaceutical industry consists of subsidiaries of multinational companies and small and medium-sized Austrian firms. Both groups have enjoyed above average growth in sales in recent years. Market leaders are Novartis, Glaxo Smith Kline, Baxter, Sanofi-Aventis, Roche, Janssen & Cilag Pharma, and Merck, Sharp & Dohme.

Products from the U.S. enjoy an excellent reputation with respect to quality and safety. The Austrian market is very receptive to U.S. imports in this field; however, U.S. exporters may find significant bureaucratic hurdles. U.S. imports of drugs and pharmaceuticals rank second only to Germany in volume, and they are ahead of France, the United Kingdom, and Switzerland. The 2008 U.S. Market Share in Austria of imported pharmaceutical products was 11.2%.

Approval of Pharmaceutical Products

Access to the Austrian pharmaceutical market is subject to strict national and EU legislation. The approving authority is the newly established "Austrian Federal Agency for Safety and Health Care" with its operational sub-unit "AGES Pharm Med." The authorization process consists of three different procedures:

Reimbursement of Pharmaceuticals and Patent Issues

A pharmaceutical firm seeking to include a product on the list of reimbursable drugs without prior authorization must first obtain the approval of the umbrella organization of social insurance funds (Hauptverband der oesterreichischen Sozialversicherungstraeger / HVB). Almost all new innovative pharmaceuticals must be individually approved by HVB physicians. According to U.S. pharmaceutical companies, the HVB approval process (particularly the long delay in securing HVB decisions) limits market access for innovative pharmaceutical products. The problem is compounded by other, relatively quick HVB approvals of generic competitor products. In 2007, the European Commission filed a suit against Austria for violating the EU's Transparency Directive, challenging the transparency of the approval process, particularly the long delays in securing decisions. As a result the approval process has been adjusted.

A recent trend has been to launch generics in Austria well before a patent expires. This is made possible by the fact that the regulatory authorities do not have a mechanism in place to confirm that a patent has expired before authorizing drugs to be sold on the Austrian market. The Austrian authorities are aware of this problem, but insist that this is a legal question and patent holders must take violations to court for a decision. The U.S. pharmaceutical industry points out legal proceedings are lengthy and expensive and that they are compelled to reduce their prices in the meantime. In some cases if the original product does not reduce its price it can even be removed from the approved reimbursement list.

Best Products and Services

Best prospects among American-made pharmaceuticals are: cancer medications; cardiovascular medications; pharmaceuticals for psychotherapy; AIDS medications; bio-technologically produced medications; and vitamin and mineral combinations such as Melatonin, DHEA, and St. John's Wort. These are classified as pharmaceuticals in Austria, not as dietary supplements as they are in the U.S.

Web Resources

http://www.statistik.at	Statistik Austria

http://www.bmg.gv.at/	Bundesministerium fuer Gesundheit (Federal Ministry for Health)
http://www.oebig.at	Austrian Institute for Health Management
http://www.sozvers.at	Association of Austrian Social Insurance Funds
http://www.pharmig.at	Association of Pharmaceutical Enterprises
http://www.apotheker.or.at	Austrian Chamber of Pharmacists
http://www.fcio.at	Association of the Austrian Chemical Industry
http://www.fopi.at	FOPI – American Association of research-based companies, including some associate members from other countries

U.S. Commercial Service Vienna, Austria
Manfred J. Weinschenk, Commercial Specialist
e-Mail: **manfred.weinschenk@mail.doc.gov**

ELECTRICAL POWER SYSTEMS (ELP)

Austrian electric power generation and distribution systems are among the most reliable and environmentally friendly in Europe. Though dependence on foreign electricity is a matter of concern for policy makers, the relatively high cost associated with local power generation (in accordance with environmental concerns and regulations) has brought a continuous shift to foreign-sourced electricity.

The market for electric power is characterized by increasing consumption, stable production levels, and increasing imports. In 2008, final domestic electricity consumption actually fell slightly from 211,623 to 211,405 Tetrajoules. This unusual result is being attributed to the economic crisis in the year's fourth quarter as well as the warm winter months of January-March of that year.

According to statistics prepared by the Austrian electricity regulator e-control in October 2009, there are currently 6,405 power generation facilities in Austria with a total installed capacity of 20,743 MW (megawatt). Here is a breakdown:

The Austrian grid network is composed of overhead and underground elements, whereby the overhead lines predominate with 95% of the transmission route and 96% of the system length. The transmission route has a total length of 9,794 kilometers, split into 110, 220 and 380kv lines. The system length is 17,334 kilometers.

Best Products and Services

The most interesting business opportunities for U.S. companies at this time are in alternative energy projects, power generation and storage projects, as well as the expansion of smart grid systems and the completion of the high voltage network. Investments upwards of 7 billion Euros ($11 billion) in alternative energy projects are planned for the time period between 2008 and 2015. Wind projects are currently seen as the most promising and benefit most from the government's financial incentive programs. Several hydropower plants, as well as pumped storage facilities, are in planning. Finally, the E.U. in its latest electricity directive, has established the goal of making a smart meter available to 80% of all electricity customers by 2020. In Austria, around 40,000 smart meters are currently in operation and there is significant interest on the part of Austria's electricity providers to move forward with the implementation of smart grid technology.

Opportunities

In addition to the plans to demand for wind energy projects and smart grid technology, there are several projects currently in planning for power generation and storage. According to the Austrian Association of Electricity Companies, there are currently over 80 hydropower projects currently in planning for a total of 7 Terawatt hours of power by 2020. Here are some examples:

Project	Utility	Output	Status	Scheduled to go online
Pumped storage hydro power station Obervermutwerk II	Illwerke, FKW	160MW	Feasibility study in progress	Not available
Pumped storage hydro power station Feldsee II	Kelag	70MW	Approval process underway	2011
Pumped storage hydropower station Reisseck	Verbund	430MW	Seeking bids	2014
Run-of-river cooperative power station Inn	Verbund, TIWAG, Engadiner	88 MW	Approval process underway	2013
Pumped storage system Kuehtai	TIWAG	Capacity increase of 180 MW	Not available	2014

Source: Der Standard, January 13, 2009, p.3 and utility websites (listed below)

Web Resources

http://www.veoe.at/start.html?L=2	Association of Austrian Electricity Companies
http://www.wifo.ac.at/	Austrian Institute for Economic Research
http://www.verbund.at/cps/rde/xchg/internet/hs.xsl/index.htm	Verbund
http://www.tiwag.at/	TIWAG
http://www.kelag.at/	Kelag
http://www.illwerke.at/	Illwerke
http://www.statistik.at	Austrian Statistical Office
http://www.e-control.at	e-Control Austria

U.S. Commercial Service Vienna, Austria
Marta Haustein, Commercial Specialist
e-Mail: **marta.haustein@mail.doc.gov**

ELECTRIC VEHICLES AND INFRASTRUCTURE (EVI)

Austria is an excellent candidate to be an early adopter of electric vehicles:

Best Prospects and Services

The most interesting business opportunities for U.S. companies at this time are in providing vehicles, software, and infrastructure to electric vehicle pilot projects currently in operation or in planning. Opportunities are also likely to arise as local automotive firms move forward with their hybrid and electric vehicle projects.

Web Resources

http://www.wk.or.at/fahrzeuge/	Wirtschaftskammer, Automotive section
www.statistik.at	Austrian Statistical Office
http://www.klimafonds.gv.at/	Climate and Energy Fund
http://www.vlotte.at/	Vlotte
http://www.salzburg-ag.at/ElectroDrive.1936.0.html	ElectroDrive
http://www.mobilityhouse.at/	Mobility House
http://www.austrian-mobile-power.at/en/101.htm	Austrian Mobile Power

U.S. Commercial Service Vienna, Austria
Marta Haustein, Commercial Specialist
E-Mail: **marta.haustein@mail.doc.gov**

MEDICAL DEVICES (MED)

	2008	2009 (estimated)	2013 (estimated)
Total Market Size	1105.8	1129.2	1163.6
Total Domestic Production	851.0	855.3	867.3
Total Exports	1,263.5	1,282.5	1,313.5
Total Imports	1,518.3	1,556.4	1,609.8
Imports from the U.S.	253.1	262.0	273.6

This best prospects report deals with market opportunities for medical devices in Austria, used in hospitals and doctors' medical practices, including dental, as well as home healthcare.

In 2008, Austrian imports of medical equipment were $1,518.3 million. For 2009 we expect these imports to show an increase to $1,556.4 million. Total demand for medical devices in Austria added up to $1,105.8 million, while exports of this equipment amounted to $1,263.5 million. Austria is a transit-trade country with strong trade relationships with Central, Eastern and Southeastern Europe, as well as the Near and Middle East. Re-exporting products is quite common here; hence the volume of imports exceeds the total market. Taking into consideration these re-exports, imports are expected to increase at an average annual real growth rate of 2%. Despite the present economic crisis, the size of the market in Austria for medical equipment should also still increase about by 2% annually over the next three years.

Presently, Austria provides its citizens with universal or nearly universal medical service. Participation in public health insurance programs is essentially mandatory. Some 5.9 million Austrians contribute to the public health insurance companies (Krankenkassen), providing health care coverage for these workers and their families, or about 8 million persons. Insurance costs are shared between employers and employees. Insurance for hospital treatment, however, falls short of the actual costs, and the difference has to be met from public funds.

According to the Austrian Insurance Association (Vesicherungsverband Oesterreich) http://www.vvo.at/krankenversichering-in-osterreich.html , in 2008, approximately 2.83 million people living in Austria participated in private health insurance. Despite the current economic crisis, there has been an increase in the number of private health care subscribers. Currently, there are eight companies in Austria that offer private insurance: Allianz Elementar Versicherungs-Aktiengesellschaft, Call Direct Versicherung AG/UNIQA Personenversicherung AG, Generali Versicherung AG, Merkus Versicherung Aktiengesellscht, MuKi Versicherungsverein auf Gegenseitigkeit, Wiener Städtische Versicherung AG (VIENNA INSURANCE GROUP), Wüstenrot Versicherungs-Aktiengesellschaft. These companies provide a number of services to their subscribers, including Temporary Disability Insurance, Hospital Daily Benefit Insurance, Care Allowance Insurance, Travel Health Insurance, Hospital Expense Insurance, Outpatient Treatment Insurance, Dental Treatment, and Prosthodontics Insurance, etc. According to the Austrian Insurance Association, main reasons behind the increasing number of Austrians purchasing private health insurance can be attributed to the quality of the benefits and services, as well as a subscriber's ability to specifically individualize their health care plan.

Some Austrians pay premiums into a private supplementary insurance, in addition to their social security contributions. For these premiums, the insured person is given better accommodation in the hospital (a single room, for example). And the costs of treatment by a doctor of choice are covered. This can mean shorter waiting periods for examinations. Private insurance also covers the cost of treatment in the private surgery of the practicing doctor, as well as any prosthetic materials and pharmaceuticals which are not fully covered by the contract with the social health insurance program, e.g. those for special dental services. The premiums for private health insurance are calculated according to actuarial principles and are partly income tax-deductible.

The great majority of medical equipment used in Austria is imported. U.S. manufacturers have seized a substantial share of the market and are now the second-largest supplier group, following German companies. German competition enjoys the advantages of geographic proximity, a common language, products with the same standards, no exchange rate problems, and duty-free access through Austria's membership in the EU.

The Austrian market for medical equipment is a sophisticated and well-served one. Against the heavy German competition in this market, American products can usually compete well on the basis of price and innovation.

Germany supplied 31.9% of Austria's imports of medical equipment in 2008. The United States ranked second with 16.7% among foreign supplier countries, followed by Switzerland with 7.6%, Japan with 4%, The Netherlands with 2.9%, and Italy with 2.3%. The German import share did shrink from 34.6% in 2005 to 31.9% in 2008.

Total Austrian imports of medical devices from the United States amounted to $253.1 million in 2008 and in 2009 should reach $262.0 million. Sales of U.S.-engineered healthcare equipment are actually much higher than are reflected in official import statistics, because many products imported into Austria from Western Europe and from the Far East were made or assembled by subsidiaries of U.S. firms.

Best Products and Services

The average Austrian still expects hospitals to have the latest technology. Thus, U.S.-made products that are on the cutting-edge will still have great potential. But the trend is to reduce the number of hospital beds and to close down some hospitals altogether. So American companies that are interested in hospital construction or in the sale of "routine" hospital equipment and supplies may find their prospects reduced over the next few years.

Projected growth rates for different imaging products vary considerably. The Austrian market for medical equipment is constantly evolving and utilizing increasingly sophisticated products.

Scanning units that offer user-friendly features like image networking, which enable the user to digitally store and project high quality images, also should have quite good prospects in Austria. Austria is also an interesting market for echography units, which are popular as the industry discovers new applications for it. Recent technological advances that incorporate Doppler technology and sophisticated probes within their designs should find a good market in Austria.

Sales of conventional radiology apparatus, which has traditionally been the most popular type of equipment, have declined over the last several years. The recent ability to digitalize this out-dated equipment, however, has sparked new interest in traditional radiology. Interventionism radiology is the most recent development in the medical imagery field and has a market in Austria. A combination of radiology and surgery, interventionism radiology has resulted from advances in vascular radiology, digitalization techniques, and catheter performance. It promises to have a strong future.

Taking into consideration the above information, as well as feedback from medical industry experts, the following products are considered to have the best sales prospects in Austria:

Opportunities

Almost all major hospital projects planned for Vienna and the Austrian provinces have been completed. However, with the expansion of the city of Vienna across the Danube River, a new tender was published for a hospital project called "Krankenhaus Nord", for a total cost of $616 million. The hospital is expected to have 850 beds and should be completed by 2012.

Replacement of obsolete hospital equipment is an ongoing process. In January 2009, the Government of the city of Vienna announced a new investment program to modernize and renovate public hospitals as an economic stimulus initiative during the economic crisis.

It should be noted, an increasing number of hospital projects in the Central and Eastern European countries of Hungary, Czech Republic, Slovakia, Romania, and Bulgaria are to be constructed by Austrian companies. These projects will result in many opportunities for American companies to penetrate these markets as suppliers or subcontractors, or in partnership with Austrian firms active in the region. Furthermore, some Austrian design and construction companies are involved in hospital projects in Middle Eastern and Asian countries, including Saudi Arabia, Kuwait, and Indonesia.

U.S. manufacturers interested in marketing their medical equipment in Austria could considerably improve their market position by aggressive marketing, and by the following:

In the past, some U.S. subsidiaries have had significant problems in this market, which has been dominated for several decades by German manufacturers who offer great incentives to decision makers and purchasing officers. Unfortunately, hospitals owned by Austria's provincial governments or cities have sometimes published tenders clearly specifying German equipment, which has created unfair competition. Advocacy efforts by the U.S. Embassy on behalf of U.S. manufacturers have improved the bidding environment. U.S. companies operating in or entering the Austrian market should notify the U.S. Commercial Service office in Vienna, Austria.

Web Resources

http://www.bmg.gv.at/	Bundesministerium für Gesundheit, (Austrian Federal Ministry for Health
http://www.sozialversicherung.at	Hauptverband der oesterreichischen Sozialversicherungstraeger (Association of Austrian Sick Funds)
http://www.oebig.at	Oesterreichisches Bundesinstitut fuer Gesundheitswesen (Austrian Federal Institute for Health)
http://www.fgoe.org	Fonds „Gesundes Oesterreich" (Foundation „Healthy Austria")
http://www.wko.at	Wirtschaftskammer Oesterreich (Austrian Federal Economic Chamber)
http://www.aek.or.at	Oesterreichische Aerztekammer (Austrian Physicians Chamber)
http://www.ameso.at	Austrian Medical Society
http://www.oegam.at	Oesterreichische Gesellschaft fuer Allgemein- und Familienmedizin (Member World Organization of Family Doctors)
http://www.tuev.at/medizin	TUEV Oesterreich (Testing and Certification Institution in Austria)
http://www.medizinprodukte.at	Oesterreichisches Medizinprodukte Handbuch (Medical Products Handbook, published by the Goeschl Publishing House)

U.S. Commercial Service Vienna, Austria
Manfred J. Weinschenk, Commercial Specialist
e-Mail: **manfred.weinschenk@mail.doc.gov**

OIL AND GAS FIELD EQUIPMENT (OGM)

Natural gas is an essential element of Austria's energy economy, providing 22% of Austrian energy consumption. In addition, Austria plays a significant role in the European gas network, acting as a hub for the distribution of Russian gas to other European countries.

Gas consumption has been rising slowly, with dips and peaks caused by variations in weather patterns and economic activity. The average yearly gas consumption in Austria is around 8 bcm, of which over half comes from Russia (via Ukraine), 17% from Norway, 15% from local production, and the remaining 18% from other sources. Usage is split between industry (37%), power generation (34%), households/agriculture (19%), and transportation/other uses (10%). It is estimated that one in four homes heats with gas. The national gas pipeline network is around 38,000 kilometers long (around 23,600 miles). Transit lines add another 1,400 kilometers (670 miles). Austria has storage capacity of around 4.17 bcm, or half of its yearly need, held at five different locations.

Austria's most important gas/oil company is OMV, a regional player with operations in 22 countries, including significant investments throughout Central and Eastern Europe. OMV operates the international gas hub at Baumgarten near the Slovak border, as well as the Central European Gas Hub (CEGH), a web-based trading platform offering commercial, logistical, and auctioneering services to gas traders. Its 100% subsidiary Austrian Gas Grid Management AG manages the Austrian pipeline network. OMV also operates three of Austria's five storage reservoirs. The company plays an important role in the Nabucco gas pipeline company, which would give EU countries access to gas resources in Azerbaijan and Turkmenistan through a pipeline that passes through Turkey, Bulgaria, Romania, Hungary to the Austrian Baumgarten station.

The second significant Austrian gas/oil company is RAG, a company that is specialized in the exploration and production of crude oil and natural gas. RAG operates two of Austria's five gas reservoirs, and is currently developing two more.

Plans to bring several gas-fired power plants online in the coming years (including Mellach, Riedersbach, Simmering, Werndorf, and Klagenfurt) will boost demand significantly, compounding existing distribution bottlenecks in the area around Vienna as well as the southern and western parts of the network. Adding capacity will clearly be necessary. The Russian/Ukrainian gas dispute in the winter of 2008/2009, which resulted in a six day cut-off of Russian gas to Austria and thus much of Europe, was hardly felt in Austria because of their well-stocked storage facilities. This crisis, however, has served to highlight the importance of gas storage (and the drawbacks to dependence on Russian gas). Due to its geological structure, Austria is well suited to accomodating additional storage capacity in depleted natural gas reservoirs and several projects are underway to do just that – in fact, the Austrian gas industry envisions Austria playing a role in storing gas for clients across Europe.

Best Products and Services

The most interesting business opportunities for U.S. companies at this time are in projects that will add volume to current storage capabilities as well as compressor stations and capacity to the existing pipeline network. Opportunities are also likely to arise from pipeline projects currently in planning, most notably the Nabucco pipeline project.

Opportunities

Austria's two primary gas industry players together have plans to more than double Austria's natural gas storage capacity from 4.2 bcm today to 9.7 bcm by 2017. OMV plans to double its gas storage capacity from 1.8 bcm to almost 4 bcm. This will involve expanding current reservoirs (Thann, Schoenkirchen, Tallesbrunn) through increasing pressure and area, as well as new construction (Schoenkirchen-Tief). RAG and its partners are also actively working to increase their storage capacity significantly through the expansion of current facilities (Haidach, Puchkirchen) and the construction of new ones (Aigelsbrunn and Seven Fields) for a total of 5.7 bcm by 2017, up from 1.2 bcm today.

In addition to these storage projects, there are a number of network expansion and upgrade projects in the pipeline, designed to accommodate increasing demand. Here is a sample from the long list of planned projects available online at the AGGM website

Project	Project Lead	Details	Completion Date
Pipeline segment Schwechat-Mannswoerth	OMV	4 km (2.5 miles) PN 70 DN 500	2012
Planning for pipeline segment Gratkorn-Werndorf	GSG	39.6 km (24.6 miles) PN 70 DN 600	2013
Planning for pipeline segment Friedburg/Haidach-Auerbach	OOeF	15 km (9.3 miles) PN 70 DN 500-800	2013
Pressure increase pipeline segment Roitham-Reitsham	OOeF	From 32 to 50 barg.	2011

The Nabucco pipeline consortium is physically located in Austria, and Austria's OMV has played a leading role in this project. The planned length of the pipeline is approximately 3,300 km (2,050 miles), from the Turkish border with Georgia all the way to Austria's Baumgarten hub. The pipeline would transport around 31 bcm yearly, and would come with a price tag of 7.9 billion Euros ($11.2 billion). The first construction phase is scheduled to begin in 2011, and will cover the route between Ankara and Baumgarten.

Web Resources

http://www.gaswaerme.at	Natural Gas and District Heat Association
http://www.omv.com	OMV
http://www.aggm.at	Austrian Gas Grid Management AG
http://www.statistik.at	Austrian Statistical Office
http://www.gashub.at	Central European Gas Hub
http://www.nabucco-pipeline.com/	Nabucco Pipeline Project

U.S. Commercial Service Vienna, Austria
Marta Haustein, Commercial Specialist
e-Mail: **marta.haustein@mail.doc.gov**

RENEWABLE ENERGY (REQ)

The renewable energy market in Austria is driven by energy price volatility, national and EU legislation, as well as various national and regional incentives designed to reduce Austrian dependence on foreign energy sources and promote cleaner energy.

Austria is heavily dependent on foreign energy sources. In 2008, imports made up 85% of gross consumption – up from 78% in 2007 and 71% in 2005. This is primarily due to the demand for fossil fuel for transportation (petroleum products) and heating (natural gas), as well as imported electrical energy, which is cheaper than locally produced electricity.

According to 2008 figures, total energy consumption (which does not include transmission losses) breaks down as follows: 41% liquid fossil fuels; 19% electricity; 17% natural gas; 14% renewables; 6% district heating (garbage or biomass/biogas fired facilities), and 2% coal.

Of the renewable energy produced in Austria, the most important source is biomass/biogas (59%) followed by hydro power (36%). Wind, geothermal, and solar energy, taken together, account for only 5% of domestic energy production.

The profitability of renewable energy projects is still determined by politics more than economics. While the feasibility of grid-based projects depends on green energy quotas imposed on energy providers and feed-in tariffs, projects external to the grid such as biomass systems and residential solar collectors have a somewhat more complex calculation that includes incentive schemes, the price of alternative sources, and local legislation.

Best Products and Services

Wind

Wind energy is expected to benefit most from the newest amendments to the eco-electricity law, which is scheduled to go into effect this year and foresees a 20% increase in the support for wind power. Experts believe that this could bring investments totalling up to 200 million EUR ($282 million) in new projects that would add 120 MW per year to the wind electricity generated yearly. Currently, there are 618 wind turbines online in Austria with a total capacity of 995 MW. In total, these produce around 2.1 Terrawatt hours of clean electricity.

Solar: PV

The Austrian market for photovoltaic systems is limited, and many argue that this technology is not suitable for the Austrian climate – on average, Austria charts only 1,891 hours of sunlight per year, which breaks down to an average of 5.2 hours/day. Average sun hours per day run as low as 1.5 in December. Compare this to Spain, where the yearly sunlight hours number 2,910 and even in December an average of over 4.3 hours is maintained.

Though the domestic market is limited, the Austrian PV industry is growing – with export rates of up to 100%. Though only around 4.5 MW of new PV capacity was installed in 2008, Austrian PV systems with a capacity of 65 MW were produced. Opportunities for cooperation exist.

Solar: Solar Thermal

Though the PV market remains somewhat dormant, the solar thermal market is growing at an impressive pace. The combination of financial incentives offered on both federal and provincial levels (covering approximately 45% of the initial investment), volatile energy prices, and legislation mandating installation in new buildings in some regions has brought double-digit growth over the past several years. In 2008, the market grew by another 25% with 362,923 square meters newly installed. As with PV systems, the export rate in this sector is also high at just under 80%. Although it is a highly competitive market, significant opportunities exist.

Opportunities

In addition to the opportunities likely to arise for new wind installations and the growing solar thermal market, Austria has established itself as a sort of competence-center for renewable energy technologies, presenting interesting opportunities for U.S. companies to establish partnerships for expansion throughout Europe. Austrian companies are particularly strong in these sub-sectors:

Web Resources

http://www.biomasseverband.at/biomasse?cid=37412	Austrian Biomass Association
http://www.pvaustria.at/content/page.asp?id=57	Photovoltaic Association Austria
http://www.umweltbundesamt.at/en/	Federal Environmental Agency
http://www.lebensministerium.at	Federal Ministry for Environment
http://www.statistik.at	Austrian Statistics Office
http://www.e-control.at/	e-Control Austria
http://igwindkraft.at	Austrian Wind Energy Association
http://www.kfp.at/scripts/active.asp	Kreutzer Fischer Partner (Market Analysis)

U.S. Commercial Service Vienna, Austria
Marta Haustein, Commercial Specialist
e-Mail: **marta.haustein@mail.doc.gov**

SECURITY AND SAFETY EQUIPMENT (SEC)

	2008	2009 (estimated)	2013 (estimated)
Total Market Size	421.4	442.9	457.2
Total Local Production	365.0	370.5	379.5
Total Exports	200.9	205.9	213.0
Total Imports	257.3	278.3	290.7
Imports from the U.S.	5.0	5.2	5.4

Property crime in Austria is rising rapidly and there is a growing unease by public. In the context of a European Union comparison, Austria can still be viewed as a country with relatively little crime, but citizens and law enforcement officials realize that crime is on the increase. Differentiation must be made however between violent crime, which is rising but still relatively low, and property crime, which has risen quite dramatically in the past years. A total of 88,904 violent crime offences were recorded in 2008 with a detection rate of 84.2%. With regard to property crime, the number of criminal offenses has risen to a total of 591,597 in 2009, which is 3.30% more than in 2008. According to Austrian officials, the detection rate is 39.85%. Vienna is still the main region affected by crime followed by Lower Austria. Specifically, a sharp increase in incidence can be seen in the number of burglaries in both private and commercial properties as well as cybercrime and financial fraud have been affected by a sharp increase. A Master plan set up for 2013 has been designed to specifically combat the high number of burglaries in private properties. However people's sense of security has declined: According to a current survey, only 28% of the population is completely satisfied with the performance of the police, and 45% of Vienna's citizens state that they fear being out on the streets alone at night.

The political and economic consequences resulting from ongoing integration in Europe as well as the evident globalization of economic systems in conjunction with a continuous increase in migration are considered by Austrians to have had significant impact on increasing crime. The rise in criminal offences, especially burglaries, has lead to ongoing political discussions including the possible role of the removal of border controls due to the Schengen Agreement, as most Austrians blame foreigners for the increased crime. In this regard, cross-border investigations are highly significant. Austria was the first country in the EU to have converted to the Schengen pan-European criminal search system, "SISone4ALL" which will be followed by "SIS II" in 2013. Other international co-operations include OCTA 2008 against drug trafficking and fraud, close collaboration with Europol against financial crime as well as with Eurojust with emphasis on the fight against human trafficking, and representation on various Interpol committees. The threat of terrorism in Austria plays an important role in defining the domestic security market. Austria was directly affected by Islamist radicalization influenced by Al Qaeda's ideology when two Austrian citizens were held hostage from February to October 2008. Additionally, world media outlets reported on a campaign for municipal elections which heavily criticized Islam and lead to direct threats against Austria as well as proceedings against two individuals found guilty and sentenced for the spreading of the ideology of Islamist terrorists. Although the terrorism threat potential continues to be high in Europe in 2009, 80% of Austrians do not fear terrorist attacks in their country, yet only 30% believe that Austria is well prepared for such a contingency.

The security market in Austria has become a growth industry with 440 firms involved in security systems, 170 firms involved in safety engineering and 150 in providing support functions. Surveillance companies dealing with the protection of persons and property, electronic monitoring, fire detection as well as armored–car manufacture and services generate strong turnover figures. The lion's share of the surveillance business is comprised of the Austrian Security Service (2400 employees), Securitas (1350 employees), which is a part of a Swedish concern and Group4S (2300 employees). In 2009, the total Austrian market for safety and security equipment is estimated to have been $442.9 million. Despite the present economic crisis, the market is still expected to grow at an estimated annual real growth rate of 3% over the next three years. Austrian imports from the United States in this sector were approximately $5.2 million in 2009. 2008 Austrian import market shares for Security and Safety Equipment in Austria were as follows:

Country	Market Share (of imports only)
Germany	47.8%
Switzerland	6.2%
China	4.8%
Slovakia	3.3%
Italy	2.7%
Slovenia	2.5%
USA	1.9%

Two leading U.S. manufacturers of sophisticated security solutions are already well established in the Austrian market: GE Security and ADT of Tyco International.

Austrian local production with this sector consists of manufacturing of all sizes of safes, some electronic security devices and a wide range of sophisticated locks and locking systems for all applications.

Best Products and Services

The Austrian security market offers many opportunities for U.S. firms. In general, it is a desirable, affluent test market for advanced U.S. technology. In particular, access control systems, including biometric identification systems, and video surveillance equipment, including CCTV systems have considerable potential. IP-based security is highly attractive to the trade and is currently growing at an annual rate of 40%. From this perspective, the greatest potential can be realized in the retail and public sectors – governmental authorities, schools and public areas. Additional growth possibilities exist in products such as explosives and metal detectors (X-Ray, handheld), residential alarms, forensic equipment, perimeter protection systems, ICT security (firewall, anti-virus software, Spam filters), fire-related protection and work-wear protection.

Opportunities

The Government of Austria and some semi-governmental institutions are working on several infrastructure projects (e.g. a large "Central Railway Station" in Vienna) which may soon increase the demand for safety and security equipment.

Web Resources

http://www.vsoe.at	Association of Austrian Security Companies
http://www.bmi.gv.at	Austrian Ministry of the Interior
http://www.elektrotechniker.at	Association of Austrian Electronic, Audio-Video,and Alarm Equipment Companies

U.S. Commercial Service Vienna, Austria
Manfred J. Weinschenk, Commercial Specialist
e-Mail: **manfred.weinschenk@mail.doc.gov**

TRAVEL AND TOURISM SERVICES (TRA)

	2008	2009 (estimated)	2013 (estimated)
Total Arrivals to the United States	158,768	161,943	162,429

Austrians took a total of 15.4 million trips and 7.5 million trips abroad in 2008, which is the most recent year for which we have complete records. In general, Austrians prefer to spend their vacations abroad. They spent a record € 7.7 billion ($10.7 billion) traveling abroad in 2008. They spent € 186 million ($259 million) for travel to the United States. We expect 2009, to show a momentary pause in these rates of decline because of the relatively strong Euro.

The United States enjoyed the highest popularity among long-haul destinations (meaning a destination outside Europe) for Austrian travelers. We expect the number of Austrian travelers to the United States to increase about 2% in 2013. For 2009 we expect an increase in travelers but a decrease in spending due to the downturn of the economy. Total arrivals from Austria in 2008 were 158,768. Austria ranked 33rd overall for arrivals to the United States in 2008. The top ports of entry for Austrian travelers are, in order, New York, Washington D.C., Los Angeles, San Francisco, Boston, Atlanta, Miami, Chicago and Dallas.

The most popular U.S. destinations are New York, Florida (Orlando, Miami), California (San Francisco, Los Angeles, and San Diego), Nevada, Massachusetts, Illinois, Pennsylvania, New Jersey, Texas and the national parks. The most popular attractions while in the United States are amusement/theme parks like Disney World, Disneyland, Universal Studios, Sea World, cities, visit of museums and art galleries, cultural heritage sites, ranches, shopping malls, restaurants, water sports and golfing. Travel industry representatives see potential for adventure trips to Alaska, Washington State, Oregon, Colorado, Montana, Texas and Louisiana. New York, Florida, California and Las Vegas will remain strong attractions. Repeat travelers choose secondary destinations like New England, the Carolinas, Tennessee, Georgia and the Great Lakes.

In 2008, the Austrian long-haul sector of the outbound market increased by 23%, however only 10% of all trips abroad were long-haul trips. There was less demand for packages offered to South East Asia, South America, Africa and the Middle East. However, the United States had an increase of 21% of visitors from Austria. The appreciation of the Euro against the U.S. dollar and attractive packages offered by tour operators stimulated long-haul travel to the United States. The correlation between the weaker U.S. currency and the Austrian visitor to the United States was particularly noticeable, especially during the second half of the year. Industry experts forecast that Austrian long-haul pleasure travel will grow by 2% annually over the next 3 years if the dollar does not appreciate too much against the Euro. Expenditures will not rise at the same rate since the average length per trip and cost is declining due to the economic downturn. Expenditures per person traveling to the United States amounted to approximately € 3,360 ($4,670) in 2008 vis-à-vis € 2,826 ($3,928) in 2007. Visitors to the United States stayed an average of 14 days per trip in 2008, which is one more day compared to 2007 and they spent €240 ($334) per day compared to €213 ($296) in 2007, which is an increase 12.7 % over the previous year.

Austrians who travel to the United States are generally 20-50 years of age with about 50% belonging to the upper middle class. Their length of stay in 2008 was approximately 14.0 days vis-à-vis 13.0 days in 2007. Travel mostly takes place during June, July, August and September. Almost 50% of all pleasure travel takes place during the months of July and August. About half are repeat travelers. About 53% of Austrian bookings to the United States are for pleasure, 21% for business, 18% for visiting friends and 4% for attending a conference/convention. Another 10% combine business and pleasure. Vienna and its surroundings account for the major part of travel to the United States.

Stiff competition among the direct service carriers Austrian Airline's Group, which is now owned by Lufthansa, in cooperation with United Airlines (Star Alliance), Delta Air Lines, Air France KLM in cooperation with Northwest Airlines, British Airways in cooperation with American Airlines, is expected to keep airfares low and attractive. In 2009, several carriers offered return trips to New York and Washington D.C. for € 439 ($610) excluding taxes. The Star Alliance group and British Airways pick up the highest number of passengers originating from Vienna across the Atlantic. A strong Euro may encourage some people to take a trip to the United States in order to take advantage of the attractive packages offered by travel suppliers, which are about ten% less compared to the previous year. In fall 2008, the Austrian Airline's Group discontinued the flight to Chicago. Delta Air Lines also discontinued its non-stop service from Atlanta to Vienna in October 2008.

Airfares increased from € 349 ($485) in 2007 to € 439 ($610) for a round trip to New York in 2008. The dollar declined vis-à-vis the Euro during the same period. Austrians in the past have discovered the United States as a shopping paradise and very often considered the U.S. a bargain. Austrians also discovered excellent wines and cuisine as well as a broad offering of cultural events, which now rank among the main attractions. Sports are in very high in demand, as is adventure travel. Most Austrians, with the exception of older people, prefer to travel individually. The majority of Austrian travelers rent a car.

The United States is in a strong position, as long as the dollar does not increase too much vis-à-vis the Euro, which would make traveling to the United States expensive for middle-class

Austrians. Competition from the Caribbean, South East Asia, Middle East, South Africa and South America is increasing and continuous marketing is necessary to meet these challenges.

Paid vacation is generally between 5-6 weeks depending upon industry and years of service. English is widely spoken and is not generally a barrier for Austrian travel to the United States.

The Austrian outbound travel market is wide open with virtually no restrictions. The use of credit cards by Austrians is fairly widespread, but not as common as in the U.S., with VISA, MasterCard, American Express and Diners Club being the most popular.

Tour operators and travel agencies do extensive promotional work and absorb most promotion costs. Increasing pressure comes from tourists who like to make their own arrangements and reservations (Internet, etc.). Tour operators have been successful so far in competing with packaged air travel, hotels and car rentals at very competitive prices, due to their annual purchasing power. E-specials and last minute offers are very popular due to the attractive prices.

The Visit USA Committee is a registered Association in Austria. The Association comprises approximately 30 members and is funded primarily by membership dues and profits generated from events. The Visit USA Committee's website is www.visit-usa.at

ESTA – Electronic System for Travel Authorization

ESTA registration is mandatory for citizens of all Visa-Waiver countries, including Austria, as of January 20, 2013.

Best Products and Services

Fly and drive packages, short city trips for shopping and cultural events, guided tours, hotels and resorts in lesser known areas, specialties such as flights in small planes to the wilderness, river rafting, adventure trips, helicopter sightseeing etc. educational trips (language study, the MBA, other studies, pilot training, etc.) and cruises (including river cruises).

Opportunities

Given that most visitors from Austria to the United States are repeat visitors who prefer to travel independently, we expect that U.S. tour operators could profitably offer attractive fly and drive packages, short city trips for shopping and cultural events, guided tours, cruises, hotel and resort packages in lesser known areas, wilderness, river rafting or adventure trips, helicopter sightseeing, wedding packages, etc. Educational trips/stays (e.g., language, MBA programs, pilot training) may also have good potential. The traditional golf packages offered should be expanded to areas, which are less known to Austrians. The market for vacation club packages and time-share condominiums still has some potential in this market.

Web Resources

http://www.statistik.at	Statistik Austria
http://tinet.ita.doc.gov	ITA Office of Travel & Tourism Industries
http://www.visit-usa.at	Visit USA Committee Austria
http://www.usembassy.at/en/embassy/cons/niv.htm	U.S. Embassy Vienna, Austria: U.S. Consular Section (Visa Information)

https://esta.cbp.dhs.gov/esta/esta.html?_flowExecutionKey=_cB2773F62-8673-1974-2513-527DAE5A5034_k5EA55EC4-6E86-ABB4-7E6C-07221C8AF49E	ESTA Information and Application Page

U.S. Commercial Service Vienna, Austria
Ingeborg Doblinger, Commercial Specialist
e-Mail: **ingeborg.doblinger@mail.doc.gov**

AGRICULTURAL SECTORS OPPORTUNITIES

AGRICULTURAL, FISH AND FORESTRY SECTOR

In 2008, Austria's agriculture, fish and forestry imports worldwide amounted to $15.3 billion. Exports reached $17.1 billion. In total, 84% of all imported agricultural products came from the EU territory and 75% of all exported goods were delivered to EU Member States. The major trading partner is Germany followed by Italy. From the United States Austria imported $112.7 million worth of agricultural, fishery and forestry products not including significant and steadily increasing transshipments from other EU countries. In 2009, imports and exports are expected to decline by value but not by quantity.

When responding to polls, consumers usually express a preference for high quality foods; however, when it comes to actually buying, price appears to be the major purchasing factor for a majority of the population. In 2009, due to the global recession, lower food prices and a tendency to choose lower-cost alternate products, food expenditures are expected to drop by 0.8% compared to 2008. Food expenditures are predicted to recover and increase again in 2013 (Source: Euromonitor). However, for special events most people, even those with a low income, are willing to spend more for "exclusive" products. In addition, the higher income and gourmet market segments (which regularly buy high priced foods) are growing.

The traditional Austrian diet is based on pork, flour, and vegetables. Cakes and bakery products are also important parts of the diet. Austrian dishes are rich in cholesterol and fat and the most important ingredient is meat, either pork or beef. The increasing interest in a healthy lifestyle, especially among younger people, who are more concerned about their daily calorie – intake and a healthy diet, makes low-fat food more and more popular. The younger generation also appreciates trying new products with appealing image along with good taste. Because of environmental concerns, a very negative perspective of Austrian consumers towards biotech products, and food safety scares, there is a reliable and growing market for organic products. An increasing number of pets are stimulating the demand for pet food.

	Agricultural, Fish and Forestry Data Table (in $ million)		
	2008	2009 (estimated)	2013 (estimated)
Total Market Size	10,600	10,700	10,900
Total Local Production	12,400	12,500	13,200
Total Exports	17,100	16,300	17,500
Total Imports	15,300	14,500	15,200
Imports from the U.S.	113	105	117

Best Products and Services

Despite the fact that foods and beverages from Austria, Germany, and other EU countries dominate the shelves of Austrian retail outlets, there are some good market opportunities for U.S. products, particularly in the prime quality sectors. Consumer oriented food and beverage products are the most important sector. In 2008, the consumer oriented sector accounted for 52% of total imports from the United States and reached a value of $58 million, which is an increase of 38% from 2007 (Source: Global Trade Atlas). These numbers do not include significant and steadily growing transshipments of U.S. products from other EU countries.

Opportunities

Market opportunities for U.S. products include fish and seafood products, nuts, wine, pet foods, dried fruits, fruit juices, snack foods, and hormone free high quality beef, game and exotic meat for the upper scale gastronomy.

DRIED FRUITS AND NUTS

There is growing demand for wholesome/natural foods by Austrian consumers. Austrian imports of nuts and dried fruits are constantly growing. Those products are mostly used as ingredients by the food-processing sector for the production of pastries and breakfast cereals. Dried fruits and prepared nuts are also popular as a snack. Austrian production of dried fruits and nuts is limited to locally grown products like pears and walnuts. Demand for organically/sustainably produced dried fruits and nuts is also on a sharp increase.

The statistics below show actual Austrian imports from the United States not including EU transshipments. A large share of Austria's cereal, fruits and nut mixtures consumption is sourced from Germany where these items are processed and packed and then exported to Austria. Therefore, the actual import value of U.S. dried fruits and nuts to Austria is estimated to be much higher. The EU and Turkey are the largest suppliers of these products to Austria.

The United States is the third most important supplier of nuts to Austria. Almonds are the most important commodity within this category. Further products with good sales potential include walnuts, pistachios, pecans, hazelnuts, raisins, prunes, apricots, and cranberries.

	2008	2009 (estimated)	2013 (estimated)
Total Market Size	118	108	126
Total Local Production	20	20	21
Total Exports	44	42	45
Total Imports	142	130	150
Imports from the U.S.	13	13	15

FISH AND SEAFOOD

The Austrian market offers small but lucrative opportunities for fish and seafood products. Fish consumption in Austria is growing as consumers associate fishery products with a modern healthy diet. Domestic fish production is marginal and limited to fresh water fish like trout and carp. Since Austria is a landlocked country, all marine fish, shellfish, and crustaceans must be imported. The main suppliers are Germany, Netherlands, Italy, and Denmark.

Consumption of seafood is rising. The reason for the general upward trend is the rising standard of living, health awareness, and the growing number of restaurants serving seafood. Austrian per capita consumption of fish rose from 6 kg in 2003 to almost 8 kg in 2008.

Due to transshipment within the EU, the real value of imports from the United States is thought to be much higher than indicated in customs statistics. Major U.S. seafood products are imported through Germany.

Best prospects for U.S. fish and seafood exports are salmon, lobster, shrimps, crabs, caviar substitutes, catfish and scallops.

	2008	2009 (estimated)	2013 (estimated)
Total Market Size	431	396	436
Total Local Production	25	25	26
Total Exports	23	24	25
Total Imports	429	395	435
Imports from the U.S.	1.5	1.9	2.2

WINE

Austria's average wine output is about 2.5 million hectoliters/year, which corresponds roughly to the annual domestic wine consumption. Large quantities of wine are imported and exported. The predominant suppliers are Italy, France, Germany, and Spain, which supply mostly red wines.

A large share of California wines is imported through German wholesalers and does not appear as a U.S. import in the official trade statistics. The numbers below show only wines imported directly into Austria.

Austria has traditionally a high share of domestic wine consumption. However, good prospects exist for "new world wines" including those from the United States. In 2008, the United States was the sixth most important supplier of wine (by value) in Austria. U.S. wine sales increased in retail stores including discounter who mainly carry inexpensive U.S. wines. Demand for good quality, inexpensive U.S. wine priced from $5 to $10 a bottle is increasing. The main competitors for U.S. wines are Chilean and Australian wines.

	2008	2009 (estimated)	2013 (estimated)
Total Market Size	805	741	825
Total Local Production	721	680	740
Total Exports	167	156	170
Total Imports	251	217	255
Imports from the U.S.	4.1	4.1	4.5

PET FOODS

Due to the increasing number of single households and the rising number of older people seeking companionship, the number of pets continues its upward trend. This stimulates the demand for pet food.

Austria is a net exporter of dog and cat foods. However, there are good market opportunities for prime quality, organic and nutritional pet food products. As consumers seek healthier lifestyles for themselves, many seek the same for their pets. The trend towards eating more natural and organic foods for humans has already been emulated in pet foods and an increase in organic pet food sales can be seen. As an increasing number of owners look for ways to extend their pets' lives, sales for nutritional pet food products containing vitamins and supplements are on a rising trend.

	2008	2009 (estimated)	2013 (estimated)
Total Market Size	374	371	388
Total Local Production	388	391	400
Total Exports	198	190	200
Total Imports	184	170	188
Imports from the U.S.	3.6	3.7	3.9

Web Resources

http://www.lebensministerium.at	Bundesministerium fuer Land- und Forstwirtschaft, Umwelt und Wasserwirtschaft (Federal Ministry of Agriculture, Forestry, Environment and Water Management)
http://www.bmg.gv.at	Bundesministerium fuer Gesundheit (Federal Ministry of Health)
http://wko.at	Wirtschaftskammer Oesterreich (Austrian Federal Economic Chamber)
http://www.ages.at	Oesterreichische Agentur fuer Gesundheit und Ernaehrungssicherheit (Austrian Agency for Health and Food Safety)
http://www.statistik.at	Statistik Austria (Statistics Austria)
http://useu.usmission.gov	The United States Mission to the European Union
http://gain.fas.usda.gov/Pages/Default.aspx	U.S. Department of Agriculture's Global Agricultural Information Network (GAIN)

For further information on these sectors, please contact the U.S. Department of Agriculture's Foreign Agricultural Service (FAS) in Vienna, Austria: agvienna@fas.usda.gov

Contacts

U.S. Commercial Service - Austria

U.S. Commercial Service U.S. Embassy Boltzmanngasse 16, 1091 Vienna, Austria Tel. ++43 1 313 39-0 Fax: ++43 1 310 6917 e-Mail: vienna.office.box@mail.doc.gov
Web: http://www.buyusa.gov/austria/en/contact_cs_ vienna.html

U.S. Mission to the E.U. - Foreign Commercial Service

Rue Zinner 13, B-1000 Brussels, Belgium
Fax: ++32 2 513 1228
Contacts: Mr. Louis Santamaria – Standards Attaché
Tel.: ++32 2 508 2674
e-Mail: louis.santamaria@mail.doc.gov
Ms. Sylvia Mohr – Standards Specialist
Tel.: ++32 2 508 2675, Fax: ++32 2 513 1228
e-Mail: sylvia.mohr@mail.doc.gov

CEN – European Committee for Standardization

Rue de Stassart 36, B-1050 Brussels, Belgium

Tel.: ++32 2 550 08 25-550 08 11, Fax: ++32 2 550 08 19
Web: http://www.cen.eu/cenorm/index.htm

CENELEC – European Committee for Electrotechnical Standardization

Rue de Stassart 35, B-1050 Brussels, Belgium
Tel.: ++32 2 519 68 71, Fax: ++32 2 519 69 19
Web: http://www.cenelec.org

ETSI – European Telecommunications Standards Institute

Route des Lucioles 650
F-06921 Sophia Antipolis Cedex, France
Tel.: ++33 4 92 94 42 12, Fax: ++33 4 93 65 22 99
Web: **http://www.etsi.org**

European Commission: Enterprise Directorate-General

Rue de la Science 15; B-1040 Brussels, Belgium
Tel.: ++32 2 299 56 72, Fax: ++32 2 299 16 75
Web: **http://europa.eu.int/comm/enterprise/standards_policy/**

EFTA – European Free Trade Association

Rue de Trèves 74, B-1040 Brussels
Tel.: ++32 2 286 17 41, Fax: ++32 2 286 17 42
Web: **http://www.efta.int/**

NORMAPME – European Office of Crafts, Trades and Small and Medium-Sized Enterprises for Standardization

Rue Jacques de Lalaing 4, B-1040 Brussels, Belgium
Tel.: ++32 2 282 05 31, Fax: ++32 2 282 05 35
Web: **http://www.normapme.com**

ANEC – European Association for the Co-ordination of Consumer Representation in Standardization

Avenue de Tervueren 36, Box 4
B-1040 Brussels, Belgium
Tel.: ++32 2 743 24 70, Fax: ++32 2 706 54 30
Web: **http://www.anec.org**

ECOS – European Environmental Citizens Organization for Standardization

Boulevard de Waterloo 34, B-1000 Brussels, Belgium
Tel.: ++32 2 289 10 93, Fax: ++32 2 289 10 99

EOTA – European Organization for Technical Approvals (for construction products)

Avenue des Arts 40, B-1040 Brussels, Belgium
Tel.: ++32 2 502 69 00, Fax: ++32 2 502 38 14
Web: **http://www.eota.be** , e-Mail: **info@eota.be**

Austria's International Investment Position (in EUR billion)

	2007	*2008**	*2009***
FDI in Austria	108.1	117.6	122.9
Austrian FDI Abroad	102.6	122.6	125.4

TRADE AND PROJECT FINANCING

How Do I Get Paid? (Methods of Payment)

It is common practice to require either (partial) payment in advance or confirmed and irrevocable letters of credit for initial transactions. Due diligence information is readily available for most companies, greatly reducing the risk of non-payment. The U.S. Commercial Service Vienna offers a due diligence service (International Company Profile or ICP) which includes, when resources permit, a personal interview with the company in question. Please contact our office for more information. Once the relationship with a customer is established, open account and extended terms will be expected. As Austria is a fully developed industrial nation, programs offered by the U.S. government and multinational institutions designed to reduce the risk of trading with developing countries do not apply here. Austria's international credit rating gives it preferred status for trade, finance, and investment guarantees. A bilateral arbitration agreement exists and can be included in contracts. In Austria, the common business practice is to allow 30 to 60 days for payment; early payments (within 14 days) are usually credited with a discount of 3 to 6%, depending on the industry. Supplier credits are common.

How Does the Banking System Operate?

Austria is a member of the European Monetary Union and uses the Euro as its only legal tender. The Austrian banking system is well developed, with worldwide correspondent relations, as well as offices and branches in the United States and other major financial centers, and a huge network in the countries in Central, Eastern, and Southeastern Europe (CESEE) and the former Soviet Union (FSU).

A wide range of credit and financial instruments is offered by all of Austria's banks. General financing to establish foreign operations in Austria is readily available. Foreign firms enjoy access to Austrian credit and capital markets without restriction.

IMPACT OF THE GLOBAL FINANCIAL CRISIS

Austrian banks were spared immediate fallout of the subprime crisis, but they suffered indirectly from the worldwide financial crisis through higher refinancing costs and credit scarcity, and later, due to their strong focus on CESEE/FSU countries, from huge loan losses and write-offs in the area. Most Austrian banks active in CESEE/FSU will continue to suffer loan losses in the region -- but have performed better than expected in 2009 and continue to make profits, have ramped up loan loss provisions, are taking advantage of government state aid, and appear sufficiently capitalized. Austrian banks view the situation in CESEE/FSU as difficult but manageable and all have made a strong commitment to remain in those growing markets. Even though Austrian banks have sufficient liquidity and there is no credit crunch, tighter lending conditions in reaction to the economic downturn, i.e., the solvency and risk assessment of companies applying for loans is being conducted more thoroughly than was previously the case, resulted in some credit scarcity, particularly for small and medium-sized companies. This situation is unlikely to change soon, given the outlook for slow and modest economic recovery in both Austria and CESEE markets, the strict Basel II Capital Accord requirements for banks and in general their medium-term need for additional capital.

FINANCING TRADE AND INVESTMENT IN CENTRAL AND EASTERN EUROPE

Large Austrian banks can also assist in trade and investment financing in Central and Eastern and Southeastern Europe (CESEE) and the former Soviet Union (FSU), where they operate significant networks. Western European banking groups dominate the CESEE/FSU banking markets, and three of the five largest foreign banking groups in the area are Austrian. Austrian banks can also help arrange financing for export and investment transactions in Central and Eastern Europe. The Austrian government does not have a counter trade policy or any other specific regulations in this field.

Many major foreign banks, including American banks, have operations in Austria.

Foreign-Exchange Controls

Austria has a fully liberalized foreign exchange regime. There are no limitations on cross-border payments, whether related to foreign trade, capital investments, or other transactions, except to countries under UN or EU sanctions.

U.S. BANKS AND LOCAL CORRESPONDENT BANKS

Branches / Subsidiaries of U.S. Banks in Austria

American Express Bank Ltd. TRS

Commercial & Private Banking
Kärntnerstrasse 21-23, A-1015 Vienna, Austria
Tel.: ++43 1 515 67-0, Fax: ++43 1 515 67-15
Web:
http://www.americanexpress.com/austria/homepage.shtml

Citibank International PLC, Austria Branch

Corporate & Investment Banking (no retail services)
Kärntnerring 11-13, A-1010 Vienna, Austria
Tel.: ++43 1 717 17-0, Fax: ++43 1 712 97 07
Web: **http://www.citigroup.com**

Western Union International Bank

Consumer Financial Services
Maderstrasse 1, A-1040 Vienna, Austria
Tel.: ++43 1 506 17 120, Fax: ++43 1 506 17 897
Web: **http://www.westernunionbank.com**

Austrian Banks with Subsidiaries in the United States

Erste Bank der oesterreichischen Sparkassen AG

In Austria:
Graben 21, A-1010 Vienna, Austria
Tel.: ++43 50100-10100, Fax: ++43 501009-10100
Web: **http://www.sparkasse.at/erstebank**

In the United States:
Erste Bank der oesterreichischen Sparkassen AG
New York Branch
280 Park Avenue, West Building, 32nd Floor
New York, NY 10017, USA
Tel.: (212) 984-5600, Fax: (212) 986-1423

Raiffeisen Zentralbank AG

In Austria:
Am Stadtpark 9, A-1030 Vienna, Austria
Tel.: ++43 1 717 07-0, Fax: ++43 1 717 07-1715
Web: **http://www.rzb.at**

In the United States:
RZB Finance LCC
1133 Avenue of the Americas
New York, NY 10036, USA
Tel.: (212) 845-4100, Fax: (212) 944-2093
Web: **http://www.rzbfinance.com**

PROJECT FINANCING

EU financial assistance programs provide a wide array of grants, loans, loan guarantees and co-financing for feasibility studies and infrastructure projects in a number of key sectors (e.g., environmental, transportation, energy, telecommunications, tourism, public health). From a commercial perspective, these initiatives create significant market opportunities for U.S. businesses, U.S.-based suppliers, and subcontractors.

The EU supports projects within its Member States, as well as EU-wide "economic integration" projects that cross both internal and external EU borders. In addition, the EU provides assistance to accession countries in Eastern and Southern Europe and Turkey, as well as some of the former Soviet republics.

The European Union provides project financing through grants from the European Commission and loans from the European Investment Bank. Grants from the Structural Funds are distributed through the Member States' national and regional authorities, and are only available for projects in the 27 EU Member States. All grants for projects in non-EU countries are managed through the EuropeAid Cooperation agency in conjunction with various European Commission departments, called "Directorates-General.

The CSEU Tenders Database

The U.S. Commercial Service at the U.S. Mission to the European Union offers a tool on its website to help U.S.-based companies identify European public procurement opportunities. The database features all current public procurement tenders issued by all national and regional public authorities in the 27 Member States of the European Union, plus four other European countries, and that are open to U.S.-based firms under the terms of the Government Procurement Agreement (GPA) implemented in 1995. The database is updated twice weekly and is easy to use with a range of search options, including approximately 20 industry sectors. The database also contains tenders for public procurement contracts relating to structural funds. Readers may access the database at http://www.buyusa.gov/europeanunion/eu_tenders.html .

EU Structural Funds

The EU Structural Funds, including the European Regional Development Fund, were created in 1975 to assist economically depressed regions of the European Union that required industrial restructuring. The EU earmarked EUR 308 billion for projects under the Structural Funds and the Cohesion Fund programs for the 2007-2013 period for the EU-27. In addition to funding economic development projects proposed by Member States or local authorities, EU Structural Funds also support specialized projects promoting EU socioeconomic objectives. Member States negotiate regional and "sectoral" programs with officials from the regional policy Directorate-General at the European Commission. For information on approved programs that will result in future project proposals, please visit: http://ec.europa.eu/regional_policy/atlas2007/fiche_index_en.htm .

For projects financed through the Structural Funds, Member State officials are the key decision-makers. They assess the needs of their country; investigate projects; evaluate bids; and award contracts. To become familiar with available financial support programs in the Member States, it is advisable for would-be contractors to meet with local officials to discuss local needs.

Tenders issued by Member States' public contracting authorities for projects supported by EU grants are subject to EU public procurement legislation if they meet the EU minimum contract value requirement for the eligible sector. Below this threshold, tender procedures are subject to national procurement legislation. There are no overt prohibitions against the participation of U.S. companies, either as developers or concessionaires of projects supported partially by the Structural Funds, or as bidders on subsequent public tenders related to such projects, but it is advisable to team up with a local partner. All Structural Fund projects are co-financed by national authorities and most may also qualify for a loan from the European Investment Bank. The private sector is also involved in project financing. For more information on these programs, please see the market research section on the website of the US Mission to the EU: http://www.buyusa.gov/europeanunion/mrr.html

The Cohesion Fund

The Cohesion Fund is another instrument of EU structural policy. Its EUR 61.5 billion (2007-2013) budget seeks to improve cohesion within the EU by funding transport infrastructure and environmental projects in Portugal, Spain, Greece and the twelve new (since 2004) EU Member States from Central and Eastern Europe. These projects are generally co-financed by national authorities, the European Investment Bank, and the private sector.

The Trans-European Networks

The European Union also provides financial support to the Trans-European Networks (TENs) to develop infrastructure, strengthen cohesion and increase employment across greater Europe. Launched at the Essen Counsel (Germany) in 1994, the TENs are a series of transport, telecommunications and energy projects that are continually being expanded and upgraded. The TENs are largely financed by private sector and non-EU sources. The EU does, however, provide grants from the Cohesion Fund, loans from the European Investment Bank (and loan guarantees from the European Investment Fund), and partial feasibility study grants for the TENs. There are no overt EU restrictions on the participation of U.S. firms in the TENs.

Other EU Grants for Member States

Another set of sector-specific grants offers assistance to EU Member States in the fields of science, technology, communications, energy, environmental protection, education, training and research. Tenders related to these grants are posted on the various websites of the directorates-generals of the European Commission. Conditions for participation are strict and participation is usually restricted to EU firms or tied to EU content. Information pertaining to each of these programs can be found on:

External Assistance Grants

The EuropeAid Cooperation Office is the European Commission agency in charge of managing the EU's external aid programs. This Agency is responsible for the management of the entire project cycle, from identification to evaluation, while the Directorates-General in charge of External Relations and Development, are responsible for the drafting of multi-annual programs. The EuropeAid website offers extensive information on the range of grant programs, the kind of projects that are eligible, as well as manuals to help interested parties understand the relevant contract law. However, participation to calls for tender for contracts financed by EuropeAid is reserved for enterprises located in the EU Member States and requires that the products used to respond to these projects are manufactured in the EU or in the aid recipient country. But consultants of US nationality employed by a European firm are allowed to form part of a bidding team. European subsidiaries of U.S. firms are eligible to participate in these calls for tender.

All tenders related to EU-funded programs outside the territory of the European Union (including the accession countries) are located on the EuropeAid Cooperation Office website: http://ec.europa.eu/europeaid/work/funding/index_en.htm

Two new sets of programs have been approved for the financing period 2007-2013., The EU provides specific Pre-Accession financial assistance to the accession candidate countries that seek to join the EU through the "Instrument for Pre-accession Assistance" (IPA). Also, the European Neighborhood and Partnership Instrument (ENPI) will provide assistance to countries that are the Southern Mediterranean and Eastern neighbors of the EU.

Loans from the European Investment Bank

Headquartered in Luxembourg, the European Investment Bank (EIB) is the financing arm of the European Union. Since its creation in 1958, the EIB has been a key player in building Europe. As the EIB's lending practices evolved over the years, it became highly competent in assessing, reviewing and monitoring projects. As a non-profit banking institution, the EIB offers cost-competitive, long-term lending in Europe. Best known for its project financial and economic analysis, the Bank makes loans to both private and public EU-based borrowers for projects in all sectors of the economy, such as telecommunications, transport, energy infrastructure and environment.

While the EIB mostly funds projects within the EU, it lends outside the EU as well (e.g., in Central, Eastern and Southeastern Europe; Latin America; and Pacific and Caribbean states). In 2007, the EIB approved loans for projects worth EUR 56.4 billion, of which around 16% was lent outside the EU. The EIB also plays a key role in supporting EU enlargement with loans used to finance improvements in infrastructure, research and industrial manufacturing to help those countries prepare for eventual EU membership.

Projects financed by the EIB must contribute to the socioeconomic objectives set out by the European Union, such as fostering the development of less favored regions; improving European transport and telecommunication infrastructure; protecting the environment; supporting the activities of SMEs; assisting urban renewal; and, generally promoting growth, competitiveness and employment in Europe. Last year, the EIB created a list of projects to be considered for approval and posted the list on its website. As such, the EIB website is a source of intelligence on upcoming tenders related to EIB-financed projects: http://www.eib.org/projects/pipeline/index.htm

The EIB presents attractive business opportunities to U.S. businesses. EIB lending rates are lower than most other commercial rates. Like all EIB customers, however, U.S. firms must apply the loan proceeds to a project that contributes to the European objectives cited above.

The EIB's i2i (Innovation 2013 Initiative) is designed to highlight projects that support innovative technology in the European Union, in particular by financing broadband and multimedia networks; the physical or virtual infrastructure providing local access to these networks; and research and development infrastructures, especially in the less developed regions of the European Union. i2i will also finance projects to computerize schools and universities and to provide information technology training in conjunction with public authorities.

The US Mission to the European Union in Brussels has developed a database to help US-based companies bid on EIB public procurement contracts in non-EU countries in particular. The EIB-financed contracts that are open to US-based companies are featured in this database. All the tenders in this database are extracted from the EU's Official Journal. The EIB database contains on average 50 to 100 tenders and is updated twice per week.

Austrian Websites

http://www.oenb.at/en/welcome_to_the_oenb.jsp	Austrian Central Bank
http://www.oekb.at/en/about-oekb/pages/default.aspx	Austrian Control Bank
http://www.fma.gv.at/cms/site/EN/index.html	Austrian Financial Market Authority
http://www.oebfa.co.at/e/index.htm	Austrian Federal Financing Agency

EU Websites

http://ec.europa.eu/regional_policy/atlas2007/fiche_index_en.htm .	Future project proposals
http://ec.europa.eu/regional_policy/index_en.htm	The EU regional policies, the EU Structural and Cohesion Funds
http://ec.europa.eu/ten/transport/index_en.htm	The Trans-European Networks (TENs)
http://ec.europa.eu/grants/index_en.htm	EU Grants and Loans index
http://ec.europa.eu/europeaid/index_en.htm	EuropeAid Co-operation Office
http://ec.europa.eu/enlargement/how-does-it-work/financial-assistance/index_en.htm	IPA
http://www.eib.org/	The European Investment Bank
http://www.eib.org/projects/index.htm?lang=-en	EIB-financed projects
http://www.eib.org/Attachments/thematic/innovation_2013_initiative_en.pdf	The EIB's i2i (Innovation 2013 Initiative)

US Websites

http://www.buyusa.gov/europeanunion/eu_tenders.html	CSEU Tender Database
http://www.buyusa.gov/europeanunion/mrr.html	Market research section on the website of the US Mission to the EU
http://www.buyusa.gov/europeanunion/euopportunities.html	European Union Tenders Database
http://www.exim.gov	Export-Import Bank of the United States
http://www.exim.gov/tools/country/country_limits.html	Country Limitation Schedule
http://www.opic.gov	OPIC
http://www.tda.gov/	Trade and Development Agency
http://www.sba.gov/oit/	SBA's Office of International Trade
http://www.fsa.usda.gov/ccc/default.htm	USDA Commodity Credit Corporation
http://www.usaid.gov	U.S. Agency for International Development

BUSINESS TRAVEL

BUSINESS CUSTOMS

Business practice and etiquette are similar in Austria to American customs; however, there are some important differences. For example, it is worth noting the relatively formal environment in which business is generally conducted in Austria. When making appointments with prospective buyers or clients it is customary to make initial contact well in advance, either in writing or by phone, and to offer to meet on the premises of the person in question. Another manifestation of Austrian formality is the widespread use of titles, be they in recognition of a university degree, a position in a firm or in the government. The most common titles are "Doktor" (abbreviated form: “Dr.”; a university degree similar to the U.S. Doctorate), "Magister" (abbreviated form: “Mag.”; similar to the U.S. Master of Arts), "Diplom-Ingenieur" (abbreviated form: “DI” or “Dipl. Ing.”; similar to the U.S. Master of Science), and “Ingenieur” (abbreviated form: “Ing.”; literally meaning ‘Engineer”). The use of titles adheres to a system and it is not uncommon for one to have several titles and the highest title will come first, i.e. Dr. Mag. Schmidt or Dr. Dipl. Ing. Steinbock. In addition to Austrian titles, academic degrees which were previously only seen in the English speaking world are being increasingly awarded by Austrian universities. Therefore, titles such as B.A., M.A. and M.B.A may not necessarily mean that the individual has studied in an English speaking country. However, these titles will come after one’s name.

At a function, Austrians would prefer to have the host introduce them to the other guests rather than to introduce themselves. When Austrians do introduce themselves, they usually just give their family name. First names may or may not come later in a relationship. Although first names are used immediately in social situations in the United States, with many employees calling their bosses by their first names, this is not done in Austria. There are, of course, exceptions, particularly among the younger generation. The newcomer should take his or her cue from the people around them.

Austrians shake hands whenever they greet or leave acquaintances; this is done with everyone in a group. A woman offers her hand first to the man, and the older person to the younger. Handshakes are firm with direct eye contact. It is considered rude to have one’s hands in one’s pockets while being introduced or while talking to anyone. Also, Americans inexperienced in negotiations and discussions with Austrians may initially find some Austrians overly direct in initial meetings, however, one should keep in mind that directness is seen in the same light as honesty in Austria.

Overall, Austrians are generally well disposed towards the United States and Americans. Showing understanding for the Austrian way of doing things will prove rewarding.

SELLING FACTORS/TECHNIQUES

Possibly because of the many years of shortage during World War II and the post-war period, and certainly because of Austria’s monarchical authoritarian history, the traditional buyer-seller relationship in Austria may seem strange to the American. The customer wants or needs something and is thus at a disadvantage, while the seller, who is holding the item that the customer wants, is in a position of power. Though it is true that this traditional interpersonal part of the commercial relationship is losing its hold here as the older generations move into retirement and more sophisticated communications and competition take hold, the sense that the customer is asking a favor of the seller still persists to some degree.

Why is this information important? Because it will help U.S. firms avoid making simple mistakes when communicating with potential partners and customers. Two rules of thumb are worth remembering: First, companies should refrain from hard sell practices, which could backfire if the Austrian customer feels that the products are less desirable because the sales approach is so strong. And second, companies should stick to simple American friendliness and transparency, which usually make a good impression.

Another interesting difference in the way Austrians make purchasing decisions is the relative importance here of preciseness. While Americans like a product to be tough and easy to use, Austrians want a product to be perfectly engineered and very precise.

In addition to cultural considerations, price has become a key factor in purchasing. More and more sectors are now price-driven, a development that has accelerated with the globalization of the local economy. Where product quality and personal relationships once played a larger role in purchasing decisions, the focus has shifted increasingly to pricing and the bottom line. However, emphasis on quality and personal relationships still play a comparatively stronger role in decisions than in the U.S.

Tipping

In some Austrian restaurants and hotels a 10% service charge may be included and it will be itemized on the bill ('Rechnung') as a service charge ('Bedienungszuschlag'). Where this is the case, only a small amount of extra change needs to be left as an additional tip. The common practice is to round up to the next even amount or to leave a tip of about 10 to 15% of the total if a service charge has not been included. If the service charge has been included, it is accepted to round up to the next Euro. In a restaurant, the tip is always handed to the waiter or waitress directly and never left on the table. It is good practice to tell the server what you would like back in change rather than to wait until after they have handed you the change.

For example, if the bill is 25 Euros and you intend to leave the server a 2 Euro tip, you might hand the server 30 Euros and say "27 please". They will understand that you intend to give them a 2 Euro tip. This interaction works in all tipping situations. Again, avoid leaving a tip on the table.

Misc. Services	Tipping Guidelines
Taxis:	10% of the fare, more if the driver has helped with baggage.
Hotels:	Moderate tips, such as EUR 1 to 2 per bag or suitcase handled, are in order for bellhops or others who perform special services for guests.
Barber:	About 10% for a man's haircut.
Hairdresser:	About 10% is customary, plus EUR 2 to 3 for the assistant who washes one's hair. However, it is regarded as an insult to tip the owner of the shop.

TRAVEL ADVISORY

There are no general travel advisories specifically for Austria.

Travel warnings are issued when the U.S. State Department recommends that citizens either avoid travel altogether, or exercise various cautions, when visiting a specific country. Countries where this is recommended will have a travel warning as well as Consular Information Sheets. These sheets are available for every country of the world and can be found online at http://travel.state.gov/travel/warnings_consular.html

In addition, travelers can refer to the U.S. Department of State's pamphlet, A SAFE TRIP ABROAD, for ways to promote a trouble-free trip. The pamphlet is available from the Superintendent of Documents, U.S. Government Printing Office, Washington, D.C. 20402. This document can also be viewed online at: http://travel.state.gov/travel/tips/safety/safety_1747.html

Austria is a predominantly mountainous, landlocked Central European country, with an area of 32,378 mi² (83,859 km²) and a population of 8.3 million. It is divided into nine federal provinces: Wien (Vienna), Niederösterreich (Lower Austria), Burgenland, Steiermark (Styria), Oberösterreich (Upper Austria), Salzburg, Kärnten (Carinthia), Tirol (Tyrol) and Vorarlberg. For a map of Austria and its 9 provinces, please see page 17 of this Country Commercial Guide.

The climate varies considerably from the Alpine region to the eastern plain. Summers can be hot, humid and long; cold winters bring snow and ice.

Electrical Voltage

The European standard is 230 volts/50 cycles. All 110 or 120 volt U.S. appliances will need a transformer. Clocks and other appliances that require 60 cycle current will not function properly, even with a transformer. Austria uses a plug with two small and elongated round prongs. More exact information can be found here: Electrical Plug/Outlet and Voltage Information for Austria (Republik Österreich): Adaptelec.com, International Electrical Specialists . Adapters and converters for small appliances are available at luggage or travel stores and at Radio Shack in the United States and can also be found quite easily at any electronic store in Austria.

Safety

Although statistics show crime has risen in recent years, Vienna is often cited as one of the safest cities in Europe, and Austria is considered one of the safest countries in the world. Violent crime in Austria is very rare. The most worrisome crime in urban areas is having one's pocket picked or purse stolen. As in any big city, the visitor should take care when walking alone, avoiding dark and isolated places. For the most part, the visitor will be safe any time of the day or night. There are three separate emergency numbers, all of which are free of charge:

Arrival At VIE Vienna International Airport

Vienna International Airport, also called Schwechat International, is located about 12 miles east of Vienna near the town of Schwechat. It is a short 20 to 30 minute ride by taxi, bus, or train from the airport to the city center. An Airportbus is probably the easiest and most efficient means of public transportation to get from the airport to your hotel. A shuttle bus departs every 20 or 30 minutes from the lower level of the airport, with 4 buses, one of each stopping at Schwedenplatz, Kaisermühlen VIC & Kagraner Platz, at train stations Wien Miedling & Westbahnhof, and a bus runs to the neighboring town of Baden. More exact information can be found here: ÖBB-Postbus GmbH: Vienna AirportLines . Tickets can be bought on the bus for 6 for EUR 6 one-way (EUR 11 round trip). There is also the S-7 Schnellbahn (train) that runs from Wien Nord, via Wien Mitte, to Vienna International Airport and back, about every half hour. The trip takes 30 minutes and costs EUR 3,60 but can only be bought before getting on the train.

The City Airport Train (CAT) is an express train service to and from "Wien Mitte". The ride lasts 16 minutes and costs EUR 9 one-way (EUR 16 round trip) for adults and EUR 5 one-way (EUR 8 round-trip) for children. Trains leave every 30 minutes. Luggage can be checked in the city at Wien Mitte. Further information on CAT: CAT - City Airport Train .

Additional information on how to get to and from the Airport is available on the following websites: **http://www.schnellbahn-wien.at/english/index.htm**

Tourist information is available in the arrival area of Vienna International Airport, as well as at train stations. The Vienna Tourist Information Office is located behind the State Opera House at Kärntner Strasse 38 in the 1st district. There is also a City Information Office at the City Hall (Rathaus).

The currency used in Austria is the Euro (EUR) and Euro Cents (1 Euro = 100 cents).

The Austrian National Tourist Office, Inc. in North America conducts nationwide and regional promotions and co-op marketing programs, and offers numerous support services. Details are available on their website: http://www.austria-tourism.at/us

Business travelers to Austria seeking appointments with U.S. Embassy Vienna officials should contact the U.S. Commercial Service Vienna well in advance, as visitors are accepted on an appointment basis only. Please feel free to contact the U.S. Commercial Service at the American Embassy in Vienna:

The U.S. Commercial Service in Vienna, Austria
Tel.: ++43 1 313 39 – 0, Fax: ++43 1 310 69 17
e-Mail: **vienna.office.box@mail.doc.gov**
Web: **http://www.buyusa.gov/austria/en**

VISA REQUIREMENTS

A visa is not required for U.S. citizens who wish to stay in Austria for up to two three-month periods during one calendar year. At the conclusion of the six-month stay, the visitor must leave the country. The exception is if he or she has already submitted and received a residence permit.

For further detailed information, visitors should consult the website of the Consular Section of the U.S. Embassy in Vienna: http://www.usembassy.at/en/embassy/cons/niv.htm

U.S. Companies that require travel of foreign businesspersons to the United States should be advised that security options are handled via an interagency process. Visa applicants should go to the following links. State Department Visa Website: http://travel.state.gov/visa/index.html

TELECOMMUNICATIONS

Telecommunications services are reliable in Austria. The phone system is fully automated, and direct dialing is available to most countries in the world at varying international rates. The system was for many years monopolized by the government- owned and operated company Telekom Austria. A few years ago the government deregulated the system and new companies entered the market. Telekom Austria still exists as a partially government-run agency, but now it has competition.

Public telephone booths are becoming less common as almost every Austrian older than ten has a mobile phone. However, a public phone is available in most post offices. You can use coins or a pre-paid calling card (Telefonwertkarte). The card can be bought at post offices or tobacco shops (Trafik).

Direct Long Distance Calls

To make a direct call outside Austria, the caller should first dial "00" and then the country code (e.g. 001 for the United States and Canada), the area or city code, and finally the phone number. International country codes are listed at the front of the white pages in the Vienna telephone book. The country names in the telephone book are in German. Area codes for major cities within the specific countries are also listed. The list also provides the time difference (Zeitunterschied) given in numbers of hours between Austria and the destination country. For credit card calls, the caller should dial 0802 34 56 or 0800 287 874 21 (toll-free). For long distance information, he should call 11 88 77 for Austria, Germany and the EU countries, and countries bordering Austria. For other countries, the caller should call 0900 11 88 77. The Herold Business Data AG also provides online telephone information for Austria: http://www.herold.at/telefonbuch/

Internet Calling

For inexpensive Internet phone service, the caller should consult the following websites: http://www.dialpad.com or

Callback Long Distance Services

There are also callback long-distance carriers that offer reasonably priced calls to the United States. They are known as "call-back" services because the caller calls a phone number, hangs up, and waits for it to call back. It then connects the caller to an open U.S. phone line. For this service, visitors should contact the following provider (English is spoken):

InCom Austria

Contact: Ms. Claudia Poelzl
Tel.: ++43 1 979 23 98
e-Mail: **claudiainaustria@hotmail.com**

Cell Phones

"Cell" phones are called "Handys" in the German speaking areas of Europe. Austria uses the GSM standard for its cellular service. Unless the visitor is in a very remote area, he will most likely have coverage. A tri-frequency cell phone will provide service in Austria and the United States. Drivers are not allowed to drive and use a hand-held cell phone at the same time. If caught without a hands-free system (Freisprechanlage), the driver will be fined. During traffic jams, drivers are exempt from this law.

The following cell phone service providers / networks are used in Austria:

A1 (Telekom Austria)	http://www.mobilkom.at or http://www.a1.net
Orange	http://www.orange.at
Tele-ring	http://www.telering.at
T-Mobile	http://www.t-mobile.at
Drei	http://www.drei.at
Bob	http://bob.at/

Internet

Visitors to Austria can also use numerous Internet Cafés throughout the country. The visitor should check with the hotel receptionist or the yellow pages of the local telephone directory.

TRANSPORTATION

Direct flights connect Vienna to several U.S. cities. Austria's modern highways link most cities, and numerous border crossings into neighboring countries are easily accessible. Unlike highways in America, Austrian highways do not indicate their route through direction, i.e. I-95N or Rt. 30W, but rather which major cities it runs towards, i.e. A9 Salzburg or A4 Bratislava. Air travel connections between major cities in Austria and in the region are available and frequent, and land travel by train or bus is comfortable and reliable. Travelers can save money by using second class, which most travelers consider adequate and comfortable. If extensive travel is planned, Austrian and European wide rail passes may be the best value. The Austrian Railpass offers three days of unlimited travel in a 15-day period and includes some major shipping lines. For those including Austria on a multi-nation itinerary, Eurailpasses are honored in 18 countries. For people wanting unlimited travel, the Eurail ticket provides the option to travel in and between 27 countries in Europe. For detailed rail information as well as purchases of rail tickets, call:

For travel itineraries, train schedules and prices for rail trips within Austria (and to some neighboring countries); please visit the Austrian Railways' website (Oesterreichische Bundesbahnen, OeBB): http://www.oebb.at/en/index.jsp

Toll stickers (Vignette) are required on all vehicles on Austria's major highways. They can be obtained from the Austrian Automobile Clubs as well as at post offices, gasoline stations and borders. The following fees apply:

Validity	Private Car	Motor Home (weighing up to 3.5 tons)	Motorcycle
1 year	EUR 76.20	EUR 76.20	EUR 30.40
2 months	EUR 22.90	EUR 22.90	EUR 11.50
10 days	EUR 7.90	EUR 7.90	EUR 4.50

Stickers must be applied on the upper middle or left side of the windshield in cars and on motorcycles on any good visible part. Motorists who do not possess the appropriate sticker are subject to a fine. Cars rented in neighboring countries may or may not be equipped with the sticker, so travelers should remember to obtain one from their car rental agency.

Contact information for the Austrian Automobile Clubs:

OEAMTC

Tel.: ++43 1 71199-0 (information) and ++43 1 120 (24-hour road service)
Web: **http://www.oeamtc.at**

ARBOE

Tel.: ++43 1 891 21-0 (information) and ++43 1 123 (24-hour road service)
Web: **http://www.arboe.at**

All of the major *car rental companies* can be found at the Vienna International Airport. Some also offer offices in the city of Vienna:

AVIS Autovermietung Ges.m.b.H.

Laaer-Berg-Str. 43, A-1100 Vienna, Austria
Tel.: ++43 1 601 870, Fax: ++43 1 601 87- 61
Web: **http://www.avis.at** , e-Mail: **kundenservice@avis.at**

Hertz Autovermietung

Kaerntner Ring 17, A-1010 Vienna, Austria
Tel.: ++43 1 795 32, Fax: ++43 1 795 42 696
Web: **http://www.hertz.at** , e-Mail: **reservierung@hertz.at**

In Vienna, districts 1, 2, 3, 4, 5, 6, 7, 8, 9 and 20, as well as parts of district 15 are so-called "Kurzparkzonen" - Short Time Parking Zones. On weekends, parking is free. Monday through Friday the parking time is limited to 2 hours from 9:00 am to 10:00 pm in the in the above districts. The same system is used in many other Austrian cities. To use Short Time Parking Zones, tickets have to be displayed on the dashboard. They can be purchased at tobacco shops or banks. Throughout the provinces, regulations for short time parking vary and other methods are used. Numerous cities have pay meters, and some use cardboard clocks indicating arrival and departure time, which must be displayed on the car dashboard.

Public transportation is excellent throughout the country, and particularly good in larger cities. In Vienna, a public transportation ticket is valid on any form of public transportation – U-Bahn, Schnellbahn, trams, or buses, even within the same trip. The honor system is used here; however, periodic checks by controllers, potential embarrassment and the hefty fine dissuade most people from riding without a ticket. Tickets can be bought in advance (less expensive) at "Vorverkaufsstellen", ticket machines, and from tobacco shops. Trams and buses have integrated machines. There are single tickets, 24-hour and 72-hour tickets, 8-day tickets, weekly and monthly travel passes, and annual travel passes. Information is available online: Wiener Linien or one could visit Wiener Linien Ticket Prices for details on different kinds of public transportation tickets, and please also see Wiener Linien Maps for public transportation maps within Vienna.

LANGUAGE

For a traveler, it is no problem to get around the country with little or no knowledge of the German language. Many Austrians speak English (mandatory in school) and are quite willing to help.

Water

Vienna's water is not only safe to drink from the tap, but is recommended. It comes from alpine springs and is very refreshing. However, the water supply is not fluoridated. This is true throughout Austria.

Public Hospitals

Travelers needing to consult a doctor should check with the receptionist at their hotel or make use of the yellow pages of the local telephone directory.

Emergency room service is not offered at private hospitals, but only at public facilities, and there is often more than one emergency room in a hospital managing different types of problems and age groups. The ambulance may be instructed to transport an individual to a specific center. Private citizens are not usually permitted to drive up to the ambulance entrance in their own car. For urgent assistance, the individual should call an ambulance.

Allgemeines Krankenhaus der Stadt Wien (AKH)

Währinger Guertel 18-20, A – 1090 Vienna, Austria
Tel.: ++43 1 404 00-0, Tel. of Children's Clinic: ++43 1 404 00-3232, Fax: ++43 1 404 00-1212
Web: **http://www.akhwien.at**

Wilhelminenspital der Stadt Wien

Montleartstrasse 37, A – 1160 Vienna, Austria
Tel.: ++43 1 491 50-0, Tel. of Children's Clinic: ++43 1 491 50-2924, Fax: ++43 1 491 50-1009
Web: **http://www.wienkav.at/kav/wil/**

Dental Emergencies

The weekend edition of the Viennese daily newspapers lists the on-call dentists and dental surgeons available for dental emergencies (Zahnärzte und Dentisten) under the heading "Notdienst". Also available is the

Dental University Clinic (Zahnklinik)

Waehringer Strasse 25 a, A – 1090 Vienna, Austria
Tel.: ++43 1 4277 67131, Fax: ++43 1 4277 67139
Web: **http://www.meduniwien.ac.at/zahnklinik/**
e-Mail: **aufnahme-zmk@meduniwien.ac.at**

American physicians expect their patients to ask lots of questions and seek explanations, as partners in health care. This is not as common in Austria as in the U.S.

Pharmacies in Austria are not open 24 hours a day. They usually have hours from 8:00 am through 6:00 pm, and on Saturday from 8:00 am through 12:00 noon. There is a rotating schedule of pharmacies that provide services after these hours, and their location will be posted at the entrance to a closed pharmacy. You may also look up the Austrian pharmacies' weekend schedule online (province by province) by putting your address into this website's search engine:

http://www.apotheker.or.at/Internet/OEAK/NewsPresse_1_0_0a.nsf/agentEmergency!OpenAgent&p=0078BC2D78F93AF2C1256F2C004B35F5&fsn=fsStartHomeFachinfo&iif=0

Local Time, Business Hours, and Holidays

Central European Time is used in Austria. There is a time difference of +6 hours between Vienna and New York City, except for a couple weeks in the Spring and Fall when European and American daylight savings times differ. Austrians use the 24-hour clock. For example, 5 p.m. is written as "17:00 Uhr". Variations may be: 17 U, 17.00, 17h or 17h00. Times (especially in movie and theater listings) are distinctly Austrian: ¼ 4 = 3:15, ½ 4 = 3:30, ¾ 4 = 3:45, and so on. Austria follows European Daylight Savings Time, which begins the first Sunday in April and ends in October.

The following holidays will be observed in Austria in calendar year 2013 (If "U.S." is indicated in the column on the right, the respective Holiday is also celebrated by the official American community in Austria):

January 1 (Friday)	***New Year's Day***	Austria & U.S.
January 6 (Wednesday)	***Epiphany***	Austria
January 18 (Monday)	***Martin Luther King's Birthday***	U.S.

	(3rd Monday in January)	
February 15 (Monday)	Washington's Birthday	U.S.
	(3rd Monday in February)	
April 2 (Friday)	Good Friday	Austria
April 4 (Sunday)	Easter Sunday	Austria & U.S.
April 5 (Monday)	Easter Monday	Austria
May 1 (Saturday)	Labor Day	Austria
May 13 (Thursday)	Ascension Day	Austria
May 23 (Sunday)	Whit–Sunday	Austria
May 24 (Monday)	Whit–Monday	Austria
May 31 (Monday)	Memorial Day	U.S
	(last Monday in May)	
June 3 (Thursday)	Corpus Christi Day	Austria
July 4 (Sunday)	Independence Day	U.S.
July 5 (Monday)*	Independence Day (observed)	U.S.
August 15 (Sunday)	Assumption Day	Austria
September 6 (Monday)	Labor Day	U.S.
	(1st Monday in September)	
October 11 (Monday)	Columbus Day	U.S.
	(2nd Monday in October)	
October 26 (Tuesday)	National Day	Austria
November 1 (Monday)	All Saints' Day	Austria
November 11 (Thursday)	Veteran's Day	U.S.
November 25 (Thursday)	Thanksgiving	U.S.
December 8 (Wednesday)	Immaculate Conception	Austria
December 24 (Friday)	Christmas Eve	Austria & U.S.
December 25 (Saturday)	Christmas Day	Austria & U.S.
December 26 (Sunday)	St. Stephen's Day	Austria

Business visitors should note that the Austrian vacation season is in July and August, and that many decision-makers take extended vacations during that time -- sometimes four weeks or more. Business visits or events are not recommended during these two months. Many offices and businesses are closed Friday afternoons, reflecting the widely implemented 38.5-hour workweek.

TEMPORARY ENTRY OF MATERIALS AND PERSONAL BELONGINGS

Computers Used for Business Purposes

When entering Austria, visitors should go through Customs, declare their laptop or notebook, and state that it is used for doing business only (e.g. for PowerPoint presentations). It is advisable to have the value of the electronic equipment (evidenced on a copy of the invoice) available. The visitor will be issued a Customs paper called "Verwendungsschein", which will also include the visitor's departure date (there is an upper limit of 12 months). When leaving Austria, the visitor should go through Customs again for a checkout.

Web Resources

http://travel.state.gov/travel/warnings_consular.html	U.S. State Department Travel Warning
http://travel.state.gov/travel/tips/safety/safety_1747.html	Safe Trip Abroad Pamphlet
http://www.buyusa.gov/austria/en	The U.S. Commercial Service in Vienna, Austria
http://www.viennaairport.com	Vienna International Airport
http://www.schnellbahn-wien.at/english/index.htm	Schnellbahn Vienna
http://www.cityairporttrain.com/	Vienna City Airport Train (CAT)
http://www.austria-tourism.at/us	Austrian National Tourist Office
http://www.advantageaustria.org/us/zentral/about_austria/reisen-nach-oesterreich.en.jsp	Austrian Trade Portal: Travelling to Austria
http://www.usembassy.at/en/embassy/cons/index.html	U.S. Embassy Visa Information
http://travel.state.gov/visa/index.html	State Department Visa Website
http://www.herold.at/telefonbuch/	Online Telephone Information in Austria
http://www.skype.com	Internet Phone Service
http://www.dialpad.com	Internet Phone Service
http://www.iconnecthere.com	Internet Phone Service
http://www.mobilkom.at ,	Cell Phone Service
http://www.a1.net	Cell Phone Service
http://www.orange.at	Cell Phone Service
http://www.telering.at	Cell Phone Service
http://www.t-mobile.at	Cell Phone Service
http://www.drei.at	Cell Phone Service
http://www.bob.at	Cell Phone Service
http://www.raileurope.com	Rail Europe
http://www.oebb.at/en/index.jsp	Austrian Railways
http://www.oeamtc.at	Austrian Automobile Club
http://www.arboe.at	Austrian Automobile Club
http://www.avis.at	Avis Rent-a-Car in Austria
http://www.hertz.at	Hertz Rent-a-Car in Austria
http://www.wienerlinien.at	Public Transportation Information in Vienna
http://www.akhwien.at/	Vienna University Hospital
http://www.wienkav.at/kav/wil/	Wilhelminen Hospital Vienna
http://www.rudolfinerhaus.at/en.html	Rudolfinerhaus Private Hospital Vienna
http://www.meduniwien.ac.at/zahnklinik/	Dental University Clinic

CONTACTS

Contacts

United States Government Agencies in Austria:

The U.S. Commercial Service - Austria

Please use the following mailing address for mail sent from the United States:	The U.S. Commercial Service at the American Embassy, Austria Boltzmanngasse 16, A–1090 Vienna, Austria Tel.: ++43 1 313 39 22 97 Fax: ++43 1 310 69 17 e-Mail: **Vienna.office.box@mail.doc.gov** Web: **http://www.buyuse.gov/austira/en** and **http://www.export.gov/cs** The U.S. Commercial Service Vienna 9900 Vienna Place Washington, D.C., 20521-9900

The United States Embassy in Austria

Please use the following mailing address for mail sent from the United States:	United States Embassy in Austria Boltzmanngasse 16, A–1090 Vienna, Austria Tel.: ++43 1 313 39-0 Fax: ++43 1 310 69 17 e-Mail: **embassy@usembassy.at** Web: **http://vienna.usembassy.gov/en/index.html** The U.S. Commercial Service Vienna 9900 Vienna Place Washington, D.C., 20521-9900

Austrian Government Agencies:

Embassy of Austria in the United States

Press and Information Service: Consular Section:	3524 International Court N.W. Washington, DC 20008-3027, USA Tel.: (202) 895-6700, Fax: (202) 895-6750 e-Mail: **austrianembassy@washington.nu** Web: **http://www.austria.org/** and **http://www.austrianinformation.org/** Tel.: (202) 895-6711, Fax: (202) 895-6773 e-Mail: **consularsection.washington@mailbox.as**

Austria's Official Consultant for Foreign Investment:

ABA - Invest in Austria, the Foreign Investment Promotion Agency of the Austrian government, is the international investor's first business address in Austria providing free-of-charge support and assistance to foreign investors planning business establishments or acquisitions in Austria.

ABA – Invest in Austria

In the United States: In Austria:	ABA – Invest in Austria 120 West 45th Street, 9th floor New York, NY 10036, USA Tel.: (212)-398 1221, Fax: (212) 398 151 e-Mail: **office-usa@aba.gv.at** Web: **http://www.aba.gv.at/EN/ABA-Invest+in+Austria.aspx** ABA – Invest in Austria Opernring 3 A – 1010 Vienna, Austria Tel.: ++43 1 588 58-0, Fax: ++43 1 586 86-59 e-Mail: **office@aba.gv.at**

Austrian Federal Ministries:

Federal Ministry of Economics and Labor of the Republic of Austria

Stubenring 1
A – 1011 Vienna, Austria
Tel.: ++43 1 711 00-0, Fax: ++43 1 713 79 95
e-Mail: **service@bmwa.gv.at**
Web: **http://www.bmwa.gv.at/EN/default.htm**

Federal Ministry of Agriculture, Forestry, Environment and Water Management

Stubenring 1
A – 1011 Vienna, Austria
Tel.: ++43 1 711 00-0, Fax: ++43 1 711 00-2127
e-Mail: **office@lebensministerium.at**
Web: **http://www.lebensministerium.at**

The Austrian Trade Association in the United States:

The Austrian Trade Commission operates offices in the U.S. at the below listed locations. The following phone number can be used for all Austrian Trade Delegates in the United States: **1-800-VIP-AHST**

The Austrian Trade Commission

New York: Austrian Trade Commission, New York
120 West 45th Street, 9th Floor
New York, NY 10036, USA
Tel.: (212) 421 52 50, Fax: (212) 421 52 51
e-Mail: **newyork@austriantrade.org**
Web: **http://www.advantageaustria.org/us/**

Washington, D.C.: Austrian Embassy/Commercial Section, Washington, D.C.
818 18th Street, Suite 500, N.W.
Washington, D.C. 20006, USA
Tel.: (202) 537 50 47, Fax: (202) 537 50 48
e-Mail: **washington@austriantrade.org**
Web: **http://www.advantageaustria.org/us/**

Illinois: Austrian Trade Commission, Illinois
500 North Michigan Avenue, Suite 1950
Chicago, IL 60611-3722, USA
Tel.: (312) 644 55 56, Fax: (312) 644 65 26
e-Mail: **chicago@austriantrade.org**
Web: **http://www.advantageaustria.org/us/**

The Austrian Trade Commission (Cont'd)

California: Austrian Trade Commission, California
11601 Wilshire Blvd., Suite 2420
Los Angeles, CA 90025, USA
Tel.: (310) 477 99 88, Fax: (310) 477 16 43
e-Mail: **losangeles@austriantrade.org**
Web: **http://www.advantageaustria.org/us/**

Chambers of Commerce

American Chamber of Commerce in Austria

Porzellangasse 35
A – 1090 Vienna, Austria
Tel.: ++43 1 319 57 51, Fax: ++43 1 319 51 51
e-Mail: **office@amcham.at**
Web: **http://www.amcham.at**

Wirtschaftskammer Oesterreich (Austrian Federal Economic Chamber, North America

Desk):

Wiedner Hauptstrasse 63
A – 1040 Vienna, Austria
Tel.: ++43 5 90 900-4181, Fax: ++43 5 90 900-114181
e-Mail: **awo.amerika@wko.at**
Web: **http://wko.at/awo**

U.S.–Austrian Chamber of Commerce, Inc.

165 West 46th Street
New York, NY, 10036, USA
Tel.: (212) 819-0117, Fax: (212) 819-0345
Web: **http://www.usatchamber.com/**

Austrian Associations

Pharmaceutical Industry

Oesterreichische Apothekerkammer (Austrian Pharmacists' Association)

Spitalgasse 31, Postfach 87
A – 1090 Vienna, Austria
Tel.: ++43 1 404 14-100, Fax: ++43 1 408 84 40
e-Mail: **info@apotheker.or.at**
Web: **http://www.apotheker.or.at/**

Pharmaceutical Industry (Cont'd)

Forum der forschenden pharmazeutischen Industrie – **FOPI** (Association of the research-based Pharmaceutical Industry)

Wyeth-Lederle Pharma GmbH
Storchengasse 1
A - 1150 Vienna, Austria
Tel.: ++43 1 89 114-0, Fax: ++43 1 89 11-600
e-Mail: **office@wyeth.at**
Web: **http://www.fopi.at/**

Pharmig – Verband der pharmazeutischen Industrie Oesterreichs (Austrian Association of the Pharmaceutical Industry)

Garnisongasse 4 / 1 / 6
A – 1090 Vienna, Austria
Tel.: ++43 1 40 60 290, Fax: ++43 1 40 60 290-9
e-Mail: **office@pharmig.at**
Web: **http://www.pharmig.at**

Dental Industry

Landeszahnaerztekammer Wien (National Dental Association, Vienna)

Kohlmarkt 11 / 6
A – 1010 Vienna, Austria
Tel.: ++43 5 05 11, Fax: ++43 5 05 11-1167
e-Mail: **office@zahnaerztekammer.at**
Web: **http://www.zahnaerztekammer.at/**

Medical Industry

Oesterreichische Aerztekammer (Austrian Medical Association; International Office)

Weihburggasse 10-12
A - 1010 Vienna, Austria
Tel.: ++43 1 51406-0, Fax: ++43 1 51406-933
e-Mail: **post@aerztekammer.at**
Web: **http://www.aerztekammer.at**

Electric / Electronic Industry

Fachverband der Elektro- und Elektronikindustrie

Mariahilfer Str. 37-39

- FEEI (Association of the Electric and Electronic Industry in Austria)	A – 1060 Vienna, Austria Tel.: ++43 1 588 39-0, Fax: ++43 1 586 69 71 e-Mail: **info@feei.at** Web: **http://www.feei.at/en/home/**
IT-Sector / Computer Industry	
Arbeitsgemeinschaft fuer Datenverarbeitung – ADV (Austrian Association for Electronic Data Processing)	Trattnerhof 2 A – 1010 Vienna, Austria Tel.: ++43 1 533 09 13, Fax: ++43 1 533 09 13-77 e-Mail: **office@adv.at** Web: **http://www.adv.at**
Oesterreichische Computer Gesellschaft (Austrian Computer Society)	Wollzeile 1 – 3 A – 1010 Vienna, Austria Tel.: ++43 1 5120235-0, Fax: ++43 1 5120235-9 e-Mail: **ocg@ocg.at** Web: **http://www.ocg.at/en/index.html**
Environmental Technology	
Oesterreichische Gesellschaft fuer Umwelt und Technik – OEGUT (Austrian Association for Environment and Technology)	Hollandstrasse 10 / 46 A – 1020 Vienna, Austria Tel.: ++43 1 315 63 93, Fax: ++43 1 315 63 93-22 e-Mail: **office@oegut.at** Web: **http://www.oegut.at**

Austrian Commercial Banks / Branch Offices of Austrian Banks in the U.S.

Bank Austria (Member of UniCredit Group)

In Austria: In the United States:	Bank Austria, UniCredit Group Schottengasse 6 – 8 A – 1010 Vienna, Austria Tel.: ++43 5 0505-25, Fax: ++43 1 711 91-56155 e-Mail: **info@unicreditgroup.at** Web: **http://www.bankaustria.at/en/** Swift: BKAUATWW, Bank Austria's Bank Code: 12000 HVB Capital Markets, Inc., New York 150 East 42nd Street New York, NY 10017, USA Tel.: (202) 672 6000, Fax: (202) 672 5529 Business Activities: Corporate Banking

Erste Bank der Oesterreichischen Sparkassen AG

In Austria: In the United States:	Erste Bank / Sparkasse Graben 21 A – 1010 Vienna, Austria Tel.: ++43 5 0100–10100, Fax: ++43 5 0100-910100 e-Mail: **service@s-servicecenter.at** Web: **https://www.sparkasse.at/erstebank** Swift Code / BIC: GIBAATWW, Bank Code: 20111

Erste Bank
280 Park Ave # 32W
New York, NY 10017, USA
Tel.: (212) 984-5600 , Fax: (212) 986-1423

Raiffeisen Zentralbank Oesterreich AG

In Austria:	Raiffeisen Zentralbank Oesterreich AG Am Stadtpark 9, A-1030 Vienna, Austria Tel.: ++43 1 71707-0, Fax: ++43 1 71707-1715 Web: **http://www.rzb.at/** Swift Code: RZBA AT WW, Bank Code: 31000
In the United States:	RZB Finance LCC 1133 Avenue of the Americas, 16th Floor New York, NY 10036, USA Tel.: (212) 845-4100, Fax: (212) 944-2093 Web: **http://www.rzbfinance.com/**

BAWAG P.S.K. - Bank fuer Arbeit und Wirtschaft und Oesterreichische Postsparkasse AG

In Austria: **NO** branch office in the U.S.	BAWAG P.S.K. Georg-Coch-Platz 2, A-1018 Vienna, Austria Tel.: ++43 1 534 53-0 e-Mail: **info@bawagpsk.com** Web: **http://www.bawagpsk.com/** Swift Codes: BAWAATWW and OPSKATWW Bank Codes: 14000 and 60000

U.S.-Based Associations

The associations listed below represent some of the industries offering the best prospects for U.S. products and services in Austria. This should not be considered a conclusive list of all trade associations. These associations do not have offices in Austria. For an extensive listing of International Trade Associations, please visit the website of the Federation of International Trade Associations (FITA) at: **http://www.fita.org**

Medical Technology Industry

Advanced Medical Technology Association	701 Pennsylvania Ave, N.W., Suite 800 Washington, D.C. 20004-2654, USA Tel.: (202) 783-8700, Fax: (202) 783-8750 Web: **http://www.advamed.org/** e-Mail: **info@advamed.org**

Electronics Industry

American Electronics Association Santa Clara, CA:	AeA, Advancing the Business of Technology 5201 Great America Parkway #400 Santa Clara, CA 95054, USA Tel.: (408) 987 4200, Fax: (408) 987 4298
Washington, D.C.:	AeA, Advancing the Business of Technology 601 Pennsylvania Avenue NW Suite 600, North Building Washington, D.C. 20004, USA Tel.: (202) 682 9110, Fax: (202) 682 9111 e-Mail: **csc@aeanet.org** Web: **http://www.aeanet.org/**

Dental Industry Association

Dental Trade Alliance	2300 Clarendon Boulevard, Suite 1003 Arlington, VA 22201, USA

Tel.: (703) 379-7755, Fax: (703) 931-9429
e-Mail: **info@dentaltradealliance.org**
Web: **http://www.dentaltradealliance.org/**

Environmental Industry Associations: http://www.envasns.org

National Solid Wastes Management Association – NSWMA	4301 Connecticut Avenue, NW, Suite 300 Washington, D.C. 20008-2304, USA Tel.: (202) 244-4700, Fax: (202) 364-3792 e-Mail: **membership@envasns.org** Web: **http://www.nswma.org/**
Waste Equipment Technology Association – WASTEC	4301 Connecticut Avenue, NW, Suite 300 Washington, D.C. 20008-2304, USA Tel.: (202) 244-4700, Fax: (202) 966-4824 e-Mail: **membership@envasns.org** Web: **http://www.wastec.org/**

Electrical Industry

National Electrical Manufacturers Association – NEMA	1300 North 17th Street, Suite 1752 Rosslyn, Virginia 22209, USA Tel.: (703) 841-3200, Fax: (703) 841-5900 Web: **http://www.nema.org/**

Telecommunications Industry

Telecommunications Industry Association – TIA	2500 Wilson Boulevard, Suite 300 Arlington, VA 22201, USA Tel.: (703) 907 7700, Fax: (703) 907 7727 Web: **http://www.tiaonline.org/**

Washington-Based U.S. Government Contacts

Trade Information Center in Washington, D.C.

Tel.: 1-800-USA-TRADE (1-800-872-8723)
Fax: (202) 482 44 73
Web: **http://www.export.gov**

U.S. Department of Commerce

The U.S. Department of Commerce
International Trade Administration
Mr. Alexander Gorshenin, M.B.A.
(Desk Officer for Austria and Germany)
1401 Constitution Avenue, N.W.
Washington, D.C. 20230, USA
Tel.: (202) 482 24 34
e-Mail: **alexander.gorshenin@mail.doc.gov**
Web: **http://www.commerce.gov/**

U.S. Department of Agriculture

The U.S. Department of Agriculture
Foreign Agriculture Service
Office of Country and Regional Affairs (OCRA)
Europe Division
Ms. Sharynne Nenon, Director
Room 5527 – S
Washington, D.C. 20250, USA
Tel.: (202) 720 1330, Fax: (202) 690 0876
e-Mail: **nenon.sharynne@fas.usda.gov**
Web: **http://www.fas.usda.gov**

The U.S. Department of Agriculture (APHIS)
Sanitary and Phytosanitary Management Team
Ms. Mary Lisa Madell
14th and Independence Avenue S.W., Room 1132
Washington, D.C. 20250, USA
Tel.: (202) 720 0318 , Fax: (202) 690 2861
e-Mail: **mary.l.madell@aphis.usda.gov**
Web: **http://www.aphis.usda.gov**

TRAVEL TO AUSTRIA

US STATE DEPARTMENT SUGGESTIONS

COUNTRY DESCRIPTION: Austria is a highly developed stable democracy with a modern economy.

ENTRY REQUIREMENTS: A passport is required. A visa is not required for business or tourist stays up to three months. For more information concerning entry requirements for Austria, travelers should contact the Embassy of Austria at 3524 International Court, N.W., Washington, D.C. 20008, tel: (202) 895-6767, or the nearest Austrian Consulate General in Chicago, Los Angeles, or New York. The Austrian Embassy to the United States maintains a Web page in English that answers in detail, questions concerning the laws and regulations of Austria, including residency, driver's license requirements, and permission to work: www.austria.org/index.html.

CRIME INFORMATION: Austria has a low crime rate, and violent crime is rare. However, crimes involving theft of personal property have increased in recent years. Travelers can become targets of pickpockets and purse-snatchers who operate where tourists tend to gather; favorite spots include Vienna's two largest train stations. The loss or theft of a U.S. passport overseas should be reported immediately to the local police and the nearest U.S. embassy or consulate. U.S. citizens can refer to the Department of State's pamphlet "A Safe Trip Abroad" for ways to promote a more trouble-free trip. The pamphlet is available from the Superintendent of Documents, U.S. Government Printing Office, Washington, D.C. 20402.

MEDICAL FACILITIES: Good medical care is widely available. U.S. medical insurance is not always valid outside the United States. Travelers have found that in some cases, supplemental medical insurance with specific overseas coverage, including coverage for medical evacuation by air, has proven to be useful. Serious medical problems requiring hospitalization and/or medical evacuation to the United States can cost thousands of dollars or more. Doctors and hospitals often expect immediate cash payment for health services.

MEDICAL INSURANCE: U.S. medical insurance is not always valid outside the United States. U.S. Medicare and Medicaid programs do not provide payment for medical services outside the United States. Uninsured travelers who require medical care overseas may face extreme difficulties. Please check with your own insurance company to confirm whether your policy applies overseas, including provision for medical evacuation. Please ascertain whether payment will be made to the overseas hospital or doctor or whether you will be reimbursed later for expenses that you incur. Some insurance policies also include coverage for psychiatric treatment and for disposition of remains in the event of death. Useful information on medical emergencies abroad, including overseas insurance programs, is provided in the Department of State's Bureau of Consular Affairs brochure, "Medical Information for Americans Traveling Abroad," available via the Bureau of Consular Affairs home page or autofax: (202) 647-3000.

OTHER HEALTH INFORMATION: Information on vaccinations and other health precautions may be obtained from the Centers for Disease Control and Prevention's hotline for international travelers at 1-877-FYI-TRIP (1-877-394-8747); fax 1-888-CDC-FAXX (1-888-232-3299), or via CDC's Internet site at http://www.cdc.gov.

TRAFFIC SAFETY AND ROAD CONDITONS: While in a foreign country, U.S. citizens may encounter road conditions which differ significantly from those in the United States. The information below concerning Austria is provided for general reference only, and may not be totally accurate in a particular location or circumstance.

Safety of Public Transportation: Excellent
Urban Road Conditions/Maintenance: Excellent
Rural Road Conditions/Maintenance: Excellent
Availability of Roadside Assistance: Excellent

According to the Austrian Automobile Association (OAMTC), road conditions and traffic safety are very good throughout Austria. During the winter, however, road conditions in the alpine area may change drastically due to snow and ice. In times of unusually heavy snowfalls or danger of avalanches, roads in the mountain areas may be closed for several days or longer. On many mountain roads the use of chains are required by law during periods of heavy snowfall. Highways, city streets, and major roads are cleaned of snow around the clock. Drivers should exercise caution during winter vacation (December to February), Easter, and summer vacation (July and August) due to heavier traffic. Traffic information and road conditions are broadcast on the English language channel FM4, located between 91 and 105 FM depending on the locale.

A U.S. driver's license is not sufficient to drive in Austria. The U.S. driver's license must be accompanied by an international driver's license, or by an official translation of the U.S. driver's license, which can be easily obtained at one of the Austrian automobile clubs (OAMTC or ARBO). This arrangement is only acceptable for the first six months of driving in Austria, after which all drivers must obtain an Austrian license.

Austria requires all vehicles using the Autobahn and other major highways to display a highway tax sticker "Autobahn Vignette" on the inside windshield of the vehicle. The sticker may be purchased at border crossings, gas stations on highways leading into Austria, gas stations in Austria, as well as small "Tabak" shops located in Austrian towns. Fines for failing to display a valid Autobahn Vignette on the windshield of the car are usually $85.00.

Tourists driving rented vehicles should pay close attention to the provisions of their rental contract. Many contracts prohibit drivers from taking rented vehicles into Eastern European countries. Drivers attempting to enter countries listed as "prohibited" on the car rental contract may be arrested, fined, and/or convicted of attempted auto theft. The vehicle can be held by Austrian police for the car rental company.

AVIATION SAFETY OVERSIGHT: The U.S. Federal Aviation Administration (FAA) has assessed the Government of Austria's Civil Aviation Authority as Category 1 -- in compliance with international aviation safety standards for oversight of Austria's air carrier operations. For further information, travelers may contact the Department of Transportation within the U.S. at tel. 1-800-322-7873, or visit the FAA's Internet website at http://www.faa.gov/avr/iasa.htm. The U.S. Department of Defense (DOD) separately assesses some foreign air carriers for suitability as official providers of air services. For information regarding the DOD policy on specific carriers, travelers may contact the DOD at tel. (618) 229-4801.

CUSTOMS REGULATIONS: Austria customs authorities encourage the use of an ATA (Admission Temporaire/Temporary Admission) Carnet for the temporary admission of professional equipment, commercial samples, and/or goods for exhibitions and fair purposes. ATA Carnet Headquarters, located at the U.S. Council for International Business, 1212 Avenue of the Americas, New York, NY 10036, issues and guarantees the ATA Carnet in the United States. For additional information, please call (212) 354-4480, or send an e-mail to atacarnet@uscib.org, or visit www.uscib.org for details.

DRUG PENALTIES: U.S. citizens are subject to the laws of the country in which they are traveling. Penalties for possession, use, or trafficking in illegal drugs in Austria are strict, and convicted offenders can expect jail sentences and fines.

CHILDREN'S ISSUES: For information on international adoption of children and international parental child abduction, please refer to our Internet site at http://travel.state.gov/children's_issues.html or telephone (202) 736-7000.

REGISTRATION AND EMBASSY/CONSULATE LOCATION: U.S. citizens are encouraged to register at the Consular Section of the U.S. Embassy or Consular Agency and obtain updated information on travel and security in Austria. The U.S. Embassy in Vienna is located at Boltzmanngasse 16 in the Ninth District. The Consular Section of the U.S. Embassy is located on the fourth floor of Gartenbaupromenade 2 in the First District. The telephone number for both the U.S. Embassy and the Consular Section is (43)(1) 31-339. There is also a Consular Agency in Salzburg at Alter Markt 1, telephone (43) (662) 84-87-76, open Monday, Wednesday, and Thursday from 9:00 A.M. to 12:00 noon. U.S. citizens in Salzburg who require assistance outside of these hours may contact the U.S. Embassy in Vienna. The Embassy also maintains a web site at http://www.usembassy-vienna.at, with information helpful to American citizens.

BUSINESS TRAVELLER TO AUSTRIA

OFFICE HOURS

Business and industry:	Monday - Friday 8 a.m. - 4 p.m
Banks:	Monday - Friday 8 a.m. - 3 p.m.
Shops:	Monday - Friday 8 a.m. - 6 p.m. Saturday 8 a.m. - 13 p.m. the first Saturday in the month shops may be open until 5 p.m.

Time: CET (GMT + 2 hour)

IMMIGRATION REQUIREMENTS

All visitors are required to have passports. Contact the Austrian Embassy or Consulate for further information concerning visa. Austria has no vaccination requirements.

A residence longer than 3 months requires a special residence permit. An alien who wishes to accept employment must first obtain a work permit.

TRANSPORT

Austria's international airports in Vienna, Graz, Linz, Salzburg, Klagenfurt and Innsbruck are operated by a number of international airlines. Within Austria it is convenient to use the railway system or rental cars, which are available at airports, hotels and agencies.

ACCOMMODATION

Major hotels in Vienna (http://www.nethotels.com):

Hotel Ambassador
Neuer Markt 5
A-1010 Vienna
Tel.: +43/1/514 66
Fax: +43/1/513 29 99

Ana Grand Hotel
Kärntner Ring 9
A-1010 Vienna
Tel.: +43/1/515 80-0
Fax: +43/1/513 13 13

Vienna Hotel Bristol
Kärntner Ring 1
A-1015 Vienna
Tel.: +43/1/515 16
Fax: +43/1/515 16-550

Hotel De France
Schottenring 3
A-1010 Vienna
Tel.: +43/1/313 68-0
Fax: +43/1/319 59-69

Vienna Hilton Hotel
Am Stadtpark
A-1030 Vienna
Tel.: +43/1/717 00-0
Fax: +43/1/713 06 91

Hotel Im Palais Schwarzenberg
Schwarzenbergplatz 9
A-1030 Vienna
Tel.: +43/1/798 45 15
Fax: +43/1/798 47 14

Hotel Imperial
Kärntner Ring 16
A-1010 Vienna
Tel.: +43/1/501 10-0
Fax: +43/1/501 10-410

Inter-Continental Hotel
Johannesgasse 28
A-1037 Vienna
Tel.: +43/1/711 22-0
Fax: +43/1/713 44 89

Vienna Marriott Hotel
Parkring 12a
A-1010 Vienna
Tel.: +43/1/515 18-0
Fax: +43/1/515 18-6736

Vienna Plaza Hotel
Schottenring 11
A-1010 Vienna
Tel.: +43/1/313 90-0
Fax: +43/1/313 90-160

Radisson SAS Palaishotel
Parkring 16
A-1010 Vienna
Tel.: +43/1/51517-0
Fax: +43/1/512 22 16

Hotel Renaissance
Linke Wienzeile–Ullmannstr. 71
A-1150 Vienna
Tel.: +43/1/85 04-0
Fax: +43/1/85 04-100

Hotel Sacher
Philharmonikerstrasse 4
A-1010 Vienna
Tel.: +43/1/514 56
Fax. +43/1/514 57-810

A complete list of hotels is available at your nearest Austrian Trade Commission.

LEGAL HOLIDAYS

New Year's Day	January 1
Epiphany	January 6
Easter Monday	April 5, 1999

Labour Day	May 1
Ascension Day	May 13, 1999
Whit Monday	May 24, 1999
Corpus Christi	June 3, 1999
Maria Ascension Day	August 15
National Day	October 26
All Saint's Day	November 1
Immaculate Conception	December 8
Christmas	December 25 and 26

MEDICAL SERVICES

Good medical care is widely available. Medical insurance with supplemental overseas coverage is recommended.

For additional information or special enquiries contact the

Austrian Doctor's Board (*Ärztekammer*)
A-1010 Vienna, Weihburggasse 10-12
Tel.: +43/1/51406 Fax: +43/1/51406-42

USEFUL HINTS FOR YOUR STAY IN AUSTRIA

Tipping:	10% for waiters, taxi etc.
Postage, Telephone:	letters (Europe) ATS 7,-
	letters (overseas) ATS 13,-
	registered mail ATS 25,-
	express mail ATS 30,-
telephone charges/min:	within Austria ATS 4,-/min
	within Europa ATS 8,-/min
	overseas (USA, Japan) ATS 18,-/min
	In hotels etc. these telephone charges are subject to additional charges.
Voltage:	230 V/50 cycles
Average Daily Expenses:	approximately ATS 3.000,- per day, based on accomodation in a four-star - hotel

SELECTED BUSINESS CONTACTS

AUSTRIA TRADE REPRESENTATIONS WORLD

ABU DHABI

Zustelladresse:
The Commercial Counsellor at the Austrian Embassy
Postfach P.O.B. 3095, Abu Dhabi
UNITED ARAB EMIRATES

Büroadresse:
Adnic Building, 6th floor, Sheikh Khalifa Street, Abu Dhabi
UNITED ARAB EMIRATES

Kommunikation:

Telefon:	+971 2 626 77 55
Fax:	+971 2 626 71 33
Email:	abudhabi@wko.at

Bürozeiten:	Samstag bis Mittwoch: 8:00 - 16:00 Uhr
Zeitverschiebung:	MEZ + 3 Stunden

Handelsdelegierte/-r: Seiwald Dkfm.Dr. Nikolaus

Betreuungsbereich:	**zuständige Länderreferate in der Wirtschaftskammer Österreich:**
Vereinigte Arabische Emirate	Referat Nahost
Oman	Referat Nahost
Katar	Referat Nahost

AMMAN

Zustelladresse:
The Commercial Counsellor at the Austrian Embassy
Postfach P.O.B. 5287, Amman 11183
JORDAN

Büroadresse:
Burqah Street 3, Jabal Amman, Near Prince Abdalla Square (former 4th Circle) (next to South Korean Embassy), Amman 11183
JORDAN

Kommunikation:

Telefon: +962 6 593 07 50, 593 18 52

Fax: +962 6 593 05 31

Email: amman@wko.at

Bürozeiten: Sonntag bis Donnerstag: 8:00 - 16:00 Uhr

Zeitverschiebung: MEZ + 1 Stunde

Handelsdelegierte/-r: Altmann Dr. Kurt

Betreuungsbereich:	**zuständige Länderreferate in der Wirtschaftskammer Österreich:**
Jordanien	Referat Nahost

ANKARA

Zustelladresse:
Avusturya Ticaret Müstesari
P.K. 46 Kavaklidere, TR-06692 Ankara
TÜRKEI

Büroadresse:
Kircicegi Sokak 8/2, Gaziosmanpasa, TR-06700 Ankara
TÜRKEI

Lokale Homepage: http://www.austriatrade.org/ankara

Kommunikation:

Telefon: +90 312 447 71 77 (PBX)

Fax: +90 312 446 21 22

Email: ankara@wko.at

Bürozeiten: Montag bis Freitag: 8:30 - 17:00 Uhr

Zeitverschiebung: MEZ + 1 Stunde

Handelsdelegierte/-r: Sedlmayer Mag. Peter

Betreuungsbereich:	**zuständige Länderreferate in der Wirtschaftskammer Österreich:**
Türkei	Referat Europa 2

Provinzen: Türkei mit Ausnahme des europäischen Teils und der Marmara-Region

ATHEN

Büroadresse:
Empor. Symvoulos Presvias Avstrias
Tritis Septemvriou 43 A, GR-104 33 Athen
GRIECHENLAND

Kommunikation:

Telefon:	+30 1 884 37 11
Fax:	+30 1 882 79 13
Email:	athen@wko.at

Bürozeiten: Montag bis Freitag: 7:30 - 15:30 Uhr

Zeitverschiebung: MEZ + 1 Stunde

Handelsdelegierte/-r: Galathovics Dr. Wilhelm

Betreuungsbereich:	**zuständige Länderreferate in der Wirtschaftskammer Österreich:**
Griechenland	Referat Europa 2
Zypern	Referat Europa 2

ATLANTA

Büroadresse:
Atlanta, GA 30327, 4200 Nothside Parkway, NW, Bldg. 1, Ste. 300
USA

Lokale Homepage: http://www.austriantradeus.org/

Kommunikation:

Telefon:	+1 404 995 93 47
Fax:	+1 404 995 93 48
Email:	atlanta@wko.at

BARCELONA

Büroadresse:
Oficina Comercial de Austria
Balmes, 200-7/1 a, E-08006 Barcelona
ESPANA

Lokale Homepage: http://www.austriatrade.org/barcelona

Kommunikation:

Telefon:	+34 93 292 23 78
Fax:	+34 93 237 76 21
Email:	barcelona@wko.at

Bürozeiten: Montag bis Freitag: 8:30 - 17:00 Uhr, 1.7. - 31.8.: Montag bis Freitag: 8:00 - 16:30 Uhr

Zeitverschiebung: keine

Handelsdelegierte/-r: Walter Dr. Heinz

Betreuungsbereich:	**zuständige Länderreferate in der Wirtschaftskammer Österreich:**
Andorra	Referat Europa 2
Spanien	Referat Europa 2

Provinzen: Katalonien, Balearen, Valencia

BANGKOK

Zustelladresse:
The Commercial Counsellor at the Austrian Embassy
G.P.O.B. 495, Bangkok 10501
THAILAND

Büroadresse:
Chartered Square Building, 14th Floor, Suite 1403, 152 North Sathorn Road, Bangkok 10500
THAILAND

Lokale Homepage: http://www.austriacom.or.th

Kommunikation:

Telefon:	+66 2 268 22 22
Fax:	+66 2 268 22 26
Email:	bangkok@wko.at

Bürozeiten: Montag bis Freitag: 8:00 - 16:00 Uhr
Zeitverschiebung: MEZ + 6 Stunden (MESZ + 5 Stunden)

Handelsdelegierte/-r: Renner Dkfm. Herwig

Betreuungsbereich:	**zuständige Länderreferate in der Wirtschaftskammer Österreich:**
Kambodscha	Referat Asien 3
Myanmar (Burma)	Referat Asien 3
Vietnam	Referat Asien 3
Laos	Referat Asien 3
Thailand	Referat Asien 3

BAGHDAD

Zustelladresse:
The Commercial Counsellor at the Austrian Embassy
P.O.B. 2079 Alwiyah, Baghdad
IRAQ

Büroadresse:
(Austrian Embassy - Commercial Section), Babil Area 923, House No. 23, Street No. 3, Jadriyah, Baghdad
IRAQ

Kommunikation:

Telefon: +87 3 761 35 38 67 (Sat-Tel)

Fax: +87 3 761 35 38 69 (Sat-Fax)

Bürozeiten: So - Do: 8:00 - 16:00 Uhr

Zeitverschiebung: MEZ + 2 Stunden

Handelsdelegierte/-r: Schröder Dr. Franz

Anmerkung: Sat-Tel: +87 3 761 35 38 67, Sat-Fax: +87 3 761 35 38 69

Betreuungsbereich:	**zuständige Länderreferate in der Wirtschaftskammer Österreich:**
Irak	Referat Nahost

BANGKOK

Zustelladresse:
The Commercial Counsellor at the Austrian Embassy
G.P.O.B. 495, Bangkok 10501
THAILAND

Büroadresse:
Chartered Square Building, 14th Floor, Suite 1403, 152 North Sathorn Road, Bangkok 10500
THAILAND

Lokale Homepage: http://www.austriacom.or.th

Kommunikation:

Telefon: +66 2 268 22 22

Fax: +66 2 268 22 26

Email: bangkok@wko.at

Bürozeiten: Montag bis Freitag: 8:00 - 16:00 Uhr

Zeitverschiebung: MEZ + 6 Stunden (MESZ + 5 Stunden)

Handelsdelegierte/-r: Renner Dkfm. Herwig

Betreuungsbereich:	zuständige Länderreferate in der Wirtschaftskammer Österreich:
Kambodscha	Referat Asien 3
Myanmar (Burma)	Referat Asien 3
Vietnam	Referat Asien 3
Laos	Referat Asien 3
Thailand	Referat Asien 3

BEIRUT

Zustelladresse:
The Commercial Counsellor at the Austrian Embassy
P.O.Box 11-420, Riad el Solh 1107 2040, Beirut
LEBANON

Büroadresse:
Sammakieh Bldg. (near Hotel Bristol), Rue Madame Curie 382, Beirut
LEBANON

Kommunikation:

Telefon: +961 1 35 42 38, 35 42 14
Fax: +961 1 34 53 07
Email: beirut@wko.at

Bürozeiten: Montag: 7:30 - 17:30 Uhr, Dienstag bis Freitag: 7:30 - 15:00 Uhr
Zeitverschiebung: MEZ + 1 Stunde

Handelsdelegierte/-r: Festin Dr. Peter

Betreuungsbereich:	zuständige Länderreferate in der Wirtschaftskammer Österreich:
Libanon	Referat Nahost

BEIJING

Büroadresse:
The Commercial Counsellor at the Austrian Embassy
Suite 2280 Beijing Sunflower Tower, No. 37 Maizidian Street
Chaoyang District, Beijing 100026
THE PEOPLE'S REPUBLIC OF CHINA

Kommunikation:

Telefon: +86 10 85 27 50 50, 85 27 50 41, 85 27 50 42, 85 27 50 43

Fax:	+86 10 85 27 50 49
Email:	peking@wko.at

Bürozeiten: Montag bis Freitag: 9:00 - 17:30 Uhr
Zeitverschiebung: MEZ + 7 Stunden

Handelsdelegierte/-r: Lanz Dr. Wolfgang

Betreuungsbereich:	zuständige Länderreferate in der Wirtschaftskammer Österreich:
Mongolei	Referat Asien 1
China	Referat Asien 1
Korea, Demokratische Volksrepublik (Nord)	Referat Asien 1

Provinzen: Betreuung der chinesischen Provinzen: Beijing, Gansu, Hebei, Heilongjiang, Henan, Hubei, Inner Mongolia A.R., Jilin, Liaoning, Ningxia Hui A.R., Quinghai, Shaanxi, Shandong, Shangdong, Shanxi, Sichuan, Tianjin, Tibet A.R., Xinjiang Uygur A.R.

BELGRAD

Zustelladresse:
Trgovinski savetnik pri Ambasadi Austrije za SR Jugoslaviju
Postanski fah 361, YU-11001 Beograd
JUGOSLAVIJA

Büroadresse:
Genex Center, Vladimira Popovica 6, YU-11070 Novi Beograd
JUGOSLAVIJA

Kommunikation:

Telefon:	+381 11 301 58 50
Fax:	+381 11 311 21 39
Email:	belgrad@wko.at

Bürozeiten: Montag bis Freitag: 7:30 - 16:30 Uhr, Juni-August: 7:30 - 15:30 Uhr
Zeitverschiebung: keine

Handelsdelegierte/-r: Preclik Dr. Herbert

Betreuungsbereich:	zuständige Länderreferate in der Wirtschaftskammer Österreich:
Jugoslawien	Referat Mittel- und Osteuropa 3
Mazedonien, ehem. Jugoslawische Republik	Referat Mittel- und Osteuropa 3

Provinzen: Serbien, Montenegro

BERLIN

Büroadresse:
Der österreichische Handelsdelegierte
Wilhelmstraße 65, D-10117 Berlin
DEUTSCHLAND

Lokale Homepage: http://www.oesterreich.org

Kommunikation:

Telefon:	+49 30 238 62 00
Fax:	+49 30 391 36 01
Email:	berlin@wko.at

Bürozeiten: Montag bis Donnerstag: 8:00 - 17:00 Uhr, Freitag: 8:00 - 16:00 Uhr
Zeitverschiebung: keine

Handelsdelegierte/-r: Schragl Dr. Alfred

Betreuungsbereich:	zuständige Länderreferate in der Wirtschaftskammer Österreich:
Deutschland	Referat Europa 1

Provinzen: Berlin, Mecklenburg-Vorpommern, Brandenburg, Sachsen-Anhalt, Thüringen, Sachsen

BOGOTA

Zustelladresse:
El Consejero Comercial de la Embajada de Austria
Apartado Aéreo 12308, Santafé de Bogotá D.C.
COLOMBIA

Büroadresse:
Calle 100 Nr. 8 A-55, Oficina 708, World Trade Center, Torre C,
Santafé de Bogotá D.C.
COLOMBIA

Kommunikation:

Telefon:	+57 1 644 19 60, 655 07 95, 655 07 85, 655 07 90, 616 08 50, 616 08 29
Fax:	+57 1 616 09 64
Email:	bogota@wko.at

Bürozeiten: Montag bis Freitag: 8:00 - 16:30 Uhr
Zeitverschiebung: MEZ - 6 Stunden (MESZ - 7 Stunden)

Handelsdelegierte/-r: Harm Mag. Christian

Betreuungsbereich:	zuständige Länderreferate in der Wirtschaftskammer Österreich:
Ecuador	Referat Lateinamerika
Kolumbien	Referat Lateinamerika
Panama	Referat Lateinamerika

BRÜSSEL

Büroadresse:
Le Conseiller Commercial de l'Ambassade d'Autriche
479, Avenue Louise, Boîte 52, B-1050 Bruxelles
BELGIQUE

Lokale Homepage: http://www.austria.be

Kommunikation:

Telefon: +32 2 645 16 50
Fax: +32 2 640 12 69
Email: bruessel@wko.at

Bürozeiten: Montag bis Freitag: 8:30 - 17:00 Uhr
Zeitverschiebung: keine

Handelsdelegierte/-r: Gressel Dr. Gustav

Betreuungsbereich:	zuständige Länderreferate in der Wirtschaftskammer Österreich:
Belgien	Referat Europa 1
Luxemburg	Referat Europa 1

BUDAPEST

Büroadresse:
Az Osztrák Nagykövetség Kereskedelmi Tanácsosa
Délibáb utca 21, H-1062 Budapest VI
UNGARN

Lokale Homepage: http://www.austriatrade.org/hungary

Kommunikation:

Telefon: +36 1 351 11 96
Fax: +36 1 351 12 04
Email: budapest@wko.at

Bürozeiten: Montag bis Donnerstag: 8.00 - 17.00 Uhr, Freitag: 8.00 - 14.30 Uhr
Zeitverschiebung: keine

Handelsdelegierte/-r:	Rejtö Dr. Peter
Betreuungsbereich:	**zuständige Länderreferate in der Wirtschaftskammer Österreich:**
Ungarn	Referat Mittel- und Osteuropa 2

BUENOS AIRES

Zustelladresse:
El Consejero Comercial de la Embajada de Austria
Casilla Correo Central 523, C 1041 WAF Buenos Aires
ARGENTINA

Büroadresse:
Cerrito 1294, piso 15, C1010 AAZ Buenos Aires
ARGENTINA

Lokale Homepage: http://www.austria.com.ar

Kommunikation:

Telefon:	+54 11 48 16 04 79, 48 14 36 69
Fax:	+54 11 48 14 36 70
Email:	buenosaires@wko.at
Bürozeiten:	Montag bis Freitag: 9:00 - 17:30 Uhr, 24.12. - 15.3.: 8:00- 16:00 Uhr
Zeitverschiebung:	MEZ - 4 Stunden

Handelsdelegierte/-r:	Schwald Dkfm. Josef
Betreuungsbereich:	**zuständige Länderreferate in der Wirtschaftskammer Österreich:**
Argentinien	Referat Lateinamerika
Paraguay	Referat Lateinamerika
Uruguay	Referat Lateinamerika

BUENOS AIRES

Zustelladresse:
El Consejero Comercial de la Embajada de Austria
Casilla Correo Central 523, C 1041 WAF Buenos Aires
ARGENTINA

Büroadresse:
Cerrito 1294, piso 15, C1010 AAZ Buenos Aires
ARGENTINA

Lokale Homepage: http://www.austria.com.ar

Kommunikation:

Telefon:	+54 11 48 16 04 79, 48 14 36 69
Fax:	+54 11 48 14 36 70
Email:	buenosaires@wko.at
Bürozeiten:	Montag bis Freitag: 9:00 - 17:30 Uhr, 24.12. - 15.3.: 8:00- 16:00 Uhr
Zeitverschiebung:	MEZ - 4 Stunden

Handelsdelegierte/-r: Schwald Dkfm. Josef

Betreuungsbereich:	**zuständige Länderreferate in der Wirtschaftskammer Österreich:**
Argentinien	Referat Lateinamerika
Paraguay	Referat Lateinamerika
Uruguay	Referat Lateinamerika

BUKAREST

Büroadresse:
Consilierul Comercial al Ambasadei Austriei
Strada Clopotarii Vechi 4, RO-71126 Bukarest
RUMÄNIEN

Kommunikation:

Telefon:	+40 1 312 03 35, 312 67 85
Fax:	+40 1 312 06 14
Email:	bukarest@wko.at
Bürozeiten:	Montag: 8.00 - 17.30 Uhr, Dienstag - Donnerstag: 8.00 - 17.00 Uhr, Freitag: 8.00 - 14.00 Uhr
Zeitverschiebung:	MEZ + 1 Stunde

Handelsdelegierte/-r: Bachleitner Mag. Franz

Betreuungsbereich:	**zuständige Länderreferate in der Wirtschaftskammer Österreich:**
Moldau	Referat Mittel- und Osteuropa 2
Rumänien	Referat Mittel- und Osteuropa 2

CAIRO

Zustelladresse:
The Commercial Counsellor at the Austrian Embassy
P.O.Box 2470, Cairo
ARAB REPUBLIC OF EGYPT

Büroadresse:
8, Ismail Mohamed Street - Zamalek, Cairo

ARAB REPUBLIC OF EGYPT

Lokale Homepage: http://www.austria.org.eg

Kommunikation:

Telefon:	+20 2 736 1150
Fax:	+20 2 736 2892
Email:	kairo@wko.at

Bürozeiten: Sonntag bis Donnerstag: 7:30 - 15:30 Uhr

Zeitverschiebung: MEZ + 1 Stunde

Handelsdelegierte/-r: Glatz Dr. Martin

Betreuungsbereich:	**zuständige Länderreferate in der Wirtschaftskammer Österreich:**
Somalia	Referat Nahost
Sudan	Referat Nahost
Ägypten	Referat Nahost
Äthiopien	Referat Nahost
Dschibuti	Referat Nahost
Eritrea	Referat Nahost

CARACAS

Zustelladresse:
El Consejero Comercial de la Embajada de Austria
Apartado 14 027, Caracas 1011-A
VENEZUELA

Büroadresse:
Edificio Plaza C/PH, Calle Londres entre Caroni y Nueva York Las
Mercedes, Caracas
VENEZUELA

Lokale Homepage: http://www.austriantrade.org.ve

Kommunikation:

Telefon:	+58 212 993 98 44, 993 85 37
Fax:	+58 212 993 99 35
Email:	caracas@wko.at

Bürozeiten: Montag - Freitag: 8.00 - 16.30 Uhr

Zeitverschiebung: MEZ - 5 Stunden

Handelsdelegierte/-r: Schmid Dr. Andreas

Betreuungsbereich:	**zuständige Länderreferate in der Wirtschaftskammer Österreich:**
Aruba	Referat Lateinamerika
Venezuela	Referat Lateinamerika
Antigua und Barbuda	Referat Lateinamerika
Barbados	Referat Lateinamerika
Dominica	Referat Lateinamerika
Dominikanische Republik	Referat Lateinamerika
Französisch Guayana	Referat Lateinamerika
Grenada	Referat Lateinamerika
Guyana	Referat Lateinamerika
Haiti	Referat Lateinamerika
Jamaika	Referat Lateinamerika
Niederländische Antillen	Referat Lateinamerika
St. Kitts und Nevis	Referat Lateinamerika
St. Lucia	Referat Lateinamerika
St. Vincent und die Grenadinen	Referat Lateinamerika
Suriname	Referat Lateinamerika
Trinidad und Tobago	Referat Lateinamerika
Anguilla	Referat Lateinamerika
Britische Jungferninseln	Referat Lateinamerika
Guadeloupe	Referat Lateinamerika
Montserrat	Referat Lateinamerika
Martinique	Referat Lateinamerika

CASABLANCA

Zustelladresse:
Le Conseiller Commercial auprés de l'Ambassade d'Autriche
B.P. 13822, 20001 Casablanca
MAROC

Büroadresse:
45, Avenue Hassan II, 20000 Casablanca
MAROC

Kommunikation:

Telefon:	+212 2 222 32 82, 226 69 04, 222 47 70
Fax:	+212 2 222 10 83
Email:	casablanca@wko.at

Bürozeiten: Montag bis Donnerstag: 8:00 - 17:00 Uhr, Freitag: 8:00 - 13:00 Uhr

Zeitverschiebung: MEZ - 1 Stunde

Handelsdelegierte/-r: Paumgarten Dr. Heinz

Betreuungsbereich:	zuständige Länderreferate in der Wirtschaftskammer Österreich:
Cote D'Ivoire	Referat Afrika
Gambia	Referat Afrika
Guinea-Bissau	Referat Afrika
Kap Verde	Referat Afrika
Niger	Referat Afrika
Senegal	Referat Afrika
Marokko	Referat Afrika
Burkina Faso	Referat Afrika
Guinea	Referat Afrika
Mali	Referat Afrika
Mauretanien	Referat Afrika

CHICAGO

Büroadresse:
The Austrian Trade Commissioner
500 North Michigan Avenue, Suite 1950, Chicago, IL 60611-3794
USA

Lokale Homepage: http://www.austriantradeus.org/

Kommunikation:

Telefon: +1 312 644 55 56

Fax: +1 312 644 65 26

Email: chicago@wko.at

Bürozeiten: Montag bis Freitag: 8:30 - 17:00 Uhr

Zeitverschiebung: MEZ - 7 Stunden

Handelsdelegierte/-r: Hager Mag. Gudrun

Anmerkung: In den USA und Puerto Rico erreichen Sie die AHStn unter der Telefonnummer 1-800 VIP AHST kostenlos

Betreuungsbereich:	zuständige Länderreferate in der Wirtschaftskammer Österreich:

USA (Vereinigte Staaten von Amerika)	Referat Nordamerika

Provinzen: Betreuungsbereiche: Illinois, Indina, Iowa, Kansas, Kentucky, Michigan, Minnesota, Missouri, Nebraska, North Dakota, Ohio, South Dakota, Wisconsin

DAMASKUS

Zustelladresse:
The Commercial Counsellor at the Austrian Embassy
P.O.B. 7659, Damascus
SYRIA

Büroadresse:
Mezze, Eastern Villas, Farabi Street 116a, Damascus
SYRIA

Kommunikation:

Telefon:	+963 11 611 4616
Fax:	+963 11 613 2078
Email:	damaskus@wko.at

Bürozeiten: Sonntag bis Donnerstag: 7:00 - 15:00 Uhr

Zeitverschiebung: MEZ + 1 Stunde

Handelsdelegierte/-r: Machu Dr. Horst

Betreuungsbereich:	zuständige Länderreferate in der Wirtschaftskammer Österreich:
Syrien	Referat Nahost

DRESDEN

Büroadresse:
D-01309 Dresden, Loschwitzer Straße 50
DEUTSCHLAND

Lokale Homepage: http://www.oesterreich.org

Kommunikation:

Telefon:	+49 351 311 07 10
Fax:	+49 351 311 07 11
Email:	ahst-dresden@t-online.de

DÜSSELDORF

Büroadresse:

Der österreichische Handelsdelegierte
Bahnstraße 9, D-40212 Düsseldorf
DEUTSCHLAND

Lokale Homepage: http://www.oesterreich.org

Kommunikation:

Telefon:	+49 211 32 40 36
Fax:	+49 211 32 64 01
Email:	duesseldorf@wko.at

Bürozeiten:	Montag bis Donnerstag: 8:00 - 17:00 Uhr, Freitag: 8:00 - 16:00 Uhr
Zeitverschiebung:	keine

Handelsdelegierte/-r: Janschek Dkfm. Klaus

Betreuungsbereich:	**zuständige Länderreferate in der Wirtschaftskammer Österreich:**
Deutschland	Referat Europa 1

Provinzen: Nordrhein-Westfalen

DUBLIN

Büroadresse:
The Commercial Counsellor at the Austrian Embassy
Merrion Centre, Nutley Lane, Dublin 4
IRLAND

Lokale Homepage: http://www.austriatrade.org/ie

Kommunikation:

Telefon:	+353 1 283 04 88
Fax:	+353 1 283 05 31
Email:	dublin@wko.at

Bürozeiten:	Montag bis Freitag: 8:00 - 16:30 Uhr
Zeitverschiebung:	MEZ - 1 Stunde

Handelsdelegierte/-r: Dückelmann-Dublany Dr. Gerd

Betreuungsbereich:	**zuständige Länderreferate in der Wirtschaftskammer Österreich:**
Irland	Referat Europa 1

FRANKFURT

Büroadresse:
Der österreichische Handelsdelegierte
Unterlindau 21 - 29, D-60323 Frankfurt am Main
DEUTSCHLAND

Lokale Homepage: http://www.oesterreich.org

Kommunikation:

Telefon: +49 69 97 10 12 0
Fax: +49 69 97 10 12 29
Email: frankfurt@wko.at

Bürozeiten: Montag bis Donnerstag: 8:00 - 17:00 Uhr, Freitag: 8:00 - 16:00 Uhr
Zeitverschiebung: keine

Handelsdelegierte/-r: Kuen Dkfm. Friedrich

Betreuungsbereich:	**zuständige Länderreferate in der Wirtschaftskammer Österreich:**
Deutschland	Referat Europa 1

Provinzen: Baden-Württemberg, Hessen, Rheinland-Pfalz, Saarland

HAAG

Büroadresse:
De Handelsraad, Ambassade van Oostenrijk
Lange Voorhout 58 a, 2514 EG Den Haag
NEDERLAND

Lokale Homepage: http://www.austriantrade.nl

Kommunikation:

Telefon: +31 70 365 49 16
Fax: +31 70 365 73 21
Email: denhaag@wko.at

Bürozeiten: Montag bis Freitag: 8.00 - 16.30 Uhr
Zeitverschiebung: keine

Handelsdelegierte/-r: Mühlberger Dr. Günter

Betreuungsbereich:	zuständige Länderreferate in der Wirtschaftskammer Österreich:
Niederlande	Referat Europa 1

HAMBURG

Büroadresse:
Der österreichische Handelsdelegierte
Poststraße 23, D-20354 Hamburg
DEUTSCHLAND

Lokale Homepage: http://www.oesterreich.org

Kommunikation:

Telefon:	+49 40 34 06 39
Fax:	+49 40 35 44 28
Email:	hamburg@wko.at

Bürozeiten: Montag bis Donnerstag: 8:00 - 17:00 Uhr, Freitag: 8:00 - 16:00 Uhr
Zeitverschiebung: keine

Handelsdelegierte/-r: Larcher Dr. Walter

Betreuungsbereich:	zuständige Länderreferate in der Wirtschaftskammer Österreich:
Deutschland	Referat Europa 1

Provinzen: Hamburg und Bremen, Niedersachsen, Schleswig-Holstein sowie Fragen des Überseegeschäftes, der Seehäfen und damit zusammenhängender Verkehrspolitik

HARARE

Zustelladresse:
The Commercial Counsellor at the Austrian Embassy
P.O.B. 1850, Harare
SIMBABWE

Büroadresse:
51 Jason Moyo Avenue, Globe House, 6th Floor Harare
SIMBABWE

Kommunikation:

Telefon:	+263 4 75 24 14
Fax:	+263 4 75 14 38
Email:	harare@wko.at

Bürozeiten: Montag bis Freitag: 8:00 - 16:00 Uhr

Zeitverschiebung: MEZ + 1 Stunde (keine Sommerzeit)

Handelsdelegierte/-r: Lenz Mag. Alf-Peter

Betreuungsbereich:	zuständige Länderreferate in der Wirtschaftskammer Österreich:
Kenia	Referat Afrika
Simbabwe	Referat Afrika
Malawi	Referat Afrika
Mosambik	Referat Afrika
Ruanda	Referat Afrika
Tansania	Referat Afrika
Uganda	Referat Afrika
Angola	Referat Afrika
Burundi	Referat Afrika
Sambia	Referat Afrika

HELSINKI

Büroadresse:
The Commercial Counsellor at the Austrian Embassy
Mannerheimintie 15 a B, FIN-00260 Helsinki
FINNLAND

Lokale Homepage: http://www.austria.fi

Kommunikation:

Telefon:	+358 9 43 66 33 0
Fax:	+358 9 43 66 33 99
Email:	helsinki@wko.at

Bürozeiten: Montag bis Freitag: 8:30 - 16:30 Uhr, Juni/Juli/August: 8:00 - 16:00 Uhr

Zeitverschiebung: MEZ + 1 Stunde

Handelsdelegierte/-r: Karabaczek Mag. Georg

Betreuungsbereich:	zuständige Länderreferate in der Wirtschaftskammer Österreich:
Estland	Referat Europa 1
Finnland	Referat Europa 1

HONGKONG

Büroadresse:
The Austrian Trade Commissioner
13/F, Diamond Exchange Building, 8-10 Duddell Street, Central,
Hongkong
CHINA

Kommunikation:

Telefon:	+852 25 22 23 88
Fax:	+852 28 10 64 93
Email:	hongkong@wko.at

Bürozeiten:	Montag bis Freitag: 9:00 - 17:30 Uhr
Zeitverschiebung:	MEZ + 7 Stunden

Handelsdelegierte/-r:	Mayer Dr. Alfred

Betreuungsbereich:	zuständige Länderreferate in der Wirtschaftskammer Österreich:
Hongkong, China	Referat Asien 1
Macau	Referat Asien 1
China	Referat Asien 1

Provinzen: Südchinesischen Provinzen: Guangdong, Guangxi, Guizhou, Hainan, Hunan, Yunnan

ISTANBUL

Büroadresse:
Ticari Konsolos
Avusturya Dis Ticaret Ofisi, Büyükdere Caddesi 100-102, Maya Aker
Center B Blok Kat 14 No. 51 TR-80280 Esentepe - Istanbul
TÜRKEI

Lokale Homepage: http://www.wk.or.at/aw/atc/ankara

Kommunikation:

Telefon:	+90 212 211 14 76 77
Fax:	+90 212 212 01 33
Email:	istanbul@wko.at

Bürozeiten:	Montag bis Freitag: 8:00 - 16:30 Uhr
Zeitverschiebung:	MEZ + 1 Stunde

Handelsdelegierte/-r:	Teoman-Brenner Dr. Erika

Betreuungsbereich:	**zuständige Länderreferate in der Wirtschaftskammer Österreich:**
Türkei	Referat Europa 2

Provinzen:	Provinzen Istanbul, Edirne, Kirklareli, Tekirdag, Kocaeli, Balikesir, Bursa und Çanakkale

JAKARTA

Zustelladresse:
The Commercial Counsellor at the Austrian Embassy
P.O.Box 4955/JKTM 12049, Jakarta
INDONESIA

Büroadresse:
Menara Kadin Indonesia, 19th Floor, Jalan H.R. Rasuna Said Blok X-5, Kav. 2&3, Jakarta 12950
INDONESIA

Kommunikation:

Telefon:	+62 21 25 50 01 86
Fax:	+62 21 527 47 07
Email:	jakarta@wko.at

Bürozeiten:	Montag bis Freitag: 8:00 - 16:30 Uhr
Zeitverschiebung:	MEZ + 6 Stunden

Handelsdelegierte/-r:	Gradt Mag. Raymund

Betreuungsbereich: **zuständige Länderreferate in der Wirtschaftskammer**

	Österreich:
Indonesien	Referat Asien 3
Osttimor	-

JEDDAH

Zustelladresse:
The Austrian Consular Office Commercial Section
P.O.B. 1706, Jeddah 21441
SAUDI-ARABIA

Büroadresse:
New Jeddah Chamber of Commerce & Industry Building, Al-RUWAIS,
Jeddah 21441
SAUDI-ARABIA

Lokale Homepage: http://www.austriantrade.org.sa

Kommunikation:

Telefon:	+966 2 651 18 16, 651 23 04
Fax:	+966 2 653 37 64
Email:	jeddah@wko.at

Bürozeiten:	Samstag bis Mittwoch: 8:00 - 16:00 Uhr
Zeitverschiebung:	MEZ + 2 Stunden (Winterzeit), MEZ + 1 Stunde (Sommerzeit)
Handelsdelegierte/-r:	Friedl Ing.Mag. Walter

Betreuungsbereich:	zuständige Länderreferate in der Wirtschaftskammer Österreich:
Jemen	Referat Nahost
Saudi-Arabien	Referat Nahost

Provinzen: Asir (Abha, Khamis Mushayt), Baha, Qurayyat, Jizan, Medina, Makkah (Jeddah, Makkah, Taif, Yanbu), Najran, Tabuk

JOHANNESBURG

Zustelladresse:
The Austrian Trade Commissioner
Private Bag X18, Parklands (Johannesburg) ZA-2121 Rep. of South

Africa
REP. OF SOUTH AFRICA

Büroadresse:
Cradock Heights, 2nd Floor, 21, Cradock Avenue (Corner Tyrwhitt Avenue), Rosebank (Johannesburg)
REP. OF SOUTH AFRICA

Lokale Homepage: http://www.austriatrade.org/za

Kommunikation:

Telefon:	+27 11 442 71 00
Fax:	+27 11 442 83 04
Email:	johannesburg@wko.at

Bürozeiten:	Montag bis Freitag: 8:00 - 16:30 Uhr
Zeitverschiebung:	MEZ + 1 Stunde

Handelsdelegierte/-r: Pöschl Dr. Walter

Betreuungsbereich:	zuständige Länderreferate in der Wirtschaftskammer Österreich:
Botsuana	Referat Afrika
Südafrika	Referat Afrika
Komoren	Referat Afrika
Lesotho	Referat Afrika
Madagaskar	Referat Afrika
Mauritius	Referat Afrika
Mayotte	Referat Afrika
Namibia	Referat Afrika
Reunion	Referat Afrika
Seychellen	Referat Afrika
Swasiland	Referat Afrika

KARACHI

Büroadresse:
The Commercial Counsellor at the Austrian Embassy
F-27/1, Block-9, Clifton, Karachi-75600
PAKISTAN

Kommunikation:

Telefon:	+92 21 586 65 01, 586 65 02, 587 51 19, 587 53 96
Fax:	+92 21 587 03 43
Email:	karachi@wko.at

Bürozeiten: Montag bis Freitag: 8:00 - 16:30 Uhr
Zeitverschiebung: MEZ + 4 Stunden (MESZ + 3 Stunden)

Handelsdelegierte/-r: De Colle Dipl.-Ing. Dr. Carl

Betreuungsbereich:	zuständige Länderreferate in der Wirtschaftskammer Österreich:
Pakistan	Referat Asien 1
Afghanistan	Referat Asien 1

KIEW

Zustelladresse:
Torhowi Radnik Posolstwa Awstrii
Holowposchtamt, a/c 62, 01001 Kiew
UKRAINE

Büroadresse:
wul. Volodimirska, 48 A, 2. St., 01034 Kiew
UKRAINE

Lokale Homepage: http://www.austria.com.ua

Kommunikation:

Telefon:	+380 44 235 13 41, 235 03 18
Fax:	+380 44 230 25 37
Email:	kiew@wko.at

Bürozeiten: Montag bis Freitag: 9:00 - 17:30 Uhr
Zeitverschiebung: MEZ + 1 Stunde

Handelsdelegierte/-r: Gessl Mag. Christian

Betreuungsbereich:	**zuständige Länderreferate in der Wirtschaftskammer Österreich:**
Ukraine	Referat Mittel- und Osteuropa 1

KOPENHAGEN

Büroadresse:
Handelsraden ved den Ostrigske Ambassade
Gronningen 5, III, DK-1270 Kobenhavn K.
DANMARK

Kommunikation:

Telefon:	+45 33 11 14 12
Fax:	+45 33 91 14 13
Email:	kopenhagen@wko.at

Bürozeiten:	Montag bis Freitag: 8:00 - 16:00 Uhr
Zeitverschiebung:	keine

Handelsdelegierte/-r: König Dr. Heinz

Betreuungsbereich:	**zuständige Länderreferate in der Wirtschaftskammer Österreich:**
Dänemark	Referat Europa 1
Färöer Inseln	Referat Europa 1
Grönland	Referat Europa 1

KUALA LUMPUR

Zustelladresse:
Austrian Embassy Office at the Commercial Counsellor
P.O.B. 10.555, 50716 Kuala Lumpur
MALAYSIA

Büroadresse:
Suite 14.1, Level 14, Menara IMC, No. 8, Jalan Sultan Ismail, 50250
Kuala Lumpur
MALAYSIA

Lokale Homepage: http://www.austrian-trade.org.my/austrian-trade

Kommunikation:

Telefon:	+60 3 20 32 28 30
Fax:	+60 3 20 32 31 30
Email:	kualalumpur@wko.at

Bürozeiten:	Montag bis Freitag: 8:00 - 16:30 Uhr
Zeitverschiebung:	MEZ + 7 Stunden

Handelsdelegierte/-r:	Astegher Mag. Hubert

Betreuungsbereich:	**zuständige Länderreferate in der Wirtschaftskammer Österreich:**
Brunei	Referat Asien 1
Malaysia	Referat Asien 3

LAGOS

Zustelladresse:
The Commercial Counsellor at the Austrian Embassy
P.O.B. 56085 Falomo/Ikoyi, Lagos
NIGERIA

Büroadresse:
65A, Oyinkan Abayomi Drive, Ikoyi, Lagos
NIGERIA

Kommunikation:

Telefon:	+234 1 263 68 27, 269 62 12, 269 62 13
Fax:	+234 1 269 42 29
Email:	lagos@wko.at

Bürozeiten:	Montag bis Freitag: 8.30 - 16.30 Uhr
Zeitverschiebung:	keine

Handelsdelegierte/-r:	Stock Mag. Guido

Betreuungsbereich:	**zuständige Länderreferate in der Wirtschaftskammer Österreich:**
Gabun	Referat Afrika
Ghana	Referat Afrika

Kamerun	Referat Afrika
Liberia	Referat Afrika
Sierra Leone	Referat Afrika
Togo	Referat Afrika
Tschad	Referat Afrika
Zentralafrikanische Republik	Referat Afrika
Nigeria	Referat Afrika
Äquatorial Guinea	Referat Afrika
Benin	Referat Afrika
Kongo, Republik	Referat Afrika
Kongo, Demokratische Republik	Referat Afrika
Sao Tome und Principe	Referat Afrika

LISSABON

Büroadresse:
O Conselheiro Comercial da Embaixada da Austria
Rua Rodrigues Sampaio, 18-5, P-1169-027 Lisboa
PORTUGAL

Lokale Homepage: http://www.austriatrade.org/lissabon

Kommunikation:

Telefon:	+351 213 17 10 10
Fax:	+351 213 17 10 19
Email:	lissabon@wko.at

Bürozeiten:	Mo - Do: 8.30 - 17.30 Uhr, Fr: 8.30 - 15.30; Juli - August: Mo - Do: 8.00 - 16.45, Fr: 8.00 - 15.30 Uhr
Zeitverschiebung:	MEZ - 1 Stunde

Handelsdelegierte/-r: Fellner Dr. Dietmar

Betreuungsbereich:	**zuständige Länderreferate in der Wirtschaftskammer Österreich:**
Portugal	Referat Europa 2

Provinzen: Azoren, Madeira

LJUBLJANA

Büroadresse:
Avstrijsko Veleposlanistvo Gospodarski oddelek
Nazorjeva 6, Postni predal 1595, SI-1000 Ljubljana
SLOVENIJA

Lokale Homepage: http://www.austriantrade.si

Kommunikation:

Telefon:	+386 1 425 22 54, 425 22 44
Fax:	+386 1 425 32 61
Email:	laibach@wko.at

Bürozeiten: Montag bis Donnerstag: 8:00 - 17:00 Uhr, Freitag: 8:00 - 14:30 Uhr
Zeitverschiebung: keine

Handelsdelegierte/-r: Krauchenberg Mag. Georg

Betreuungsbereich:	zuständige Länderreferate in der Wirtschaftskammer Österreich:
Slowenien	Referat Mittel- und Osteuropa 3

LONDON

Büroadresse:
The Austrian Trade Commissioner
45, Princes Gate (Exhibition Road), London SW7 2QA
GREAT BRITAIN

Lokale Homepage: http://www.austriatrade.org/uk

Kommunikation:

Telefon:	+44 20 75 84 44 11
Fax:	+44 20 75 84 25 65
Email:	london@wko.at

Bürozeiten: Montag bis Freitag: 9:00 - 17:00 Uhr
Zeitverschiebung: MEZ - 1 Stunde

Handelsdelegierte/-r: Engel Dr. Rudolf J.

Betreuungsbereich:	zuständige Länderreferate in der Wirtschaftskammer Österreich:
Grossbritannien	Referat Europa 1

Gibraltar	Referat Europa 1

LOS ANGELES

Büroadresse:
The Austrian Trade Commissioner
11601 Wilshire Blvd., Suite 2420, Los Angeles/California 90025
USA

Lokale Homepage: http://www.austriantradeus.org/

Kommunikation:

Telefon:	+1 310 477 99 88
Fax:	+1 310 477 16 43
Email:	losangeles@wko.at

Bürozeiten:	Montag bis Freitag: 9:00 - 17:00 Uhr
Zeitverschiebung:	MEZ - 9 Stunden

Handelsdelegierte/-r:	Schwetz DDr. Hubert H.

Anmerkung:	In den USA und Puerto Rico erreichen Sie die AHStn unter der Telefonnummer 1-800 VIP AHST kostenlos

Betreuungsbereich:	**zuständige Länderreferate in der Wirtschaftskammer Österreich:**
USA (Vereinigte Staaten von Amerika)	Referat Nordamerika

Provinzen:	Alaska, Arizona, California, Colorado, Hawaii, Idaho, Montana, Nevada, New Mexico, Oregon, Ozeanien (USA), Utah, Washington (Staat), Wyoming

MADRID

Büroadresse:
Embajada de Austria - Oficina Comercial
Orense, 11-6, E-28020 Madrid
ESPANA

Lokale Homepage: http://www.oficina-comercial-de-austria.com

Kommunikation:

Telefon:	+34 91 556 43 58

Fax:	+34 91 556 99 91
Email:	madrid@wko.at

Bürozeiten:	Montag bis Freitag: 8:30 - 17:00 Uhr, 1.7. - 31.8.: Montag bis Freitag: 8:00 - 16:30 Uhr
Zeitverschiebung:	keine

Handelsdelegierte/-r: Resl Dr. Walter

Betreuungsbereich:	**zuständige Länderreferate in der Wirtschaftskammer Österreich:**
Spanien	Referat Europa 2

Provinzen: Einschließlich der Kanarischen Inseln alle jene Autonomen Regionen, die nicht zur AHSt. Barcelona gehören

MANILA

Zustelladresse:
The Commercial Counsellor at the Austrian Embassy
P.O.B 1215, Makati Central Post Office, 1252 Makati City, Metro Manila
PHILIPPINES

Büroadresse:
14th Floor, The Pacific Star Bldg., Sen. Gil J. Puyat Ave./Corner Makati Ave., 1200 Makati City, Metro Manila
PHILIPPINES

Lokale Homepage: http://www.austriatrade.org/manila

Kommunikation:

Telefon:	+63 2 818 61 16, 818 15 81, 818 16 14
Fax:	+63 2 810 37 13
Email:	manila@wko.at

Bürozeiten:	Montag bis Freitag: 8:00 - 16:30 Uhr
Zeitverschiebung:	MEZ + 7 Stunden

Handelsdelegierte/-r: Harwalik Dr. Wolfgang

Betreuungsbereich:	zuständige Länderreferate in der Wirtschaftskammer Österreich:
Philippinen	Referat Asien 3

MEXIKO

Zustelladresse:
El Consejero Comercial de la Embajada de Austria
Apartado Postal CAP Polanco 242, 11550 México, D.F.
MÉXICO

Büroadresse:
Col. Chapultepec Morales, Delegación Miguel Hidalgo, Av. Presidente Masaryk 101, 9. St., 11570 México, D.F. (Polanco)
MÉXICO

Kommunikation:

Telefon:	+52 52 54 44 18, 52 54 44 28, 52 54 44 38
Fax:	+52 52 55 16 65
Email:	mexiko@wko.at

Bürozeiten:	Montag bis Freitag: 8:30 - 16:30 Uhr
Zeitverschiebung:	MEZ - 7 Stunden

Handelsdelegierte/-r: Koren Dr. Walter

Betreuungsbereich:	zuständige Länderreferate in der Wirtschaftskammer Österreich:
Mexiko	Referat Lateinamerika
Belize	Referat Lateinamerika
Guatemala	Referat Lateinamerika
El Salvador	Referat Lateinamerika
Honduras	Referat Lateinamerika
Nicaragua	Referat Lateinamerika
Costa Rica	Referat Lateinamerika
Kuba	Referat Lateinamerika

MILANO

Büroadresse:

Sezione Commerciale del Consolato Generale d'Austria
Piazza del Duomo 20, I-20122 Milano
ITALIA

Lokale Homepage: http://www.austriatrade.it

Kommunikation:

Telefon:	+39 02 86 61 68
Fax:	+39 02 87 73 19
Email:	mailand@wko.at

Bürozeiten: Montag bis Freitag: 8:30 - 17:00 Uhr, Juli/August: 8:00- 16:00 Uhr
Zeitverschiebung: keine

Handelsdelegierte/-r: Pötscher Dr. Michael

Betreuungsbereich:	**zuständige Länderreferate in der Wirtschaftskammer Österreich:**
Italien	Referat Europa 2
San Marino	Referat Europa 2

Provinzen: Norditalien, ausgenommen Friaul/Julisch-Venetien und Venetien; Trentino-Südtirol, Lombardei, Piemont, Aostatal, Ligurien, Emilia-Romagna, San Marino
Postleitzahlen: 10010-29199, 38010-44199, 46010-48199

MONTREAL

Büroadresse:
Le Délégue Commercial d'Autriche
1010 ouest, Rue Sherbrooke, Suite 1410, Montréal Que. H3A 2R7
CANADA

Lokale Homepage: http://www.austriantrade.org

Kommunikation:

Telefon:	+1 514 849 37 08 9
Fax:	+1 514 849 95 77
Email:	montreal@wko.at

Bürozeiten: Montag bis Freitag: 9:00 - 17:00 Uhr
Zeitverschiebung: MEZ - 6 Stunden

Handelsdelegierte/-r: Grabmayr Dr. Christoph

Betreuungsbereich:	**zuständige Länderreferate in der Wirtschaftskammer Österreich:**
Kanada	Referat Nordamerika

Provinzen: Betreuungsbereich: New Brunswick, Newfoundland, Nova Scotia, Prince Edward Island, Québec

MOSCOW

Büroadresse:
Torgowyi Sowetnik Posoljstwa Awstrii
Starokonjuschennyi per. 1, 119 034 Moskau
RUSSLAND

Kommunikation:

Telefon:	+7 095 201 73 08, 201 28 44
Fax:	+7 095 230 26 87
Email:	moskau@wko.at

Bürozeiten: Montag bis Freitag: 9:00 - 18:00 Uhr
Zeitverschiebung: MEZ + 2 Stunden

Handelsdelegierte/-r: Kausl Mag. Johann

Betreuungsbereich:	**zuständige Länderreferate in der Wirtschaftskammer Österreich:**
Russische Föderation (Rußland)	Referat Mittel- und Osteuropa 1
Armenien	Referat Mittel- und Osteuropa 1
Kasachstan	Referat Mittel- und Osteuropa 1
Kirgisistan	Referat Mittel- und Osteuropa 1
Turkmenistan	Referat Mittel- und Osteuropa 1
Usbekistan	Referat Mittel- und Osteuropa 1
Belarus (Weißrußland)	Referat Mittel- und Osteuropa 1
Georgien	Referat Mittel- und Osteuropa 1
Aserbaidschan	Referat Mittel- und Osteuropa 1

Tadschikistan	Referat Mittel- und Osteuropa 1

MÜNCHEN

Büroadresse:
Der österreichische Handelsdelegierte
Promenadeplatz 12/V, D-80333 München
DEUTSCHLAND

Lokale Homepage: http://www.oesterreich.org

Kommunikation:

Telefon:	+49 89 22 52 88
Fax:	+49 89 22 58 87
Email:	muenchen@wko.at

Bürozeiten: Montag bis Donnerstag: 8:00 - 17:00 Uhr, Freitag: 8:00 - 16:00 Uhr

Zeitverschiebung: keine

Handelsdelegierte/-r: Meschke Ing.Mag. Gerhard

Betreuungsbereich:	zuständige Länderreferate in der Wirtschaftskammer Österreich:
Deutschland	Referat Europa 1

Provinzen: Betreuungsbereich: Bayern

NEW DELHI

Büroadresse:
The Commercial Counsellor at the Austrian Embassy
12a, Amrita Shergill Marg, New Delhi 110 003
INDIA

Lokale Homepage: http://http://www.wko.at/aw/atc/india

Kommunikation:

Telefon:	+91 11 469 17 80, 469 17 81, 469 17 82
Fax:	+91 11 461 87 42
Email:	newdelhi@wko.at

Bürozeiten: Montag bis Freitag: 7:30 - 16:30 Uhr
Zeitverschiebung: MEZ + 4,5 Stunden, keine Sommerzeit

Handelsdelegierte/-r: Dabringer Dr. Sepp

Betreuungsbereich:	zuständige Länderreferate in der Wirtschaftskammer Österreich:
Indien	Referat Asien 1
Bangladesch	Referat Asien 1
Bhutan	Referat Asien 1
Malediven	Referat Asien 1
Nepal	Referat Asien 1
Sri Lanka	Referat Asien 1

NEW YORK

Büroadresse:
The Austrian Trade Commissioner
150 East 52nd Street, 32nd Floor, New York, N.Y. 10022
USA

Lokale Homepage: http://www.austriantradeus.org/

Kommunikation:
Telefon: +1 212 421 52 50
Fax: +1 212 751 46 75
Email: newyork@wko.at

Bürozeiten: Montag bis Freitag: 9:00 - 17:00 Uhr
Zeitverschiebung: MEZ - 6 Stunden

Handelsdelegierte/-r: Freytag Mag. Bruno

Anmerkung: In den USA und Puerto Rico erreichen Sie die AHST unter der Telefonnummer: 1-800 VIP AHST kostenlos.

Betreuungsbereich:	zuständige Länderreferate in der Wirtschaftskammer Österreich:

USA (Vereinigte Staaten von Amerika)	Referat Nordamerika
Bermuda	Referat Nordamerika

Provinzen: Betreuungsbereich: Bermuda-Inseln, Connecticut, Delaware, Maine, Massachusetts, New Hampshire, New York (Staat), New Jersey, North Carolina, Pennsylvania, Rhode Island, Vermont, West Virginia

OSAKA

Büroadresse:
Osaka 541-0053, Hoover Honmachi Bldg. 9F, 3-2-6 Honmachi, Chuo-ku
JAPAN

Lokale Homepage: http://www.austriatrade-jp.org

Kommunikation:

Telefon:	+81 6 62 41 84 11
Fax:	+81 6 62 41 84 15
Email:	osaka@wko.at

OSLO

Büroadresse:
Den Osterrikske Ambassade Handelsraden
Oscars gate 81, N-0256 Oslo
NORGE

Lokale Homepage: http://www.austria.no

Kommunikation:

Telefon:	+47 22 55 57 30, 22 55 56 51, 22 55 56 65
Fax:	+47 22 55 66 22
Email:	oslo@wko.at

Bürozeiten: Montag bis Freitag: 8:00 - 16:00 Uhr
Zeitverschiebung: keine

Handelsdelegierte/-r: Luck Dr. Robert

Betreuungsbereich: **zuständige Länderreferate in der Wirtschaftskammer Österreich:**

Norwegen	Referat Europa 1
Island	Referat Europa 1

PADUA

Büroadresse:
Sezione Commerciale dell'Ambasciata d'Austria - Ufficio di Padova
Via E. Filiberto, 3, I-35122 Padova
ITALIA

Lokale Homepage: http://www.austriatrade.it

Kommunikation:

Telefon:	+39 049 876 25 30, 876 26 98, 876 27 21
Fax:	+39 049 876 27 76
Email:	padua@wko.at

Bürozeiten:	Montag bis Freitag: 8:30 - 17.00 Uhr, Juli/August: 8:00 - 16.00 Uhr
Zeitverschiebung:	keine

Handelsdelegierte/-r:	Valentini-Wanka Dr. Ingrid
Sekretariat:	Stromberger Jutta

Betreuungsbereich:	**zuständige Länderreferate in der Wirtschaftskammer Österreich:**
Italien	Referat Europa 2

Provinzen: Friaul/Julisch-Venetien, Venetien Postleitzahlen: 30010-37199, 45010-45199 Auf dem Lebensmittelsektor zuständig für ganz Italien

PRAG

Büroadresse:

Obchodní rada Rakouského velvyslanectví
Krakovská 7, P.O.B. 493, CZ-111 21 Praha 1
TSCHECHIEN

Lokale Homepage: http://www.austriantrade.cz

Kommunikation:

Telefon:	+420 2 22 21 02 55
Fax:	+420 2 22 21 12 86
Email:	prag@wko.at

Bürozeiten: Montag bis Donnerstag: 8.00 - 17.00 Uhr, Freitag: 8.00 - 14.30 Uhr
Zeitverschiebung: keine

Handelsdelegierte/-r: Angerer Dr. Michael

Betreuungsbereich:	zuständige Länderreferate in der Wirtschaftskammer Österreich:
Tschechische Republik	Referat Mittel- und Osteuropa 4

PRESSBURG

Zustelladresse:
Obchodný radca Rakúskeho vel'vyslanectva
P.O.B. 138, SK-814 99 Bratislava/SR
SLOWAKEI

Büroadresse:
Grösslingova ulica 7, SK-811 00 Bratislava/SR
SLOWAKEI

Lokale Homepage: http://internet.sk/austriantrade/

Kommunikation:

Telefon:	+421 2 57 10 17 00
Fax:	+421 2 57 10 17 99
Email:	pressburg@wko.at

Bürozeiten: Montag bis Donnerstag: 8.00 - 17.00 Uhr, Freitag: 8.00 - 14.30 Uhr
Zeitverschiebung: keine

Handelsdelegierte/-r: Altenburger Dkfm.Ing. Josef

Betreuungsbereich:	**zuständige Länderreferate in der Wirtschaftskammer Österreich:**
Slowakei	Referat Mittel- und Osteuropa 4

RIYADH

Zustelladresse:
The Austrian Embassy Commercial Section
P.O.B. 94362, Riyadh 11693
SAUDI-ARABIA

Büroadresse:
Chamber of Commerce Building, Prince Abdul-Aziz Bin, Musaid Bin
Jallawi Street (formerly: Dhabab Street), 5th floor, Suite 2, Riyadh
11693
SAUDI-ARABIA

Lokale Homepage: http://www.austriantrade.org.sa

Kommunikation:

Telefon:	+966 1 404 10 10, 404 03 34, 401 52 11
Fax:	+966 1 404 29 75
Email:	riyadh@wko.at

Bürozeiten: Samstag bis Mittwoch: 8.00 - 16.00 Uhr
Zeitverschiebung: MEZ + 2 Stunden (Winterzeit), MEZ + 1 Stunde (Sommerzeit)

Handelsdelegierte/-r: Friedl Ing.Mag. Walter

Betreuungsbereich:	**zuständige Länderreferate in der Wirtschaftskammer Österreich:**
Saudi-Arabien	Referat Nahost
Bahrain	Referat Nahost
Kuwait	Referat Nahost

Provinzen: Betreuungsbereich: Eastern Province (Dammam, Al Kobar, Dhahran, Jubail, Hufuf), Hail, Jawf, Northern Province Frontier (Arar), Quasim (Buraydah), Riyadh

RIO DE JANEIRO

Zustelladresse:
O Cônsul Comercial da Austria
Caixa Postal 62.529, BR-22257-970 Rio de Janeiro - RJ
BRASIL

Büroadresse:
Praia de Botafogo, 228 sala 614, BR-22359-900 Rio de Janeiro - RJ
BRASIL

Lokale Homepage: http://www.austria.org.br

Kommunikation:

Telefon:	+55 21 553 02 85
Fax:	+55 21 551 01 42
Email:	riodejaneiro@wko.at

Bürozeiten:	Montag bis Freitag: 8:00 - 16:30 Uhr
Zeitverschiebung:	MEZ: - 4 Stunden (Allgemein), - 3 Stunden (Ende Okt. - Anfang Feb.), MESZ: - 5 Stunden

Handelsdelegierte/-r:	Dorn Mag. Franz

Betreuungsbereich:	**zuständige Länderreferate in der Wirtschaftskammer Österreich:**
Brasilien	Referat Lateinamerika

ROM

Büroadresse:
Sezione Commerciale dell'Ambasciata d'Austria
Via Flaminia, 158, I-00196 Roma
ITALIA

Internet Homepage: http://wko.at/aw/rom

Lokale Homepage: http://www.austriatrade.it

Kommunikation:

Telefon:	+39 06 320 16 59
Fax:	+39 06 361 35 79
Email:	rom@wko.at

Bürozeiten: Montag bis Freitag: 8.30 - 17.00 Uhr, Juli/August: 8.00- 16.00 Uhr

Zeitverschiebung: keine

Handelsdelegierte/-r: Geissler Dr. Herbert

Betreuungsbereich:	zuständige Länderreferate in der Wirtschaftskammer Österreich:
Italien	Referat Europa 2
Albanien	Referat Mittel- und Osteuropa 3
Malta	Referat Europa 2
Vatikan (Heiliger Stuhl)	Referat Europa 2

Provinzen: Mittel- und Süditalien; Postleitzahlen: 00010-09199, 50010-98199

SAN PAULO

Büroadresse:
BR-01412-100 São Paulo, Rua Augusta 2516-10° - conj. 103
BRASIL

Kommunikation:

Telefon:	+55 11 30 85 62 11
Fax:	+55 11 30 64 27 45
Email:	saopaulo@wko.at

SANTIAGO

Zustelladresse:
Consejero Comercial de la Embajada de Austria
Casilla 239 Correo 10, Santiago
CHILE

Büroadresse:
Of. 601, Las Condes, Isidora Goyenecha 2934, Santiago
CHILE

Lokale Homepage: http://www.austriatrade.org/chile

Kommunikation:

Telefon: +56 2 233 05 57

Fax: +56 2 233 69 71

Email: santiago@wko.at

Bürozeiten: Montag bis Freitag: 9:00 - 17:00 Uhr

Zeitverschiebung: MEZ - 5 Stunden

Handelsdelegierte/-r: Hofer Mag. Josef

Betreuungsbereich:	**zuständige Länderreferate in der Wirtschaftskammer Österreich:**
Chile	Referat Lateinamerika
Bolivien	Referat Lateinamerika
Peru	Referat Lateinamerika

SARAJEVO

Büroadresse:
Trgovinski Savetnik Austrijske Ambasade
Marsala Tita 38/II, BiH-71000 Sarajevo
BOSNIEN-HERZEGOWINA

Lokale Homepage: http://www.austrijainfo.org

Kommunikation:

Telefon: +387 33 26 78 40, 26 78 50

Fax: +387 33 23 14 97

Email: sarajevo@wko.at

Bürozeiten: Montag - Donnerstag: 8:30 - 17:00 Uhr, Freitag: 8:30 - 16:00 Uhr

Zeitverschiebung: keine

Handelsdelegierte/-r: Scherz Dr. Michael

Betreuungsbereich:	**zuständige Länderreferate in der Wirtschaftskammer Österreich:**
Bosnien Herzegowina	Referat Mittel- und Osteuropa 3

SARAJEVO

Büroadresse:
Trgovinski Savetnik Austrijske Ambasade
Marsala Tita 38/II, BiH-71000 Sarajevo
BOSNIEN-HERZEGOWINA

Lokale Homepage: http://www.austrijainfo.org

Kommunikation:

Telefon:	+387 33 26 78 40, 26 78 50
Fax:	+387 33 23 14 97
Email:	sarajevo@wko.at

Bürozeiten:	Montag - Donnerstag: 8:30 - 17:00 Uhr, Freitag: 8:30 - 16:00 Uhr
Zeitverschiebung:	keine

Handelsdelegierte/-r:	Scherz Dr. Michael

Betreuungsbereich:	**zuständige Länderreferate in der Wirtschaftskammer Österreich:**
Bosnien Herzegowina	Referat Mittel- und Osteuropa 3

SEOUL

Zustelladresse:
The Commercial Counsellor at the Austrian Embassy
C.P.O. Box 6417, Seoul 100-664
REPUBLIC OF KOREA

Büroadresse:
Kyobo Building, Room 1914, 1-1, Chong-ro, 1-ka, Chongro-ku, Seoul
110-714
REPUBLIC OF KOREA

Lokale Homepage: http://www.austria.or.kr

Kommunikation:

Telefon:	+82 2 732 73 31
Fax:	+82 2 732 43 37
Email:	seoul@wko.at

Bürozeiten:	Montag bis Freitag: 9.00 - 17.30 Uhr
Zeitverschiebung:	MEZ + 8 Stunden

Handelsdelegierte/-r:	Kesberg Dr. Christian

Betreuungsbereich:	**zuständige Länderreferate in der Wirtschaftskammer Österreich:**
Korea, Republik (Süd)	Referat Asien 2

SHANGHAI

Büroadresse:
Austrian Consulate General - Commercial Section
American International Centre at Shanghai Centre (West), Suite 514,
P.O.Box 155, 1376 Nanjing Xi Lu, Shanghai 200040
THE PEOPLE'S REPUBLIC OF CHINA

Kommunikation:

Telefon:	+86 21 62 79 71 97
Fax:	0086 21 62797198
Email:	shanghai@wko.at

Bürozeiten:	Montag bis Freitag: 9.00 - 17.30 Uhr
Zeitverschiebung:	MEZ + 7 Stunden

Handelsdelegierte/-r:	Somweber Mag. Werner
Sekretariat:	Jiang Hilda

Betreuungsbereich:	**zuständige Länderreferate in der Wirtschaftskammer Österreich:**
China	Referat Asien 1

Provinzen: Betreuungsbereich: Anhui, Fujian, Jiangsu, Jiangxi, Shanghai, Zhejiang

SYDNEY

Büroadresse:

Austrian Foreign Trade Office
19th floor, 1, York Street, Sydney NSW 2000
AUSTRALIA

Lokale Homepage: http://www.austriatrade.org/sydney

Kommunikation:

Telefon:	+61 2 92 47 85 81
Fax:	+61 2 92 51 10 38
Email:	sydney@wko.at

Bürozeiten:	Montag bis Freitag: 8.30 - 17.00 Uhr
Zeitverschiebung:	MEZ + 9 Stunden (bzw. + 8 Stunden im europ. Sommer und + 10 Stunden im europ. Winter)

Handelsdelegierte/-r:	Rauch Mag. Roman

Betreuungsbereich:	**zuständige Länderreferate in der Wirtschaftskammer Österreich:**
Australien	Referat Asien 1
Cookinseln	Referat Asien 1
Fidschi	Referat Asien 1
Mikronesien, Föderation	Referat Asien 1
Französisch Polynesien	Referat Asien 1
Kiribati	Referat Asien 1
Marianen	Referat Asien 1
Marshallinseln	Referat Asien 1
Nauru	Referat Asien 1
Neukaledonien (Französisch)	Referat Asien 1
Neuseeland	Referat Asien 1
Niue	Referat Asien 1
Palau (Belau)	Referat Asien 1
Papua Neuguinea	Referat Asien 1
Salomonen	Referat Asien 1
Samoa	Referat Asien 1
Tonga	Referat Asien 1
Tuvalu	Referat Asien 1
Vanuatu	Referat Asien 1
Heard und McDonald Inseln	-

SINGAPUR

Zustelladresse:
The Commercial Counsellor at the Austrian Embassy
Tanglin P.O.B. 238, Singapore 912408
REP. OF SINGAPORE

Büroadresse:
1, Scotts Road, #24-05/06 Shaw Centre, Singapore 228208
REP. OF SINGAPORE

Lokale Homepage: http://www.austria.org.sg

Kommunikation:

Telefon:	+65 235 40 88, 235 40 89, 734 50 04
Fax:	+65 737 12 02
Email:	singapur@wko.at

Bürozeiten: Montag bis Freitag: 9.00 - 17.30 Uhr
Zeitverschiebung: MEZ + 7 Stunden

Handelsdelegierte/-r: Mayerhofer Dkfm. Wolfgang

Betreuungsbereich:	zuständige Länderreferate in der Wirtschaftskammer Österreich:
Singapur	Referat Asien 3

SOFIA

Büroadresse:
Targovski savetnik pri Avstriisko posolstvo
ul. Khan Krum 3, BG-1000 Sofia
BULGARIEN

Lokale Homepage: http://www.wko.at/aw/atc/bulgaria

Kommunikation:

Telefon:	+359 2 980 44 80 (Serie)
Fax:	+359 2 980 20 44
Email:	sofia@wko.at

Bürozeiten: Montag bis Donnerstag: 8:15 - 17:00 Uhr, Freitag: 8:15 - 13:00 Uhr
Zeitverschiebung: MEZ + 1 Stunde

Handelsdelegierte/-r: Ortner Dr. Hermann

Betreuungsbereich:	**zuständige Länderreferate in der Wirtschaftskammer Österreich:**
Bulgarien	Referat Mittel- und Osteuropa 4

STOCKHOLM

Büroadresse:
Handelsradet vid Österrikes Ambassad
Karlaplan 12, SE-115 20 Stockholm
SCHWEDEN

Lokale Homepage: http://www.austriatrade.org/sweden

Kommunikation:

Telefon:	+46 8 667 01 30
Fax:	+46 8 660 83 78
Email:	stockholm@wko.at

Bürozeiten: Montag bis Freitag: 8.30 - 16.30 Uhr
Zeitverschiebung: keine

Handelsdelegierte/-r: Höfle Dr. Walter

Betreuungsbereich:	**zuständige Länderreferate in der Wirtschaftskammer Österreich:**
Schweden	Referat Europa 1
Litauen	Referat Europa 1
Lettland	Referat Europa 1

STRAßBURG

Büroadresse:
Section Commerciale du Consulat Général d'Autriche
14, Quai Kléber, F-67000 Strasbourg Cédex
FRANCE

Kommunikation:

Telefon:	+33 3 88 52 29 62
Fax:	+33 3 88 52 29 61
Email:	strassburg@wko.at

Bürozeiten: Montag bis Freitag: 8.45 - 17.15 Uhr
Zeitverschiebung: keine

Handelsdelegierte/-r: Berger Dr. Michael

Betreuungsbereich:	zuständige Länderreferate in der Wirtschaftskammer Österreich:
Frankreich	Referat Europa 2

Provinzen: Betreuungsbereich: Französischen Departements: 08 Ardennes, 10 Aube, 25 Doubs, 39 Jura, 51 Marne, 52 Marne (Haut), 54 Meurthe et Moselle, 55 Meuse, 57 Moselle, 67 Rhin (Bas), 68 Rhin (Haut), 70 Saône (Haute), 88 Vosges, 90 Belfort (Territoire de)

TAIPEI

Zustelladresse:
The Austrian Trade Delegate
P.O.B. 118-171, Taipei 105,
TAIWAN

Büroadresse:
Bank Tower, Suite 608, 205, Tun Hwa North Road, Taipei 105
TAIWAN

Lokale Homepage: http://www.austriatrade.org/taipei

Kommunikation:

Telefon:	+886-2-27155220
Fax:	+886-2-27173242
Email:	taipei@wko.at

Bürozeiten: Montag bis Freitag: 8.30 - 17.00 Uhr
Zeitverschiebung: MEZ + 7 Stunden

Handelsdelegierte/-r: Lochschmidt Dr. Ingomar

Betreuungsbereich:	zuständige Länderreferate in der Wirtschaftskammer Österreich:
Taiwan	Referat Asien 2

TAIPEI

Zustelladresse:
The Austrian Trade Delegate
P.O.B. 118-171, Taipei 105,
TAIWAN

Büroadresse:
Bank Tower, Suite 608, 205, Tun Hwa North Road, Taipei 105
TAIWAN

Lokale Homepage: http://www.austriatrade.org/taipei

Kommunikation:

Telefon:	+886-2-27155220
Fax:	+886-2-27173242
Email:	taipei@wko.at

Bürozeiten:	Montag bis Freitag: 8.30 - 17.00 Uhr
Zeitverschiebung:	MEZ + 7 Stunden

Handelsdelegierte/-r: Lochschmidt Dr. Ingomar

Betreuungsbereich:	zuständige Länderreferate in der Wirtschaftskammer Österreich:
Taiwan	Referat Asien 2

TEHERAN

Zustelladresse:
The Commercial Counsellor at the Austrian Embassy
P.O.B. 19395/1575, Teheran
IRAN

Büroadresse:
Africa Expressway, Golgasht Street 21, Teheran
IRAN

Kommunikation:

Telefon:	+98 21 205 18 20, 204 77 91, 201 66 28
Fax:	+98 21 205 18 16
Email:	teheran@wko.at

Bürozeiten: Sonntag bis Donnerstag: 7.30 - 15.30 Uhr
Zeitverschiebung: MEZ + 2,5 Stunden

Handelsdelegierte/-r: Smrzka Dkfm. Oskar

Betreuungsbereich:	zuständige Länderreferate in der Wirtschaftskammer Österreich:
Iran	Referat Asien 3

TEL AVIV

Zustelladresse: The Commercial Counsellor at the Austrian Embassy
P.O.B. 3510, 61034 Tel Aviv
ISRAEL

Büroadresse:
Hayarkonstraße 198, Tel Aviv
ISRAEL

Kommunikation:

Telefon:	+972 3 522 66 41, 524 64 43, 524 06 39
Fax:	+972 3 522 40 71
Email:	telaviv@wko.at

Bürozeiten: Montag bis Donnerstag: 7.30 - 16.30 Uhr, Freitag: 7.30 - 14.00 Uhr
Zeitverschiebung: MEZ + 1 Stunde

Handelsdelegierte/-r: Love Mag. Michael

Betreuungsbereich:	zuständige Länderreferate in der Wirtschaftskammer Österreich:
Israel	Referat Nahost
Palästinensische Autonomiegebiete	Referat Nahost

TOKIO

Zustelladresse:
The Austrian Trade Commissioner
P.O.B. Azabu 4, Tokyo 106-8691
JAPAN

Büroadresse:
13-3, 3 Chome, Motozabu, Minato-ku, Tokyo 106-0046
JAPAN

Lokale Homepage: http://www.austriatrade-jp.org

Kommunikation:

Telefon:	+81 3 34 03 17 77, 34 03 17 79
Fax:	+81 3 34 03 34 07
Email:	tokio@wko.at

Bürozeiten:	Montag bis Freitag: 9:00 - 18:00 Uhr
Zeitverschiebung:	MEZ + 8 Stunden (Winterzeit), MEZ + 7 Stunden (Sommerzeit)

Handelsdelegierte/-r:	Penzias Dr. Wolfgang
Sekretariat:	Trattner Susanne

Betreuungsbereich:	**zuständige Länderreferate in der Wirtschaftskammer Österreich:**
Japan	Referat Asien 2

TORONTO

Büroadresse:
Consulate General of Austria Commercial Section
2 Bloor Street West, Suite 400, Toronto, ON M4W 3E2
CANADA

Lokale Homepage: http://www.austriantrade.org

Kommunikation:

Telefon:	+1 416 967 33 48, 967 33 80
Fax:	+1 416 967 41 01
Email:	toronto@wko.at

Bürozeiten: Montag bis Freitag: 9.00 - 17.00 Uhr

Zeitverschiebung: MEZ - 6 Stunden

Handelsdelegierte/-r: Müller Dkfm. Gerhard

Betreuungsbereich:	zuständige Länderreferate in der Wirtschaftskammer Österreich:
Kanada	Referat Nordamerika

Provinzen: Betreuungsbereich: Manitoba, Northwest Territories, Nunavut, Ontario, Saskatchewan

TRIPOLI

Zustelladresse:
The Commercial Counsellor at the Austrian Embassy
P.O.B. 5072, Tripoli,
LIBYA

Büroadresse:
11-13 Shara el Amir, Abdulkader el Jazairi, Tripoli
LIBYA

Kommunikation:

Telefon: +218 21 333 51 76, 333 51 77, 333 04 16

Fax: +218 21 333 73 22

Email: tripolis@wko.at

Bürozeiten: Sonntag bis Donnerstag: 7.30 - 15.30 Uhr

Zeitverschiebung: MEZ + 1 Stunde

Handelsdelegierte/-r: Knappitsch Dr. Franz Otto

Betreuungsbereich:	zuständige Länderreferate in der Wirtschaftskammer Österreich:
Libyen	Referat Afrika

TUNIS

Büroadresse:
Le Conseiller Commercial d'Autriche

21, Avenue Charles Nicolle 1002, TN-1002 Tunis-Belvedere
TUNISIE

Kommunikation:

Telefon:	+216 1 79 78 75, 79 99 30, 79 98 48
Fax:	+216 1 78 83 68
Email:	tunis@wko.at

Bürozeiten:	Montag bis Freitag: 8.00 - 16.00 Uhr
Zeitverschiebung:	keine

Handelsdelegierte/-r:	Wimpissinger Dr. Heinz

Betreuungsbereich:	zuständige Länderreferate in der Wirtschaftskammer Österreich:
Tunesien	Referat Afrika
Algerien	Referat Afrika

VANCOUVER

Büroadresse:
The Austrian Trade Commissioner
200 Granville Street, Suite 1380, Vancouver B.C.
CANADA V6C 1S4

Lokale Homepage: http://www.austriantrade.org

Kommunikation:

Telefon:	+1 604 683 58 08, 683 86 95, 683 24 50
Fax:	+1 604 662 85 28
Email:	vancouver@wko.at

Bürozeiten:	Montag bis Freitag: 8.00 - 17.00 Uhr
Zeitverschiebung:	MEZ - 9 Stunden

Betreuungsbereich:	zuständige Länderreferate in der Wirtschaftskammer Österreich:
Kanada	Referat Nordamerika

Provinzen: Betreuungsbereich: Alberta, British Columbia, Yukon Territory

WARSCHAU

Zustelladresse:
Radca Handlowy Ambasady Austrii
skrytka pocztowa Nr. 78, PL-00976 Warszawa
POLEN

Büroadresse:
ul. Idzikowskiego 7/9, PL-02704 Warszawa
POLEN

Kommunikation:

Telefon:	+48 22 843 79 09, 843 99 32, 843 99 42, 843 30 58
Fax:	+48 22 843 95 05
Email:	warschau@wko.at

Bürozeiten:	Montag bis Freitag: 8:00 - 16:30 Uhr
Zeitverschiebung:	keine

Handelsdelegierte/-r:	Thaler Dr. Rudolf

Betreuungsbereich:	**zuständige Länderreferate in der Wirtschaftskammer Österreich:**
Polen	Referat Mittel- und Osteuropa 4

WASHINGTON

Büroadresse:
The Commercial Counsellor at the Austrian Embassy
1350 Connecticut Avenue N.W., Suite 501, Washington D.C. 20036
USA

Lokale Homepage: http://www.austriantradeus.org/

Kommunikation:

Telefon:	+1 202 835 89 62
Fax:	+1 202 835 89 60
Email:	washington@wko.at

Bürozeiten:	Montag bis Freitag: 9.00 - 17.00 Uhr

Zeitverschiebung: MEZ - 6 Stunden

Handelsdelegierte/-r: Seitinger DDr. Heinz

Anmerkung: In den USA und Puerto Rico erreichen Sie die AHStn unter der Telefonnummer 1-800 VIP AHST kostenlos.

Betreuungsbereich:	zuständige Länderreferate in der Wirtschaftskammer Österreich:
USA (Vereinigte Staaten von Amerika)	Referat Nordamerika
Bahamas	Referat Nordamerika
Puerto Rico	Referat Nordamerika
Jungferninseln (U.S.)	Referat Nordamerika

Provinzen: Betreuungsbereich: Washington (Stadt), Metropolitan Area (Groß-Washington), Weltbank und Interamerikanische Entwicklungsbank, Militärisches Beschaffungswesen (Pentagon), US-Bundesbehörden, Alabama, Arkansas, Bahamas, Florida, Georgia, Louisiana, Maryland, Mississippi, Oklahoma, Puerto Rico, South Carolina, Tennessee, Texas, Virginia, US-Virgin Islands

ZAGREB

Zustelladresse:
Veleposlanstvo Republike Austrije Ured Savetnika za trgovinske odnose
Postanski pretinac 25, HR-10001 Zagreb
KROATIEN

Büroadresse:
Ilica 12/2. St., HR-10000 Zagreb
KROATIEN

Lokale Homepage: http://www.atembassy.hr/atc

Kommunikation:

Telefon:	+385 1 488 19 00
Fax:	+385 1 488 19 12
Email:	zagreb@wko.at

Bürozeiten: Montag bis Freitag: 8:00 - 16:30 Uhr

Zeitverschiebung: keine

Handelsdelegierte/- Palla Dr. Franz M.

r:

Betreuungsbereich:	zuständige Länderreferate in der Wirtschaftskammer Österreich:
Kroatien	Referat Mittel- und Osteuropa 3

ZÜRICH

Zustelladresse:
Der österreichische Handelsdelegierte
CH-8039 Zürich
SCHWEIZ

Büroadresse:
Talstraße 65, CH-8001 Zürich
SCHWEIZ

Lokale Homepage: http://www.austriatrade.org/ch

Kommunikation:

Telefon:	+41 1 212 48 00
Fax:	+41 1 212 28 38
Email:	zuerich@wko.at

Bürozeiten:	Montag: 8.00 - 17.00 Uhr, Dienstag - Donnerstag: 8.00 - 16.30 Uhr, Freitag: 8.00 - 16.00 Uhr
Zeitverschiebung:	keine

Handelsdelegierte/-r: Zyla Dr. Klaus

Betreuungsbereich:	zuständige Länderreferate in der Wirtschaftskammer Österreich:
Schweiz	Referat Europa 2
Liechtenstein	Referat Europa 1

FEDERATION OF AUSTRIAN INDUSTRY

House of Industry
Schwarzenbergplatz 4
A-1031 Vienna

Phone: 43-1-711 35/0

	Phone	eMail
Lorenz Fritz **Secretary General**	01-711 35/2100	l.fritz@iv-net.at
Berthold Berger-Henoch **Brussels Office & Europe**	0032-2-231 18 47	b.berger@iv-net.at
Dieter Drexel **Environmental Policy**	01-711 35/2394	d.drexel@iv-net.at
Martin Eichtinger **International Relations**	01-711 35/2412	m.eichtinger@iv-net.at
Erhard Fürst **Industrial Policy & Economy**	01-711 35/2400	e.fuerst@iv-net.at
Edgar Kilian **Personnel & Financial Affairs**	01-711 35/2200	e.kilian@iv-net.at
Werner Lanthaler **Marketing & Communication**	01-711 35/2300	w.lanthaler@iv-net.at
Stefan Mara **Legal Policy**	01-711 35/2389	s.mara@iv-net.at
Christoph Neumayer **IV-Newsroom**	01-711 35/2311	c.neumayer@iv-net.at
Gerhard Riemer **Education, Innovation & Research**	01-711 35/2360	g.riemer@iv-net.at
Wolfgang Seitz **Public Sector & Fiscal Policy**	01-711 35/2340	w.seitz@iv-net.at
Wolfgang Tritremmel **Labour & Social Policy**	01-711 35/2320	w.tritremmel@iv-net.at
Erika Wedorn **Facility Management**	01-711 35/2220	e.wedorn@iv-net.at

ADDRESS

A-1031 Vienna, Schwarzenbergplatz 4

Fax: + 43-1-711 35/2910

eMail: iv.office@iv-net.at

ASSOCIATIONS REPRESENTING THE INTERESTS OF THE EUROPEAN AUTOMOTIVE INDUSTRY

CLEPA is the umbrella organisation for the European automotive supply industry and represents suppliers and national associations in the European Union towards the global automotive industry.

CLEPA's headquarters are in Brussels, Belgium. Its members cover all products and services within the automotive supply chain.

CLEPA embraces 18 national supply associations from most European countries and over 80 corporate members, which include the world's most prominent suppliers for car parts, systems and modules.

www.clepa.be

ASSOCIATIONS REPRESENTING THE INTERESTS OF THE EUROPEAN AUTOMOTIVE INDUSTRY

ACEA

ACEA is the representative body of thirteen European car, lorry and bus manufacturers at European and international levels.

www.acea.be

NATIONAL ASSOCIATIONS

The countries indicated below are represented within CLEPA through national associations:

- Belgien - AGORIA www.agoria.be
- Dänemark - AUTIG www.autig.dk
- Deutschland -VDA www.vda.de
- Frankreich - FIEV www.fiev.fr
- Holland - RAI www.autovak.nl
- Holland - NEVAT www.nevat.nl
- Italien - ANFIA www.anfia.it
- Austria - AOEM www.aoem.at
- Schweden - SAS www.fordonskomponentgruppen.se
- Spanien - SERNAUTO www.sernauto.es
- UK - SMMT www.smmt.co.uk
- Portugal - AFIA www.afia-afia.pt

Associated Members:

MAJOSZ
Könyves Kálmán Krt. 76
H - 1087 Budapest
phone +361.303.9007
Fax +361.303.9007

TAYSAD
Tosb-Taysad Organize Sanayi B

41491 Sekerpinar-Gebze/Kocaeli
Phone +90.216.373.22.75
Fax +90.216.361.62.84
www.taysad.org.tr

INA
Av. Colonia del Valle #607
C.P. 03100 México D.F.
Phone +52.5682.58.62
Fax +52.5669.38.42
www.ina.com.mx

SINDIPEÇAS
Rua Abilio Soares 1487
BR-04005-005 S.Paulo/SP, Brasil
Phone +55.11.884.45.99
Fax +55.11.884.05.84
www.sindipecas.org.br

Affiliated Members:

EUROBAT
Avenue Marcel Thiry, 204
B-1200 Brussels
Phone +32.2.774.96.10
Fax +32.2.774.96.90
www.eurobat.org

EUWA
E. Ambrosetti & Sons Ltd
CH-6928 Manno, Switzerland
Phone +41.91.611.15.15
Fax +41.91.611.15.30

EPMA
Old Bank Building, Bellstone
GB-Shrewsbury SY1 1HU, United Kingdom
Phone +44.1743.248.899
Fax +44.1743.362.968
www.epma.com

February 2001

AUTOMOTIVE ASSOCIATIONS WORLDWIDE

- Brasil - (www.sindipecas.org.br)
- South Africa - (www.naamsa.com)
- MEMA - (www.mema.org)
- JAPAN - (www.japanauto.com)
- Nordamerika - (www.mem.org)

Tschechien - (www.autosap.cz)

AUSTRIA OFFICES IN THE US

AUSTRIAN TRADE COMMISSION NEW YORK

Scope of activities:
Main office (coordination)
covered areas:
Connecticut, Delaware, Maine, Massachusetts,
New Hampshire, New York, New Jersey,
North Carolina, Pennsylvania, Rhode Island,
Vermont, West Virginia, and the Bermudas

Trade Commissioner
Bruno FREYTAG
Deputy Trade Commissioner
Robert PUNKENHOFER
Gerd BOMMER
Peter GATSCHA (Technology)
Address:
The Austrian Trade Commission
150 East 52nd Street
32nd Floor
New York, NY 10022
Telephone: 1(212) 421-5250
Telefax: 1(212) 751-4675
newyork@wko.at

AUSTRIAN TRADE COMMISSION WASHINGTON D.C.

scope of activities: Trade Policy and Promotion

covered area:
Washington D.C., Maryland, Virginia
Alabama, Arkansas, Bahamas, Florida, Georgia,
Louisiana, Maryland, Mississippi, Oklahoma,
Puerto Rico, South Carolina, Tennessee,
Texas, Virginia, US-Virgin Islands

Trade Commissioner
Heinz SEITINGER
Deputy Trade Commissioner
Guenter KLEEDORFER
Address:

The Commercial Counsellor
at the Austrian Embassy
1350 Connecticut Avenue NW
Suite 501

Washington DC 20036 / USA
Telephone: 1(202) 835-8962
Telefax: 1(202) 835-8960
washington@wko.at

AUSTRIAN TRADE COMMISSION CHICAGO

covered area:
Illinois, Indiana, Iowa, Kansas, Kentucky,
Michigan, Minnesota, Missouri, Nebraska,
North Dakota, Ohio, South Dakota, Wisconsin

Trade Commissioner
Ms. Gudrun HAGER
Address:
The Austrian Trade Commission
500 North Michigan Avenue
Suite 1950
Chicago, IL 60611-3704 / USA
Telephone: 1(312) 644-5556
Telefax: 1(312) 644-6526
chicago@wko.at

AUSTRIAN TRADE COMMISSION LOS ANGELES

covered area:
Alaska, Arizona, California, Colorado, Hawaii,
Idaho, Montana, Nevada, New Mexico, Oregon,
Utah, Washington, Wyoming, Pacific Islands

Trade Commissioner
Hubert H. SCHWETZ
Deputy Trade Commissioner
Nikolaus BERG
Anton EMSENHUBER (Technology)
Address:
The Austrian Trade Commission
11601 Wilshire Blvd.
Suite 2420
Los Angeles, CA 90025 / USA
Telephone: 1(310) 477-9988
Telefax: 1(310) 477-1643
losangeles@wko.at

Austrian Trade Commission Atlanta
Covered Area:
Alabama, Arkansas, Bahamas, Florida, Georgia,
Louisiana, Maryland, Mississippi, Oklahoma,
Puerto Rico, South Carolina, Tennessee,
Texas, Virginia, US-Virgin Islands

Trade Commissioner
Heinz SEITINGER
Address:

The Austrian Trade Commission
4200 Northside Parkway, NW
Bldg.1, Ste. 300
Atlanta, Georgia 30327 / USA
Telephone: 1(404) 995-9347
Telefax: 1(404) 995-9348
atc-atl@mindspring.com

AUSTRIAN FEDERAL ECONOMIC CHAMBER

The Austrian Federal Economic Chamber
Wiedner Hauptstrasse 63
P.O.Box 150
A-1045 Wien
Austria/Europe
Telephone: 011-43-1-50105
Telefax: 011-43-1-50105-255
e-mail: aw.leitung@wko.at
Website:www.wko.at

Austrian Federal Economic Chamber
North America Desk
covered areas:
Canada, United States of America, Bahamas,
the Bermudas, Puerto Rico, US Virgin Islands

Head of the North American Desk
Peter ATHANASIADIS
Address:
The Austrian Federal Economic Chamber
Wiedner Hauptstrasse 63
P.O.Box 150
A-1045 Wien
Austria/Europe
Telephone: 011-43-1-50105 ext. 4204, 4228
Telefax: 011-43-1-50105-255
e-mail: aw.nordamerika@aw.wk.or.at
Website:www.wko.at
Office Hours: Monday to Friday 08 A.M. to 04.30 P.M.

AUSTRIA TRADE REPRESENTATIVES

A. Kuehner & Sohn KG
34 East 64th Street, Ste. 4
New York, NY 10021-7351
Phone: (212) 223-4996
Fax: (212) 223-4997

e-mail: none
website: none

For further information please contact:

A.R. Haire Truck Designs

28 Cub Drive
Thomasville, NC 27360
Phone: (336) 882-5937
Fax: (336) 601-0665

e-mail: none
website: none

Abrasive and Cutting Technology, Inc.
11285 Elkins Rd.,Suite B3
Roswell, GA 30076
Phone: (404) 664-0084
Fax: (404) 664-0085

e-mail: none
website: none

Accent Awning
1600 East Str. Gertrude
Santa Ana, CA 92705
Phone: (714) 540-7899
Fax: (714) 708-1399

THE AUSTRIAN IMPORT MARKET

ECONOMIC STRUCTURE

In 1998, Austria's Gross Domestic Product will reach ATS 2.633,7 billion. Austria ranks among the wealthiest nations in the world with a per capita incomeof ATS 330.000 in 1998 (1$ ... 11,50 ATS).

At the beginning of the nineties the Austrian economy experienced high rates of economic growth despite the global recession. Since1995, however, the weak economic growth in Austria´s neighbouring countries and main trading partners, and the government´s measures to consolidate the budget have had an unfavourable impact on the Austrian economy. Growth forecasts predict a growth of 3,3% for 1998 and of 2,8% for 1999. The principal growth sectors include high tech manufacturing and the service industry (tourism excluded).

Since 1987 the government has gradually reduced its role in the economy. On the basis of privatization programs state owned industries have been sold , merged with other industrial partners, or converted into public companies.

INDUSTRY

The Austrian industry consists mostly of small and medium sized enterprises. Roughly 85% of all companies have less than 100 employees. Another 12% employ up to 500 people, 1.6% up to 1.000, and only 1% have 1.000 or more people on the payroll.

The dominant industries today are machine tools and steel, electronics and chemicals. In general, considerable productivity gains have been achieved in the past years.

SERVICES

As a gateway to all parts of Europe and the rest of the world Austria has developed a widely diversified and efficient service sector. In 1996 a total of 54.000 trade firms employed approximately 444.000 people. This figure includes both wholesale and retail trade as well as domestic and import-export trade. The total turnover of Austria's trade firms reached US$ 45 million in retail and US$ 80 million in wholesale in 1995. There are many small businesses, particularly in retail trade: 22% of all trading firms are one-person businesses, 70% employ up to 10 people, 7% up to 50, and only 1% have more than 50 employees.

Austria, and especially Vienna, enjoys an excellent reputation as an East-West trading centre, thanks to the expertise accumulated over the years. The experience of trading companies in barter-trade and complex financing arrangements are essential to the success of business transactions, even with today's open markets in Eastern Europe.

AGRICULTURE

Although only about 19% of Austria's surface is covered by arable land and 26% by grassland, 252.000 farms (1997) cover Austria's food needs. Modern techniques of food production have led to a high level of self-sufficiency. However, as in most industrialized countries, the agricultural surplus remains to be of major concern.

The principal agricultural production areas of Austria are located to the north of the Alps and along both banks of the Danube to the plains of the eastern border areas.

50 % of Austria's agriculture and forestry is accounted for by small scale units (less than 20 acres); only 3% are large scale units (200 acres or more). Farms are almost exclusively family

USEFUL ADDRESSES

FEDERAL AGENCY FOR INDUSTRIAL COOPERATION AND DEVELOPMENT

Austrian Business Agency
Opernring 3
A-1010 Vienna
Tel.: +43/1/588 58-0
Fax: +43/1/586 86 59

BANKS

Bank Austria AG
Vordere Zollamtsstrasse 13
A-1030 Vienna
Tel.: +43/1/711 91
Fax: +43/1/711 91-6155

Creditanstalt-Bankverein AG
Schottengasse 6-8
A-1010 Vienna
Tel.: +43/1/531 31-0
Fax: +43/1/531 31-44699

BAWAG
Seitzergasse 2-4
A-1010 Vienna
Tel.: +43/1/534 53-0
Fax: +43/1/534 53-2840

Die Erste österreichische Spar-Casse AG
Graben 21
A-1010 Vienna
Tel.: +43/1/531 00-0
Fax: +43/1/531 00-2272

Raiffeisen Zentralbank Österreich AG
Am Stadtpark 9

Österreichische Postsparkasse
Georg-Coch-Platz 2

A-1030 Vienna
Tel.: +43/1/717 07
Fax: +43/1/717 07-1715

A-1018 Vienna
Tel.: +43/1/514 00-0
Fax: +43/1/514 00-1700

LARGEST AUSTRIA EXPORTERS: ALPHABETICAL LISTING

	Company Name
A	AAT GmbH & Co.
A	Achenseebahn
	AE Austria
	ALD Aichelin GmbH
A	Alpina GmbH
	Amann GmbH
	Amaco GmbH
	ASW WarenhandelsgmbH
	Austria Mikro Systeme GmbH
	Austrian Academy of Sciences Press
	Austrian Research Centers
	Austrian Wine Export Center
	Austroplan GmbH
	Austroplast GmbH
B	Bachmann Electronic GmbH
	Backaldrin (Augendopler GmbH)
	B.A.N.K. Austria
	Banner GmbH
	Baumann Dekor Austria
	Beisteiner GmbH
	Bema GmbH
	Beton- u. Monierbau
	Binder Interiors
	Biomin Austria GmbH
	Boehler Bleche GmbH
	Boesendorfer GmbH
	Bouda GmbH

A	Brainforce Software AG
	Braun Maschinenfabrik
	BST Fire Protection Systems
C	Candol GmbH
	Cargo Partner AG
	CISS Consulting GmbH
	Creation Stummer GmbH
D	Darbo AG
	Delacon Biotechnik GmbH
	Digicard GmbH
	Doppelmayr GmbH
	DSM Chemie
E	Ebner GmbH
	Economos GmbH
	Ecus GmbH
	Eder Engineering GmbH
	E+E Elektronik GmbH
	Egger's Sohn GmbH
	Elfenhof Weingut
	Elsner & Co
	Enco GmbH
	Engel Group
	Entec GmbH
	Electro-Terminal GmbH
	Eurotrade Handelsagentur
	EVVA GmbH
	Eybl Krems Textilwerke AG
F	Feldmarschall Radetzky
	Fehrer AG
	Feller GmbH
	Fittydent GmbH
	FMW AG
	Food & Commerce HandelsgmbH

	Forst Service
	Framag Industrieanlagenbau GmbH
	Fronius AG
	Funder GmbH
G	Gantner GmbH
	Geislinger & Co GmbH
	Glaunach GmbH
	Gleitbau Salzburg GmbH
	Gmundner Fertigteile GmbH & Co KG
	Grabner Instruments Messtechnik GmbH
	Grass AG
	Greiner Labortechnik GmbH
H	Hackler GmbH & Co KG
	Hajek GmbH & Co KG
	Hafner Weine
	Hantronic GmbH
	Hartl Crushtek GmbH
	H.C.Koenig GmbH
	Heraklith GmbH
	Hertwich Engineering GmbH
	Hirsch GmbH
	HMH GmbH
	Hoepler GmbH
	Hoerbiger-Origa GmbH
	Hornstein Glastextil AG
	Hueck Folien GmbH
I	IFE AG
	IGM Robotersysteme AG
	Infuehr Sektkellerei
	Interchim Austria GmbH
	Int. Sommerschule Gmunden
	IPT Austria
	Isovolta AG

	ITM Krems
J	Jako GmbH
	Josef Resch GmbH
K	Kaiser GmbH
	Kastner GmbH
	Katarga GmbH
	Kattus GmbH
	KCS Industrie-Holding AG GmbH
	KEBA GmbH
	KIM GmbH
	Kisch GmbH
	Koeck Indoor Design GmbH & Co KG
	Koelbl GmbH
	Koenig Maschinen GmbH
	Kral GmbH & Co
	Kresta GmbH
L	Lamotrading KEG
	Lasermed Ltd.
	Laska GmbH
	Legrand GmbH
	Leica AG
	Leitner Design GmbH
	Lico GmbH
	Liebherr Haushaltsgeräte GmbH
	Liendl Import Export
	Linex GmbH
	Lobmeyr GmbH
	Loruenser Leichtmetall GmbH & CO KG
M	MAG AG
	MAM GmbH
	Manner AG
	Mayreder GmbH
	Medek & Schoerner GmbH

	Mepla GmbH & Co KG
	Metternich-Sandor
	Miba Frictec GmbH & Co. KG
	Moidl GmbH
	Monolith GmbH
	Montes Vertriebs GmbH
N	Natex GmbH
	Neuhofer Holz
	Neuhold GmbH
	Nogler GmbH
	Nordkettenbahnen GmbH
O	Oberdorfer GmbH
	Obernosterer
	Omicron Electronics GmbH
	OMV AG
	Ottakringer Brauerei AG
P	Paar GmbH
	Pacal AG
	Palfinger Kran
	Papst GmbH
	Patria AG
	Joh. Pengg AG
	Perner Handelsagentur
	Pessl Instruments GmbH
	Pfanner GmbH
	Plansee AG
	Pletterbauer GmbH
	Polyfelt
	Praher Kunststofftechnik GmbH
	Purkert
R	ReSound Viennatone AG
	Robamat GmbH
	Rusi Kristall

	Richard Felsinger Int. GmbH
	Rosenbauer International AG
	RSB Schalungstechnik GmbH
	Ruebig GmbH & Co KG
S	Salm & Co GmbH
	Sanamed GmbH
	Sartori & Ruchswurm
	Saubermacher AG
	SBM Wageneder GmbH
	Scheiber GmbH
	Schiebel GmbH
	Schoeler GmbH
	Schwaz Schausilberbergwerk
	Schweighofer GmbH
	Scotty Tele-Transport Corporation
	Seebach GmbH
	Sigl Naturbett
	Silberquelle GmbH & Co KG
	SML MaschinengmbH
	Stallinger GmbH & Co KG
	Starmann GmbH
	Strebel GmbH
	STS Consulting & Trading GmbH
	Creation Stummer GmbH
	Sumetzberger GmbH
	Supervac GmbH & Co KG
	Swaromed Nessler Medizintechnik
	Swarovski Crystal Worlds
	Swarovski Optik KG
T	Thurnhofer Brot
	Tigerwerk
	Time Sharing Betrieb-AG
	Toufar GmbH

	Treibacher AG
	Treibacher Schmiermittel
	Trenka GmbH
	Trodat GmbH
W	Vimex GmbH
	VOEST Alpine Austria Draht GmbH
	Vogelbusch GmbH
	Voith Sulzer Papiermaschinen AG
	Voith Verfahrenstechnik GmbH & Co KG
	VRD Asia Pacific
W	Wallmann Export GmbH
	Walter Heindl
	Weber & Weber Modulhydraulik
	Wernig
	Wintersteiger GmbH
	Wintex International
	WM-Electronic GmbH
	Wurzer GmbH
Z	Zillertalbahn
	Zuegner - Imperial Torte
	Zumtobel Licht Gmbh

MAIN EXPORT PRODUCTS FROM AUSTRIA

Food & Health	Machinery and Equipment A-E
Austrian Wine Export Center Adolf Darbo AG Backaldrin Beisteiner GmbH A. Egger's Sohn Elfenhof Wine Estate Hafner Weine H.C. Koenig GmbH Hoepler GesmbH Infuehr KG Kastner Kattus GmbH Lamotrading Laurenz Moser KEG Montes Vertriebs GmbH Ottakringer Brauerei Pfanner GmbH Pletterbauer GmbH Feldmarschall Radetzky Sanamed Silberquelle GmbH & Co KG Thurnhofer Brot Time Sharing Betriebs-AG Walter Heindl Zuegner - Imperial Torte	ALD Aichelin GmbH Alpina Sicherheitssysteme GmbH Amaco GmbH AMAG GmbH Andritz AG Anton Paar Aquaconsult GmbH Banner GmbH BEMA GmbH Beton- und Monierbau Biopac (Franz Haas Waffelmaschinen GmbH) Boehler Bleche GmbH Bouda GmbH Braun Maschinenfabrik BST Brandschutztechnik GmbH Doppelmayr GmbH Ebner GmbH Economos GmbH Engel Group Ernst Fehrer AG EVVA GmbH
Electronics, Software, E-commerce	**Machinery and Equipment F-M**
AE Austria AMS - Austria Mikro Systeme Bachmann GmbH Brainforce Software AG Digicard GmbH E+E GmbH Electro Terminal GmbH Hantronic GmbH Legrand GmbH Omicron Electronics GmbH Schiebel GmbH Scotty Tele-Transport Corporation WM Electronic GmbH	Felsinger International GmbH Fronius GmbH FMW AG Geislinger & Co GmbH Glaunach Laermschutz GmbH Grabner Instruments Messtechnik GmbH Heinrich Hajek GesmbH & Co Hertwich Engineering GmbH Hoerbiger-Origa GmbH Hueck Folien GmbH IFE Aktiengesellschaft IGM Robotersysteme AG IPT Austria Isovolta AG Jako GmbH KEBA GmbH

	KIM GmbH Koenig Maschinen GmbH Kral GmbH & Co Kresta GmbH Laska GmbH Leica Mikrosysteme AG Lico GmbH Liebherr-Haushaltsgeraete GmbH Loruenser Leichtmetall GmbH & CO. KG Medek & Schoerner GmbH Miba Frictec GmbH & Co. KG
Luxury Goods, Clothing, Textiles, Sport	**Machinery and Equipment N -Z**
Boesendorfer GmbH Candol GmbH ECUS Papierspezialitaeten Eybl Krems Textilwerke AG Hirsch GmbH Katarga GmbH Koelbl GmbH MAM GmbH Monolith GmbH Sartori & Ruchswurm Schoeler GmbH Resch GmbH Rusi Kristall Obernosterer-Strickstoffe GmbH Scheiber GmbH Stummer GmbH & Co KG Wallmann Export GmbH Wurzer GmbH	Natex GmbH Oberdorfer GmbH Patria AG Joh. Pengg AG Pessl Instruments GmbH Plansee AG Polyfelt Praher Kunststofftechnik GmbH Robamat Automatisierungstechnik GmbH Rosenbauer International AG Ruebig GmbH & Co KG O. SALM & Co. Seebach GmbH Seeber Engineering GmbH SML MaschinengmbH Starmann GmbH Steiner FRP Technology Strebel GmbH Swarovski Optik KG Trodat GmbH ReSound Viennatone AG Veitsch Radex Didier VOEST Alpine Austria Draht GmbH Voith VT GmbH & Co KG Voith Sulzer Papiermaschinen AG Wintersteiger GmbH
Furniture, Fittings, Tapestry, Interior Design	**Environmental Technology and Biotech**
B.A.N.K. Austria Baumann Dekor Austria Binder Interiors Funder GmbH	AAT GmbH & Co. Biopac (Franz Haas Waffelmaschinen GmbH) Delacon Biotechnik GmbH Environment Technology

Grass Group Hackler GmbH & Co KG Hornstein Glastextil AG Koeck Indoor Design GmbH & Co KG Leitner Design GmbH J & L Lobmeyr Mepla-Werke GmbH & Co KG Neuhofer Holz Sigl Naturbett	Neuhold Ges.m.b.H. Papst GmbH SAD GmbH Saubermacher Dienstleistungs AG Vogelbusch GmbH
Trading & Transportation	**Chemicals, Pharmaceuticals and Medical Equipment**
ASW Albert Sigl WarenhandelsgmbH Cargo Partner AG Elsner & Co Eurotrade Handelsagentur Food & Commerce HandelsgmbH Forst Service Liendl Import Export Linex GmbH Mag. Gottfried Wernig Vimex Import Export	Amann GmbH Dental Equipment Austroplan GmbH Biomin Austria GmbH DSM Chemie Linz Fittydent GmbH Greiner Labortechnik GmbH Interchim Austria GmbH Lasermed Ltd. Swaromed Nessler Medizintechnik GmbH OMV Aktiengesellschaft Pacal Chemicals GmbH Tigerwerk Toufar GmbH Treibacher AG Treibacher Schleifmittel Trenka GmbH
Construction & Materials	**Service, Education, Publishing, Tourism**
Gleitbau Salzburg GmbH Gmundner Fertigteile GmbH & Co KG Hartl Crushtek GmbH HMH GmbH Mayreder GmbH Moidl GmbH RSB GmbH SBM Wageneder GmbH Schweighofer Holzindustrie Stallinger GmbH & Co. KG	Achenseebahn Austrian Research Centers International Institute of Tourism and Management Internationale Sommerschule Gmunden Kisch GmbH Nordkettenbahnen GmbH STS Consulting & Trading GmbH Swarovski Crystal Worlds Schwaz Silver Mine Verlag d. Akad. d. Wissenschaften Zillertalbahn

SUPPLEMENTS

AUTTORNEYS

VIENNA

(telephone: prefix 01 in-country, or internationally 1)

Dr. Markus A. Andreewitch, Stallburggasse 4/1, 1010 Vienna, Tel.: 533 31 58, Fax: 533 20 91, graduated from the University of Vienna in 1980, was admitted to the bar in April 1986. His specialties are corporate, commercial, tax, unfair competition, antitrust, contract, estate and computer law, as well as international transactions. Dr. Andreewitch has practiced law with the U.S. law firms of Barnes, Richardson & Colburn (1980), and Cleary, Gottlieb, Steen & Hamilton (1981). He speaks English and French.

DDr. Georg Bahn, of Freshfields Bruckhaus Deringer, Seilergasse 16, 1010 Vienna, Tel: 515 15-0, Telefax: 512 63 94, e-mail: vienna@freshfields.com, homepage: http://www.freshfields.com, graduated from the University of Vienna in November 1965, was admitted to the Bar in December 1973. He has a general practice, excluding criminal cases and narcotics offenses. His specialties are corporate law and real estate. Dr. Bahn has been handling various M&A transactions and real estate transactions concerning hotels, office buildings and shopping centers including dispute matters. In dealing with corporate matters he has broad experience with the problems of the automotive industry and the construction industry. Dr. Bahn speaks English and has a working knowledge of French.

Dr. Gerd Baumgartner, Nibelungengasse 1, 1010 Vienna, Tel.: 587 41 14, Fax: 587 89 14, graduated from the University of Vienna in March 1965, was admitted to the bar on January 29, 1974. He has a general practice, specializing in collection cases (according to tariff), lease contracts and estate cases. He handles criminal cases only as an exception, never accepting drug cases. He speaks fluent English.

Dr. Gerhard Benn-Ibler, of Weiss-Tessbach law firm, Rotenturmstrasse 13, 1010 Vienna, Tel.: 53178-0, Fax: 533 52 52, e-mail: office@weisstessbach.com, homepage: http://www.weisstessbach.com, graduated from the University of Vienna in 1964, admitted to the bar in 1970. He has a general practice, excluding criminal cases and narcotics offenses. His specialties are corporate, administrative and constitutional law, general civil law, as well as collection cases, estates and trade disputes. Dr. Benn-Ibler is the vice president of the Austrian Bar Association and is fluent in English.

Dr. Karl Bernhauser, Schmerlingplatz 3/III, 1010 Vienna, Tel.: 402 12 27 or 402 44 28, Fax: 408 55 38, graduated from the University of Vienna in 1966, was admitted to the bar in 1975. He has a general practice, specializing in criminal law including drug offenses. He speaks English.

Dr. Brigitte Birnbaum, Beatrixgasse 3, 1030 Vienna, Tel.: 713 13 57, Fax: 713 77 76, graduated from the University of Vienna in 1975 and was admitted to the bar in 1981. She has a general practice specializing in family, marriage and divorce law, child abduction cases, real estate law and inheritance law. Dr. Birnbaum is fluent in English.

Dr. Jürgen Brandstätter, of Foglar-Deinhardstein & Brandstätter law firm, Plankengasse 7, 1010 Vienna, Tel.: 511 15 71 0, Fax: 513 43 42, e-mail: office@fdblawyers.com, graduated from the University of Vienna in 1979, was admitted to the bar in 1985. He has a general practice, excluding criminal cases and narcotics offenses. He is specialized in arbitration, chemicals, European Community Law, industrial property rights, corporate law and unfair competition. Dr.

Brandstaetter is a member of the International Bar Association and the Legal Committee of the Austrian Federation of Industrialists. He is fluent in English, French and Italian.

Dr. Martin Bordey, LL.M., of Dorda Brugger & Jordis law firm, Dr. Karl Lueger Ring 12, A-1010 Vienna, Tel.: 533 47 95 38, Fax: 533 47 95 56, email: martin.bordey@dbj.at.
Information about the law firm Dorda Brugger & Jordis is available at the website: www.dbj.at.
Dr. Bordey graduated from the University of Vienna in 1988 and the University of Virginia in 1989 and was admitted to the bar in Austria in 1994. He has a general practice, excluding criminal and narcotics cases. He is specialized in mergers and acquisitions, competition law, telecommunication law and collection cases. The law firm also handles business and trade law, general advice to corporate clients and individuals in all business-related areas of Austrian and EU law and transactions (M&A, banking & finance, etc.). He is a member of the law firm's steering committee and a member of the board of director of several private trusts. Dr. Bordey speaks fluent English and French.

Dr. Roland Deissenberger, of Deissenberger & Partners, Dominikanerbastei 4, 1010 Vienna, Tel.: 516 37, Fax: 512 28 18, e-mail: rd@deissenberger.at. Dr. Deissenberger graduated from the University of Vienna in 1981 and was admitted to the bar in 1988. He has a general practice, excluding criminal cases. His specialties are intellectual property, trade, unfair competition, trademarks, licensing, communications, media corporate law, international commercial and business law, tax, banking and finance, as well as litigation and arbitration. Dr. Deissenberger is fluent in English and corresponds in Russian and also speaks French and Italian.

Mag. Ivo Deskovic, of Weiss-Tessbach law firm, Rotenturmstrasse 13, 1010 Vienna, Tel.: 531 78 0, Fax: 533 52 52, e-mail: office@weisstessbach.com, homepage: http://www.weisstessbach.com graduated from the University of Vienna in 1988, was admitted to the bar in 1993. He has a general practice excluding criminal cases and narcotics offenses. His specialties are real estate, property, environmental law, investment funds, collection cases, estates and trade disputes. Dr. Deskovic speaks fluent English.

Dr. Helge Doczekal, Wickenburggasse 3/11, 1080 Vienna, Tel.: 403 44 04, Fax: 403 44 04-40, graduated from the University of Vienna on June 12, 1980, was admitted to the bar on April 14, 1987. He has a general practice, with special emphasis on criminal (including narcotics) and civil cases and family law. He speaks fluent English and also speaks Italian.

Dr. Stefan Eder, of Weiss-Tessbach law firm, Rotenturmstrasse 13, 1010 Vienna, Tel.: 531 78 0, Fax: 533 52 52, e-mail: office@weisstessbach.com, homepage: http://www.weisstessbach.com, graduated from the University of Vienna in 1984, was admitted to the bar in 1992. He has a general practice excluding criminal cases and narcotics offenses. His specialties are financing, corporate, tax law, Eastern European investments, estates and trade disputes. Dr. Eder speaks fluent English.

Dr. Thomas G. Eustacchio, M.A., Währingerstrasse 26, 1090 Vienna, Tel.: 319 97 00, Fax: 319 97 00-22, e-mail: t.g.eustacchio@telecom.at, homepage: http://members.nextra.at/rategs graduated from the University of Graz in 1991 and the College of Europe in Bruges, Belgium in 1993, and was admitted to the bar in Austria in 1997. He has a general practice, including international civil trade procedure and arbitration cases as well as criminal cases (including narcotics). His specialties are intellectual property, law of damages, inheritance and pharmaceutical law. Dr. Eustacchio is fluent in English and also speaks French, Italian and Spanish.

Dr. Klaus Galle, of Weiss-Tessbach law firm, Rotenturmstrasse 13, 1010 Vienna, Tel.: 53178 0, Fax: 533 52 52, e-mail: office@weisstessbach.com, homepage: http://www.weisstessbach.com, graduated from the University of Vienna in 1957, was admitted to the bar in 1964. He has a general practice excluding criminal cases and narcotics offenses. His specialties are building society law, general civil law, personal tax, litigation, collection cases, estates and trade disputes. Dr. Galle speaks fluent English.

Dr. Christian Gassauer-Fleissner, of Gassauer-Fleissner law firm, Wallnerstrasse 4, 1010 Vienna, Tel.: 205 206 100, Fax: 205 206 207, e-mail: c.gassauer@gassauer.at, homepage: http://www.gassauer.at, graduated from the University of Vienna in 1980, was admitted to the bar in 1985. He has a general practice, excluding criminal cases and narcotics offenses. His specialties are corporate law, general commercial law, intellectual property, EC-law, collection cases, estates and trade disputes. Dr. Gassauer-Fleissner is a member of the Law Committee of the Federation of Austrian Industry. He speaks fluent English and French.

Dr. Christoph Gottesmann, LL.M., of Kunz Schima Wallentin & Partner, Porzellangasse 4, 1090 Vienna, Tel.: 313 74, Telefax: 313 74 80, e-mail: christoph.gottesmann@ksw.at, graduated from the University of Vienna in 1989 and was admitted to the bar in 1994. He graduated from the New York University School of Law in 2001 and was admitted to the New York bar in 2002. He has a general practice, specializing in civil law, commercial and business law, including media law, intellectual property, unfair competition, landlord and tenant law, cross-border transactions, European Union law and civil rights. He speaks fluent English.

Dr. Ferdinand Graf, LL.M., of Graf, Maxl, Pitkowitz law firm, Stadiongasse 2, 1010 Vienna, Tel.: 401 17, Fax: 401 17 40, e-mail: graf@gmp.at, graduated from the University of Vienna in 1989 and the New York University School of Law in 1991, was admitted to the bar in Austria 1994 and the New York bar in 1993. He has a general practice excluding criminal cases and narcotics offenses. His specialties are private law, distribution law, Austrian and European Antitrust law, protection of industrial property (legislation against unfair competition, trademark and design law) labor law, industrial law and banking law. Dr. Graf speaks fluent English.

Dr. Alexander Grohmann, of Lambert, Grohmann, Stolitzka & Röhsner, Laurenzerberg 2, 1010 Vienna, Tel.: 515 50 110, Telefax: 515 50 50. Dr. Grohmann graduated from the University of Vienna in 1978, was admitted to the bar in 1984. He has a general practice, excluding criminal cases. His specialties are franchising (author on "The Practice of Franchising in Austria, Manz 1992), international commercial and business law, trade, tax, unfair competition, intellectual property, real estate, administrative, estate and probate law, as well as litigation and arbitration. Dr. Grohmann is fluent in French and has a working knowledge of English.

Dr. Rudolf Gürtler, Seilergasse 3, 1010 Vienna, Tel.: 512 75 75, Fax: 513 83 03, e-mail: guertler@rechtsanwalt-wien.at or guertler@anwalt-wien.at, studied at the University of Vienna, graduated in December 1966, was admitted to the bar in February 1973. Dr. Gürtler has a general practice, including criminal cases. His specialties are international private law, trade register law, housing rental and hunting and game law. Dr. Gürtler serves as legal consultant for and as president or member of supervisory boards of several companies. He speaks fluent English and French.

Dr. Wulf Gordian Hauser, LL.M., Seilerstätte 18-20, 1010 Vienna, Tel.: 512 29 00, Fax: 513 77 42, e-mail: office@wulf-g-hauser.com, graduated from the University of Vienna in 1974, and the Georgetown University Law Center in 1983. He was admitted to the bars of New York State (Jan. 1984), District of Columbia (June 1984), and Austria (Jan. 1986). Dr. Hauser has a general practice, excluding criminal cases and narcotic offenses, specializing in Corporate, commercial and international law. He speaks English and French.

Drs. Johannes Hock Sr. and Jr., Stallburggasse 4, 1010 Vienna, Tel.: 533 50 62, Fax: 533 09 89, studied at the University of Vienna. Father, admitted to the bar in 1952, also holds a B.S. in Economics from the University of Oregon. Son, admitted to the bar in January 1987, did additional studies at the Columbia School of Law. Dr. Johannes Hock, Sr. has a general practice, including criminal cases, specializing in corporation law, trade mark law and divorce cases with international background. Dr. Johannes Hock, Jr. specializes in commercial and corporate law, unfair competition and trade marks, lease contracts and litigations in rent matters. He handles criminal cases only in connection with Food Act matters and copyright infringements. Father and son are fluent in English. Son also speaks French.

Dr. Wolfgang Hofer, Freyung 6/11, 1010 Vienna, Tel.: 533 87 26-0, Fax: 533 87 26-34, Telex: 11 59 47, graduated from the University of Vienna in 1975, was admitted to the bar in 1980. He has a general practice, excluding criminal cases and narcotics offenses. His specialties are commercial law, distribution, corporate and banking law, industrial property, contracts and estate, real property and construction. Dr. Hofer is fluent in English.

DDr. Paul Hopmeier, Rathausstrasse 15, 1010 Vienna, Tel.: 405 33 82, Fax: 408 84 67, graduated from the University of Vienna and from the Vienna School of Economics in 1974, was admitted to the bar in 1980. He has a general practice, excluding criminal cases and narcotics offenses. His specialties are tax law and company law. He is a court interpreter for the English language and also speaks French and Spanish.

Dr. Günther J. Horvath, of Freshfields Bruckhaus Deringer, Seilergasse 16, 1010 Vienna, Tel.: 515 15-0, Fax: 512 63 94, e-mail: vienna@freshfields.com, homepage: http://www.freshfields.com, graduated from University of Graz in June 1976, was admitted to the bar in December 1981. He has a general practice, excluding criminal cases and narcotics offenses. His specialties are corporate, commercial, tax, contract and estate, as well as international transactions and arbitration. Dr. Horvath speaks English and has a working knowledge of Italian.

Dr. Christoph H. Kerres, LL.M., of Kerres & Diwok, Stubenring 18, 1010 Vienna, Tel.: 516 60, Fax: 516 60 60, e-mail: office@kerres-diwok.com. Dr. Kerres graduated from the University of Vienna in 1982 and from Georgetown University in 1986. He practiced in Washington, D.C. with the law firm of Seifman, Semo & Slevin 1986 and was admitted to the bar in both New York and Austria in 1988. Dr. Kerres has a general practice, excluding criminal cases. His specialties are international business transactions, commercial and business law, trade, tax and finance, energy an environmental law, unfair competition, intellectual property and administrative law, as well as litigation and arbitration. Dr. Kerres is fluent in English and Spanish, speaks French, and is Chairman of the New York Bar Association's Vienna Chapter.

Dr. Helene Klaar, of Dr. Helene Klaar, Mag. Norbert Marschall Rechtsanwälte OEG, Prinz Eugen-Strasse 34, 1040 Vienna, Tel.: 505 04 62, Fax: 504 39 50, graduated from the University of Vienna in 1972, was admitted to the bar in 1976. Her specialties are family law, labor law, and real estate law. She is proficient in English.

Dr. Alexander Klauser, of Brauneis, Klauser & Prändl, Bauernmarkt 2, 1010 Vienna, Tel.: 532 12 10 0, Fax: 532 12 10 20, e-mail: viennalaw@bkp.at, homepage: http://www.bkp.at graduated from the University of Vienna in 1983, was admitted to the bar in 1990. He practiced European Competition Law as an intern at the European Commission (DG IV) in Brussels. Dr. Klauser has a general practice, primarily in civil and commercial matters, antitrust, intellectual property, copyright, administrative, real estate, tenancy, family, insolvency and litigation. He is a lecturer at the McGeorge School of Law (Salzburg) in Private International Law. He accepts criminal cases only as an exception. Dr. Klauser speaks fluent English, French and Italian.

Dr. Gerhard Kornek, Ferstelgasse 1, 1090 Vienna, Tel.: 401 51-0, Fax: 401 51-20, graduated from the University of Vienna in January 1970, was admitted to the bar in 1974. He has a general practice, including criminal cases, and specializes in divorce law, traffic accidents, insurance claims, trade and labor. He speaks English.

Dr. Elmar Kresbach, LL.M., Schottengasse 4/4/29, 1010 Vienna, Tel.: 533 26 90, Fax: 533 27 90, graduated from the Univerity of Graz in 1982 and the McGeorge School of Law in Sacramento, California in 1984, was admitted to the bar in Austria in 1992. He has a general practice with special emphasis in criminal cases (including narcotics), divorce cases, collection cases, general litigation practice and unfair trade practices. Dr. Kresbach speaks fluent English and French.

Dr. Rudolf Krilyszyn, Porzellangasse 39, 1090 Vienna, Tel.: 319 94 70, Fax: 319 94 70 70, e-mail: krilyszyn@online.edvg.co.at or rudolf@krilaw.at, graduated from the University of Vienna in 1973, admitted to the bar in 1978. He has a general practice, excluding criminal cases and narcotics offenses. His specialties are commercial, banking, labor, estate, arbitration, litigation, collection cases and trade disputes. Dr. Krilyszyn speaks fluent English.

Dr. Peter Lambert, of Lambert, of Grohmann, Stolitzka & Röhsner, Laurenzerberg 2, 1010 Vienna, Tel.: 515 50 120, Fax: 515 50 50. Dr. Lambert graduated from the University of Vienna and McGeorge School of Law, Sacramento, California in 1979, was admitted to the bar in 1983. He practiced in San Francisco, California with the law firm of Maron, Reed & Sheehy from 1982 to 1983. Dr. Lambert has a general practice, excluding criminal cases. His specialties are international commercial and business law, trade, tax, unfair competition, intellectual property, real estate, administrative, estate and probate law, as well as litigation and arbitration. Dr. Lambert is fluent in English, speaks French, and is Chairman of the American Bar Association's Vienna Chapter.

DDDr. Franz Langmayr, Langmaisgasse 7/3, 1010 Vienna, Tel: 944 77 24, Fax: 789 03 54-20, graduated from the University of Vienna in July 1967, was admitted to the bar in December 1972. He has a general practice, including all types of civil and criminal cases. His specialties are commercial law, citizenship matters, and insurance financing. He speaks English and French.

Dr. Andreas Lintl, Lugeck 7, 1010 Vienna, Tel.: 512 60 50, Fax: 512 86 05, e-mail: a.lintl@lintl-law.at, graduated from the University of Vienna in 1983 and was admitted to the bar in 1991. He has a general practice, with special emphasis on Austrian inheritance, estate, trade disputes, personal injury and insurance matters. He is court interpreter for the English language.

Dr. Werner J. Loibl, Riemergasse 14, 1010 Vienna, Tel.: 512 88 82-0, Fax: 512 88 62, e-mail: office@law.co.at, graduated from the University of Vienna in 1981, was admitted to the bar in 1988. Dr. Loibl also holds a master's degree from New York University. He has a general practice, specializing in international business law, corporate law, intellectual property, commercial litigation. He does not handle criminal cases. Dr. Loibl speaks English, French and Spanish.

Dr. Paul Luiki, of Freshfields Bruckhaus Deringer, Seilergasse 16, 1010 Vienna, Tel.: 515 15-0, Fax: 512 63 94, e-mail: vienna@freshfields.com, homepage: http://www.freshfields.com, received his first legal education at the University of Iowa. He obtained a law degree from the University of Vienna in 1993 as well as a doctoral degree from the same University in 1996. He is admitted to the Austrian and Ohio Bars and has a general practice, excluding criminal cases and narcotics offenses. His specialties are M&A, joint ventures, banking and finance law as well as general corporate law. Dr. Luiki speaks English and German.

Dr. Friedrich W. Mosing, Mölker Bastei 5, 1010 Vienna, Tel.: 533 56 09, Fax: 533 07 21, graduated from the University of Vienna in 1951, subsequently obtained a LL.M. at the Yale School of Law, then did additional studies at the Universities of Geneva and Paris. He was admitted to the bar in 1960. His specialties are commercial law, industrial property and international law. He does not handle criminal cases. He speaks fluent English and French.

Dr. Peter Philipp, Graben 17, 1010 Vienna, Tel.: 533 80 01, Fax: 533 09 59, graduated from the University in Vienna 1970 and was admitted to the bar in 1975. He has a general practice, with special emphasis in criminal cases, including narcotic offenses and family law. Dr. Philipp speaks English, French and Italian.

Dr. Peter Pöch, of Ortner, Pöch, Foramitti, Strauchgasse 1-3, 1010 Vienna, Tel.: 535 37 21, Fax: 533 15 55, e-mail: opf.vienna@aon.at, homepage: http://www.opf.at studied at the Universities of Vienna, Grenoble and Kansas, graduated in Vienna in 1964. He was admitted to the bar in 1972. With the exclusion of criminal cases he has a general practice, specializing in industrial property, unfair competition, banking, commercial and corporate. He is Austrian advisor for the *European Intellectual Property Review* and the *Journal of International Banking Law*. He speaks fluent English and some French.

Dr. Peter M. Polak, LL.M., Getreidemarkt 1, 1060 Vienna, Tel.: 582 58-0, Fax: 582 58-2, e-mail: f-p-vienna@lex.co.at or fplp@fplp.at, graduated from the University of Vienna in 1982 and the University of California at Berkeley in 1984. He was admitted to the bar in California in 1985 and in Austria in 1989. He has a general practice, excluding criminal cases and narcotics offenses. His specialties are corporate, commercial, tax, industrial property, unfair competition, anti- trust, contract, estate, real estate and administrative law, as well as international transactions. He is an Associate Professor with Webster University (Vienna campus). Dr. Polak is a certified translator for the English language and also speaks French. Dr. Polak's partner, Dr. Rudolf Fiebinger, speaks English, French and Spanish.

Jenny Power, of Freshfields Bruckhaus Deringer, Seilergasse 16, 1010 Vienna, Tel.: 515 15-0, Fax: 512 63 94, e-mail: vienna@freshfields.com, homepage: http://www.freshfields.com, holds a J.D. (*juris doctor*) degree from the University of Miami School of Law. She has no Austrian law decree and is therefore not authorized to practice law in Austria. She is a member of the Florida and American Bar Associations. She has a general practice, excluding criminal cases and narcotics offenses. The primary focus of her practice is the representation of clients as counsel in international arbitration including those conducted under the auspices of the ICC and the International Arbitral Center of the Austrian Economic Chamber as well as in *ad hoc* proceedings. Jenny Powers speaks English and German.

Dr. Michael Prager, Seilergasse 9, 1010 Vienna, Tel.: 512 62 20, Fax 512 62 21, graduated from the University of Vienna in June 1984, was admitted to the bar in June 1992. He has a general practice, specializing in corporate law & civil disputes including company formation, business licensing, real estate conceptions, rental agreements, employment relations, trade disputes, trademark matters, agency and distribution, joint venture set up, M & A, aviation & insurance. Dr. Prager does not accept criminal cases. He speaks fluent English.

Dr. Felix Prändl, LL.M., J.S.M., of Brauneis, Klauser and Prändl, Bauernmarkt 2, 1010 Vienna, Tel.: 532 12 10 0, Fax: 532 12 10 20, e-mail: viennalaw@bkp.at, homepage: http://www.bkp.at, graduated from the University of Vienna in 1982, from Tulane Law School, New Orleans, in 1984 and from Stanford Law School in 1986. He was admitted to the bar in 1992. Dr. Prändl practiced law in a San Francisco law firm and in a Brussels EC-law firm. He has a general practice, primarily in corporate and commercial matters, contracts, mergers and acquisitions, European Community, probate, wills, computers and software, agency and distributorships and cross-border transactions. He does not handle criminal cases. Dr. Prändl speaks fluent English.

Dr. Peter Prettenhofer, of Prettenhofer & Jandl, Oppolzergasse 6, 1010 Vienna, Tel.: 533 36 19, Fax: 533 36 19-24, e-mail: prettenhofer.jandl@telecom.at or office@lawco.at, homepage: http://www.lawco.at graduated from the University of Vienna in 1960, was admitted to the bar in

1967. He has a general practice, specializing in corporation and commercial law, including industrial property, trade mark, unfair competition and tax matters, and international law. He does not accept criminal cases. He speaks fluent English and French.

Dr. Rose-Marie Rath, Weißgerber Lände 40, 1030 Vienna, Tel.: 713 13 79, Fax: 713 02 62, studied law at the universities of Vienna and Graz, graduated from the latter in January 1983. She was admitted to the bar in 1988. She has a general practice and, with the exception of narcotics offenses, accepts all criminal and civil cases. Dr. Rath speaks English.

Dr. Axel Reidlinger, of Freshfields Bruckhaus Deringer, Seilergasse 16, 1010 Vienna, Tel.: 515 15-0, Fax: 512 63 94, e-mail: vienna@freshfields.com, homepage: http://www.freshfields.com, obtained an LLM/DEA in European Community Law from the College of Europe in Bruges. He is a member of the Austrian Bar and has a general practice, excluding criminal cases and narcotics offenses. His specialties are the antitrust competition & trade, more precisely competition law in energy sector liberalization as well as Austrian and European telecommunications and e-commerce law. Dr. Reidlinger speaks English and has a working knowledge of French.

Dr. Andreas Reiner, Helferstorferstr 4/Freyung 6/12, 1010 Vienna, Tel.: 532 23 32 0, Fax: 532 23 32 10, e-mail: reiner@aon.at, graduated from the University of Vienna in 1975, and from the University of Orleans, France, in 1980. In addition, Dr. Reiner did post-graduate studies in EC-law at the University of Paris. From 1981 to 1985 he worked as a Counsel at the International Court of Arbitration of the International Chamber of Commerce. He was admitted to the bar in 1989. Dr. Reiner has a general practice, excluding criminal cases and narcotics offenses. His specialties are commercial, distribution, corporate, unfair competition, industrial property, labor arbitration. He lectures at the Vienna School of Economics and is fluent in English and French.

Dr. Wieland Schmid-Schmidsfelden, of Weiss-Tessbach law firm, Rotenturmstrasse 13, 1010 Vienna, Tel.: 533 16 51 0, Fax: 533 52 52, e-mail: office@weisstessbach.com, homepage: http://www.weisstessbach.com, graduated from the University of Vienna in 1984, admitted to the bar in 1989. He has a general practice, excluding criminal cases and narcotic offenses. His specialties are corporate law, mergers and acquisitions, corporate finance, joint ventures in Austria and Central Europe and trade disputes. Dr. Schmid-Schmidsfelden is the Secretary General of the Austrian Joint Venture Association and speaks fluent English.

Mag. Harald Schuster, Wickenburggasse 13, 1080 Vienna, Tel.: 406 61 47 Fax: 406 61 47-15, e-mail: advocat.schuster@aon.at, graduated from the University of Vienna in 1989, was admitted to the bar in 1994. He has a general practice with special emphasis in criminal cases (including narcotics offenses) and civil law. Mag. Schuster speaks fluent English.

Dr. Friedrich Schwank, Law Offices, Stock Exchange Building, Wipplingerstraße 34, 1010 Vienna, Tel.: 533 57 04, Fax: 533 57 06, e-mail: offices@schwank.com, homepage: http://www.schwank.com, graduated from the University of Innsbruck in 1972 and was admitted to the bar in 1976. Dr. Schwank did postgraduate work in London and Paris. He has a general practice, handling, inter alia, antitrust, banking, competition, EC law, copyright, trademark litigation, and capital taxation. Dr. Schwank does not accept criminal cases. He speaks English, French and Spanish. With three additional lawyers working for him, the firm can also handle Singhalese and Italian.

Dr. Michael Sedlaczek, of Freshfields Bruckhaus Deringer, Seilergasse 16, 1010 Vienna, Tel.: 515 15-0, Fax: 512 63 94, e-mail: vienna@freshfields.com, homepage: http://www.freshfields.com, holds the degree of Master of Laws (*Mag. iur.*) from the University of Vienna and the degree of PhD in law (*Dr. iur.*) from the University of Innsbruck. He has a general practice, excluding criminal cases and narcotics offenses. His area of practice is tax, includes tax related corporate law, and investment fund law. He specialises in structuring national and international M&A transactions; corporate tax planning and group reorganisations (including domestic and cross-border mergers, spin-offs, split-ups, contributions in kind, post acquisition tax planning); financial instruments, their tax driven structures (including derivatives, swaps, stock lending and repo transactions, hybrid instruments, etc.) and investment funds; international taxation (e.g. tax planning for artists). Dr. Sedlaczek speaks English and has a working knowledge of Italian.

Dr. A. Nicholas Simon, Stallburggasse 4, 1010 Vienna, Tel.: 533 31 58, Fax: 533 20 91, graduated from the Boston University School of Law in 1980 and from the University of Vienna in December 1985. He was admitted to the bar of the Massachusetts Supreme Judicial Court and the United States Court, Massachusetts in 1980 and 1981, respectively. In January 1990, he was admitted to the bar in Austria. Dr. Simon's practice specializes in international business law. He is fully bilingual in English and German.

Dr. Harald Sitta, Piaristengasse 2, 1080 Vienna, Tel.: 408 85 24-0, Fax: 409 55 26, e-mail: office@sitta.at, homepage: http://www.sitta.at, graduated from the University of Vienna in 1978, was admitted to the bar in 1991. Dr. Sitta has a general civil law practice, specializing in commercial and company law, computer law, consumer protection law, product liability and labor law. He is a member of several professional associations and has written legal articles in a number of professional publications. Dr. Sitta speaks English.

Hon.Prof. DDr. Hellwig Torggler, of Schönherr, Barfuss, Torggler & Partner, Tuchlauben 13, 1010 Vienna, Tel.: 534 37-0, Fax: 533 25 21, e-mail: h.torggler@schoenherr.at, is a graduate of the Law School of the University of Graz, Austria. He also has a Master of Comparative Law from the Law School of the Southern Methodist University, Dallas, Texas. Dr. Torggler has general practice, primarily in corporate matters, commercial law and tax law and industrial property rights. He does not handle criminal cases. Dr. Torggler is an official interpreter for the English language.

Dr. Michaela Tulipan, LL. M., Keplerplatz 13, 1100 Vienna, Tel.: 602 06 55, Fax: 602 06 55-90, e-mail: kanzlei@tulipan.at, graduated from the University of Vienna in 1976. After postgraduate studies in comparative law in Paris, legal practice in Germany and additional studies in the U.S. She was admitted to the bar in 1986. Her practice covers civil matters including international law and family law. She speaks fluent French and English and has a fair knowledge of Italian.

Dr. Peter Wagesreiter, LL. M., of Schneider & Wagesreiter law firm, Seilerstätte 13, 1010 Vienna, Tel.: 512 90 55, Fax: 512 90 55 55, e-mail: wagesreiter@s-w-attorneys.com, graduated from the University of Vienna in 1991 and the University of Pennsylvania in 1994 and was admitted to the bar in Austria in 1998 and New York in 2001. He has a general practice, specializing in international business transactions and contract law, collection cases, estates and trade disputes. He does not handle criminal cases. He speaks fluent English.

Dr. Erhart Weiss, Kohlmarkt 1, 1010 Vienna, Tel.: 533 99 03, Fax: 535 63 37, graduated from the University of Vienna in 1962. After postgraduate studies at Oxford and legal practice in London he was admitted to the bar at the end of 1972. He has a general practice, specializing in commercial and corporation law including tax, currency and industrial property matters. He does not handle criminal cases. He speaks fluent English.

Dr. Ingrid Weisz, LL.M., Florianigasse 7/9, 1010 Vienna, Tel.: 406 00 51, Fax: 406 00 52 22, e-mail: weisz@magnet.at, graduated from the University of Vienna in 1984 and the New York University School of Law in 1991 and was admitted to the bar in Austria in 1991 and New York in 1992. She has a general practice, specializing in litigation (civil and commercial law), administrative law, insurance and product liability law. She also accepts criminal cases except narcotics cases. Dr. Weisz speaks fluent English.

Dr. Richard Wibiral, Parkring 10/1, 1010 Vienna, Tel.: 513 83 24-0, Fax: 513 83 24 14, graduated from the University of Vienna in 1981 and was admitted to the bar in 1986. He has a general practice, specializing in civil law, compensation, commercial law, companies legislation, formation of associations, joint ventures, restoration to profitability, contracts of sale and gift regarding real estate and apartments, estate proceedings and administration, contracts of lease, land register, trade marks registration act, foundations and trusts. He also handles criminal cases including narcotics offenses. Dr. Wibiral speaks fluent English.

Dr. Wolfgang Winkler, Gigergasse 6 (entrance Henslerstrasse 3), 1030 Vienna, Tel.: 710 79 29 0, Fax 710 79 19 19, graduated from the Paris-Lodron-University of Salzburg in 1985 and was admitted to the bar in 1992. He has a general practice, specializing in contractual right law, trade disputes and criminal law (including narcotis). He speaks fluent English and also speaks French.

DDr. Hans-Georg Zeiner, Schellinggasse 6, 1010 Vienna, Tel.: 512 23 64, Fax: 512 33 25, graduated from the Vienna University in July 1967, also studied at the Institut d'Etudes Politiques in Paris and the New York University. He practiced law in New York for one year. His fields of specialization are corporate law, tax law, cartel law, unfair competition, patent and trademark law. He does not handle criminal cases. He is a court interpreter for the English language and also speaks French.

BURGENLAND

Eisenstadt

telephone: prefix 02682 in-country, or internationally 2682)

Dr. Martin Beck, of Beck & Dörnhöfer, Franz Liszt Gasse 1, 7000 Eisenstadt, Tel.: 62468, Fax: 66214, graduated from the University of Vienna in 1990 and was admitted to the bar in 1996. He has a general practice with special emphasis on civil law (divorce and tort law) and criminal law, including narcotic offenses. He is a member of the Disciplinary Division of the Burgenland Bar Association. Dr. Beck speaks English.

Dr. Klaus Dörnhöfer, of Beck and Dörnhöfer, Franz Liszt Gasse 1, 7000 Eisenstadt Tel.: 62468, graduated from the University of Vienna in 1979 and was admitted to the bar in 1985. He has a general practice and is specialized in insolvency law and bancruptcy cases. He does not handle criminal cases. He is a member of the Burgenland Bar Association, a member of the Austrian Bar Association and a General Manager of a Holding Company owing hotel operating companies. Dr. Dönrnhöfer speaks English.

Dr. Peter Hajek, Blumengasse 5, 7000 Eisenstadt, Tel.: 62 740, Fax: 65 640, e-mail: hajek@eurojuris.at, homepage: http://www.eurojuris.at/hajek.hajek.htm, graduated from the University of Vienna in 1973, was admitted to the bar in 1978. He has a general practice, including all civil and criminal cases (including narcotics), and specializes in traffic accidents. Dr. Hajek speaks English.

Dr. Thomas Schreiner, of Schreiner & Lackner Rechtsanwäte OEG, Esterhazyplatz 6a, 7000 Eisenstadt, Tel.: 64044, Fax: 64044-30, e-mail: schreiner@rechtsanwaelte.co.at or ra.schreiner@aon.at, graduated from the University of Vienna in 1975, was admitted to the bar in 1982. Dr. Schreiner has a general practice, excluding criminal cases, and specializes in commercial, corporate, real estate, rental and bank securities law. He is a member of the disciplinary board of the Burgenland bar association. Dr. Schreiner speaks English and French.

CARINTHIA

KLAGENFURT

(telephone: prefix 0463 in-country, or internationally 463)

Dr. Hanno Burger-Scheidlin, Villacher Straße 1a/14, 9020 Klagenfurt, Tel.: 55056, Telefax: 56055, e-mail: office@burger-scheidlin.at, studied at the Universities of Innsbruck and Vienna, graduated in 1976 and was admitted to the bar in 1980. He has a general practice including civil and commercial law, contracts, collections, estates and probate cases, bancruptcy and also handles trade disputes He does not accept criminal and narcotics cases. He speaks English.

Dr. Herwig Jasbetz, Karfreitstraße 3/II, 9020 Klagenfurt, Tel.: 51 24 75, Fax: 51 22 59, studied law at the University of Graz, graduated in 1957, was admitted to the bar in 1965. He has a general practice, including criminal cases (also narcotics offenses), specializing in contract law. He speaks English and some Italian.

Dr. Günther Moshammer, Dr. A. Lemischplatz 4/II, 9020 Klagenfurt, Tel. and Fax: 55 4 80, studied at the University of Graz, graduated in 1952, was admitted to the bar in 1963. He has a general practice, handling all civil and criminal cases, estates, collections and trade disputes. He is specialized in traffic accident cases and banking law. Also handles narcotics offenses. He acts as disciplinary counsel for the bar association. He speaks English.

Dr. Heinz Walther, Alter Platz 23/I, 9020 Klagenfurt, Tel.: 572 63, Fax: 572 63-14, graduated from the University of Vienna in 1961, was admitted to the bar in 1970. He has a general practice, handling all civil and criminal cases (including narcotics offenses), estates, collections and trade disputes. He speaks English and has some knowledge of French and Italian.

VILLACH

(telephone: prefix 04242 in-country, or internationally 4242)

Dr. Peter Gradischnig, Moritschstrasse 7, 9500 Villach, Tel.: 251 32-0, Fax: 251 32-9. e-mail: gradischnig.gradischnig@utanet.at, homepage: http://www.top-10.at/recht/gradischnig, Dr. Gradischnig graduated from the University of Graz in 1954. He was admitted to the bar in 1961. He has a general practice, including criminal cases and drug offenses. He is specialized in estate cases and traffic accidents. He speaks English, French, Italian and Spanish.

Dr. Karl Heinz Kramer, Moritschstrasse 2/I, 9500 Villach, Tel.: 23 203, Fax: 23 203 3. Dr. Kramer graduated from the University of Vienna in 1985 and was admitted to the bar in 1991. He has a general practice, including criminal cases (also narcotics offenses). He speaks English and Italian.

LOWER AUSTRIA

ST. PÖLTEN

(telephone: prefix 02742 in-country, or internationally 2742)

Dr. Franz Amler, of Amler & Schwarz, Brunngasse 12/2, 3100 St. Pölten, Tel.: 35 27 18, Fax: 35 27 18-5, e-mail: michael_schwarz@online.edvg.co.at, graduated from the University of Vienna in 1982, was admitted to the bar in 1987. Dr. Amler has a general practice, handling all civil and criminal cases (including narcotics offenses). His specialties are traffic accidents and contracts. He speaks English.

Dr. Michael Schwarz, of Amler & Schwarz, Brunngasse 12/2, 3100 St. Pölten, Tel.: 35 27 18, Fax: 35 27 18 5, e-mail: michael_schwarz@online.edvg.co.at. He graduated from the University of Vienna in 1982, was admitted to the bar in 1988. Dr. Schwarz has a general practice regarding all civil law areas, with criminal cases being accepted only in connection with trade law (bankruptcy cases, etc.). Dr. Schwarz is a lecturer at the International College for Tourism and Management (Krems and Semmering, Lower Austria). He speaks English.

Dr. Max Urbanek, Riemerplatz 4, 3100 St. Pölten, Tel.: 35 35 75, Fax: 35 26 78. He graduated from the University of Vienna in 1966 and was admitted to the bar in 1973. Dr. Urbanek has a general practice regarding all civil law areas, with criminal law cases being accepted only in connection with trade law (bankruptcy cases, etc.). Dr. Urbanek is a member of the American Bar Association. He speaks fluent English.

BADEN BEI WIEN

(telephone: prefix 02252 in-country, or internationaly 2252)

Dr. Richard Heller, Wassergasse 14, 2500 Baden, Tel.: 432 34, Fax: 219 53, graduated from the University of Vienna on April 14, 1957, was admitted to the bar in 1963. He has a general practice, handling all civil and criminal cases (including narcotics offenses). Dr. Heller speaks English and Spanish.

Dr. Alexander Knotek, of Wolczik, Knotek & Wurst, Rathausgasse 9, 2500 Baden, Tel.: 430 56-0, Fax: 430 56-20, graduated from the University of Vienna in 1973, was admitted to the bar in 1979. Dr. Knotek has a general practice, handling all civil and criminal cases (including narcotics offenses). He speaks English.

Dr. Viktor Wolczik, of Wolczik, Knotek & Wurst, Rathausgasse 9, 2500 Baden, Tel.: 430 56-0, Fax: 430 56-20, graduated from the University of Vienna in 1954, was admitted to the bar in 1961. Dr. Wolczik has a general practice, handling all civil and criminal cases (including narcotics offenses). He speaks English.

Dr. Stefan Wurst, of Wolczik, Knotek & Wurst, Rathausgasse 9, 2500 Baden, Tel.: 430 56-0, Fax: 430 56-20, graduated from the University of Linz in 1985, was admitted to the bar in 1991. Dr. Wurst has a general practice, handling all civil and criminal cases (including narcotics offenses). He speaks English.

Dr. Erich Heliczer, Anton-Bauer-Strasse 2a, 2540 Bad Vöslau, Tel.: 715 73, Fax: 715 73-13, graduated from the University of Vienna in 1972, was admitted to the bar in 1980. Dr. Heliczer has a general practice, handling all civil and criminal cases. He specializes in estate matters, copyright law and press law. Dr. Heliczer speaks English, French and Italian.

PERCHTOLDSDORF

(telephone: prefix 01 in-country, or internationally 1)

Dr. Stefan Prokop, Walzengasse 2 (corner of Hochstrasse 29/2), 2380 Perchtoldsdorf, Tel.: 865 71 72, Fax: 865 71 73, graduated from the University of Vienna in 1983, was admitted to the bar in 1990. With the exception of narcotics matters, Dr. Prokopp has a general practice, handling all civil and criminal cases. He speaks English, French and Spanish.

STOCKERAU

(telephone: prefix 02266 in-country, or internationally 2266)

Dr. Manfred Dimmy, Schiessstattgasse 27, 2000 Stockerau, Tel.: 65697, graduated from the

University of Vienna in 1979, was admitted to the bar in 1985. Dr. Dimmy has a general practice, handling all civil and criminal cases (except narcotics offenses). He speaks English.

WIENER NEUSTADT

(telephone: prefix: 02622 in-country, or internationally 2622)

Dr. Doris Hohler-Rössel, Grazer Strasse 90, 2700 Wiener Neustadt, Tel.: 210 33-0, Fax: 210 33-14, e-mail: hohlerroesselra@aon.at, graduated from the University of Vienna in 1980, was admitted to the bar in 1986. Dr. Hohler-Rössel has a general practice, handling both civil and criminal cases (with the exception of narcotics matters). Her specialty is trade law. She speaks English.

Dr. Norbert Kosch, of Kosch & Partners, Hauptplatz 31, 2700 Wiener Neustadt, Tel.: 270 41, Fax: 292 46, homepage: http://www.kosch-partner.com, graduated from the University of Vienna in June 1952, was admitted to the bar in 1959. His law corporation includes three additional attorneys. He has a general practice, accepts all civil and criminal cases (including narcotics matters), as each of his associates has an area of specialization, also handles estate and collection cases. Dr. Kosch is a member of the disciplinary board of the Vienna bar association. He speaks English and French.

SALZBURG

CITY OF SALZBURG

(telephone: prefix 0662 in-country, or internationally 662)

Dr. Wolfgang Berger, Jr., of Berger & Aichlreiter, Sterneckstraße 55/I, 5020 Salzburg, Tel.: 87 08 36-0, Fax: 87 97 17, graduated from the University of Vienna in 1972, was admitted to the bar in 1977. Except for criminal cases, he has a general practice, specializing in business law and real estate matters. He speaks English.

Dr. Peter Cardona, Kaigasse 20, 5020 Salzburg, Tel.: 84 75 35, Fax: 84 75 354, graduated from the University of Vienna in 1967 and was admitted to the bar in 1975. He has a general practice, specializing in criminal law (including narcotics offenses), labor law, divorce law and traffic accidents. He is the president of the Austrian Automobile Association ARBÖ - Salzburg. He is fluent in English and speaks Italian, French and Spanish.

Dr. Norman Dick, of Norman Dick & Michael Dyck, Imbergstraße 15/I, 5020 Salzburg, Tel.: 87 14 85-0, Fax: 87 14 85-6, studied at the University of Salzburg, graduated in December 1972 and was admitted to the bar in July 1977. He has a general practice, specializing in corporation law, commercial law and unfair competition cases. He speaks English and French.

Dr. Friedrich Gehmacher, of Gehmacher & Hüttinger, Alter Markt 7, 5020 Salzburg, Tel.: 84 11 41-0, Fax: 84 84 15, e-mail: gehmacher-huettinger@aon.at, graduated from the University of Innsbruck in 1957, was admitted to the bar in 1964. He has a general practice, handling all criminal (including narcotics) and civil cases. He speaks English.

Mag. Carl Handlechner, Griesgasse 17/14, A-5020 Salzburg, Tel.: 84 92 30, Fax: 84 92 30 18, e-mail: carl.handlechner@mh.sbg.ac.at, graduated from the University of Salzburg in 1990 and was admitted to the bar in 1998. He has a general practice, specializing in criminal law (including narcotics offenses) and civil law. He speaks English and Italian.

Dr. Ulrike Hauser, of Hauser & Herzog, Haunspergstrasse 33, 5020 Salzburg, Tel.: 87 00 46 0,

Fax 87 84 62, e-mail: office@raehauser-herzog.com, graduated from the University of Salzburg in 1984 and was admitted to the bar in 1991. She has a general practice specialized in criminal law (including narcotics offenses), domestic and matrimonial law, law of descent and distributions, actions for damages and contracts. Dr. Hauser speaks English and French.

Dr. Utho Hosp, of Hosp & Wamprechtshamer, Mozartplatz 4, 5020 Salzburg, Tel.: 84 31 31, Fax: 84 03 404, e-mail: hosp-partner@salzburg.co.at, graduated from the University of Salzburg in 1968 and was admitted to the bar in 1974. He has a general practice, specializing in industrial law, traffic and insurance law, damages law, family law, civil and commercial law. He also handles criminal cases including narcotics offenses, Dr. Hosp speaks English.

Dr. Manfred Jokesch, Kaigasse 11, 5020 Salzburg, Tel.:84 21 24, Fax: 84 00 81, e-mail: ra-jokesch@rechtsanwaelte.co.at, graduated from the University of Graz in 1969 and was admitted to the bar in 1976. He has a general practice, specializing in bancruptcy, family law, divorce law and criminal law (including narcotics offenses). Dr. Jokesch speaks English, Italian and French.

Dr. Stefan Vargha, Georg-Wagner-Gasse 5, 5020 Salzburg, Tel.: 82 93 160, Fax: 82 93 11 32, e-mail: ra-waltl-vargha-law@aon.at, graduated from the University of Innsbruck in 1968 and was admitted to the bar in 1975. He has a general practice, specialized in civil law, commercial law and company law. He does not accept criminal cases. Dr. Vargha speaks English and Hungarian.

Dr. Karl Wampl, of Wampl & Mühlberger, Künstlerhausgasse 4, 5020 Salzburg, Tel.: 84 15 41, Fax: 84 15 41-4, graduated from the University of Salzburg in 1975 and was admitted to the bar in 1983. He has a general practice, specializing in criminal cases (including narcotics offenses) and foreign law. Dr. Wampl speaks English.

ZELL AM SEE

(telephone: prefix 06542 in-country, or internationally 6542)

Dr. Rüdiger Hanifle, Schillerstraße 22, 5700 Zell am See, Tel.: 722 04, Fax: 732 44, e-mail: ra-dr.hanifle@EUnet.at. He studied at the University of Innsbruck, graduated in 1982 and was admitted to the bar in 1987. Succeeding his father who recently retired, Dr. Hanifle maintains a general practice, including civil and criminal matters, but excluding narcotics offenses. His areas of specialization are trade and traffic law as well as contract matters. He speaks English.

STYRIA

GRAZ

(telephone: prefix 0316 in-country, or internationally 316)

Dr. Anton Cuber, of Bartl & Cuber, Hauptplatz 3, 8010 Graz, Tel.: 83 75 17 0, Fax: 83 75 17-20, e-mail: p.bartl@bartl-cuber.at or kanzlei@bartl-cuber.at, homepage: http://www.bartl-cuber.at, graduated from the University of Graz in 1989 and was admitted to the bar in 1995. He has a general practice, specializing in trade law excluding criminal cases. Dr. Cuber speaks English and French.

Dr. Ulrich O. Daghofer, LL.M., Albrechtgasse 3, 8010 Graz, Tel.: 82 43 42, Fax: 83 77 68, e-mail: dahofer@vip.rdp.at, graduated from the University of Graz in 1969 and from Southern Methodist University in 1971 and was admitted to the bar in June 1975. He specializes in commercial, private, inheritance, and product liability law. He handles criminal cases only under exceptional circumstances. Dr. Daghofer is a member of the Executive Council of the Styrian Bar and a court interpreter for the English language.

Dr. Manfred Eichholzer, Schmiedgasse 19, 8010 Graz, Tel.: 83 02 71, Fax: 81 13 59, graduated from the University of Graz in 1970 and was admitted to the bar in 1971. Dr. Eichholzer specializes in business, contract and international law. He does not accept criminal cases. Dr. Eichholzer speaks English, Italian and French.

Dr. Ralph Forcher, of Eisenberger, Herzog, Nierhaus, Forcher & partner, Tel.: 36 47, Fax: 36 47 58, e-mail: ehnfr@sime.com, graduated from the University of Graz in 1984 and was admitted to the bar in 1989. He has a general practice, specializing in corporate and commercial law, litigations, arbitrations and contracts. He handles only "white collar crime" criminal cases. Dr. Forcher speaks English.

Dr. Harald Gerl, Radetzkystraße 6, 8020 Graz, Tel.: 83 04 42, Fax: 82 11 28, e-mail: dr.gerl@aon.at graduated from the University of Graz in 1955 and was admitted to the bar in 1963. Dr. Gerl has a general civil law practice. He does not accept criminal cases. He holds offices in the Styrian Bar Association and with the German Chamber of Commerce in Austria. Dr. Gerl speaks English.

Dr. Gunter Griss, of Griss, Krenn, Mächler & Holler, Glacisstraße 67, 8010 Graz, Tel.: 83 03 04, Fax: 83 81 17, e-mail: g.griss@griss.at, homepage: http://www.griss.at, graduated from the University of Graz in 1967 and from the University of Chicago (M.L.C.) in 1970, studied and practiced also in England and France. Dr. Griss has a general practice, handling all civil and criminal cases (including narcotics offenses). He specializes in international private and commercial law, regulation of real property and natural resources, including expropriations. He is an official court interpreter for English and French.

Dr. Alexander Isola, of Schönherr, Barfuss, Torggler & Partner, Marburgerkai 47, 8010 Graz, Tel.: 833 777 0, Fax: 833 777 33, e-mail: a.isola@schoenherr.at, graduated from the University of Graz in 1981 and from the New York University School of Law in 1984. He was admitted to the bar in 1986. Dr. Isola has a general civil law practice, specializing in commercial law and bankruptcy proceedings. He is a member of the American Chamber of Commerce in Austria. Dr. Isola speaks fluent English.

Dr. Rainer Kurbos, Rosegger Kai 5, 8010 Graz, Tel.: 82 77 22, Fax: 82 77 22-16, graduated from the University of Graz in 1979 and was admitted to the bar in 1984. Dr. Kurbos does not accept criminal cases. His specialties are contracts, building regulations, business licenses and product liability. Dr. Kurbos speaks English.

Dr. Hans Werner Schmidt, Brockmanngasse 63, 8010 Graz, Tel.: 82 54 28, Fax: 82 33 86, e-mail: hw_schmidt@son.at, graduated from the University of Graz in 1986 and was admitted to the bar in 1992. He has a general practice, specializing in actions for damages and warranty claims, traffic accident cases and criminal cases (including narcotics offenses). Dr. Schmidt speaks English and Italian.

Dr. Fritz Starnberg, Kaiserfeldgasse 19, 8010 Graz, Tel.: 82 20 21, Fax: 82 20 21 4, e-mail: ra-dr.starnberg.law.office@aon.at, graduated from the University of Graz in 1985 and was admitted to the bar in 1990. He has a general practice, specializing in criminal cases (including narcotics offenses), divorce law, estate cases and contracts. Dr. Starnberg speaks English.

LEOBEN

(telephone: prefix 03842 in-country, or internationally 3842)

DDr. Manfred Erschen, of Erschen & Jesser, Parkstraße 3, 8700 Leoben, Tel.: 43 4 43, Fax: 45 2 30, e-mail: jesser-erschen@t-online.at, graduated from the University of Graz, where he obtained his Ph.D.(1948) and his Jur.D.(1951). He was admitted to the bar in 1958. He has a general practice, including criminal cases (handling also narcotics offenses). Dr. Erschen specializes in commercial and tax law. He speaks English.

Dr. Harald W. Jesser, of Erschen & Jesser, Parkstraße 3, 8700 Leoben, Tel.: 43 4 43, Fax: 45 2 30, e-mail: jesser-erschen@t-online.at, graduated from the University of Graz in 1948 and was admitted to the bar in 1955. He has a general practice, also handling criminal cases (including narcotics offenses), and specializes in international civil law, especially for the countries of Eastern Europe. He speaks English.

UPPER AUSTRIA

LINZ

(telephone: prefix 0732 in-country, or internationally 732)

Dr. Herwig Anderle, Kaisergasse 18/II, 4020 Linz, Tel.: 77 62 76, Fax 77 62 76 81, graduated from the University of Innsbruck in 1987, and was admitted to the bar in 1988. He has a general practice and accepts criminal cases only in connection with trade disputes. His specialties are real estate sales, divorce suits, contracts, tenancy agreements, estates and trade disputes. Dr. Anderle speaks fluent English.

Dr. Ludwig Beurle, of Beurle, Oberndorfer, Mitterlehner, Landstraße 9, 4020 Linz, Tel.: 77 16 53-0, Fax: 77 16 53-18, e-mail: office@bom.at, graduated from the University of Innsbruck in 1981 and was admitted to the bar in 1985. Except for criminal cases, Dr. Beurle has a general practice, specializing in commercial and civil law. Dr. Beurle speaks English.

Dr. Wolfgang Moringer, of Moringer & Moser, Hauptstrasse 33/2, 4040 Linz, Tel.: 73 65 14, Fax: 73 65 14-9, e-mail: office@mormos.com, homepage: http://www.mormos.com, graduated from the University of Linz and was admitted to the bar in 1977. He has a general practice specializing in commercial law, penal law concerning business offenses, European law and criminal law (including narcotics offenses). He is a member of the Committee of the Upper Austrian Bar Association. Dr. Moringer speaks English.

Dr. Hans Oberndorfer, of Beurle, Oberndorfer, Mitterlehner, Landstrasse 9, 4020 Linz, Tel.: 77 16 53-0, Fax: 77 16 53-18, e-mail: office@bom.at, graduated from the University of Vienna in 1955 and was admitted to the bar in 1963. Except for criminal cases, Dr. Oberndorfer has a general practice, specializing in commercial and civil law. Dr. Oberndorfer speaks English.

Mag. Harald Pisar, of Eigl & Pisar, Lederergasse 33b, 4020 Linz, Tel.: 79 39 00, Fax: 79 39 00-15, e-mail: eigl.pisar@eunet.at, graduated from the University of Linz in 1991 and was admitted to the bar in 1997. He has a general practice, specializing in criminal cases (including narcotics offenses), collection cases, family law, accidents, contracts, compensation law, liability law and company start-up. Mag. Pisar speaks English and French.

Mag. Thomas P. Schweiger, LL.M. (Duke), of MRS (Meyndt, Ransmayr, Schweiger) & Partners law firm, Kaplanhofstrasse 2, 4020 Linz, Tel.: 79 69 00 0, Fax: 79 69 06, e-mail: t.schweiger@m-r-s-.at, graduated from the University of Linz in 1993 and the Duke University School of Law in 1996, and was admitted to the bar in 1999. He has a general practice, specializing in corporate and other transactions, corporate counsel, arbitration and litigations (mostly for corporations), trade disputes and estates. He is a member of the Austrian Franchise Federation, German Arbitration Association, German Lawyers Association, Moot Alumni Association. Mag. Schweiger speaks fluent English and Russian.

Dr. Gerhard Wagner, of Wagner & Reitmayr, Spittelwiese 6, 4020 Linz, Tel.: 77 58 00, Fax: 77 58 00-15, e-mail: ra-wagreit@tbxa.telecom.at or office@rechtsanwalt-wagner.com, graduated from the University of Linz in 1981 and was admitted to the bar in 1987. Dr. Wagner has a general practice, handling criminal cases (except narcotics) as well as all types of civil cases. His areas of specialization are trade law, contracts, collection cases, and human rights. He speaks English.

GMUNDEN

(telephone: prefix 07612 in-country, or internationally)

Dr. Heinz Ortner, of Ortner & Ortner, Kirchengasse 6, 4810 Gmunden, Tel.: 64 511, Fax: 64 511-10, e-mail: ra-ortner-gmunden@aon.at, graduated from the University of Graz in 1957 and was admitted to the bar in 1967. He has a general practice, also handling criminal cases (including narcotics offenses), collection cases and trade disputes. He is a member of the Gmunden City Council. He speaks fluent English.

WELS

(telephone: prefix 07242 in-country, or internationally 7242)

Dr. Friedrich W. Ganzert, of the law firm Ganzert & Ganzert, Dr. Koss-Straße 1, 4600 Wels, Tel.: 41 1 22, Fax: 41 1 22 32, e-mail: office@ganzert.at, graduated from the University of Graz in 1966. He also holds a master's degree in International Relations from the University of Denver, Colorado. Dr. Ganzert was admitted to the bar in 1976. He has a general practice, handling all types of civil and criminal cases (including narcotics offenses), specializing in business law. He speaks English and French.

Dr.Johannes Kirschner, Fabrikstrasse 26, 4600 Wels, Tel.: 6 73 73, Fax: 6 82 70, e-mail: kanzlei.kirschner@merlin.at, homepage: http://www.meinanwalt.at/kirschner graduated from the University of Salzburg in 1980 and was admitted to the bar in 1986. He has a general practice specializing in criminal law (including narcotics offenses), family law, especially divorce law, maintenance, custody, traffic law, insurance law, especially compensation (Member of the Pan-European Organization of Personal Injury Lawyers). Dr. Kirschner speaks English.

Dr. Christopher Straberger, Maria-Theresia-Strasse 19, 4600 Wels, Tel.: 471 75 or 472 44, Fax: 641 222, e-mail: straberger.law@aon.at, graduated from the University of Vienna in 1986 and was admitted to the bar in 1996. He has a general practice specializing in contract law (e.g. joint ventures, distribution agreements), trademark law, insolvency law, business law in general, question relating to regulations of the European Union, trade disputes and estate cases. He does not handle criminal cases. Dr. Straberger speaks fluent English.

VORARLBERG

BREGENZ

(telephone: prefix 05574 in-country, or internationally 5574)

Dr. Walter Derganz, Weiherstraße 3, 6900 Bregenz, Tel.: 423 76-0, Fax: 423 76-4, studied at the Universities of Vienna and Innsbruck, graduated in 1965, was admitted to the bar in 1973. He has a general practice, handling all civil and criminal cases (including narcotics offenses). He is an official court interpreter for the English language.

Dr. Meinrad Einsle, of Stolz-Manhart-Einsle, Römerstrasse 19, 6900 Bregenz, Tel.: 42 3 64, Fax: 42 3 64 20, e-mail: stolz.manhart.einsle@vol.at, graduated from the University of Innsbruck in 1991 and was admitted to the bar in 1997. He has a general practice, specializing in criminal law (including narcotics offenses), civil law, trade law, tax and tariff law and European law. Dr. Einsle speaks English.

Dr. Alexander Matt, of Matt & Matt, Belruptstrasse 8, 6900 Bregenz, Tel.: 46 6 08, Fax; 46 6 08 4, e-mail: justitia@aon.at, graduated from the University of Innsbruck in 1981 and was admitted to the bar in 1986. He has a general practice, specializing in contract law, business law and real estate law. He does not handle criminal cases. Dr. Matt speaks English.

Dr. Katja Matt, of Matt & Matt, Belruptstrasse 8, 6900 Bregenz, Tel.: 46 6 08, Fax: 46 6 08 4, e-mail: justitia@aon.at, graduated from the University of Innsbruck in 1983 and was admitted to the bar in 1998. She has a general practice, specializing in criminal law (including narcotics offenses) and family law. Dr. Matt speaks English.

Dr. Helgar Georg Schneider, LLM , of Preisl & Schneider, Reichsstrasse 5a, 6900 Bregenz, Tel.: 44943-0, Fax: 44943-3, e-mail: schneider@preisl-schneider.at, graduated from the University of Innsbruck School of Law in 1987, from the University of Virginia School of Law in 1988 and from the University of Graz School of Law in 1992 and was admitted to the bar in 1996. He has a general practice, specializing in business law, competition law, company law, family law and inheritance law. He is co-author of the book *ABC der Vertrags- und Testamentsmuster* or *ABC of Contract and Last Will Models* Linde Publishers, Vienna. He is an official court interpreter for the English language.

FELDKIRCH

(telephone: prefix 05522 in-country, or internationally 5522)

Dr. Christian Cerha, Mühletorplatz 2, 6800 Feldkirch, Tel.: 328 70, Fax: 328 71. Dr. Cerha studied at the Universities of Vienna, Innsbruck and London, graduated from the University of Innsbruck in 1973 and from the University of London (LL.M.) in 1974 and was admitted to the bar in 1985. He has a general practice, handling all civil matters, out-of-court settlements, criminal and commercial cases. He is a court interpreter for the English language.

Dr. Gerold Hirn, of Hirn & Hirn, Gilmstraße 2, 6800 Feldkirch, Tel.: 757 01, Fax: 779 03, e-mail: hirn@hirn.cable.vol.at, studied law at the University of Innsbruck and was admitted to the bar in May 1974. He has a general practice, handling civil and criminal cases (including drug offenses) and specializing in commercial law. He speaks English.

US AND COUNTRY CONTACTS

1. AUSTRIAN GOVERNMENT AGENCIES

Embassy of Austria in the United States
3524 International Court N.W.
Washington, DC 20008
Phone: (202) 895-6700
Fax: (202) 895-6750
Consular Section:
Phone: (202) 895-6767
Fax: (202) 895-6773

Federal Agency for Industrial Cooperation and Development

In the U.S.: In Austria:

Austrian Business Agency Austrian Business Agency
150 East 52nd Street, 32nd floor Opernring 3-5
New York, NY 10022 A-1010 Vienna, Austria
Phone: (212) 980 7970 Phone: (43 1) 588 58-0
Fax: (212) 980 7975 Fax: (43 1) 586 86 59
E-mail: austrian.business@telecom.at

Website: http://www.telecom.at/AustrianBusinessInfo/

Federal Ministry of Economics and Labor
Stubenring 1
A-1010 Vienna
Phone: (43 1) 711 00-0
Fax: (43 1) 713 93 11 or 713 79 95
Website: www.bmwa.gv.at

Federal Ministry of Agriculture, Forestry, Environment and Water Management
Stubenring 1
A-1010 Vienna
Phone: (43 1) 711 00-0
Fax: (43 1) 711 00-2127
Website: www.bmlf.gv.at/ge

2. AUSTRIAN TRADE ASSOCIATIONS/ CHAMBERS OF COMMERCE

Austrian Trade Commission operates offices in the U.S. at the following locations:

New York: 150 East 52nd Street
32nd floor
New York, NY 10022
Phone: (212) 421 5250
Fax: (212) 751 4675
E-mail: atc_ny@ix.netcom.com

Illinois: 500 North Michigan Avenue
Suite 1950
Chicago, IL 60611
Phone: (312) 644 5556
Fax: (312) 644 6526
E-mail: atc-chi@ix.netcom.com

California: 11601 Wilshire Blvd.
Suite 2420
Los Angeles, CA 90025
Phone: (310) 477 9988
Fax: (310) 477 1643
E-mail: atc-la@ix.netcom.com

Washington, D.C.: 1350 Connecticut Avenue N.W.
Suite 501
Washington, DC 20036
Phone: (202) 835-8962
Fax: (202) 835-8960
E-mail: atc-wdc@austriantradedc.org

The following telephone number can be used for all Austrian Trade Delegates: 1-800-VIP-AHST.
Website: http://www.austriantrade.org

American Chamber of Commerce in Austria
Porzellangasse 35
A-1090 Vienna, Austria
Phone: (43 1) 319 57 51
Fax: (43 1) 319 51 51
E-mail: office@amcham.or.at
Website: www.amcham.or.at

Wirtschaftskammer Oesterreich
(Austrian Federal Economic Chamber)
Wiedner Hauptstrasse 64
A-1045 Vienna, Austria
Phone: (43 1) 501 05-4204
Fax: (43 1) 502 06-255
E-mail: aw.nordamerika@aw.wk.or.at
Website: www.wko.at/aw

Fachverband der Elektro- und Elektronikindustrie Oesterreichs
(Association of the Electric and Electronic Industry)
Mariahilfer Strasse 37-39
A-1060 Vienna, Austria
Phone: (43 1) 588 39-0
Fax: (43 1) 586 69 71
Website: www.feei.at

ADV Arbeitsgemeinschaft fuer Datenverarbeitung
(EDP Association)
Tratternhof 2
A-1010 Vienna, Austria
Phone: (43 1) 533 09 13
Fax: (43 1) 533 09 13-77
Website: www.adv.at

Oesterreichische Computer Gesellschaft
(Austrian Computer Association)
Wollzeile 1-3
A-1010 Vienna, Austria
Phone: (43 1) 512 02 35
Fax: (43 1) 512 02 35-9
E-mail: ocg@ocg.at
Website: www.ocg.at

OEGUT - Oesterreichische Gesellschaft fuer Umwelt und Technik
(Austrian Association for Environment and Technology)
Türkenstrasse 9/21
A-1090 Vienna, Austria
Phone: (43 1) 315 63 93-0
Fax: (43 1) 315 63 93-22
Website: www.oegut.at

3. AUSTRIAN MARKET RESEARCH FIRMS

Consent Betriebsberatung Ges.m.b.H
Dommayergasse 4
A-1130 Vienna, Austria
Phone: (43 1) 877 30 03-0
Fax: (43 1) 876 47 04
E-mail: consult@consent.at
Dr. Fessel GfK Institut fuer Marktforschung
Hainburger Strasse 33
A-1030 Vienna, Austria
Phone: (43 1)71710-0
Fax: (43 1) 71710-194
E-mail: fessel@gfk.at
Website: www.gfk.at

GMB Gesellschaft fur Marketingberatung
Arnethgasse 50
A-1160 Vienna, Austria
Phone: (43 1) 485 57 01
Fax: (43 1) 485 49 57

Integral Markt- und Meinungsforschungs Ges.m.b.H.
Mohsgasse 2/4A
A-1030 Vienna, Austria
Phone: (43 1) 799 19 94-0
Fax: (43 1) 799 19 94-18
E-mail: office@integral.co.at
Website: integral.co.at

Institut fuer Markt- und Meinungsforschung Ges.m.b.H.
Kaiserstrasse 55
A-1070 Vienna, Austria
Phone: (43 1) 526 55 84-0
Fax: (43 1) 526 55 84-42
E-mail: austria@research-int.com
Website: research-int.com

4. AUSTRIAN COMMERCIAL BANKS

Creditanstalt AG Bank Austria AG
Schottengasse 6 Am Hof 2
A-1010 Vienna A-1010 Vienna
Austria Austria

Phone: (43 1) 531 31-0 Phone (43 1) 711 91-0
Fax: (43 1) 531 31-4699 Fax: (43 1) 711 91-56155
Website: www.creditanstalt.co.at Website: www.bankaustria.com

Erste Bank der Raiffeisen Zentralbank
oesterreichischen Oesterreich AG
Sparkassen AG Am Stadtpark 9
Graben 21 A-1030 Vienna
A-1010 Vienna Austria
Austria Phone: (43 1) 717 07-0
Phone: (43 1) 531 00-0711 Fax: (43 1) 717 07-1648
Fax: (43 1) 531 00-2272 Website: www. rzb.at
Website: www.erstebank.at Website: www.raiffeisen.at

5. U.S. COMMERCIAL SERVICE

U.S. Embassy in Austria To mail from the United States:
Boltzmanngasse 16 Commercial Service Vienna
A-1091 Vienna, Austria 9900 Vienna Place
Phone: (43 1) 313 39-0 Washington, DC 20521-9900
Fax: (43 1) 310 69 17
E-mail: vienna.office.box@mail.doc.gov
Website: www.usembassy-vienna.at/cs.html

6. U.S.-BASED MULTIPLIERS

The Association for Manufacturing Technology
7901 Westpark Dr.
McLean, VA 22102
Phone: (703) 893-2900
Fax: (703) 893-1151
E-mail: amt@mfg.tech.org
Website: www.mfg.tech.org

Health Industry Manufacturers Association
1200 G. Street, N.W. Suite 400
Washington, DC 20005
Phone: (202) 783-8700
Fax: (202) 783-8750
E-mail: hima@himanet.org
Website: www.himanet.com

American Electronics Association
5201 Great America Pkwy, Suite 520
Santa Clara, CA 95054
Phone: (408) 970-4200
Fax: (408) 986 1247
E-mail: csc@aeanet.org
Website: www.aeanet.org

Dental Manufacturers of America
123 S. Broad Street, Suite 2030
Philadelphia, PA 19109-1020.
Phone: (215) 731-9975
Fax: (215) 731-9984
Internet: www.dmanews.org
E-mail: staff@dmanews.org

National Electrical Manufacturers Association
Diagnostic Imaging & Therapy Systems Div.
1300 N. 17th Street, Suite 1847
Rosslyn, VA 22209
Phone: (703) 841 3200
Fax: (703) 841 3300
E-mail: webmaster@nema.org
Website: www.nema.org

Telecommunications Industry Association
Suite 300
2500 Wilson Blvd.
Arlington, VA 22201-3834
Tel.: (703) 907 7700
Fax: (703) 907 7727
Website: www.tiaonline.org

Telecommunications Industry Association
Government Relations and International Affairs
Suite 350
1300 Pennsylvania Ave, N.W.
Washington, D.C. 20004
Phone: (202) 383-1480
Fax: (202) 383-1495
Website: www.tiaonline.org

Environmental Industry Associations
4301 Connecticut Ave, N.W., Suite 300
Washington, D.C. 20008
Phone: (202) 244 4700
Fax: (202) 966 4818
Website: www.envasns.org

U.S.-Austrian Chamber of Commerce, Inc.
165 West 46th Street, Suite 1112
New York, NY 10036
Phone and Fax: (212) 819-0117

7. WASHINGTON-BASED U.S. GOVERNMENT CONTACTS

Lisa Tomlinson
Austria Desk, Room 3036
U.S. Department of Commerce

14th & Constitution Ave, N.W.
Washington, DC 20230
Phone: (202) 482-2434
Fax: (202) 482-2897

Europe Team Leader
Foreign Agricultural Service
Room 5517S
U.S. Department of Agriculture
Washington, DC 20250-1024
Phone: (202) 720-1322
Fax: (202) 720-0069
Website: www.fas.usda.gov

U.S. Department of Agriculture
Foreign Agricultural Service
attn: Maureen Quinn
Director, Information Div.
Room 5074-S
Washington, D.C. 20250-1024
Phone: (202) 720-3448
Fax: (202) 720-1727
E-mail: quinn@fas.usda.gov
Website: www.fas.usda.gov

John Greifer, Director
Trade Support Team
U.S. Department of Agriculture
APHIS
Room 1132, SO. Bldg.
12th and Independence Ave., SW
Washington, DC 20252
Phone: (202) 720-7677 or 78
Fax: (202) 690-2861
E-Mail: john.k.greifer@usda.gov

Janet Thomas
Director
Multilateral Development Bank Operations
U.S. Department of Commerce
USA Trade Center
14th Street N.W.
Washington, D.C. 20230
Phone: (202) 482-3399
Fax.: (202) 482-3914
E-mail: Janet.Thomas@mail.doc.gov

TPCC Trade Information Center number in Washington: 1-800-USA-TRADE
1-800-872-8723, Fax: (202) 482-4473.
ITA's Home Page: http://www.ita.doc.gov
Natioanl Trade Data Bank (NTDB): http://www.stat.usa.gov/

Austria information: http://www.austria.org./ausinfo.shtml
Economic news from Austria: http://www.austria.org/econ11.shtml

AUSTRIA OFFICES IN THE US

AUSTRIAN TRADE COMMISSION NEW YORK

Scope of activities:
Main office (coordination)

covered areas:
Connecticut, Delaware, Maine, Massachusetts, New Hampshire, New York, New Jersey, North Carolina, Pennsylvania, Rhode Island, Vermont, West Virginia, and the Bermudas

Trade Commissioner

Bruno FREYTAG

Deputy Trade Commissioner

Robert PUNKENHOFER
Gerd BOMMER
Peter GATSCHA (Technology)

Address:

The Austrian Trade Commission
150 East 52nd Street
32nd Floor
New York, NY 10022
Telephone: 1(212) 421-5250
Telefax: 1(212) 751-4675
newyork@wko.at

AUSTRIAN TRADE COMMISSION WASHINGTON D.C.

scope of activities: Trade Policy and Promotion

covered area:
Washington D.C., Maryland, Virginia
Alabama, Arkansas, Bahamas, Florida, Georgia, Louisiana, Maryland, Mississippi, Oklahoma, Puerto Rico, South Carolina, Tennessee, Texas, Virginia, US-Virgin Islands

Trade Commissioner

Heinz SEITINGER

Deputy Trade Commissioner

Guenter KLEEDORFER

Address:

The Commercial Counsellor
at the Austrian Embassy
1350 Connecticut Avenue NW
Suite 501
Washington DC 20036 / USA
Telephone: 1(202) 835-8962
Telefax: 1(202) 835-8960
washington@wko.at

AUSTRIAN TRADE COMMISSION CHICAGO

covered area:
Illinois, Indiana, Iowa, Kansas, Kentucky,
Michigan, Minnesota, Missouri, Nebraska,
North Dakota, Ohio, South Dakota, Wisconsin

Trade Commissioner

Ms. Gudrun HAGER

Address:

The Austrian Trade Commission
500 North Michigan Avenue
Suite 1950
Chicago, IL 60611-3704 / USA
Telephone: 1(312) 644-5556
Telefax: 1(312) 644-6526
chicago@wko.at

AUSTRIAN TRADE COMMISSION LOS ANGELES

covered area:
Alaska, Arizona, California, Colorado, Hawaii,
Idaho, Montana, Nevada, New Mexico, Oregon,
Utah, Washington, Wyoming, Pacific Islands

Trade Commissioner

Hubert H. SCHWETZ

Deputy Trade Commissioner

Nikolaus BERG
Anton EMSENHUBER (Technology)

Address:

The Austrian Trade Commission
11601 Wilshire Blvd.
Suite 2420
Los Angeles, CA 90025 / USA
Telephone: 1(310) 477-9988
Telefax: 1(310) 477-1643
losangeles@wko.at

Austrian Trade Commission Atlanta

Covered Area:
Alabama, Arkansas, Bahamas, Florida, Georgia,
Louisiana, Maryland, Mississippi, Oklahoma,
Puerto Rico, South Carolina, Tennessee,
Texas, Virginia, US-Virgin Islands

Trade Commissioner

Heinz SEITINGER

Address:

The Austrian Trade Commission
4200 Northside Parkway, NW
Bldg.1, Ste. 300
Atlanta, Georgia 30327 / USA
Telephone: 1(404) 995-9347
Telefax: 1(404) 995-9348
atc-atl@mindspring.com

AUSTRIAN FEDERAL ECONOMIC CHAMBER

The Austrian Federal Economic Chamber
Wiedner Hauptstrasse 63
P.O.Box 150
A-1045 Wien
Austria/Europe

Telephone: 011-43-1-50105
Telefax: 011-43-1-50105-255
e-mail: aw.leitung@wko.at
Website:www.wko.at

Austrian Federal Economic Chamber
North America Desk

covered areas:
Canada, United States of America, Bahamas,
the Bermudas, Puerto Rico, US Virgin Islands

Head of the North American Desk

Peter ATHANASIADIS

Address:

The Austrian Federal Economic Chamber
Wiedner Hauptstrasse 63
P.O.Box 150
A-1045 Wien
Austria/Europe

Telephone: 011-43-1-50105 ext. 4204, 4228
Telefax: 011-43-1-50105-255
e-mail: aw.nordamerika@aw.wk.or.at
Website:www.wko.at

Office Hours: Monday to Friday 08 A.M. to 04.30 P.M.

TAX TREATY NETWORK

Austria has concluded tax treaties with the following countries:

Argentina
Australia
Belgium
Brazil
Bulgaria
Canada
China
Cyprus
Czechoslovakia

The tax treaty with Czechoslovakia is now being applied to both the Czech Republic and to Slovakia.

Denmark
Egypt
Finland
France
Germany
Greece
Hungary
India
Indonesia
Republic of Ireland
Israel
Italy
Japan
Republic of Korea
Liechtenstein
Luxembourg
Malaysia
Malta
The Netherlands
Norway
Pakistan
The Philippines
Poland
Portugal
Romania
Slovenia
South Africa
Spain
Sweden
Switzerland
Thailand
Tunisia
Turkey
UK
Ukraine
USA
USSR

The tax treaty with the USSR is now being applied to all states that formerly belonged to the Soviet Union, except the Baltic States.

The purpose of the above treaties is to avoid double taxation. For royalties, interest and dividends the credit method, in which the country of residence grants a tax credit for tax paid at source is generally used. With regard to other income, under some treaties the exemption method is used, in which the country of residence exempts other income from taxation. In a few cases the credit method applies to all types of income. Tax treaties regularly reduce the rate of withholding taxes on royalties, interest and dividends.

Austria has entered into tax treaties with regard to **inheritance tax** with

France
Germany
Hungary
Liechtenstein
Sweden
Switzerland
USA

If no treaty exists, the Ministry of Finance may grant unilateral relief from double taxation

BASIC TITLES ON AUSTRIA

IMPORTANT!
All publications are updated annually!
Please contact IBP, Inc. at ibpusa3@gmail.com for the latest ISBNs and additional information

TITLE
Austria A "Spy" Guide - Strategic Information and Developments
Austria A Spy" Guide"
Austria Air Force Handbook
Austria Air Force Handbook
Austria Aviation and Aerospace Industry Handbook
Austria Aviation and Aerospace Industry Handbook
Austria Banking & Financial Market Handbook
Austria Banking & Financial Market Handbook
Austria Business and Investment Opportunities Yearbook
Austria Business and Investment Opportunities Yearbook
Austria Business and Investment Opportunities Yearbook Volume 1 Strategic Information and Opportunities
Austria Business Intelligence Report - Practical Information, Opportunities, Contacts
Austria Business Intelligence Report - Practical Information, Opportunities, Contacts
Austria Business Law Handbook - Strategic Information and Basic Laws
Austria Business Law Handbook - Strategic Information and Basic Laws
Austria Business Law Handbook - Strategic Information and Basic Laws
Austria Business Law Handbook - Strategic Information and Basic Laws
Austria Business Success Guide - Basic Practical Information and Contacts
Austria Clothing & Textile Industry Handbook
Austria Clothing & Textile Industry Handbook
Austria Company Laws and Regulations Handbook
Austria Company Laws and Regulations Handbook - Strategic Information and Basic Laws
Austria Constitution and Citizenship Laws Handbook - Strategic Information and Basic Laws
Austria Country Study Guide - Strategic Information and Developments
Austria Country Study Guide - Strategic Information and Developments
Austria Country Study Guide - Strategic Information and Developments Volume 1 Strategic Information and Developments
Austria Country Study Guide Volume 1 Strategic Information and Developments
Austria Criminal Laws, Regulations and Procedures Handbook - Strategic Information, Regulations, Procedures
Austria Customs, Trade Regulations and Procedures Handbook
Austria Customs, Trade Regulations and Procedures Handbook
Austria Diplomatic Handbook - Strategic Information and Developments
Austria Diplomatic Handbook - Strategic Information and Developments
Austria Ecology & Nature Protection Handbook
Austria Ecology & Nature Protection Handbook
Austria Ecology & Nature Protection Laws and Regulation Handbook
Austria Economic & Development Strategy Handbook

TITLE
Austria Economic & Development Strategy Handbook
Austria Economic Assistance to Developing Countries Handbook
Austria Economic Assistance to Developing Countries Handbook
Austria Economic Assistance to Developing Countries Handbook
Austria Economic Assistance to Developing Countries Handbook
Austria Education System and Policy Handbook
Austria Electoral, Political Parties Laws and Regulations Handbook - Strategic Information, Regulations, Procedures
Austria Energy Policy, Laws and Regulation Handbook
Austria Export-Import Trade and Business Directory
Austria Export-Import Trade and Business Directory
Austria Foreign Policy and Government Guide
Austria Foreign Policy and Government Guide
Austria Immigration Guide
Austria Immigration Guide
Austria Immigration Laws and Regulations Handbook - Strategic Information and Basic Laws
Austria Industrial and Business Directory
Austria Industrial and Business Directory
Austria Insolvency (Bankruptcy) Laws and Regulations Handbook - Strategic Information and Basic Laws
Austria Internet and E-Commerce Investment and Business Guide - Strategic and Practical Information: Regulations and Opportunities
Austria Internet and E-Commerce Investment and Business Guide - Strategic and Practical Information: Regulations and Opportunities
Austria Investment and Business Guide - Strategic and Practical Information
Austria Investment and Business Guide - Strategic and Practical Information
Austria Investment and Business Guide - Strategic and Practical Information
Austria Investment and Business Guide - Strategic and Practical Information
Austria Investment and Business Profile - Basic Information and Contacts for Succesful investment and Business Activity
Austria Investment and Trade Laws and Regulations Handbook
Austria Investment, Trade Strategy and Agreements Handbook - Strategic Information and Basic Agreements
Austria Justice System and National Police Handbook
Austria Justice System and National Police Handbook
Austria Land Ownership and Agriculture Laws Handbook
Austria Medical & Pharmaceutical Industry Handbook
Austria Medical & Pharmaceutical Industry Handbook
Austria Mineral & Mining Sector Investment and Business Guide - Strategic and Practical Information
Austria Mineral & Mining Sector Investment and Business Guide - Strategic and Practical Information
Austria Mining Laws and Regulations Handbook
Austria National Development Strategy Handbook: Important Programs and Developments
Austria President and Political System Handbook

TITLE
Austria Recent Economic and Political Developments Yearbook
Austria Recent Economic and Political Developments Yearbook
Austria Recent Economic and Political Developments Yearbook
Austria Research & Development Policy Handbook
Austria Research & Development Policy Handbook
Austria Research & Development Policy Handbook
Austria Space Agency and Programs Handbook
Austria Space Agency and Programs Handbook
Austria Space Programs and Exploration Handbook
Austria Starting Business (Incorporating) in....Guide
Austria Tax Guide - Corporate Taxation
Austria Tax Guide - Personal Taxation
Austria Tax Guide Volume 1 Strategic Information and Basic Regulations
Austria Taxation Laws and Regulations Handbook
Austria Telecom Laws and Regulations Handbook
Austria Telecommunication Industry Business Opportunities Handbook
Austria Telecommunication Industry Business Opportunities Handbook
Austria Transportation Policy and Regulations Handbook
Austria: Business in Austria for Everyone: Practical Information and Contacts for Success
Austria: Doing Business and Investing in Austria Guide
Austria: How to Invest, Start and Run Profitable Business in Austria Guide - Practical Information, Opportunities, Contacts
Austrian Space Programs and Exploration Handbook

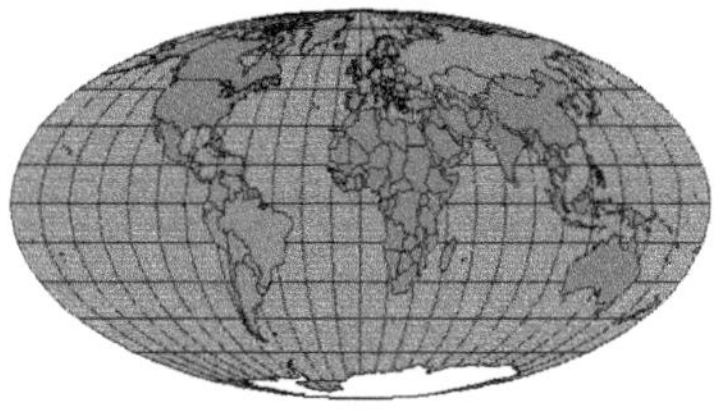

WORLD MEDICAL & PHARMACEUTICAL INDUSTRY LIBRARY

Price: $149.95 Each

Title *
1. Australia Medical & Pharmaceutical Industry Handbook
2. Austria Medical & Pharmaceutical Industry Handbook
3. Bangladesh Medical & Pharmaceutical Industry Handbook
4. Belgium Medical & Pharmaceutical Industry Handbook
5. Canada Medical & Pharmaceutical Industry Handbook
6. China Medical & Pharmaceutical Industry Handbook
7. Costa Rica Medical & Pharmaceutical Industry Handbook
8. Cuba Medical & Pharmaceutical Industry Handbook
9. Czech Republic Medical & Pharmaceutical Industry Handbook
10. Egypt Medical & Pharmaceutical Industry Handbook
11. Estonia Medical & Pharmaceutical Industry Handbook
12. Finland Medical & Pharmaceutical Industry Handbook
13. France Medical & Pharmaceutical Industry Handbook
14. Germany Medical & Pharmaceutical Industry Handbook
15. Greece Medical & Pharmaceutical Industry Handbook
16. Hungary Medical & Pharmaceutical Industry Handbook
17. India Medical & Pharmaceutical Industry Handbook
18. Indonesia Medical & Pharmaceutical Industry Handbook
19. Israel Medical & Pharmaceutical Industry Handbook
20. Italy Medical & Pharmaceutical Industry Handbook
21. Japan Medical & Pharmaceutical Industry Handbook
22. Korea, South Medical & Pharmaceutical Industry Handbook
23. Kuwait Medical & Pharmaceutical Industry Handbook
24. Laos Medical & Pharmaceutical Industry Handbook
25. Latvia Medical & Pharmaceutical Industry Handbook

For additional analytical, business and investment opportunities information, please contact Global Investment & Business Center, USA at (202) 546-2103. Fax: (202) 546-3275. E-mail: rusric@erols.com

Title *
26. Lithuania Medical & Pharmaceutical Industry Handbook
27. Malaysia Medical & Pharmaceutical Industry Handbook
28. Mexico Medical & Pharmaceutical Industry Handbook
29. Myanmar Medical & Pharmaceutical Industry Handbook
30. Pakistan Medical & Pharmaceutical Industry Handbook
31. Palau Medical & Pharmaceutical Industry Handbook
32. Palestine Medical & Pharmaceutical Industry Handbook
33. Philippines Medical & Pharmaceutical Industry Handbook
34. Russia Medical & Pharmaceutical Industry Handbook
35. Singapore Medical & Pharmaceutical Industry Handbook
36. South Africa Medical & Pharmaceutical Industry Handbook
37. Sri Lanka Medical & Pharmaceutical Industry Handbook
38. Sweden Medical & Pharmaceutical Industry Handbook
39. Taiwan Medical & Pharmaceutical Industry Handbook
40. Thailand Medical & Pharmaceutical Industry Handbook
41. Turkey Medical & Pharmaceutical Industry Handbook
42. Ukraine Medical & Pharmaceutical Industry Handbook
43. United Kingdom Medical & Pharmaceutical Industry Handbook
44. United States Medical & Pharmaceutical Industry Handbook

www.ingramcontent.com/pod-product-compliance
Ingram Content Group UK Ltd.
Pitfield, Milton Keynes, MK11 3LW, UK
UKHW051458290926
15471UKWH00008B/1281

9 781438 776187